SPSS/PC+ Statistics™ 4.0

for the IBM PC/XT/AT and PS/2

Symbol	Variable	Coordinates	
1	FEMEMPLD	.012	.909
2	RETAILNG	.815	-.236
3	INDUSTZN	.794	-.364
4	UNEMPLOY	-.558	.632
5	DWELGNEW	.891	-.106
6	MIGRNPOP	.873	.083

Marija J. Norušis/SPSS Inc.

SPSS Inc.
444 N. Michigan Avenue
Chicago, Illinois 60611
Tel: (312) 329-3500
Fax: (312) 329-3668

SPSS International BV
P.O. Box 115
4200 AC Gorinchem
The Netherlands
Tel: +31.1830.36711
Fax: +31.1830.35839

For more information about SPSS/PC+™ and other software produced and distributed by SPSS Inc., please write or call

Marketing Department
SPSS Inc.
444 North Michigan Avenue
Chicago, IL 60611
Tel: (312) 329-3500
Fax: (312) 329-3668

In Europe and the Middle East, please write or call

SPSS International BV
P.O. Box 115
4200 AC Gorinchem
The Netherlands
Tel: +31.1830.36711
Twx: 21019
Fax: +31.1830.35839

SPSS/PC+ Statistics™ 4.0
Copyright © 1990 by SPSS Inc.
All rights reserved.
Printed in the United States of America.

3 4 5 6 7 8 9 0   93 92 91

ISBN 0-923967-12-5

Library of Congress Catalog Card Number: 90-070749

Preface

SPSS/PC+ is a powerful software package for microcomputer data management and analysis. The Statistics option for SPSS/PC+ 4.0 is an add-on enhancement that enables you to carry out the most widely used types of statistical analysis on your data. The procedures in Statistics must be used with the SPSS/PC+ base system and are completely integrated into that system.

The Statistics option includes procedures for *t*-tests, 1-way and *n*-way analysis of variance, correlation and regression analysis, factor analysis, cluster analysis (using two different algorithms), nonparametric statistics, and reliability analysis of additive scales. The algorithms are identical to those used in SPSS software on mainframe computers. Although the size of the problems you can analyze may be limited by the amount of memory installed on your PC, statistical results you obtain from SPSS/PC+ will be as accurate as those computed on a mainframe.

SPSS/PC+ with the Statistics option will enable you to perform many analyses on your PC that were once possible only on much larger machines. We hope that this statistical power will make SPSS/PC+ an even more useful tool in your work.

Compatibility

SPSS Inc. warrants that SPSS/PC+ and enhancements are designed for personal computers in the IBM PC and IBM PS/2™ lines with a 10MB or larger hard disk. These products also function on closely IBM-compatible machines. Contact SPSS Inc. for details about specific IBM-compatible hardware.

Serial Numbers

Your serial number is your identification number with SPSS Inc. You will need this serial number when you call SPSS Inc. for information regarding support, payment, a defective diskette, or an upgraded system.

The serial number can be found on the diskette labeled U1 that came with your base system. Before using the system, please copy this number to the **registration card.**

Registration Card

STOP! Before continuing on, *fill out and send us your registration card.* Until we receive your registration card, you have an unregistered system. Even if you have previously sent a card to us, please fill out and return the card enclosed in your SPSS/PC+ Advanced Statistics package.

Registering your system entitles you to

- Technical support on our customer hotline.
- Favored customer status.
- *Keywords*—the SPSS user newsletter.
- New product announcements.

Of course, unregistered systems receive none of the above, so *don't put it off—send your registration card now!*

Replacement Policy   Call the Micro Software Department at 312/329-3300 to report a defective diskette. You must provide us with the serial number of your system. (The normal installation procedure will detect any damaged diskettes.) SPSS Inc. will ship replacement diskettes the same day we receive notification from you. Please return the defective diskettes to the Micro Software Department, SPSS Inc., 444 North Michigan Avenue, Chicago, IL 60611.

Shipping List   The shipping list for SPSS/PC+ Statistics 4.0 is on a separate sheet in the package.

Training Seminars   SPSS Inc. provides both public and onsite training seminars for SPSS/PC+. There is a two-day introductory course to familiarize users with the basics of SPSS/PC+. In addition there is an advanced course, also two days, that deals with more sophisticated aspects of the program. Additional seminars treat specialized topics such as data entry, graphics, report writing, and time series analysis. All seminars feature hands-on workshops.

SPSS/PC+ seminars will be offered in major U.S. and European cities on a regular basis. For further information on these seminars or to schedule an onsite seminar, call the SPSS Inc. Training Department at 312/329-3557.

Additional Documentation   Additional copies of all SPSS product manuals may be purchased separately. To order additional manuals, just fill out the Documentation Card included with your system and send it to SPSS Inc. Documentation Sales, 444 N. Michigan Avenue, Chicago, IL, 60611.

Note: In Europe, additional copies of documentation can be purchased by site-licensed customers only. Please contact the European office at the address listed on the copyright page for more information.

Technical Support   The SPSS technical hotline is available to registered customers of SPSS/PC+. Customers may call the Techline for assistance in using SPSS products or for installation help for one of the warranted hardware environments.

To reach an SPSS technical support consultant, call 312/329-3410, 9:00 a.m. to 5:00 p.m. CST. Be prepared to identify yourself, your organization, and the serial number of your system.

If you are a Value Plus or Customer EXPress customer, use the priority 800 number you received with your materials. For information on subscribing to the Value Plus or Customer EXPress plan, call SPSS Inc. at 312/329-3313.

Lend Us Your Thoughts   Your comments are important. So send us a letter and let us know about your experiences with SPSS products. We especially like to hear about new and interesting applications using the SPSS/PC+ system. Write to SPSS Inc. Marketing Department, Attn: Micro Software Products Manager, 444 N. Michigan Avenue, Chicago, IL 60611.

Contacting SPSS Inc.   If you would like to be on our mailing list, write to us at one of the addresses below. We will send you a copy of our newsletter and let you know about SPSS Inc. activities in your area.

SPSS Inc.

444 North Michigan Avenue
Chicago, IL 60611
Tel: (312) 329-3500
Fax: (312) 329-3668

SPSS Federal Systems (U.S.)

800 K St., N.W.
Suite 300
Washington, DC 20001
Tel: (202) 408-7626
Fax: (202) 408-7627

SPSS Latin America

444 North Michigan Avenue
Chicago, IL 60611
Tel: (312) 329-3556
Fax: (312) 329-3668

SPSS Benelux BV

P.O. Box 115
4200 AC Gorinchem
The Netherlands
Tel: +31.1830.36711
Fax: +31.1830.35839

SPSS UK Ltd.

SPSS House
5 London Street
Chertsey
Surrey KT16 8AP
United Kingdom
Tel: +44.932.566262
Fax: +44.932.567020

SPSS GmbH Software

Steinsdorfstrasse 19
D-8000 Munich 22
Germany
Tel: +49.89.2283008
Fax: +49.89.2285413

SPSS Scandinavia AB

Sjöängsvägen 21
S-191 72 Sollentuna
Sweden
Tel: +46.8.7549450
Fax: +46.8.7548816

SPSS Asia Pacific Pte. Ltd.

26-01
78 Shenton Way
Singapore 0207
Singapore
Tel: +65.221.2577
Fax: +65.221.9920

SPSS Japan Inc.

Gyoen Sky Bldg.
2-1-11, Shinjuku
Shinjuku-ku
Tokyo 160
Japan
Tel: +81.3.33505261
Fax: +81.3.33505245

SPSS Australasia

P.O. Box 879
345 Pacific Highway
Crows Nest
Sydney, NSW 2065
Australia
Tel: +61.2.954.5660
Fax: +61.2.954.5616

Contents

Introduction

About This Manual

This manual documents the additional statistical procedures available in SPSS/PC+ Statistics™. The manual is organized similarly to the *SPSS/PC+ Base Manual* in that there are different parts designed to meet the needs of different users. For those who have limited experience with statistics, statistical overviews are available. For those who are already familiar with statistical computing, a reference section presents the procedures in SPSS/PC+ Statistics without extensive examples. You are likely to find different parts of the manual most valuable as your experience with SPSS/PC+ grows.

To use SPSS/PC+ Statistics, you should be familiar with the SPSS/PC+ language as described in the *SPSS/PC+ Base Manual.* In addition, this manual assumes that you know how to run the SPSS/PC+ system and that you are familiar with basic data entry and manipulation. If you are unfamiliar with SPSS/PC+, consult the base manual for further information.

If you have just received SPSS/PC+ Statistics, you may want to turn to the Installation Instructions, which are in a separate booklet. You need to install SPSS/PC+ Statistics only once unless you remove it from your system. (You can, however, remove and reinstall portions of the SPSS/PC+ system: see the section on SPSS MANAGER in the *SPSS/PC+ Base Manual.)*

The three basic parts to this manual are described below.

Statistics Guide. The Statistics Guide (Part B) contains overviews of the statistics and operations for the ten procedures contained in SPSS/PC+ Statistics. The SPSS/PC+ input used to create the sample output in these chapters is shown to help you understand each procedure's operation.

Command Reference. The Command Reference (Part C) is a detailed reference to the syntax and operations of the ten procedures contained in SPSS/PC+ Statistics. The individual procedures are presented in alphabetical order. For each procedure, the Command Reference provides complete syntax rules plus details of operations.

Examples. The examples presented in Part D illustrate typical uses of the ten analytical procedures contained in SPSS/PC+ Statistics. The annotated input and output are arranged not to imitate an interactive SPSS/PC+ session but to demonstrate a set of commands that carry out a complete data analysis task. You may find that these examples, with their interpretative commentary, extend your understanding of the logic of SPSS/PC+ command structure.

Statistics Guide

Contents _____

1 Testing Differences Between Two Means: Procedure T-TEST

Would you buy a disposable raincoat, vegetables in pop-top cans, or investment counseling via closed-circuit television? These products and 17 others were described in questionnaires administered to 100 married couples (Davis & Ragsdale, 1983). Respondents were asked to rate on a scale of 1 (definitely want to buy) to 7 (definitely do not want to buy) their likelihood of buying each product. Of the 100 couples, 50 received questionnaires with pictures of the products and 50 received questionnaires without pictures. In this chapter we will examine whether pictures affect consumer preferences and whether husbands' and wives' responses differ.

1.1 TESTING HYPOTHESES

The first part of the table in Figure 1.1 contains basic descriptive statistics for the buying scores of couples receiving questionnaires with and without pictures. A couple's buying score is simply the sum of all ratings assigned to products by the husband and wife individually. Low scores indicate buyers while high scores indicate reluctance to buy. The 50 couples who received questionnaires without pictures (Group 1) had a mean score of 168 while the 48 couples who received forms with pictures had an average score of 159. (Two couples did not complete the questionnaire and are not included in the analysis.) The standard deviations show that scores for the second group were somewhat more variable than those for the first.

Figure 1.1 Family buying scores by questionnaire type

```
T-TEST GROUPS=VISUAL(0,1) /VARIABLES=FAMSCORE.
```

Independent samples of VISUAL

Group 1: VISUAL EQ 0   Group 2: VISUAL EQ 1

t-test for: FAMSCORE

	Number of Cases	Mean	Standard Deviation	Standard Error
Group 1	50	168.0000	21.787	3.081
Group 2	48	159.0833	27.564	3.979

		Pooled Variance Estimate			Separate Variance Estimate		
F Value	2-Tail Prob.	t Value	Degrees of Freedom	2-Tail Prob.	t Value	Degrees of Freedom	2-Tail Prob.
1.60	0.106	1.78	96	0.078	1.77	89.43	0.080

If one is willing to restrict the conclusions to the 98 couples included in the study, it is safe to say that couples who received forms with pictures indicated a greater willingness to purchase the products than couples who received forms without pictures. However, this statement is not very satisfying. What is needed is some type of statement about the effect of the two questionnaire types for all couples—or at least some larger group of couples—not just those actually studied.

1.2
Samples and Populations

The totality of all cases about which conclusions are desired is called the *population*, while the observations actually included in the study are the *sample*. The couples in this experiment can be considered a sample from the population of couples in the United States.

The field of statistics helps us draw inferences about populations based on observations obtained from *random samples,* or samples in which the characteristics and relationships of interest are independent of the probabilities of being included in the sample. The necessity of a good research design cannot be overemphasized. Unless precautions are taken to ensure that the sample is from the population of interest and that the cases are chosen and observed without bias, the results obtained from statistical analyses may be misleading. For example, if the sample for this study contained only affluent suburban couples, conclusions about all couples might be unwarranted.

If measurements are obtained from an entire population, the population can be characterized by the various measures of central tendency, dispersion, and shape described in *SPSS/PC+ Statistics* The results describe the population exactly. Usually, however, one obtains information from a random sample, and the results serve as *estimates* of the unknown population values. Special notation is used to identify population values, termed *parameters*, and to distinguish them from sample values, termed *statistics.* The mean of a population is denoted by μ, and the variance by σ^2. The symbols $\bar{X}$ and S^2 are reserved for the mean and variance of samples.

1.3
Sampling Distributions

The sample that is actually included in a study is just one of many random samples that could have been selected from a population. For example, if the population consists of married couples in the United States, the number of different samples that could be chosen for inclusion in a study is mind-boggling. The estimated value of a population parameter depends on the particular sample chosen. Different samples usually produce different estimates.

Figure 1.3 is a histogram of 400 means. Each mean is calculated from a random sample of 25 observations, from a population which has a normal distribution with a mean value of zero and a standard deviation of 1. The estimated means are not all the same. Instead, they have a distribution. Most sample means are fairly close to zero, the population mean. The mean of the 400 means is 0.010 and the standard deviation of these means is 0.205. In fact, the distribution of the means appears approximately normal.

Figure 1.3   Means of 400 samples of size 25 from a normal distribution

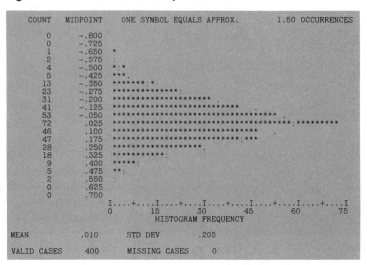

Although Figure 1.3 gives some idea of the appearance of the distribution of sample means of size 25 from a standard normal population, it is only an approximation since all possible samples of size 25 have not been taken. If the number of samples taken is increased to 1000, an even better picture of the distribution could be obtained. As the number of samples of a fixed size increases, the observed (or empirical) distribution of the means approaches the underlying, or theoretical, distribution.

The theoretical distribution of all possible values of a statistic obtained from a population is called the *sampling distribution* of the statistic. The mean of the sampling distribution is called the *expected value* of the statistic. The standard deviation is termed the *standard error*. The sampling distributions of most commonly used statistics calculated from random samples are tabulated and readily accessible. Knowing the sampling distribution of a statistic is very important for hypothesis testing, since from it one can calculate the probability of obtaining an observed sample value if a particular hypothesis is true. For example, from Figure 1.3, it appears quite unlikely that a sample mean based on a sample of size 25 from a standard normal distribution would be greater than 0.5 if the population mean were zero.

1.4
Sampling Distribution of the Mean

Since hypotheses about population means are often of interest, the sampling distribution of the mean is particularly important. If samples are taken from a normal population, the sampling distribution of the sample mean is also normal. As expected, the observed distribution of the 400 means in Figure 1.3 is approximately normal. The theoretical distribution of the sample mean, based on all possible samples of size 25, is exactly normal.

Even when samples are taken from a nonnormal population, the distribution of the sample means will be approximately normal for sufficiently large samples. This is one reason for the importance of the normal distribution in statistical inference. Consider Figure 1.4a, which shows a sample from a uniform distribution. In a uniform distribution all values of a variable are equally likely, and hence the proportion of cases in each bin of the histogram is roughly the same.

Figure 1.4a   Values from a uniform distribution

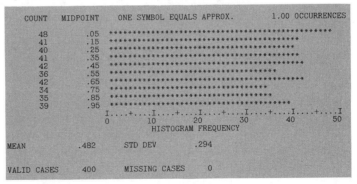

Figure 1.4b is a histogram of 400 means calculated from samples of size 25 from a uniform distribution. Note that the observed distribution is approximately normal even though the distribution from which the samples were taken is markedly nonnormal.

Figure 1.4b   Distribution of 400 means calculated from samples of size 25 from a uniform distribution

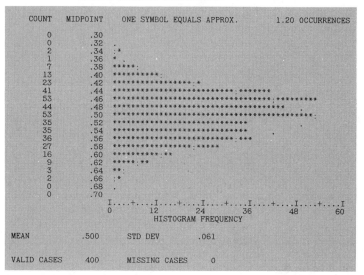

Both the size of a sample and the shape of the distribution from which samples are taken affect the shape of the sampling distribution of the mean. If samples are small and come from distributions that are far from normal, the distribution of the means will not be even approximately normal. As the size of the sample increases, the sampling distribution of the mean will approach normality.

The mean of the theoretical sampling distribution of the means of samples of size n is μ, the population mean. The standard error, which is another name for the standard deviation of the sampling distribution of the mean, is

$$\sigma_{\bar{X}} = \frac{\sigma}{\sqrt{N}}$$

Equation 1.4a

where σ is the standard deviation of the population, and N is the sample size.

The standard deviation of the observed sampling distribution of means in Figure 1.3 is 0.205. This is close to the value of the standard error for the theoretical distribution which, from Equation 1.4a, is 1/5, or 0.20.

Usually the value of the standard error is unknown and is estimated from a single sample using

$$S_{\bar{x}} = \frac{S}{\sqrt{N}}$$

Equation 1.4b

where S is the *sample* standard deviation. The estimated standard error is displayed in the FREQUENCIES procedure and is also part of the output shown in Figure 1.1. For example, for Group 1 the estimated standard error of the mean is

$$\frac{21.787}{\sqrt{50}} = 3.081$$

Equation 1.4c

This value is displayed in the column labeled STANDARD ERROR in Figure 1.1.

The standard error of the mean depends on both the sample standard deviation and the sample size. As the size of a sample increases, the standard error decreases. This is intuitively clear, since the more data are gathered, the more confident you can be that the sample mean is not too far from the population mean.

Also, as the standard deviation of the observations decreases, the standard error decreases as well. Small standard deviations occur when observations are fairly homogeneous. In this case, means based on different samples should also not vary much.

1.5
THE TWO-SAMPLE
T-TEST

Consider again whether there is evidence that the type of questionnaire administered influences couples' buying decisions. The question is not whether the two sample means are equal, but whether the two population means are equal.

To test the hypothesis that, in the population, buying scores for the two questionnaire types are the same, the following statistic can be calculated:

$$t = \frac{\overline{X}_1 - \overline{X}_2}{\sqrt{S_1^2/N_1 + S_2^2/N_2}}$$

                                                                    Equation 1.5a

$\overline{X}_1$ is the sample mean of Group 1, S_1^2 is the variance, and N_1 is the sample size.

Based on the sampling distribution of the above statistic, one can calculate the probability that a difference at least as large as the one observed would occur if the two population means (μ_1 and μ_2) are equal. This probability is called the *observed significance level*. If the observed significance level is small enough, usually less than 0.05, or 0.01, the hypothesis that the population means are equal is rejected.

The t value and its associated probability are given in Figure 1.1 in the section labeled SEPARATE VARIANCE ESTIMATE. The t value is

$$t = \frac{168.0 - 159.08}{\sqrt{\dfrac{21.787^2}{50} + \dfrac{27.564^2}{48}}} = 1.77$$

                                                                    Equation 1.5b

If $\mu_1 = \mu_2$, the probability of observing a difference at least as large as the one in the sample is estimated to be about 0.08. Since this probability is greater than 0.05, the hypothesis that mean buying scores in the population are equal for the two types of forms is not rejected. The entry under DEGREES OF FREEDOM in Figure 1.1 is a function of the sample size in the two groups and is used together with the t value in establishing the observed significance level.

Another statistic based on the t distribution can be used to test the equality of the means hypothesis. This statistic, known as the *pooled-variance t-test,* is based on the assumption that the population variances in the two groups are equal and is obtained using a pooled estimate of that common variance. The test statistic is identical to the equation for t given previously except that the individual group variances are replaced by a pooled estimate S_p^2. That is,

$$t = \frac{\overline{X}_1 - \overline{X}_2}{\sqrt{S_p^2/N_1 + S_p^2/N_2}}$$

                                                                    Equation 1.5c

where S_p^2, the pooled variance, is a weighted average of the individual variances and is calculated as

$$S_p^2 = \frac{(N_1 - 1)S_1^2 + (N_2 - 1)S_2^2}{N_1 + N_2 - 2}$$

                                                                    Equation 1.5d

From the output in Figure 1.1, the pooled t-test value for the study is 1.78. The degrees of freedom for the pooled t-test are 96, the sum of the sample sizes in both groups minus 2. If the pooled-variance t-test is used when the population variances are not equal, the probability level associated with the statistic may be in error. The amount of error depends on the inequality of the sample sizes and of the variances. However, using the separate-variance t value when the population variances are equal will usually result in an observed significance level somewhat larger than it should be. For large samples, the discrepancy between the two methods is small. In general, it is a good idea to use the separate-variance t-test whenever you suspect that the variances are unequal.

The statistic used to test the hypothesis that the two population variances are equal is the F value, which is the ratio of the larger sample variance to the smaller. In Figure 1.1, this value is $(27.6^2/21.8^2 = 1.6)$. If the observed significance level for the F test is small, the hypothesis that the population variances are equal is rejected, and the separate-variance t-test for means should be used. In this example, the significance level for the F test is large, and thus the pooled-variance t-test is appropriate.

1.6
Significance Levels

The commonsense interpretation of a small observed significance level is straight-forward: it appears unlikely that the two population means are equal. Of course, there is a possibility that the means are equal and the observed difference is due to chance. The *observed significance level* is the probability that a difference at least as large as the one observed would have arisen if the means were really equal.

When the observed significance level is too large to reject the equality hypothesis, the two population means may indeed be equal, or the means may be unequal but the difference cannot be detected. Failure to detect can be due to a true difference that is very small. For example, if a new cancer drug prolongs survival time by only one day when compared to the standard treatment, it is unlikely that such a difference will be detected, especially if survival times vary substantially and the additional day represents a small increment.

There are other reasons why true differences may not be found. If the sample sizes in the two groups are small or the variability large, even substantial differences may not be detected. Significant t values are obtained when the numerator of the t statistic is large when compared to the denominator. The numerator is the difference between the sample means, and the denominator depends on the standard deviations and sample sizes of the two groups. For a given standard deviation, the larger the sample size, the smaller the denominator. Thus, a difference of a given magnitude may be significant if obtained with a sample size of 100, but not significant with a sample size of 25.

1.7
One-Tailed vs. Two-Tailed Tests

A two-tailed test is used to detect a difference in means between two populations regardless of the direction of the difference. For example, in the study of buying scores presented in this chapter, we are interested in whether buying scores without pictures are larger *or* smaller than buying scores with pictures. In applications where one is interested in detecting a difference in one direction—such as whether a new drug is better than the current treatment—a so-called one-tailed test can be performed. The procedure is the same as for the two-tailed test, but the resulting probability value is divided by 2, adjusting for the fact that the equality hypothesis is rejected only when the difference between the two means is sufficiently large and in the direction of interest. In a two-tailed test, the equality hypothesis is rejected for large positive or negative values of the statistic.

1.8
What's the Difference?

It appears that the questionnaire type has no significant effect on couples' willingness to purchase products. Overall buying scores for the two conditions are similar. Pictures of the products do not appear to enhance their perceived desirability. In fact, the pictures actually appear to make several products somewhat less desirable. However, since the purpose of the questionnaires is to ascertain buying intent, including a picture of the actual product may help gauge true product response. Although the concept of disposable raincoats may be attractive, if they make the owner look like a walking trash bag their appeal may diminish considerably.

1.9
USING PROCEDURE CROSSTABS TO TEST HYPOTHESES

The T-TEST procedure is used to test hypotheses about the equality of two means for variables measured on an interval or ratio scale. Procedure CROSSTABS and the chi-square statistic can be used to test hypotheses about a dichotomous variable, such as purchase of a particular product (see SPSS PC+ Data Analysis).

Figure 1.9 is a crosstabulation showing the number of husbands who would definitely want to buy vegetables in pop-top cans when shown a picture and when not shown a picture of the product. The vegetables in pop-top cans were chosen by 6.0% of the husbands who were tempted with pictures and 16.0% of the husbands who were not shown pictures. The chi-square statistic provides a test of the hypothesis that the proportion of husbands selecting the vegetables in pop-top cans is the same for the picture and no-picture forms.

Figure 1.9   Husbands' preference for vegetables in pop-top cans

```
CROSSTABS TABLES=H2S BY VISUAL
   /CELLS=COUNT COLUMN /STATISTICS=CHISQ.
```

```
H2S  POP-TOP CANS HUSB SELF  by  VISUAL  PICTURE ACCOMPANIED QUESTION

                    VISUAL
            Count |
            Col Pct|NO PICTU PICTURES
                   |IRES
                   |      0 |      1 |  Row
                   |        |        |  Total
H2S         -------+--------+--------+
               1   |      8 |      3 |   11
    DEFINITELY     |   16.0 |    6.0 | 11.0
                   +--------+--------+
               2   |     42 |     47 |   89
    VERY LIKELY    |   84.0 |   94.0 | 89.0
                   +--------+--------+
           Column       50       50      100
            Total      50.0     50.0    100.0

        Chi-Square                 Value         DF        Significance
    ----------------------      -----------    -------     ------------

    Pearson                        2.55362         1          .11004
    Continuity Correction          1.63432         1          .20111
    Likelihood Ratio               2.63925         1          .10425
    Mantel-Haenszel                2.52809         1          .11184

    Minimum Expected Frequency -     5.500


    Number of Missing Observations:   0
```

The probability of 0.2011 associated with the chi-square statistic in Figure 1.9 is the probability that a difference at least as large as the one observed would occur in the sample if in the population there were no difference in the selection of the product between the two formats. Since the probability is large, the hypothesis of no difference between the two formats is not rejected.

1.10
INDEPENDENT VS. PAIRED SAMPLES

Several factors may contribute to the observed differences in response between two groups. Some of the observed difference between the scores of the picture and no-picture groups may be attributable to questionnaire type. Some of the difference may also be due to differences between individuals. Not all couples have the same buying desires, so even if the type of form does not affect buying, differences between the two groups will probably be observed due to differences between the couples within the two groups.

One method of minimizing the influence of individual variation is to choose the two groups so that the couples within them are comparable on characteristics that can influence buying behavior, such as income, education, family size, and so forth.

It is sometimes possible to obtain pairs of subjects, such as twins, and assign one member of each pair to each of the two treatments. Another frequently used experimental design is to expose the same individual to both types of conditions. (In this design, care must be taken to ensure that the sequential administration of treatments does not influence response by providing practice, decreasing attention span, or affecting the second treatment in other ways.) In both designs, subject-to-subject variability has substantially less effect. These designs are called *paired-samples designs,* since for each subject there is a corresponding, or paired, subject in the other group. In the second design, a person is paired with himself or herself. In an *independent-samples design,* there is no pairing of cases; all observations are independent.

1.11
Analysis of Paired Data

Interpreting the significance of results from paired experiments follows the same basic steps that were discussed previously for independent samples, except that different computations are used. For each pair of cases, the difference in the responses is calculated. The statistic used to test the hypothesis that the mean difference in the population is zero is

$$t = \frac{\overline{D}}{S_D/\sqrt{N}}$$

Equation 1.11

where $\overline{D}$ is the observed difference between the two means and $S_{\overline{D}}$ is the standard deviation of the differences of the paired observations. The sampling distribution of t, if the differences are normally distributed with a mean of zero, is Student's t with $N-1$ degrees of freedom, where N is the number of pairs. If the pairing is effective, the standard error of the difference will be smaller than the standard error obtained if two independent samples with N subjects each were chosen. However, if the variables chosen for pairing do not affect the responses under study, pairing may result in a test that is less powerful since true differences can be detected less frequently.

For example, to test the hypothesis that there is no difference between husbands' and wives' buying scores, a paired t-test should be calculated. A paired test is appropriate since husbands and wives constitute matched observations. Hopefully, including both members of a couple controls for some nuisance effects like socioeconomic status, age, and so forth. The observed differences are more likely to be attributable to differences in sex.

Figure 1.11 contains output from the paired t-test. The entry under number of cases is the number of pairs of observations. The mean difference is the difference between the mean scores for males and females. The t value is the mean difference divided by the standard error of the difference ($0.55/1.73=0.32$). The two-tailed probability for this test is 0.75, so there is insufficient evidence to reject the null hypothesis that married males and females have similar mean buying scores.

Figure 1.11 Husbands' versus wives' buying scores

```
T-TEST PAIRS=HSSCALE, WSSCALE.
```

Paired samples t-test:	HSSCALE	HUSBANDS BUYING SCORE
	WSSCALE	WIVES BUYING SCORE

Variable	Number of Cases	Mean	Standard Deviation	Standard Error
HSSCALE	98	82.0918	14.352	1.450
WSSCALE	98	81.5408	15.942	1.610

(Difference) Mean	Standard Deviation	Standard Error	2-Tail Corr. Prob.	t Value	Degrees of Freedom	2-Tail Prob.
0.5510	17.095	1.727	0.367 0.000	0.32	97	0.750

The correlation coefficient between husbands' and wives' scores is 0.367. A positive correlation indicates that pairing has been effective in decreasing the variability of the mean difference. The larger the correlation coefficient, the greater the benefit of pairing. See Chapter 2 for further discussion of correlation.

1.12
HYPOTHESIS TESTING: A REVIEW

The purpose of hypothesis testing is to help draw conclusions about population parameters based on results observed in a random sample. The procedure remains virtually the same for tests of most hypotheses.

• A hypothesis of no difference (called a *null hypothesis*) and its alternative are formulated.
• A test statistic is chosen to evaluate the null hypothesis.
• For the sample, the test statistic is calculated.
• The probability, if the null hypothesis is true, of obtaining a test value at least as extreme as the one observed is determined.
• If the observed significance level is judged small enough, the null hypothesis is rejected.

1.13
The Importance of Assumptions

In order to perform a statistical test of any hypothesis, it is necessary to make certain assumptions about the data. The particular assumptions depend on the statistical test being used. Some procedures require stricter assumptions than others. For *parametric tests,* some knowledge about the distribution from which samples are selected is required.

The assumptions are necessary to define the sampling distribution of the test statistic. Unless the distribution is defined, correct significance levels cannot be calculated. For the pooled t-test, the assumption is that the observations are random samples from normal distributions with the same variance.

For many procedures, not all assumptions are equally important. Moderate violation of some assumptions may not always be serious. Therefore, it is important to know for each procedure not only what assumptions are needed but also how severely their violation may influence results. For example, the F test for equality of variances is quite sensitive to departures from normality, while the t-test for equality of means is less so.

The responsibility for detecting violations of assumptions rests with the researcher. In a chemistry lab, faulty research methods can result in disaster. Fortunately, no explosions threaten the investigator who fails to comply with good statistical practice. However, from a research viewpoint, the consequences can be just as severe.

Wherever possible, tests of assumptions—often called diagnostic checks of the model—should be incorporated as part of the hypothesis-testing procedures. Throughout SPSS/PC+, attempts have been made to provide facilities for examining assumptions. For example, in the FREQUENCIES procedure, histograms and measures of skewness and kurtosis provide a convenient check for the normality assumption. Discussion of other such diagnostics is included with the individual procedures.

1.14
RUNNING
PROCEDURE T-TEST

The T-TEST procedure computes the Student's t statistic for testing the significance of a difference between means of independent or paired samples. When independent samples are used, T-TEST calculates the separate-variance and pooled-variance t statistics and the F test for homogeneity of variances. The two-tailed observed significance level is also displayed for each t statistic.

1.15
Requesting
Independent-Samples
Tests

The variable and criterion to be used to divide the sample into two independent groups are specified by the GROUPS subcommand. It is followed by the VARIABLES subcommand, which names the variable or variables to be tested.

1.16
Defining the Groups

Any of the following three methods can be used to define two groups on the GROUPS subcommand:

- If a single number in parentheses follows the grouping variable, all cases whose value for the grouping variable is greater than or equal to this number go into one group; the remaining cases go into the other group. For example, the output in Figure 1.1 could be produced by the command:

  T-TEST GROUPS=VISUAL(1)/VARIABLES=FAMSCORE.

- If two values are specified in parentheses after the grouping variable, one group consists of all cases whose value for the grouping variable is the first number, while the second group consists of all cases whose value for the grouping variable is the second number. Thus, the output in Figure 1.1 could also have been produced by the command:

  T-TEST GROUPS=VISUAL(0,1)/VARIABLES=FAMSCORE.

- If the grouping variable has only two values, 1 and 2, no value list is necessary; only the name of the grouping variable is required. If VISUAL had been coded as 1 or 2 rather than 0 or 1, the shortest command that would produce the output in Figure 1.1 would be:

  T-TEST GROUPS=VISUAL/VARIABLES=FAMSCORE.

Only one variable (numeric or string) may be named in the GROUPS subcommand. When a string variable is used, long strings are truncated to short strings to define the categories. Only one GROUPS subcommand may be used per T-TEST command.

1.17
Specifying the Variables

The VARIABLES subcommand follows the GROUPS subcommand and lists the variables to be analyzed. Up to 50 variables may be specified, but they must all be numeric. The specifications for the variable list follow the usual SPSS/PC+ conventions. The TO keyword may be used to refer to adjacent variables in the data file. Only one VARIABLES subcommand may be used per T-TEST command.

1.18
Requesting Paired-Samples Tests

To obtain a paired t-test, you must have two separate variables that indicate the values for the two members of the pairs. The only required subcommand is PAIRS, which specifies the variables being compared. String variables may not be used. For example, the output in Figure 1.11 was obtained by specifying

```
T-TEST PAIRS=HSSCALE WSSCALE.
```

If three or more variables are listed in PAIRS, each variable is compared with every other variable. For example, the command

```
T-TEST PAIRS=SURVEY1 SURVEY2 SURVEY3.
```

produces three paired t-tests, one comparing SURVEY1 and SURVEY2, one comparing SURVEY1 and SURVEY3, and one comparing SURVEY2 and SURVEY3.
    The keyword WITH can be used to request paired t-tests comparing each variable to the left of WITH to every variable to the right of WITH. Thus, the command

```
T-TEST PAIRS=SURVEY1 WITH SURVEY2 SURVEY3.
```

produces two paired t-tests, one comparing SURVEY1 with SURVEY2 and the other comparing SURVEY1 with SURVEY3.
    You can use Option 5 to specify special pairing of variables using the keyword WITH.

Option 5   *Special pairing for paired-samples test.* Must be used with the keyword WITH. The first variable before WITH is compared to the first variable after WITH and so forth.

Thus, the command

```
T-TEST SURVEY1 TO SURVEY3 WITH SURVEY4 TO SURVEY6
    /OPTIONS=5.
```

compares SURVEY1 and SURVEY4, SURVEY2 and SURVEY5, and SURVEY3 and SURVEY6.
    You can specify multiple analysis lists by separating them with a slash, as in

```
T-TEST PAIRS=SURVEY1 SURVEY2 SURVEY3/PRETEST WITH POSTTST1 POSTTST2.
```

1.19
Requesting One-Sample Tests

Although T-TEST is designed to be a two-sample procedure, it can be used to calculate one-sample t-tests if a COMPUTE command is also used. To test the null hypothesis that the mean of a population is some specified value m, you can use the commands

```
COMPUTE MEAN=m.
T-TEST PAIRS=varname MEAN.
```

where varname is the name of the variable you want to test. You can give computed variable MEAN any name you wish (as long as it conforms to the SPSS/PC+ variable-naming conventions).

1.20
Missing Values

By default, T-TEST deletes only cases with missing values for those variables necessary for a particular t-test. For independent-samples t-tests, T-TEST excludes cases with missing values for the grouping variable or the variable to be tested. For paired-samples t-tests, T-TEST excludes cases with missing values for either of the variables in a given pair. Two other missing-value treatments are available and are specified in the OPTIONS subcommand:

B

Statistics Guide

Option 1 *Include user-missing values.* User-defined missing values are included in the analysis.

Option 2 *Exclude missing values listwise.* Cases with missing values for any variables listed in T-TEST are excluded from the analysis.

1.21
Formatting Options

By default, T-TEST displays variable labels next to variable names. You can use Option 3 to suppress these labels.

Option 3 *Suppress variable labels.*

1.22
Annotated Example

The complete set of SPSS/PC+ commands needed to obtain the analyses in this chapter is the following:

```
DATA LIST / VISUAL 1 FAMSCORE 4-6 H2S 8 HSSCALE 11-13 WSSCALE 16-18.
BEGIN DATA.
0  169 2  102    67
0  206 1  109    97
0  156 2   73    83
 :
 :
 :
1  170 2   96    74
1  178 1   86    92
1  179 2   92    87
END DATA.
VAR LABELS FAMSCORE 'FAMILY BUYING SCORE'/
           WSSCALE 'WIVES BUYING SCORE'/
           HSSCALE 'HUSBANDS BUYING SCORE'.
VAL LABELS H2S 1 'DEFINITELY' 2 'VERY LIKELY'
T-TEST GROUPS=VISUAL(1)/VARIABLES=FAMSCORE/
       PAIRS=HSSCALE WSSCALE.
FINISH.
```

- The DATA LIST command gives the variable names and column locations.
- The VAR LABELS command assigns new labels to the variables FAMSCORE, WSSCALE, and HSSCALE.
- The VAL LABELS command assigns labels to the values of H2S for use with the CROSSTABS command that is shown in Figure 1.9.
- The T-TEST command requests an independent-samples test (with VISUAL as the grouping variable) and a paired t-test (comparing WSSCALE and HSSCALE).

The output for this job is shown in Figures 1.1 and 1.11.

Contents

2 Measuring Linear Association: Procedure CORRELATION

Youthful lemonade-stand entrepreneurs as well as balding executives of billion-dollar corporations share a common concern—increasing sales. Hand-lettered signs affixed to neighborhood trees, television campaigns, siblings and friends canvassing local playgrounds, and international sales forces are known to be effective tactics. However, the impact of various intertwined factors on sales can be difficult to isolate, and much effort in the business world is expended on determining exactly what makes a product sell.

Churchill (1979) describes a study undertaken by the manufacturer of Click ball-point pens on the effectiveness of the firm's marketing efforts. A random sample of forty sales territories is selected, and sales, amount of advertising, and number of sales representatives are recorded. This chapter looks at the relationship between sales and these variables.

2.1
EXAMINING RELATIONSHIPS

Figure 2.1a is a scatterplot of the amount of sales and the number of television spots in each of forty territories. A scatterplot can reveal various types of associations between two variables. Figure 2.1b contains some commonly encountered patterns. In the first panel there appears to be no discernible relationship between the two variables. The variables are related exponentially in the second panel. That is, Y increases very rapidly for increasing values of X. In the third panel, the relationship between the two variables is U-shaped. Small and large values of the X variable are associated with large values of the Y variable.

Figure 2.1a Scatterplot showing a linear relationship

PLOT PLOT=SALES WITH ADVERTIS.

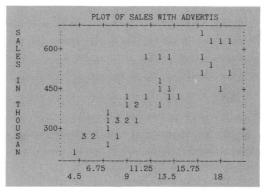

From Figure 2.1a, there appears to be a positive association between sales and advertising. That is, as the amount of advertising increases, so does the number of sales. The relationship between sales and advertising may also be termed *linear,* since the observed points cluster more or less around a straight line.

Figure 2.1b Some common relationships

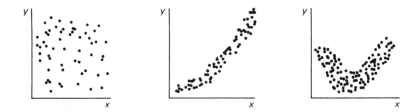

2.2
THE CORRELATION COEFFICIENT

Although a scatterplot is an essential first step in studying the association between two variables, it is often useful to quantify the strength of the association by calculating a summary index. One commonly used measure is the Pearson correlation coefficient, denoted by r. It is defined as

$$r = \frac{\sum\limits_{i=1}^{N}(X_i - \bar{X})(Y_i - \bar{Y})}{(N-1)S_X S_Y}$$

Equation 2.2

where N is the number of cases and S_x and S_y are the standard deviations of the two variables. The absolute value of r indicates the strength of the linear relationship. The largest possible absolute value is 1, which occurs when all points fall exactly on the line. When the line has a positive slope, the value of r is positive, and when the slope of the line is negative, the value of r is negative (see Figure 2.2a).

Figure 2.2a Scatterplots with correlation coefficients of +1 and −1

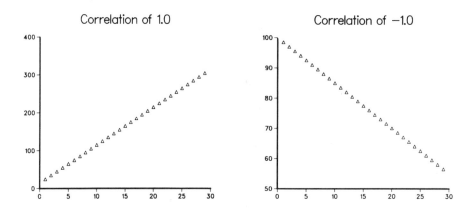

A value of 0 indicates no *linear* relationship. Two variables can have a strong association but a small correlation coefficient if the relationship is not linear. Figure 2.2b shows two plots with zero correlation.

Figure 2.2b Scatterplots with correlation coefficients of zero

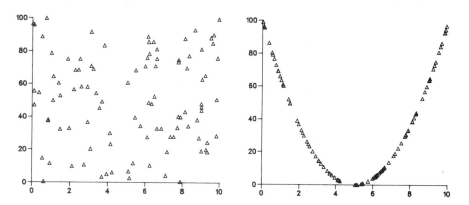

It is important to examine correlation coefficients together with scatterplots since the same coefficient can result from very different underlying relationships. The variables plotted in Figure 2.2c have a correlation coefficient greater than 0.8, as do the variables plotted in Figure 2.1a. But note how different the relationships are between the two sets of variables. In Figure 2.2c there is a strong positive linear association only for part of the graph. The relationship between the two variables is basically nonlinear. The scatterplot in Figure 2.1a is very different. The points cluster more or less around a line. Thus, the correlation coefficient should be used only to summarize the strength of linear association.

Figure 2.2c Scatterplot of percentage no facial hair with year

PLOT PLOT=CLEAN WITH YEAR.

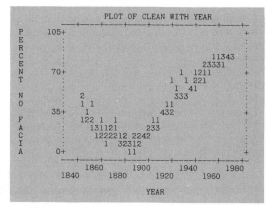

**2.3
Some Properties of the
Correlation Coefficient**

A common mistake in interpreting the correlation coefficient is to assume that correlation implies causation. No such conclusion is automatic. While sales are highly correlated with advertising, they are also highly correlated with other variables, such as the number of sales representatives in a territory. Advertising alone does not necessarily result in increased sales. For example, territories with high sales may simply have more money to spend on TV spots, regardless of whether the spots are effective.

The correlation coefficient is a symmetric measure since interchanging the two variables X and Y in the formula does not change the results. The correlation coefficient is not expressed in any units of measure, and it is not affected by linear transformations such as adding or subtracting constants or multiplying or dividing all values of a variable by a constant.

2.4
Calculating Correlation Coefficients

Figure 2.4 is a table of correlation coefficients for the number of television spots, number of sales representatives, and amount of sales. The entry in each cell is the correlation coefficient. For example, the correlation coefficient between advertising and sales is 0.8802. This value indicates that there is a fairly strong linear association between the two variables, as shown in Figure 2.1a. The table is symmetric since the correlation between X and Y is the same as the correlation between Y and X. The values on the diagonal are all 1 since a variable is perfectly related to itself. The sample size and significance levels are displayed after the table. In this example, 40 cases were used in all computations since all territories had values for the three variables.

Figure 2.4   Correlation coefficients

```
CORRELATIONS VARIABLES=ADVERTIS REPS SALES.
```

```
Correlations:  ADVERTIS    REPS       SALES

   ADVERTIS   1.0000      .7763**    .8802**
   REPS        .7763**   1.0000      .8818**
   SALES       .8802**    .8818**   1.0000
N of cases:       40               Significance:  * - .01  ** - .001

" . " is printed if a coefficient cannot be computed
```

2.5
Hypothesis Tests about the Correlation Coefficient

Although the correlation coefficient is sometimes used only as a summary index to describe the observed strength of the association, in some situations description and summary are but a first step. The primary goal may be to test hypotheses about the unknown population correlation coefficient—denoted as ρ—based on its estimate, the sample correlation coefficient r. In order to test such hypotheses, certain assumptions must be made about the underlying joint distribution of the two variables. A common assumption is that independent random samples are taken from a distribution in which the two variables are together distributed normally. If this condition is satisfied, the test that the population coefficient is 0 can be based on the statistic

$$t = r\sqrt{\frac{N-2}{1-r^2}}$$

Equation 2.5

which, if $\rho=0$, has a Student's t distribution with $N-2$ degrees of freedom. Either one- or two-tailed tests can be calculated. If nothing is known in advance, a two-tailed test is appropriate. That is, the hypothesis that the coefficient is zero is rejected for both extreme positive and extreme negative values of t. If the direction of the association can be specified in advance, the hypothesis is rejected only for t values that are of sufficient magnitude and in the direction specified.

In SPSS/PC+, coefficients with one-tailed observed significance levels less than 0.01 are designated with a single asterisk; those with one-tailed significance levels less than 0.001, with two asterisks. From Figure 2.4, the probability that a correlation coefficient of at least 0.88 is obtained when there is no linear association in the population between sales and advertising is less than 0.001. Care should be exercised when examining the significance levels for large tables. Even if there is no association between the variables, if many coefficients are computed some would be expected to be statistically significant by chance alone.

Special procedures must be employed to test more general hypotheses of the form $\rho=\rho_0$ where ρ_0 is a constant. If the assumptions of bivariate normality appear unreasonable, a variety of *nonparametric* measures, which make limited assumptions about the underlying distributions of the variables, can be calculated. See Chapter 5 for further discussion.

2.6
Correlation Matrices and Missing Data

For a variety of reasons, data files frequently contain incomplete observations. Respondents in surveys scrawl illegible responses or refuse to answer certain questions. Laboratory animals die before experiments are completed. Patients fail to keep scheduled clinic appointments.

Analysis of data with missing values is troublesome. Before even considering possible strategies, you should determine whether there is evidence that the missing-value pattern is not random. That is, are there reasons to believe that missing values for a variable are related to the values of that variable or other variables? For example, people with low incomes may be less willing to report their financial status than more affluent people. This may be even more pronounced for people who are poor but highly educated.

One simple method of exploring such possibilities is to subdivide the data into two groups—those observations with missing data on a variable and those with complete data—and examine the distributions of the other variables in the file across these two groups. The SPSS/PC+ procedures CROSSTABS and T-TEST are particularly useful for this. For a discussion of more sophisticated methods for detecting nonrandomness, see Frane (1976).

If it appears that the data are not missing randomly, use great caution in attempting to analyze the data. It may be that no satisfactory analysis is possible, especially if there are only a few cases.

If you are satisfied that the missing data are random, several strategies are available. First, if the same few variables are missing for most cases, exclude those variables from the analysis. Since this luxury is not usually available, you can alternatively keep all variables but eliminate the cases with missing values on any of them. This is termed *listwise* missing-value treatment since a case is eliminated if it has a missing value on any variable in the list.

If many cases have missing data for some variables, listwise missing-value treatment could eliminate too many cases and leave you with a very small sample. One common technique is to calculate the correlation coefficient between a pair of variables based on all cases with complete information for the two variables regardless of whether the cases have missing data on any other variable. For example, if a case has values only for variables 1, 3, and 5, it is used only in computations involving variable pairs 1 and 3, 1 and 5, and 3 and 5. This is *pairwise* missing-value treatment.

2.7
Choosing Pairwise Missing-Value Treatment

Several problems can arise with pairwise matrices, one of which is inconsistency. There are some relationships between coefficients that are impossible but may occur when different cases are used to estimate different coefficients. For example, if age and weight and age and height have a high positive correlation, it is impossible in the same sample for height and weight to have a high negative correlation. However, if the same cases are not used to estimate all three coefficients, such an anomaly can occur.

There is no single sample size that can be associated with a pairwise matrix since each coefficient can be based on a different number of cases. Significance levels obtained from analyses based on pairwise matrices must be viewed with caution since little is known about hypothesis testing in such situations.

It should be emphasized that missing-value problems should not be treated lightly. You should base your decision on careful examination of the data and not leave the choices up to system defaults.

2.8
THE REGRESSION LINE

If there is a linear relationship between two variables, a straight line can be used to summarize the data. When the correlation coefficient is $+1$ or -1, little thought is needed to determine the line that best describes the data: the line passes through all of the observations. When the observations are less highly correlated, many different lines can be drawn to represent the data.

One of the most commonly used procedures for fitting a line to the observations is the method of *least squares*. This method results in a line that minimizes the sum of squared vertical distances from the data points to the line.

The equation for the straight line that relates predicted sales to advertising is

PREDICTED SALES = a + b(ADVERTISING)   **Equation 2.8a**

The intercept, *a*, is the predicted sales when there is no advertising. The slope, *b*, is the change in predicted sales for a unit change in advertising. That is, it is the amount of change in sales per television spot.

The actual values of *a* and *b* calculated with the method of least squares are printed as part of the SPSS/PC+ PLOT output (see Figure 2.8). The least-squares equation for the line is

PREDICTED SALES = 135.4 + 25.31(ADVERTISING)   **Equation 2.8b**

Figure 2.1a shows this regression line.

Figure 2.8   Intercept and slope from PLOT

```
40 cases plotted. Regression statistics of SALES on ADVERTIS:
Correlation .88016 R Squared .77467 S.E. of Est 59.56023 Sig. .0000
Intercept(S.E.) 135.43360( 25.90649) Slope(S.E.) 25.30770( 2.21415)
```

For each pair of variables, two different regression lines can be calculated, since the values of the slope and intercept depend on which variable is dependent (the one being predicted) and which is independent (the one used for prediction). In the SPSS/PC+ PLOT output, the variable plotted on the vertical axis is considered the dependent variable in the calculation of statistics.

2.9
Prediction

Based on the regression equation, it is possible to predict sales from advertising. For example, a territory with 10 television spots per month is expected to have sales of about $388,400 (135.4 + 25.3(10)). Considerable caution is needed when predictions are made for values of the independent variable which are much larger or much smaller than those used to derive the equation. A relationship which is linear for the observed range of values may not be linear everywhere. For example, estimating *Y* values for the beginning of Figure 2.2c based on a regression line for the latter part of the plot would result in a very poor fit.

The difference between observed sales and sales predicted by the model is called a *residual*. The residual for a territory with 10 television spots and observed sales of 403.6 is 15.2:

RESIDUAL = OBSERVED − PREDICTED = 403.6 − 388.4   **Equation 2.9a**
                = 15.2

Residuals can be calculated for each of the sales territories. Figure 2.9 contains the observed value (SALES), the predicted value (*PRED), and the residual for the first 10 territories (*RESID). The residuals provide an idea of how well the calculated regression line actually fits the data.

Figure 2.9   Residuals from the regression line

```
Casewise Plot of Standardized Residual

*: Selected   M: Missing

            -3.0      0.0      3.0
    Case #   0:.......:.........:0      SALES      *PRED        *RESID
       1    .           *       .        260.3     261.9721      -1.6721
       2    .         *.        .        286.1     312.5875     -26.4875
       3    .           *       .        279.4     287.2798      -7.8798
       4    .             . *   .        410.8     363.2029      47.5971
       5    .           *       .        438.2     439.1260       -.9260
       6    .         *.        .        315.3     337.8952     -22.5952
       7    .             .   * .        565.1     413.8183     151.2817
       8    .            .*     .        570.0     540.3568      29.6432
       9    .         * .       .        426.1     464.4337     -38.3337
      10    .           *       .        315.0     312.5875       2.4125
    Case #   0:.......:.........:0      SALES      *PRED        *RESID
            -3.0      0.0      3.0
```

2.10
Goodness of Fit

Although the regression line is a useful summary of the relationship between two variables, the values of the slope and intercept alone do little to indicate how well the line actually fits the data. A goodness-of-fit index is needed.

The observed variation in the dependent variable can be subdivided into two components: the variation "explained" by the regression and the residual from the regression, or

TOTAL SS = REGRESSION SS + RESIDUAL SS   **Equation 2.10c**

The *total sum of squares* is a measure of overall variation and is given by

$$\text{TOTAL SUM OF SQUARES} = \sum_{i=1}^{N} (Y_i - \overline{Y})^2 \qquad \textbf{Equation 2.10b}$$

The total sum of squares for sales is 598,253. (It is *N*-1 times the variance.)

The *regression sum of squares*, or the sum of squares due to regression, is

$$\text{REGRESSION SUM OF SQUARES} = \sum_{i=1}^{N} (\hat{Y}_i - \overline{Y})^2 \qquad \textbf{Equation 2.10c}$$

where $\hat{Y}_i$ is the predicted value for the *i*th case. The regression sum of squares is a measure of how much variability in the dependent variable is attributable to the linear relationship between the two variables. For this example, the regression sum of squares is 463,451.

The *residual sum of squares*, sometimes called the error sum of squares, is obtained by squaring each of the residuals and then summing them.

$$\text{RESIDUAL SUM OF SQUARES} = \sum_{i=1}^{N} (Y_i - \hat{Y}_i)^2 \qquad \textbf{Equation 2.10d}$$

The residual sum of squares for sales is 134,802. The standard deviation of the residuals, called the standard error of the estimate, is

$$\text{SEE} = \sqrt{\frac{\text{RESIDUAL SUM OF SQUARES}}{N-2}} = \sqrt{\frac{134,802}{38}} = 59.56 \qquad \textbf{Equation 2.10e}$$

The standard error is displayed in Figure 2.8.

The proportion of the variation in the dependent variable that is explained by the linear regression is computed by comparing the total sum of squares and the regression sum of squares:

$$r^2 = \frac{\text{REGRESSION SUM OF SQUARES}}{\text{TOTAL SUM OF SQUARES}} = \frac{463,451}{598,253} = 0.775 \qquad \textbf{Equation 2.10f}$$

Statistics Guide

If there is no linear association in the sample, the value of r^2 is 0, since the predicted values are just the mean of the dependent variable and the regression sum of squares is 0. If Y and X are perfectly linearly related, the residual sum of squares is 0 and r^2 is 1. The square root of r^2 is r, the Pearson correlation coefficient between the two variables.

2.11
Further Topics in Regression

In this chapter, only the most basic concepts in regression analysis are discussed. Chapter 6 contains detailed descriptions of simple two-variable regression as well as multiple regression analysis.

2.12
RUNNING PROCEDURE CORRELATION

The CORRELATION procedure calculates Pearson product-moment correlations for pairs of variables. The display includes the coefficient (r), an indication of significance level, and the number of cases upon which the coefficients are computed. Means, standard deviations, cross-product deviations, and covariances are available. You can also specify optional formats and methods of handling missing data. In addition, you can write out a square matrix containing correlation coefficients and the number of cases for use in other SPSS/PC+ procedures.

2.13
Specifying the Variables

The VARIABLES subcommand lists all variables to be included in the correlation matrix. For example, to produce the correlation matrix shown in Figure 2.4, specify

```
CORRELATION VARIABLES=ADVERTIS REPS SALES.
```

The actual keyword VARIABLES can be omitted.

The order in which you name the variables is the order in which they are displayed. Use the keyword WITH to obtain the correlations of one set of variables with another set. For example, the command

```
CORRELATION VARIABLES=ADVERTIS WITH REPS SALES.
```

produces two correlations, ADVERTIS with REPS and ADVERTIS with SALES. You can specify several analysis lists by separating them with slashes.

Only numeric variables can be named on the VARIABLES subcommand. Long or short string variables on an analysis list will prevent execution of CORRELATION.

2.14
Optional Statistics

By default, the correlation matrix and the number of valid cases on which the matrix is based are displayed. A correlation that cannot be computed is displayed as a period (.). One-tailed probabilities of less than 0.01 are indicated by an asterisk (*) and those less than 0.001 by two asterisks (**). The display uses the width defined on the SET command (see SPSS/PC+ Data Analysis).

The following additional options and statistics are available using the OPTIONS and STATISTICS subcommands:

Option 3   *Display two-tailed probabilities.* Two-tailed probabilities less than 0.01 are indicated by an asterisk (*) and those less than 0.001 by two asterisks (**). When Option 5 is also specified, exact two-tailed probabilities are given.

Option 5   *Display count and probability.* The number of cases used to compute each coefficient and exact probability are displayed.

Statistic 1   *Univariate mean, standard deviation, and count.* Missing values are handled on a variable-by-variable basis, regardless of the missing-value option in effect.

Statistic 2   *Cross-product deviations and covariance.*

ALL   *Display all statistics.* Includes statistics available with Statistics 1 and 2.

For example, to obtain the statistics in Figure 2.14, specify

```
CORRELATION VARIABLES=ADVERTIS REPS SALES
   /STATISTICS=1.
```

Figure 2.14   Univariate statistics with Statistic 1

Variable	Cases	Mean	Std Dev
ADVERTIS	40	10.9000	4.3074
REPS	40	5.0000	1.6486
SALES	40	411.2875	123.8540

2.15
Missing Values

By default, SPSS/PC+ excludes a case from the calculation of all correlation coefficients if it has a missing value on any variable named on the VARIABLES subcommand. This is listwise missing-value treatment. Specify Options 1 or 2 on the OPTIONS subcommand for alternative missing-value treatments.

Option 1   *Include cases with user-missing values* in the computations.

Option 2   *Exclude cases with missing values pairwise.* All cases with valid values for the pair of variables used to compute a coefficient are included in the computation of that coefficient (see Section 2.7).

2.16
Writing Matrices

By default, matrices are written only to the display file. Use Option 4 on the OPTIONS subcommand to write matrices to the results file named on the SET command for use in other procedures.

Option 4   *Write count and correlation matrix.* The correlation matrix and number of cases used to compute each coefficient for each analysis list are written to the results file named on the SET command. You cannot use the keyword WITH in the analysis list if you specify Option 4.

2.17
Annotated Example

The following commands produce the output in Figures 2.14 and 2.17:

```
DATA LIST  / ADVERTIS 1-2 EFFIC 4 REPS 6 SALES 8-12 (1).
BEGIN DATA.
lines of data
END DATA.
CORRELATION  ADVERTIS REPS SALES/
             STATISTICS=1.
```

• The DATA LIST command defines the variable names and gives their column locations.

• The CORRELATION command asks for correlations between ADVERTIS, REPS, and SALES. Statistic 1 asks for univariate statistics.

Figure 2.17   Correlation matrix

Correlations:	ADVERTIS	REPS	SALES
ADVERTIS	1.0000	.7763	.8802
REPS	.7763	1.0000	.8818
SALES	.8802	.8818	1.0000

N of cases: 40   1-tailed Signif: * - .01 ** - .001

" . " is printed if a coefficient cannot be computed

B

Statistics Guide

Contents

3

One-Way Analysis of Variance: Procedure ONEWAY

Rotund Italians washing down carbohydrate-laden feasts with jugs of chianti, somber Jews ritualistically sipping Sabbath wine, melancholy Irish submerging grief and frustration in a bottle—all are common ethnic stereotypes. Is there any evidence to support these notions? In *Ethnic Drinking Subcultures,* Greeley et al. (1980) examine drinking habits in a sample of five ethnic populations within four major American cities.

A total of 1,107 families completed questionnaires detailing their drinking behavior and ancestral origins. Irish, Italian, Jewish, Swedish, and English families were included. The authors investigated possible differences in drinking habits and a variety of cultural and psychological explanations for them. In this chapter, only differences in total alcohol consumption are considered.

3.1 DESCRIPTIVE STATISTICS AND CONFIDENCE INTERVALS

Figure 3.2 contains basic descriptive statistics for total yearly alcohol consumption in pints for the adult males in the study. The Italians and Irish are the biggest consumers, drinking an average of 24 pints a year. The Jewish males drink the least, an average of slightly more than 9 pints a year.

The sample mean for a group provides the single best guess for the unknown population value μ_i. It is unlikely that the value of the sample mean is exactly equal to the population parameter, but it is probably not too different. Based on the sample mean, it is possible to calculate a range of values that, with a designated likelihood, includes the population value. Such a range is called a *confidence interval.* For example, as shown in Figure 3.2, the 95% confidence interval for μ_{Irish} is the range 19.61 to 28.89 pints. This means that if repeated samples are selected from a population under the same conditions and 95% confidence intervals are calculated, 95% of the intervals will contain the unknown parameter μ_{Irish}. Since the parameter value is unknown, it is not possible to determine whether a particular interval contains it.

3.2 ANALYSIS OF VARIANCE

Looking at the sample means in Figure 3.2, you might wonder whether the observed differences can be reasonably attributed to chance or whether there is reason to suspect true differences between the five groups. One of the statistical procedures commonly used to test the hypothesis that several population means are equal is *analysis of variance,* or ANOVA.

Figure 3.2 Total yearly alcohol consumption for adult males (in pints)

```
ONEWAY AMOUNT BY ETHNIC(1,5)   /STATISTICS=1
```

Group	Count	Mean	Standard Deviation	Standard Error	95 Pct Conf Int for Mean		
IRISH	119	24.2500	25.5620	2.3433	19.6097	To	28.8903
ITALIAN	84	24.3120	24.1880	2.6391	19.0629	To	29.5611
JEWISH	41	9.2500	21.6250	3.3773	2.4243	To	16.0757
SWEDISH	74	16.5630	26.7500	3.1096	10.3655	To	22.7605
ENGLISH	90	21.8750	21.5630	2.2729	17.3587	To	26.3913
Total	408	20.8373	24.6519	1.2205	18.4381	To	23.2365

Group	Minimum	Maximum
IRISH	0.0	145.0
ITALIAN	0.0	128.0
JEWISH	0.0	87.0
SWEDISH	0.0	112.0
ENGLISH	0.0	117.0
Total	0.0	145.0

Certain assumptions are required for correct application of the ANOVA test. Independent samples from normally distributed populations with the same variance must be selected. In subsequent discussion, it is assumed that the populations sampled constitute the entire set of populations about which conclusions are desired. For example, the five ethnic groups are considered to be the only ones of interest. They are not viewed as a sample from all possible ethnic groups. This is called a *fixed-effects model.*

3.3
Partitioning Variation

In analysis of variance, the observed variability in the sample is subdivided into two components—variability of the observations within a group about the group mean and variability of the group means. If the amount of alcohol consumed doesn't vary much for individuals within the same ethnic group—for example, all the Swedes seem to drink about the same—but the group means differ substantially, there is evidence to suspect that the population means are not all equal.

The *within-groups sum of squares* is a measure of the variability within groups. It is calculated as

$$\text{SSW} = \sum_{i=1}^{k} (N_i - 1)S_i^2 \qquad \text{Equation 3.3a}$$

where S_i^2 is the variance of group i about its mean, and N_i is the number of cases in group i. For the data shown in Figure 3.2, the within-groups sum of squares is

$$\begin{aligned}\text{SSW} &= 25.56^2(118) + 24.19^2(83) + 21.63^2(40) \qquad \text{Equation 3.3b}\\ &+ 26.75^2(73) + 21.56^2(89) \\ &= 237{,}986.20\end{aligned}$$

Variability of the group means is measured by the *between-groups sum of squares*, which is

$$\text{SSB} = \sum_{i=1}^{k} N_i(\bar{X}_i - \bar{X})^2 \qquad \text{Equation 3.3c}$$

The mean of the ith group is denoted $\bar{X}_i$, and the mean of the entire sample is $\bar{X}$. For the drinking study, the between-groups sum of squares is

$$\begin{aligned}\text{SSB} &= (24.25-20.84)^2(119) + (24.31-20.84)^2(84) \qquad \text{Equation 3.3d}\\ &+ (9.25-20.84)^2(41) + (16.56-20.84)^2(74) \\ &+ (21.88-20.84)^2(90) \\ &= 9{,}353.89\end{aligned}$$

The sums of squares, and other related statistics, are usually displayed in an analysis of variance table, as shown in Figure 3.3.

Figure 3.3 Analysis of variance table

ONEWAY AMOUNT BY ETHNIC(1,5).

Variable	AMOUNT	AMOUNT OF ALCOHOL CONSUMED IN PINTS			
By Variable	ETHNIC	ETHNIC BACKGROUND			

Analysis of Variance

Source	D.F.	Sum of Squares	Mean Squares	F Ratio	F Prob.
Between Groups	4	9353.8671	2338.4668	3.9599	.0036
Within Groups	403	237986.3869	590.5369		
Total	407	247340.2540			

The mean squares in Figure 3.3 are obtained by dividing the sums of squares by their degrees of freedom. The between-groups degrees of freedom are $k-1$, where k is the number of groups. The within-groups degrees of freedom are $N-k$, where N is the number of cases in the entire sample.

3.4
Testing the Hypothesis

To test the hypothesis that the five ethnic groups under study consume the same average amount of alcohol—that is, that

$$\mu_{\text{Irish}} = \mu_{\text{Italian}} = \mu_{\text{Jewish}} = \mu_{\text{Swedish}} = \mu_{\text{English}}$$ **Equation 3.4a**

the following statistic is calculated (see Figure 3.3):

$$F = \frac{\text{BETWEEN GROUPS MEAN SQUARE}}{\text{WITHIN GROUPS MEAN SQUARE}} = \frac{2338.47}{590.54} = 3.96$$ **Equation 3.4b**

When the assumptions described in Section 3.2 are met, the observed significance level is obtained by comparing the calculated F to values of the F distribution with $k-1$ and $N-k$ degrees of freedom. The observed significance level is the probability of obtaining an F statistic at least as large as the one calculated when all population means are equal. If this probability is small enough, the hypothesis that all population means are equal is rejected. In this example, the observed significance level is approximately 0.0036 (Figure 3.3). Thus, it appears unlikely that men in the five ethnic populations consume the same mean amount of alcohol.

3.5
MULTIPLE COMPARISON PROCEDURES

A significant F statistic indicates only that the population means are probably unequal. It does not pinpoint where the differences are. A variety of special techniques, termed *multiple comparison* tests, are available for determining which population means are different from each other.

You may question the need for special techniques—why not just calculate the t-test described in Chapter 1 for all possible pairs of means? The problem is that when many comparisons are made, some will appear to be significant even when all population means are equal. With five groups, for example, there are ten possible comparisons between pairs of means. When all population means are equal, the probability that at least one of the ten observed significance levels will be less than 0.05 is about 0.29 (Snedecor, 1967).

Multiple comparison tests protect against calling too many differences significant. These tests set up more stringent criteria for declaring differences significant than does the usual t-test. That is, the difference between two sample means must be larger to be identified as a true difference.

3.6
The Scheffé Test

Many multiple comparison tests are available, and they all provide protection in slightly different ways (for further discussion, see Winer, 1971). Figure 3.6a is output from the *Scheffé* multiple comparison test for the ethnic drinking data. The Scheffé method is conservative for pairwise comparisons of means. It requires larger differences between means for significance than most of the other methods.

Figure 3.6a   The Scheffé multiple comparison test

```
ONEWAY AMOUNT BY ETHNIC(1,5)
  /RANGES=SCHEFFE /OPTIONS=6.
```

```
     Variable  AMOUNT       AMOUNT OF ALCOHOL CONSUMED IN PINTS
   By Variable ETHNIC       ETHNIC BACKGROUND


Multiple Range Test


Scheffe Procedure
Ranges for the 0.050 level -

        4.38   4.38   4.38   4.38

The ranges above are table ranges.
The value actually compared with Mean(J)-Mean(I) is..
     17.1834 * Range * Sqrt(1/N(I) + 1/N(J))


  (*) Denotes pairs of groups significantly different at the 0.050 level

                           J S E I I
                           E W N R T
                           W E G I A
                           I D L S L
                           S I I H I
                           H S S   A
                             H H   N

    Mean      Group

    9.2500    JEWISH
   16.5630    SWEDISH
   21.8750    ENGLISH
   24.2500    IRISH      *
   24.3120    ITALIAN    *
```

The means are ordered and displayed from smallest to largest, as shown in Figure 3.6a. Pairs of means that are significantly different at the 0.05 level in this case are indicated with an asterisk in the lower half of the matrix at the bottom of the output. In this example, the asterisks under the vertical column labeled **JEWISH** mean that Jews are significantly different from the Irish and the Italians. No other pair is found to be significantly different. If no pairs are significantly different, a message is displayed and the matrix is suppressed.

The formula above the matrix indicates how large an observed difference must be to attain significance using the particular multiple comparison test. The table ranges are the values for the range variable in the formula.

If the sample sizes in all groups are equal, or an average sample size is used in the computations, a somewhat modified table is also displayed (Figure 3.6b). Instead of indicating which groups are significantly different, means that are not different are grouped. Subset 1 shows that Jews, Swedes, and the English are not different. Subset 2 groups Swedes, English, Irish, and Italians. Jews do not appear in the same subset as Irish and Italians since they are significantly different from these two.

Figure 3.6b   Homogeneous subsets

```
Homogeneous Subsets     (Subsets of groups, whose highest and lowest means
                         do not differ by more than the shortest
                         significant range for a subset of that size)


SUBSET  1

Group       JEWISH       SWEDISH      ENGLISH
Mean         9.2500      16.5630      21.8750
- - - - - - - - - - - - - - - - - - - - - - - - - - -

SUBSET  2

Group       SWEDISH      ENGLISH      IRISH        ITALIAN
Mean        16.5630      21.8750      24.2500      24.3120
- - - - - - - - - - - - - - - - - - - - - - - - - - -
```

3.7
EXPLANATIONS

Both cultural and psychological explanations for differences in drinking habits among ethnic groups have been suggested (Greeley, 1981). In Jewish culture, the religious symbolism associated with drinking, as well as strong cultural norms against drunkenness, seem to discourage alcohol consumption. For the Irish, alcohol is a vehicle for promotion of fun and pleasure, as well as a potent tranquilizer for dissipating grief and tension. Such high expectations of alcohol make it a convenient escape and foster dependency. Italians have accepted drinking as a natural part of daily life. Alcohol is treated almost as a food and not singled out for its special pleasures.

3.8
Tests for Equality of Variance

As previously discussed, one of the assumptions needed for applying analysis of variance properly is that of equality of variances. That is, all of the populations from which random samples are taken must not only be normal but must also have the same variance, σ^2. Several procedures are available for testing this assumption of *homogeneity of variance*. Unfortunately, many of them are not very useful since they are influenced by characteristics of the data other than the variance.

Figure 3.8   Tests for homogeneity of variance

```
ONEWAY AMOUNT BY ETHNIC(1,5)
  /STATISTICS=3.
```

```
Tests for Homogeneity of Variances

    Cochrans C = Max. Variance/Sum(Variances) =  .2479, P =  .248 (Approx.)
    Bartlett-Box F =                             1.349 , P =  .249
    Maximum Variance / Minimum Variance         1.539
```

Figure 3.8 shows the results of the three tests for homogeneity of variance available in SPSS/PC+ for the ethnic drinking study. The significance levels are relatively large, so the hypothesis that the populations have the same variance cannot be rejected. Since the variances do not appear to be unequal, there is no reason to worry. Even if the variances appeared to be different, but the sample sizes in all groups were similar, there would be no cause for alarm since the ANOVA test is not particularly sensitive to violations of equality of variance under such conditions. However, if sample sizes are quite dissimilar and variances are unequal, you should consider transforming the data or using a statistical procedure that requires less stringent assumptions (see Chapter 5).

3.9
RUNNING
PROCEDURE ONEWAY

The ONEWAY procedure produces a one-way analysis of variance. Although ANOVA (see Chapter 4) can also produce a one-way analysis of variance, ONEWAY performs several optional tests not available in ANOVA. Both ONEWAY and ANOVA calculate sums of squares, mean squares, degrees of freedom, and F tests, but only ONEWAY allows you to test for nonlinear trends, specify contrasts, and use multiple comparison tests. ONEWAY also reads and writes matrix materials.

ONEWAY operates via subcommands, including the OPTIONS and STATISTICS subcommands. You must first specify a dependent variable list and an independent variable with its range of values. The optional subcommands that produce contrasts, tests for trends, and multiple comparisons appear after this specification and can be entered in any order.

3.10
Specifying the Variables

The VARIABLES subcommand is the only required specification for ONEWAY and consists of the name of at least one dependent variable, the keyword BY, and the name of the independent variable followed by its minimum and maximum values enclosed in parentheses and separated by a comma. The actual keyword VARIABLES can be omitted. Thus, the output in Figure 3.3 could be obtained by specifying either

```
ONEWAY VARIABLES=AMOUNT BY ETHNIC(1,5).
```

or

```
ONEWAY AMOUNT BY ETHNIC(1,5).
```

The minimum and maximum values are the lowest and highest values of the independent variable to be used in the analysis. Cases with values for the independent variable outside this range are excluded from the analysis.

Only one independent variable can be used in an analysis list. When more than one dependent variable is specified, a separate one-way analysis of variance is produced for each one.

3.11
Specifying Multiple Comparison Tests

Use the RANGES subcommand to specify any of seven multiple comparison tests available in ONEWAY. You can specify multiple RANGES subcommands, and each one requests one test. The keywords for RANGES are shown below. Each specifies a type of multiple comparison test, and some can be followed by a number in parentheses indicating the significance level. If a significance level is not specified, ONEWAY uses a 0.05 significance level.

LSD(p)   *Least significant difference.* Any significance level between 0 and 1 can be specified.

DUNCAN(p)   *Duncan's multiple-range test.* Only one significance level—0.01, 0.05, or 0.10— can be specified.

SNK   *Student-Newman-Keuls test.* Only the 0.05 significance level can be used.

BTUKEY   *Tukey's alternate test.* Only the 0.05 significance level can be used.

TUKEY   *Honestly significant difference.* Only the 0.05 significance level can be used.

MODLSD(p)   *Modified LSD.* Any significance level between 0 and 1 can be specified.

SCHEFFE(p) *Scheffé's test.* Any significance level between 0 and 1 can be specified.

For example, Figures 3.6a and 3.6b were obtained by specifying

```
ONEWAY AMOUNT BY ETHNIC(1,5)
 /RANGES=SCHEFFE.
```

ONEWAY produces two types of output, depending on the design and multiple comparison test. Multiple comparisons for all groups are produced whenever RANGES is used. In this type of output, group means are listed in ascending order. Asterisks in the matrix of group names indicate which means are significantly different. For example, the asterisks in Figure 3.6a indicate that Jews are significantly different from the Irish and the Italians.

For balanced designs or when Option 10 (harmonic means) is specified, ONEWAY produces homogeneous subsets of means. Figure 3.6b shows output with homogeneous subsets of means. In this example, two subsets are produced. The first subset includes Jews and Swedes, and the second subset includes Swedes, English, Irish, and Italians. The means of the groups within a subset are *not* significantly different.

You can specify any other type of range for multiple comparisons by listing specific range values. Up to $k-1$ range values can be specified in ascending order, where k is the number of groups and where the range value times the standard error of the combined subset is the critical value. If fewer than $k-1$ values are specified, the last value is used for the remaining values. You can specify repetitions with $n*r$, where n is the number of repetitions and r is the range value. To use a single critical value for all subsets, specify one range value. For example, the command

```
ONEWAY VARIABLES=AMOUNT BY ETHNIC(1,5)
  /RANGES=4.38.
```

produces the Scheffé test shown in Figure 3.6a.

By default, the multiple comparison test uses the harmonic mean of the sizes of the two groups being compared. If you want the harmonic mean of *all* group sizes to be used, specify Option 10 on the OPTIONS subcommand. When Option 10 is specified, ONEWAY calculates homogeneous subsets.

Option 10   *Harmonic mean of all group sizes used as the sample size for each group in range tests.* If the harmonic mean is used for unbalanced designs, ONEWAY determines homogeneous subsets for all range tests.

3.12
Partitioning Sums of Squares

The POLYNOMIAL subcommand partitions the between-groups sums of squares into linear, quadratic, cubic, and higher-order trend components. Its specifications consist of a single number, which indicates the degree of the highest-order polynomial to be used. For example, the command

```
ONEWAY AMOUNT BY ETHNIC(1,5)
  /POLYNOMIAL=2.
```

specifies a polynomial of order 2 (a quadratic) as the highest-order polynomial. The number specified must be a positive integer less than or equal to 5 and less than the number of groups. The POLYNOMIAL subcommand follows the variable specifications and can be used only once.

When the design is balanced and POLYNOMIAL is used, ONEWAY computes the sum of squares for each order polynomial from weighted polynomial contrasts, using the values of the independent variable as the metric. These contrasts are orthogonal, so that the sums of squares for each order polynomial are statistically independent. If the design is unbalanced, but there is equal spacing between the values of the independent variable, ONEWAY computes sums of squares using the unweighted polynomial contrasts. These sums of squares are always calculated from the weighted sums of squares.

3.13
Specifying Contrasts

The CONTRAST subcommand specifies *a priori* contrasts to be tested by the t statistic. Its specification is simply a list of coefficients, with each coefficient corresponding to a value of the independent variable. For example, the command

```
ONEWAY AMOUNT BY ETHNIC(1,5)
  /CONTRAST=1 -2 0 0.
```

specifies comparison of the combined means of the Irish and Italians with the mean for Jews. The last two groups are not included in the contrast. Fractional coefficients can also be used, as in the command

```
ONEWAY AMOUNT BY ETHNIC(1,5)
  /CONTRAST=.5 .5 -1 0 0.
```

For most applications, the coefficients should sum to 0. Sets of coefficients that do not sum to 0 are used, but a warning message is displayed.

The notation $n*c$ can be used to specify the same coefficient for n consecutive means. For example, the command

```
ONEWAY AMOUNT BY ETHNIC(1,5)
  /CONTRAST=2*1 -2 2*0.
```

specifies a contrast coefficient of 1 for the Irish and Italians, a coefficient of -2 for Jews, and a coefficient of 0 for Swedes and the English. You must specify a contrast coefficient for every group implied by the range given for the independent variable, even if a group has no cases. Trailing zeros need not be specified, however, so that the command

```
ONEWAY AMOUNT BY ETHNIC(1,5)
  /CONTRAST=2*1 -2.
```

is equivalent to the previous command.

Only one set of contrast coefficients can be specified per CONTRAST subcommand. However, you can specify multiple CONTRAST subcommands. Output for each contrast list includes the value of the contrast, the standard error of the contrast, the t statistic, the degrees of freedom for t, and the two-tailed observed significance level of t. Both pooled-variance and separate-variance estimates are displayed.

3.14
Optional Statistics

You can specify three optional sets of statistics or the keyword ALL on the STATISTICS subcommand:

Statistic 1 *Group descriptive statistics.* For each group, the count, mean, standard deviation, standard error, minimum, maximum, and 95% confidence interval are displayed for each dependent variable.

Statistic 2 *Fixed- and random-effects statistics.* For the fixed-effects model, the standard deviation, standard error, and 95% confidence interval are displayed. For the random-effects model, the standard error, the 95% confidence interval, and the estimate of the between-component variance are displayed.

Statistic 3 *Homogeneity-of-variance-tests.* Cochran's C, the Bartlett-Box F, and Hartley's F Max are displayed.

ALL *Display all statistics.*

For example, the output in Figures 3.2 and 3.8 was obtained by specifying

```
ONEWAY AMOUNT BY ETHNIC(1,5)
  /STATISTICS=1 3.
```

3.15
Missing Values

By default, ONEWAY deletes cases with missing values on an analysis-by-analysis basis; that is, a case with missing values for the dependent variable or the independent variable is not used in that analysis. Cases with values for the independent variable outside the range specified are also excluded from the analysis. Two alternative missing-value treatments are available and are specified on the OPTIONS subcommand:

Option 1 *Include user-missing values.* Cases with user-defined missing values are included in the analysis.

Option 2 *Exclude missing values listwise.* Cases with missing values for any variable in the analysis list are excluded from the analysis.

Neither option will cause ONEWAY to include cases with values for the independent value that are outside the specified range.

3.16
Formatting Options

By default, ONEWAY displays variable labels and identifies groups as GRP1, GRP2, and so forth. The display can be modified by specifying the following options on the OPTIONS subcommand:

Option 3 *Suppress variable labels.*

Option 6 *Display value labels for groups.* Use the first eight characters of the value labels defined for the independent variable as group labels.

Option 6 was used to obtain the group identifications in Figure 3.6a.

3.17
Matrix Materials

ONEWAY can read and write matrix materials. It writes out frequencies, means, and standard deviations in a format it can read, and it also reads frequencies, means, and the pooled variance.

To write matrix materials to a file, specify Option 4 on the OPTIONS subcommand.

Option 4 *Write matrix materials to a file.* Writes a vector of category frequencies, a vector of means, and a vector of standard deviations for each dependent variable. Vectors are written 80 characters per line, with each vector beginning on a new line. The format for the frequencies vector is F10.2, and for the means and standard deviations vectors, F10.4. Thus, each line has a maximum of eight values.

If Option 4 is used, the file to which the material is written is controlled by the SET command (see *SPSS/PC+ Base Manual).*

ONEWAY reads two types of matrix materials, specified with Options 7 and 8 on the OPTIONS subcommand:

Option 7 *Read matrix of counts, means, and standard deviations.* ONEWAY expects a vector of counts for each group, followed by a vector of group means and a vector of group standard deviations like those written by Option 4.

Option 8 *Read matrix of counts, means, pooled variance, and degrees of freedom.* ONEWAY expects a vector of counts for each group, followed by a vector of means for each group, followed by the pooled variance (the within-groups mean square) and the degrees of freedom for the pooled variance. If the degrees of freedom are omitted, ONEWAY takes them to be $n-k$, where n is the number of cases and k is the number of groups. Statistics 1, 2, and 3 and the separate-variance estimate for contrasts cannot be computed.

If Option 7 or 8 is used, the MATRIX keyword must be specified on the DATA LIST command. For either option, each vector begins on a new line and can be entered in fixed or freefield format. Unless matrix materials produced by ONEWAY are to be read, it is easier to use freefield input with the FREE keyword on the DATA LIST command. (For more information, see *SPSS/PC+ Base Manual.)*

3.18
Annotated Example

The SPSS/PC+ commands used to produce the output in this chapter are

```
DATA LIST MATRIX FREE / AMOUNT ETHNIC.
VAR LABELS   AMOUNT 'AMOUNT OF ALCOHOL CONSUMED IN PINTS'/
             ETHNIC 'ETHNIC BACKGROUND'.
VALUE LABELS   ETHNIC 1 'IRISH' 2 'ITALIAN' 3 'JEWISH' 4 'SWEDISH'
                      5 'ENGLISH'.
BEGIN DATA.
119.        84.        41.        74.        90.
 24.25      24.312      9.25      16.563     21.875
 25.562     24.188     21.625     26.75      21.563
END DATA.
ONEWAY AMOUNT BY ETHNIC(1,5)
  /RANGES=SCHEFFE
  /OPTIONS=6,7
  /STATISTICS=1,3.
FINISH.
```

- The DATA LIST command indicates that the variables AMOUNT and ETHNIC are being read in as a freefield matrix.
- The VAR LABELS command assigns descriptive labels to AMOUNT and ETHNIC.
- The VALUE LABELS command assigns labels to values of ETHNIC, indicating the ethnic group represented by each value.
- The BEGIN DATA and END DATA commands enclose the matrix materials.
- The ONEWAY command names AMOUNT as the dependent variable and ETHNIC as the independent variable. The minimum and maximum values for ETHNIC are 1 and 5.
- The RANGES subcommand calculates multiple comparisons between means using the Scheffé test.
- The OPTIONS subcommand requests the display of value labels for each group and specifies matrix input.
- The STATISTICS subcommand requests descriptive statistics and homogeneity-of-variance tests.

Contents _____

4 Analysis of Variance: Procedure ANOVA

Despite constitutional guarantees, any mirror will testify that all citizens are not created equal. The consequences of this inequity are pervasive. Physically attractive persons are perceived as more desirable social partners, more persuasive communicators, and generally more likeable and competent. Even cute children and attractive burglars are disciplined more leniently than their homely counterparts (Sigall & Ostrove, 1975).

Much research on physical attractiveness focuses on its impact on heterosexual relationships and evaluations. Its effect on same-sex evaluations has received less attention. Anderson and Nida (1978) examined the influence of attractiveness on the evaluation of writings by college students. In the study, 144 male and 144 female students were asked to appraise essays purportedly written by college freshmen. A slide of the "author" was projected during the rating as part of "supplemental information." Half of the slides were of authors of the same sex as the rater; the other half were of authors of the opposite sex. The slides had previously been determined to be of high, medium, and low attractiveness. Each participant evaluated one essay for creativity, ideas, and style. The three scales were combined to form a composite measure of performance.

4.1 DESCRIPTIVE STATISTICS

Figure 4.1 contains average composite scores for the essays, subdivided by the three categories of physical attractiveness and the two categories of sex similarity. The table is similar to the summary table shown for the one-way analysis of variance in Chapter 3. The difference here is that there are two independent (or grouping) variables, attractiveness and sex similarity. The first mean displayed (25.11) is for the entire sample. The number of cases (288) is shown in parentheses. Then for each of the independent variables, mean scores are displayed for each of the categories. The attractiveness categories are ordered from low (coded 1) to high (coded 3). Evaluations in which the rater and author are of the same sex are coded as 1, while opposite-sex evaluations are coded as 2. Finally, a table of means is displayed for cases classified by both grouping variables. Attractiveness is the row variable, and sex is the column variable. Each mean is based on the responses of 48 subjects.

Figure 4.1   Table of group means

```
ANOVA  VARIABLES=SCORE BY ATTRACT(1,3) SEX(1,2)
  /STATISTICS=3.
```

```
                        * * *  C E L L   M E A N S  * * *

                    SCORE      COMPOSITE SCORE
                 BY ATTRACT    ATTRACTIVENESS LEVEL
                    SEX        SEX SIMILARITY


TOTAL POPULATION

      25.11
   (   288)


ATTRACT
        1             2             3

      22.98        25.78        26.59
   (    96)     (    96)     (    96)


SEX
        1             2

      25.52        24.71
   (   144)     (   144)


            SEX
                  1             2
ATTRACT
      1         22.79        23.17
             (    48)     (    48)

      2         28.63        22.92
             (    48)     (    48)

      3         25.13        28.04
             (    48)     (    48)
```

The overall average score is 25.11. Highly attractive individuals received the highest average score (26.59), while those rated low in physical appeal had the lowest score (22.98). There doesn't appear to be much difference between the average scores assigned to same (25.52) and opposite-sex (24.71) individuals. Highly attractive persons received an average rating of 25.13 when evaluated by individuals of the same sex and 28.04 when evaluated by students of the opposite sex.

4.2
ANALYSIS OF VARIANCE

Three hypotheses are of interest in the study: Does attractiveness relate to the composite scores? Does sex similarity relate to the scores? And is there an interaction between the effects of attractiveness and sex? The statistical technique used to evaluate these hypotheses is an extension of the one-way analysis of variance outlined in Chapter 3. The same assumptions as before are needed for correct application: the observations should be independently selected from normal populations with equal variances. Again, discussion here is limited to the situation in which both grouping variables are considered fixed. That is, they constitute the populations of interest.

The total observed variation in the scores is subdivided into four components: the sums of squares due to attractiveness, sex, their interaction, and the residual. This can be expressed as

TOTAL SS = ATTRACTIVENESS SS + SEX SS   **Equation 4.2**
          + INTERACTION SS + RESIDUAL SS

Figure 4.2 is the analysis of variance table for this study. The first column lists the sources of variation. The sums of squares attributable to each of the components are given in the second column. The sums of squares for each independent variable alone are sometimes termed the "main effect" sums of squares. The "explained" sum of squares is the total sum of squares for the main effect and interaction terms in the model.

The degrees of freedom for sex and attractiveness, listed in the third column, are one fewer than the number of categories. For example, since there are three levels of attractiveness, there are two degrees of freedom. Similarly, sex has one degree of freedom. Two degrees of freedom are associated with the interaction term (the product of the degrees of freedom of each of the individual variables). The degrees of freedom for the residual are $N-1-k$, where k equals the degrees of freedom for the explained sum of squares.

Figure 4.2   Analysis of variance table

```
ANOVA VARIABLES=SCORE BY ATTRACT(1,3) SEX(1,2).
```

```
          * * *  A N A L Y S I S   O F   V A R I A N C E  * * *
               SCORE      COMPOSITE SCORE
          by   ATTRACT    ATTRACTIVENESS LEVEL
               SEX        SEX SIMILARITY

                              Sum of                 Mean              Sig
  Source of Variation         Squares      DF        Square      F     of F

  Main Effects                733.700       3        244.567    3.276  .022
     ATTRACT                  686.850       2        343.425    4.600  .011
     SEX                       46.850       1         46.850    0.628  .429

  2-Way Interactions          942.350       2        471.175    6.311  .002
     ATTRACT  SEX             942.350       2        471.175    6.311  .002

  Explained                  1676.050       5        335.210    4.490  .000

  Residual                  21053.140     282         74.656

  Total                     22729.190     287         79.196
```

The mean squares shown in Figure 4.2 are obtained by dividing each sum of squares by its degrees of freedom. Hypothesis tests are based on the ratios of the mean squares of each source of variation to the mean square for the residual. When the assumptions are met and the true means are in fact equal, the distribution of the ratio is an F with the degrees of freedom for the numerator and denominator terms.

4.3
Testing for Interaction

The F value associated with the attractiveness and sex interaction is 6.311. The observed significance level is approximately 0.002. Therefore, it appears that there is an interaction between the two variables. What does this mean?

Figure 4.3a   Cell means
(From SPSS Graphics, a mainframe product)

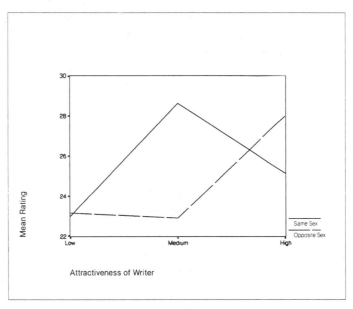

Consider Figure 4.3a, which is a plot of the cell means in Figure 4.1. Notice how the mean scores relate not only to the attractiveness of the individual and to the sex of the rater, but also to the particular combination of the values of the variables. Opposite-sex raters assign the highest scores to highly attractive individuals. Same-sex raters assign the highest scores to individuals of medium attractiveness. Thus, the ratings for each level of attractiveness depend on the sex variable. If there were no interaction between the two variables, a plot like that shown in Figure 4.3b might result, where the difference between the two types of raters is the same for the three levels of attractiveness.

**Figure 4.3b   Cell means with no interaction
(From SPSS Graphics, a mainframe product)**

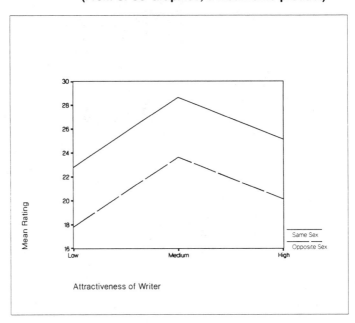

4.4
Tests for Sex and Attractiveness

Once the presence of interaction has been established, it is not particularly useful to continue hypothesis testing since the two variables *jointly* affect the dependent variable. If there is no significant interaction, the grouping variables can be tested individually. The F value associated with attractiveness would provide a test of the hypothesis that attractiveness does not affect the rating. Similarly, the F value associated with sex would test the hypothesis that sex has no main effect on evaluation.

Note that the small F value associated with sex does not indicate that response is unaffected by sex, since sex *is* included in the significant interaction term. Instead, it shows that when response is averaged over attractiveness levels, the two sex category means are not significantly different.

4.5
EXPLANATIONS

Several explanations are consistent with the results of this study. Since most people consider themselves moderately attractive, the highest degree of identification should be with same-sex individuals of moderate attractiveness. The higher empathy may result in the higher scores. An alternative theory is that moderately attractive individuals are generally perceived as more desirable same-sex friends: they have more favorable personality profiles and don't encourage unfavorable comparisons. Their writing scores may benefit from their perceived popularity.

Although we don't want friends who outshine us, handsome (and beautiful) dates provide a favorable reflection and enhance our status. Physical beauty is advantageous for heterosexual relationships, but not same-sex friendships. This prejudice may affect all evaluations of highly attractive members of the opposite sex. Regardless of the explanation, certain practical conclusions are apparent. Students, choose your instructors carefully! Authors, think twice before including your photo on the book jacket!

4.6 EXTENSIONS

Analysis of variance techniques can be used with any number of grouping variables. For example, the data in Table 4.1 originated from a more complicated experiment than described here. There were four factors—essay quality, physical attractiveness, sex of writer, and sex of subject. The original data were analyzed with a $3 \times 3 \times 2 \times 2$ ANOVA table. (The numbers indicate how many categories each grouping variable has.) The conclusions from our simplified analysis are the same as those from the more elaborate analysis.

Each of the cells in our experiment had the same number of subjects. This greatly simplifies the analysis and its interpretation. When unequal sample sizes occur in the cells, the total sum of squares cannot be partitioned into nice components that sum to the total. A variety of techniques are available for calculating sums of squares in such "non-orthogonal" designs. The methods differ in the way they adjust the sums of squares to account for other effects in the model. Each method results in different sums of squares and tests different hypotheses. However, when all cell frequencies are equal, the methods yield the same results. For discussion of various procedures for analyzing designs with unequal cell frequencies, see Kleinbaum and Kupper (1978) and Overall and Klett (1972).

4.7 RUNNING PROCEDURE ANOVA

The ANOVA procedure performs an *n*-way analysis of variance. Multiple factors (independent variables) and several dependent variables can be analyzed in one ANOVA procedure. Cell means and group sizes can be displayed in addition to the analysis of variance table.

For one-way analysis of variance, the ONEWAY procedure is often preferable (see Chapter 3). Contrasts, multiple comparisons, tests for trends, and homogeneity-of-variance statistics are produced by ONEWAY but not by ANOVA.

ANOVA operates via subcommands, including the optional STATISTICS and OPTIONS subcommands. The default model is the full factorial design, although other models can be analyzed. Covariates can be specified, but ANOVA does not perform a full analysis of covariance. There are three methods available for decomposing sums of squares, and the order of entry for covariates and factor main effects can be specified. Multiple classification analysis tables are also available.

4.8 Specifying the Variables

The only required specification is the VARIABLES subcommand with a list of one or more dependent variables, the keyword BY, and one to five factors (independent variables) followed by their minimum and maximum values enclosed in parentheses and separated by a comma. The actual keyword VARIABLES can be omitted. So the analysis of variance table in Figure 4.2 could be obtained by specifying either

```
ANOVA SCORE BY ATTRACT(1,3) SEX(1,2).
```

or

```
ANOVA VARIABLES=SCORE BY ATTRACT(1,3) SEX(1,2).
```

The values of the factors are arbitrary from a statistical point of view. They are not arbitrary, however, from a computational point of view, as they define the dimensions of the table of means and variances from which the analysis of variance is obtained. If the factor variables do not have consecutive values, they should be recoded using either the RECODE command or the AUTORECODE command (see *SPSS/PC+ Data Analysis*). before running ANOVA. Otherwise, SPSS/PC+ may not have enough computer resources to complete the job.

4.9
Specifying Full Factorial Models

The full factorial model is the default. If two or more dependent variables are named, separate analyses of variance are produced for each. They are not analyzed jointly. Interaction terms up to fifth order are analyzed.

If two or more factor variables have the same value range, the range can be listed following the last factor it applies to, as in the command

```
ANOVA CHOL BY OVERWT AGE RACE(1,4).
```

The value-range specification need not correspond exactly to a variable's actual range of values. If the specified range is smaller than the actual range, cases with values outside the specified range are excluded from the analysis. If a range larger than the actual range is specified, however, the memory required to process the ANOVA command is needlessly increased.

Only integer-valued variables should be used as factors. If a noninteger-valued variable is included in the factor list, its values will be truncated to integers. This may result in categories that are not what you intended. The RECODE command should be used before the ANOVA command to transform noninteger factor values into integer values.

More than one design can be specified on an ANOVA command by using multiple analysis lists separated by slashes, as in the command

```
ANOVA PRESTIGE BY INCOME(1,3) RACE SEX (1,2)
  /PRSTCHNG BY INCOME(1,3) RACE SEX (1,2) AGE (1,5).
```

4.10
Requesting Cell Means and Counts

The means and counts table is displayed when Statistic 3 is specified on the STATISTICS subcommand.

Statistic 3 *Display cell means and counts for the dependent variable.* For each dependent variable, a separate table is displayed, showing the means and cell counts for each combination of factor values that define the effect (ignoring all other factors). Means of covariates are not displayed.

For example, the tables in Figure 4.1 were produced by specifying

```
ANOVA SCORE BY ATTRACT(1,3) SEX (1,2)
  /STATISTICS=3.
```

Tables for the SEX, ATTRACT, and SEX by ATTRACT interaction effects are given in this output.

If Option 9 is used, this table is not available (see Section 4.13). Since Options 3 through 6 (see Section 4.11) suppress interaction terms, cell means corresponding to the suppressed interaction terms are not displayed when any of these options is used.

4.11
Suppressing Interaction Effects

By default, all interaction effects up to and including fifth-order effects are examined. You can suppress various orders of interaction effects by using the following options on the OPTIONS subcommand:

Option 3 *Suppress all interaction terms.* Only main effects and covariate effects are in the ANOVA table; the interaction sums of squares are pooled into the error (residual) sum of squares.

Option 4 *Delete all three-way and higher-order interaction terms.* The sums of squares for three-way and higher-order interactions are pooled into the error sums of squares.

Option 5 *Delete all four-way and higher-order interaction terms.* The sums of squares for four-way and higher-order interactions are pooled into the error sum of squares.

Option 6 *Delete all five-way interaction terms.* The sums of squares for the five-way and higher-order interactions are pooled into the error sum of squares.

ANOVA will not examine six-way or higher-order interactions, and the sums of squares for such terms are always pooled into the error sum of squares.

4.12
Specifying Covariates

List covariates after the factor list, following the keyword WITH, as in the command

    ANOVA SCORE BY ATTRACT(1,3) WITH SELFATRT.

By default, the covariates are assessed first, with main effects assessed after adjusting for the covariates. You can specify the order in which blocks of covariates and factor main effects are assessed with the following options:

Option 7 *Process covariates concurrently with main effects for factors.*

Option 8 *Process covariates after the main effects of the factors have been included.*

Note that the order of entry is irrelevant if Option 9 (the regression approach) is specified (see Section 4.13).

Unstandardized regression coefficients for the covariates are displayed if Statistic 2 is specified on the STATISTICS subcommand.

Statistic 2 *Display unstandardized regression coefficients for covariates.* These regression coefficients are computed when the covariates are entered into the equation. Their values depend on the design specified by Options 7 through 10 or by default. (See Section 4.13 for a discussion of Options 9 and 10.) These coefficients are displayed immediately below the analysis of variance table.

4.13
Decomposing Sums of Squares

Three methods are available for decomposing sums of squares. The default method is the *classical experimental approach,* in which each type of effect is assessed separately in the following order (unless Option 7 or 8 has been specified):

• Effects of covariates.
• Main effects of factors.
• Two-way interaction effects.
• Three-way interaction effects.
• Four-way interaction effects.
• Five-way interaction effects.

Each effect is adjusted for all other effects of that type and for all previously entered effects.

The second method, requested by specifying Option 9 on the OPTIONS subcommand, is the *regression approach.*

Option 9 *Regression approach.* All effects are assessed simultaneously, with each effect adjusted for all other effects in the model.

The following restrictions apply when this method is used:

• For each independent variable, at least one case must have the lowest value of the independent variable, since the lowest values are used as the reference category. If this does not hold, no ANOVA table is produced and a message identifying the first problematic variable is displayed.

• When the independent variables are crosstabulated, no cell defined by the smallest value of any independent variable can be empty. If this restriction is violated, one or more orders of interaction effects are suppressed, and a warning message is displayed. This constraint does not apply to cells defined by values of independent variables that do not occur in the data. For example, if two independent variables each have the values 1, 2, and 4, the (1,1), (1,2), (2,1), (4,1), and (1,4) cells can not be empty. The (1,3), (2,3), (3,3), (4,3), (3,1), (3,2), and (3,4) cells are automatically empty, however, and this does not violate the restriction. The (2,2), (2,4), (4,2), and (4,4) cells can be empty, although the degrees of freedom will be reduced accordingly if they are.

The lowest nonempty value of each independent variable should therefore be specified in the value range. Specifying a value range of (0,9) for a variable that actually has only the values 1 through 9 results in a violation of both restrictions, and no ANOVA table will be produced.

The *hierarchical approach* is the third method available for decomposing sums of squares. This method differs from the classical experimental approach only in the way covariates and factor main effects are treated.

Option 10 *Hierarchical approach.* Factor main effects and covariate effects are assessed hierarchically. The order in which they are assessed is determined by the order in which they are listed on the ANOVA command. The factor main effects are adjusted only for the factor main effects already assessed, and the covariate effects are adjusted only for the covariates already assessed.

To understand the three approaches, consider the command

```
ANOVA TESTSCOR BY SEX(1,2) MTVN(1,5) ATT(1,3).
```

Table 4.13 summarizes the way each of the three approaches would analyze the design. In the default classical experimental approach, each main effect is assessed with the two other main effects held constant. The two-way interactions are assessed with all main effects and all other two-way interactions held constant, and the three-way interaction is assessed with all main effects and two-way interactions held constant. The regression approach assesses each factor or interaction while holding all other factors and interactions constant. In the hierarchical approach, the order in which the factors are listed on the ANOVA command determines the order in which they are assessed.

Table 4.13   Terms adjusted for in each approach

Effect	Classical approach (default)	Regression approach (Option 9)	Hierarchical approach (Option 10)
SEX	MTVN, ATT	All others	None
MTVN	SEX, ATT	All others	SEX
ATTN	SEX, MTVN	All others	SEX, MTVN
SEX*MTVN	SEX, MTVN, ATT, SEX*ATT, MTVN, ATT	All others	SEX, MTVN, ATT, SEX*ATT, MTVN*ATT
SEX*ATT	SEX, MTVN, ATT, SEX*MTVN, MTVN*ATT	All others	SEX, MTVN, ATT, SEX*MTVN, MTVN*ATT
MTVN*ATT	SEX, MTVN, ATT, SEX*MTVN, SEX*ATT	All others	SEX, MTVN, ATT, SEX*MTVN, SEX*ATT
SEX*MTVN*ATT	SEX, MTVN, ATT, SEX*MTVN, SEX*ATT, MTVN*ATT	All others	SEX, MTVN, ATT, SEX*MTVN, SEX*ATT, MTVN*ATT

4.14
Summary of Analysis Methods

Various methods for decomposing sums of squares and specifying the order of entry of covariates have been discussed. Table 4.14 summarizes the types of analyses produced when combinations of these methods are used.

Table 4.14 Combinations of Options 7 through 10

Options in effect	Assessments between types	Assessments within types
Default	Covariates THEN Factors THEN Interactions	Covariates: adjust for all other covariates Factors: adjust for covariates and all other factors Interactions: adjust for covariates, factors, and all other interactions of the same and lower orders
Option 7	Factors and Covariates concurrently THEN Interactions	Covariates: adjust for factors and all other covariates Factors: adjust for covariates and all other factors Interactions: adjust for covariates, factors, and all other interactions of the same and lower orders
Option 8	Factors THEN Covariates THEN Interactions	Factors: adjust for all other factors Covariates: adjust for factors and all other covariates Interactions: adjust for covariates, factors, and all other interactions of the same and lower orders
Option 9	Covariates, Factors, and Interactions simultaneously	Covariates: adjust for factors, interactions, and all other covariates Factors: adjust for covariates, interactions, and all other factors Interactions: adjust for covariates, factors, and all other interactions
Option 10	Covariates THEN Factors THEN Interactions	Covariates: adjust for covariates that are preceding in the list Factors: adjust for covariates and factors preceding in the list Interactions: adjust for covariates, factors, and all other interactions of the same and lower orders
Options 7 and 10	Factors and Covariates concurrently THEN Interactions	Factors: adjust only for preceding factors Covariates: adjust for factors and preceding covariates Interactions: adjust for covariates, factors, and all other interactions of the same and lower orders
Options 8 and 10	Factors THEN Covariates THEN Interactions	Factors: adjust only for preceding factors Covariates: adjust for factors and preceding covariates Interactions: adjust for covariates, factors, and all other interactions

Statistics Guide

4.15
Multiple Classification Analysis

Multiple classification output consists of the grand mean of the dependent variables, a table of deviations from the grand mean for each factor level (*treatment effects*), and several measures of association. The deviations indicate the magnitude of the effect of each factor level. To obtain this output, specify Statistic 1 on the STATISTICS subcommand.

Statistic 1 *Display multiple classification analysis (MCA) table.* Three types of deviations are displayed: unadjusted deviations, deviations adjusted for the main effects of other factors if covariates are used, and deviations adjusted for the main effects of other factors and for covariates. The adjusted deviations show the effect of a particular factor level after variation due to other factors (or to other factors and covariates) has been taken into account.

The form of analysis specified by Options 7 through 10 and their defaults affects the results in the MCA table. If covariates are used, a complete table can be obtained only if Option 8, Options 8 and 10, or Options 7 and 10 are used. If a model in which factors are not assessed first is specified, deviations adjusted only for factors are not displayed in the MCA table. If Option 9 is used, the MCA table is not produced. Ordinarily, this table is of interest only when no interaction terms are significant.

Several measures of association are also displayed in the MCA table. For each factor in the table, the eta statistic is calculated. Its squared value indicates the proportion of variance "explained" by a given factor. Standardized regression coefficients, called BETA's, are also displayed. Finally, multiple R and R^2 are at the bottom of the table. R^2 indicates the proportion of variance in the dependent variable "accounted for" by all factors, covariates, and interaction terms.

4.16
Missing Values

By default, a case with missing values for any variables in the analysis list is excluded from all analyses specified by that list. With Option 1, cases with user-defined missing data are included in the analysis.

Option 1 *Include user-missing values.*

4.17
Formatting Options

By default, variable and value labels (if defined) are included in the output. The width of the output defaults to the width defined on SET (see *SPSS/PC+ Data Analysis*). Two options are available for controlling the format of the output:

Option 2 *Suppress variable and value labels.*
Option 11 *Use narrow format.*

4.18
Annotated Example

The following SPSS/PC+ commands were used to obtain the analysis in this chapter:

```
DATA LIST  / ATTRACT 1-2 SEX 3 SCORE 4-5.
BEGIN DATA.
lines of data
END DATA.
RECODE ATTRACT (1=1) (5=2) (10=3).
VARIABLE LABELS
    ATTRACT 'ATTRACTIVENESS LEVEL'/
    SEX 'SEX SIMILARITY'/
    SCORE 'COMPOSITE SCORE'.
VALUE LABELS
    ATTRACT 1 'LOW' 2 'MEDIUM' 3 'HIGH'/
    SEX 1 'SAME' 2 'OPPOSITE'.
ANOVA  SCORE BY ATTRACT(1,3) SEX(1,2)
  /STATISTICS=3.
FINISH.
```

- The DATA LIST command indicates that the data for each case is on a single record, with ATTRACT in columns 1 and 2, SEX in column 3, and SCORE in columns 4 and 5.

- The RECODE command changes the original values of ATTRACT (1, 5, and 10) to the consecutive values 1, 2, and 3, so that ANOVA processing will be more efficient.

- The VARIABLE LABELS command assigns variable labels, and the VALUE LABELS command defines labels for the new values of ATTRACT and for the values of SEX.

- The ANOVA command names SCORE as the dependent variable and ATTRACT and SEX as the factors. The minimum and maximum values for ATTRACT are 1 and 3, and for SEX, 1 and 2.

- The STATISTICS subcommand displays group means and counts for SCORE.

Contents

5 Nonparametric Tests: Procedure NPAR TESTS

Coffee and carrots have recently joined saccharin, tobacco, Laetrile, and interferon on the ever-expanding list of rumored causes of and cures for cancer. This list is necessarily tentative and complicated. The two major sources of evidence—experiments on animals and examination of the histories of afflicted persons—are fraught with problems. It is difficult to predict, based on large doses of suspect substances given to small animals, the consequences of small amounts consumed by humans over a long time span.

In studies of people, lifestyle components are difficult to isolate, and it is challenging—if not impossible—to unravel the contribution of a single factor. For example, what is the role of caffeine based on a sample of overweight, sedentary, coffee- and alcohol-drinking, cigarette-smoking, urban dwellers?

Nutrition is also thought to be an important component in cancer development and progression. For example, the per capita consumption of dietary fats is positively correlated with the incidence of mammary and colon cancer in humans (Wynder, 1976). In a recent study, King et al. (1979) examined the relationship between diet and tumor development in rats. Three groups of animals of the same age, species, and physical condition were injected with tumor cells. The rats were divided into three groups and fed diets of either low, saturated, or unsaturated fat.

One hypothesis of interest is whether the length of time until a tumor develops in rats fed saturated diets differs from the length of time in rats fed unsaturated diets. If it is tenable to assume that tumor-free time is normally distributed, the two-sample t-test described in Chapter 1 can be used to test the hypothesis that the population means are equal. However, if the distribution of times does not appear to be normal, and especially if the sample sizes are small, statistical procedures that do not require assumptions about the shapes of the underlying distributions should be considered.

5.1
THE MANN-WHITNEY TEST

The *Mann-Whitney test*, also known as the Wilcoxon test, does not require assumptions about the shape of the underlying distributions. It tests the hypothesis that two independent samples come from populations having the same distribution. The form of the distribution need not be specified. The test does not require that the variable be measured on an interval scale; an ordinal scale is sufficient.

5.2
Ranking the Data

To compute the test, the observations from both samples are first combined and ranked from smallest to largest. Consider Table 5.2, which shows a sample of the King data reported by Lee (1979). Case 4 has the shortest elapsed time to development of a tumor, 68 days. It is assigned a rank of 1. The next shortest time is for Case 3, so it is assigned a rank of 2. Cases 5 and 6 both exhibited tumors on the same day. They are both assigned a rank of 3.5, the average of the ranks (3 and 4) for which they are tied. Case 2, the next largest, is given a rank of 5, and Case 1 is given a rank of 6.

Table 5.2 Ranking the data

	Saturated			Unsaturated	
Case	Time	Rank	Case	Time	Rank
1	199	6	4	68	1
2	126	5	5	112	3.5
3	81	2	6	112	3.5

**5.3
Calculating the Test**

The statistic for testing the hypothesis that the two distributions are equal is the sum of the ranks for each of the two groups. If the groups have the same distribution, their sample distributions of ranks should be similar. If one of the groups has more than its share of small or large ranks, there is reason to suspect that the two underlying distributions are different.

Figure 5.3 shows the output from the Mann-Whitney test for the complete King data. For each group, the mean rank and number of cases is given. (The mean rank is the sum of the ranks divided by the number of cases.) Note that the unsaturated-diet group has only 29 cases since one rat died of causes unrelated to the experiment. The entry displayed under W is the sum of the ranks for the group with the smaller number of observations. If both groups have the same number of observations, W is the rank sum for the group named first on the NPAR TESTS command. For this example, W is 963, the sum of the ranks for the saturated-diet group.

Figure 5.3 Mann-Whitney output

```
NPAR TESTS M-W=TUMOR BY DIET(0,1).
```

The number identified on the output as U is the number of times a value in the unsaturated-diet group precedes a value in the saturated-diet group. To understand what this means, consider the data in Table 5.2 again. All three cases in the unsaturated-diet group have smaller ranks than the first case in the saturated-diet group, so they all precede Case 1 in the rankings. Similarly, all three cases in the unsaturated-diet group precede Case 2. Only one unsaturated-diet case (Case 4) is smaller in value than Case 3. Thus, the number of times the value for an unsaturated-diet case precedes the value for a saturated-diet case is $3+3+1=7$. The number of times the value of a saturated-diet case precedes the value of an unsaturated-diet case is 2, since Case 3 has a smaller rank than both Cases 5 and 6. The smaller of these two numbers is displayed on the output as U. If the two distributions are equal, values from one group should not consistently precede values in the other.

The significance levels associated with U and W are the same. They can be obtained by transforming the score to a standard normal deviate (Z). If the total sample size is less than 30, an exact probability level based on the distribution of the score is also displayed. From Figure 5.3, the observed significance level for this example is 0.158. Since the significance level is large, the hypothesis that tumor-free time has the same distribution for the two diet groups is not rejected.

5.4
Which Diet?

You should not conclude from these findings that it doesn't matter—as far as tumors are concerned—what kind of fat you (or rats) eat. King et al. found that rats fed the unsaturated diet had a total of 96 tumors at the end of the experiment, while rats fed the saturated diet had only 55 tumors. They also found that large tumors were more common in the unsaturated-diet group than in the saturated-diet group. Thus, unsaturated fats may be more hazardous than saturated fats.

5.5
Assumptions

The Mann-Whitney test requires only that the observations be a random sample and that values can be ordered. These assumptions, especially randomness, are not to be made lightly, but they are less restrictive than those for the two-sample t-test for means. The t-test further requires that the observations be selected from normally distributed populations with equal variances. (An approximate test for the case of unequal variances is presented in Chapter 1.)

Since the Mann-Whitney test can always be calculated instead of the t-test, what determines which should be used? If the assumptions needed for the t-test are met, the t-test is more powerful than the Mann-Whitney test. That is, the t-test will detect true differences between the two populations more often than will the Mann-Whitney test since the t-test uses more information from the data. Substitution of ranks for the actual values loses potentially useful information. On the other hand, using the t-test when its assumptions are substantially violated may result in an erroneous observed significance level.

In general, if the assumptions of the t-test appear reasonable, it should be used. When the data are ordinal—or interval but from a markedly nonnormal distribution—the Mann-Whitney test is the procedure of choice.

5.6
NONPARAMETRIC TESTS

Many statistical procedures, like the Mann-Whitney test, require limited distributional assumptions about the data. Collectively these procedures are termed *distribution-free* or *nonparametric tests.* Like the Mann-Whitney test, distribution-free tests are generally less powerful than their parametric counterparts. They are most useful in situations where parametric procedures are not appropriate: when the data are nominal or ordinal, or when interval data are from markedly nonnormal distributions. Significance levels for certain nonparametric tests can be determined regardless of the shape of the population distribution since they are based on ranks.

In the following sections, various nonparametric tests will be used to reanalyze some of the data described in previous chapters. Since the data were chosen to illustrate the parametric procedures, they satisfy assumptions that are more restrictive than those for nonparametric procedures. However, they provide an opportunity for learning new procedures with familiar data and for comparing results from different types of analyses.

5.7
One-Sample Tests

Various one-sample nonparametric procedures are available for testing hypotheses about the parameters of a population. These include procedures for examining differences in paired samples.

5.8 The Sign Test

In Chapter 1, the paired t-test for means is used to test the hypothesis that mean buying scores for husbands and wives are equal. Remember that this test requires the assumption that differences are normally distributed.

The *sign test* is a nonparametric procedure used with two related samples to test the hypothesis that the distributions of two variables are the same. This test makes no assumptions about the shape of these distributions.

To compute the sign test, the difference between the buying scores of husbands and wives is calculated for each case. Next, the numbers of positive and negative differences are obtained. If the distributions of the two variables are the same, the numbers of positive and negative differences should be similar.

Figure 5.8 Sign test output

```
NPAR TESTS SIGN=HSSCALE WITH WSSCALE.
```

```
- - - - - Sign Test

     HSSCALE    HUSBAND SELF SCALE
with WSSCALE    WIFE SELF SCALE

            Cases

               56  - Diffs (WSSCALE Lt HSSCALE)                Z =        1.6416
               39  + Diffs (WSSCALE Gt HSSCALE)
                3    Ties                             2-tailed P =         .1007
              ---
               98    Total
```

The output in Figure 5.8 shows that the number of negative differences is 56, while the number of positive differences is 39. The total number of cases is 98, including three with no differences. The observed significance level is 0.1007. Since this value is large, the hypothesis that the distributions are the same is not rejected.

5.9 The Wilcoxon Signed-Ranks Test

The sign test uses only the direction of the differences between the pairs and ignores the magnitude. A discrepancy of 15 between husbands' and wives' buying scores is treated in the same way as a discrepancy of 1. The *Wilcoxon signed-ranks test* incorporates information about the magnitude of the differences and is therefore more powerful than the sign test.

To compute the Wilcoxon signed-ranks test, the differences are ranked ignoring the signs. In the case of ties, average ranks are assigned. The sums of the ranks for positive and negative differences are then calculated.

Figure 5.9 Wilcoxon signed-ranks test output

```
NPAR TESTS WILCOXON=HSSCALE WITH WSSCALE.
```

```
- - - - - Wilcoxon Matched-pairs Signed-ranks Test

     HSSCALE    HUSBAND SELF SCALE
with WSSCALE    WIFE SELF SCALE

      Mean Rank      Cases

        45.25          56  - Ranks (WSSCALE Lt HSSCALE)
        51.95          39  + Ranks (WSSCALE Gt HSSCALE)
                        3    Ties  (WSSCALE Eq HSSCALE)
                       --
                       98    Total

        Z =     -.9428              2-tailed P =  .3458
```

From Figure 5.9, the average rank of the 56 negative differences is 45.25. The average positive rank is 51.95. The three cases that are tied have the same value for both variables. The observed significance level associated with the test is large (.3458), so again the hypothesis of no difference is not rejected.

**5.10
The Wald-Wolfowitz Runs
Test**

The runs test is a test of randomness. That is, given a sequence of observations, the runs test examines whether the value of one observation influences the values taken by later observations. If there is no influence (the observations are independent), the sequence is considered random.

A *run* is any sequence of like observations. For example, if a coin is tossed fifteen times and the outcomes recorded, the following sequence might result:

HHHTHHHHTTTTTTT

There are four runs in this sequence: HHH, T, HHHH, and TTTTTTT. The total number of runs is a measure of randomness, since too many runs, or too few, suggest dependence between observations. The Wald-Walfowitz runs test converts the total number of runs into a Z statistic having approximately a normal distribution. The only requirement for this test is that the variable tested be dichotomous (have only two possible values).

Suppose, for example, that a weather forecaster records whether it snows for twenty days in February and obtains the following sequence (1=snow, 0=no snow):

01111111010101111111100

To test the hypothesis that the occurrence or nonoccurrence of snow on one day has no effect on whether it snows on later days, the runs test is performed, resulting in the output in Figure 5.10.

Figure 5.10 Runs test

```
NPAR TESTS RUNS(1)=SNOW.
```

```
- - - - - Runs Test

    SNOW


        Runs:    7           Test Value = 1

        Cases:   5    Lt 1
                15    Ge 1               Z =  -.6243
                --
                20    Total  2-tailed P =    .5324
```

Since the observed significance level is quite large (.5324), the hypothesis of randomness is not rejected. It does not appear, from these data, that snowy (or nonsnowy) days affect the later occurrence of snow.

**5.11
The Binomial Test**

With data that are binomially distributed, the hypothesis that the probability p of a particular outcome is equal to some number is often of interest. For example, you might want to find out if a tossed coin was unbiased. To check this, you could test to see whether the probability of heads was equal to 1/2. The binomial test compares the observed frequencies in each category of a binomial distribution to the frequencies expected under a binomial distribution with the probability parameter p.

For instance, a nickel is tossed twenty times, with the following results (1=heads, 0=tails):

10011111101111011011

The output in Figure 5.11 shows a binomial test of the hypothesis that the probability of heads equals 1/2 for these data.

Figure 5.11 Binomial test

```
NPAR TESTS BINOMIAL=HEADS(0,1).
```

```
- - - - - Binomial Test

    HEADS

    Cases

         5    = 0              Test Prob. =    .5000
        15    = 1
        --                     2-tailed P =    .0207
        20    Total
```

The small (.0207) observed significance level indicates that it is not likely that *p* equals 1/2 and it appears that the coin is biased.

5.12
The Kolmogorov-Smirnov One-Sample Test

The Kolmogorov-Smirnov test is used to determine how well a random sample of data fits a particular distribution (uniform, normal, or Poisson). It is based on comparison of the sample cumulative distribution function to the hypothesized cumulative distribution function.

This test can be used with the beer data (see *SPSS/PC+ Data Analysis)* to see whether it is reasonable to assume that the ALCOHOL variable is normally distributed. The Kolmogorov-Smirnov output in Figure 5.12 shows an observed significance level of 0.05, small enough to cast doubt on the assumption of normality.

Figure 5.12 Kolmogorov-Smirnov test

```
NPAR TESTS K-S(POISSON,5)=HORSKICK.
```

```
- - - - - Kolmogorov - Smirnov Goodness of Fit Test

    ALCOHOL    ALCOHOL BY VOLUME (IN %)

    Test Distribution - Normal                    Mean:   4.577
                                    Standard Deviation:    .603

         Cases:  35

                 Most Extreme Differences
         Absolute     Positive      Negative      K-S Z      2-tailed P
         0.22941      0.15585      -0.22941       1.357         0.050
```

5.13
The One-Sample Chi-Square Test

In *SPSS/PC+ Data Analysis,* frequencies of deaths for the days of the week are examined. The FREQUENCIES output suggests that all days of the week are equally hazardous in regard to death. To test this conclusion, the *one-sample chi-square test* can be used. This nonparametric test requires only that the data be a random sample.

To calculate the one-sample chi-square statistic, the data are first classified into mutually exclusive categories of interest—days of the week in this example—and then expected frequencies for these categories are computed. Expected frequencies are the frequencies that would be expected if the null hypothesis is true. For the death data, the hypothesis to be tested is that the probability of death is the same for each day of the week. The day of death is known for 110 subjects. The hypothesis implies that the expected frequency of deaths for each weekday is 110 divided by 7, or 15.71. Once the expected frequencies are obtained, the chi-square statistic is computed as

$$\chi^2 = \sum_{i=1}^{k} (O_i - E_i)^2 / E_i$$

Equation 5.13

where O_i is the observed frequency for the ith category, E_i is the expected frequency for the ith category, and k is the number of categories.

Figure 5.13   One-sample chi-square output

```
NPAR TESTS   CHI-SQUARE=DAYOFWK.
```

```
- - - - - Chi-square Test

    DAYOFWK    DAY OF DEATH

                                       Cases
                            Category   Observed   Expected   Residual
        SUNDAY               1.00        19        15.71       3.29
        MONDAY               2.00        11        15.71      -4.71
        TUESDAY              3.00        19        15.71       3.29
        WEDNSDAY             4.00        17        15.71       1.29
        THURSDAY             5.00        15        15.71       -.71
        FRIDAY               6.00        13        15.71      -2.71
        SATURDAY             7.00        16        15.71        .29
                                       ---
                            Total       110

            Chi-Square              D.F.           Significance
              3.400                  6                0.757
```

If the null hypothesis is true, the chi-square statistic has approximately a chi-square distribution with $k-1$ degrees of freedom. This statistic will be large if the observed and expected frequencies are substantially different. Figure 5.13 shows the output from the one-sample chi-square test for the death data. The observed chi-square value is 3.4, and the associated significance level is 0.757. Since the observed significance level is large, the hypothesis that deaths are evenly distributed over days of the week is not rejected.

**5.14
The Friedman Test**

The Friedman test is used to compare two or more related samples. (This is an extension of the problem of paired data.) The k variables to be compared are ranked from 1 to k for each case, and the mean ranks for the variables are calculated and compared, resulting in a test statistic with approximately a chi-square distribution.

The Friedman test can be used to analyze data from a psychology experiment concerned with memory. In this experiment, subjects were asked to memorize first a two-digit number, then a three-digit number, and finally a four-digit number. After each number was memorized, they were shown a single digit and asked if that digit was present in the number memorized. The times taken to reach a decision for the two-, three-, and four-digit numbers are the three related variables of interest.

Figure 5.14 shows the results of the Friedman test, examining the hypothesis that the number of digits memorized has no effect on the time taken to reach a decision. The observed significance level is extremely small, so it appears that the number of digits does affect decision time.

Figure 5.14   Friedman test

```
NPAR TESTS FRIEDMAN=P2DIGIT P3DIGIT P4DIGIT.
```

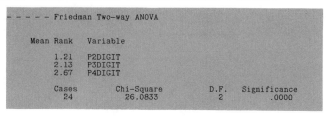

```
- - - - - Friedman Two-way ANOVA

    Mean Rank    Variable

        1.21     P2DIGIT
        2.13     P3DIGIT
        2.67     P4DIGIT

    Cases          Chi-Square         D.F.    Significance
     24             26.0833            2          .0000
```

5.15
Tests for Two or More Independent Samples

A variety of nonparametric tests involve comparisons between two or more independent samples. (The Mann-Whitney test is one such test.) In this respect, these tests resemble the t-tests and one-way analyses of variance described in Chapters 1 and 3.

5.16
The Two-Sample Median Test

The two-sample median test is used to determine whether two populations have the same median. The two samples are combined and the median for the total distribution is calculated. The number of observations above this median, as well as the number of observations less than or equal to this median, is counted for each sample. The test statistic is based on these counts.

This test can be used to determine whether median sodium levels are the same for the highest-rated and lowest-rated beers in the beer data. The output in Figure 5.16 shows the largest possible p value, 1. Therefore, there is no reason to suspect different medians.

Figure 5.16   Median test of sodium by rating

```
NPAR TESTS MEDIAN=SODIUM BY RATING(3,1).
```

```
- - - - - Median Test

    SODIUM      SODIUM PER 12 FLUID OUNCES IN MG
   by RATING


                             RATING
                          3        1
                     ----------------------
             Gt Median    4        5
   SODIUM            ----------------------
             Le Median    6        6
                     ----------------------

        Cases          Median          Exact Probability
         21              15                  1.0000
```

5.17
The Two-Sample Wald-Wolfowitz Runs Test

A runs test can be used to test the hypothesis that two samples come from populations with the same distributions. To perform this test, the two samples are combined and the values sorted. A run in this combined and sorted sample consists of a sequence of values belonging to the first sample or a sequence of values belonging to the second sample. If there are too few runs, it suggests that the two populations have different distributions.

The Wald-Wolfowitz test can be used with the beer data to compare calories for the highest-ranked and lowest-ranked beers. The output in Figure 5.17 shows an observed significance level of 0.0119. Since this is small, the distribution of calories for the highest-ranked beers appears to differ from the distribution of calories for the lowest-ranked beers.

Figure 5.17   Wald-Wolfowitz runs test

```
NPAR TESTS W-W=CALORIES BY RATING(3,1).
```

```
- - - - - Wald-Wolfowitz Runs Test

    CALORIES   CALORIES PER 12 FLUID OUNCES
   by RATING


        Cases

          10   RATING = 3  FAIR
          11   RATING = 1  VERY GOOD
         ---
          21   Total
                                                    Exact
                         Runs        Z        1-tailed P
   Minimum Possible:       6      -2.2335        .0119
   Maximum Possible:       6      -2.2335        .0119

      WARNING -- There are   1 Inter-group Ties involving    5 cases.
```

5.18
The Two-Sample
Kolmogorov-Smirnov Test

The Kolmogorov-Smirnov test for two samples provides another method for testing whether two samples come from populations with the same distributions. It is based on a comparison of the distribution functions for the two samples.

This test can be used with the beer data to compare the alcohol content of the highest-ranked and lowest-ranked beers. Since the observed significance level in Figure 5.18 is small, the alcohol distributions do not appear to be the same. The approximation used to obtain the observed significance level may be inadequate in this case, however, because of the small sample size.

Figure 5.18   Kolmogorov-Smirnov two-sample test

```
NPAR TESTS K-S=ALCOHOL BY RATING(3,1).
```

```
- - - - Kolmogorov - Smirnov 2-Sample Test
     ALCOHOL    ALCOHOL BY VOLUME (IN %)
   by RATING


        Cases

          10  RATING = 3  FAIR
          11  RATING = 1  VERY GOOD
          --
          21  Total
WARNING - Due to small sample size, probability tables should be consulted.

          Most Extreme Differences
     Absolute        Positive        Negative        K-S Z        2-tailed P
     0.60000          0.0            -0.60000         1.373           0.046
```

5.19
The *k*-Sample Median Test

An extension of the two-sample median test, the *k*-sample median test compares the medians of three or more independent samples. Figure 5.19 shows a *k*-sample median test comparing median prices for the highest-, middle-, and lowest-quality beers. The observed significance level is fairly large (.091), indicating no real difference in the median price of the three types of beer.

Figure 5.19   k-sample median test

```
NPAR TESTS MEDIAN=PRICE BY RATING(1,3).
```

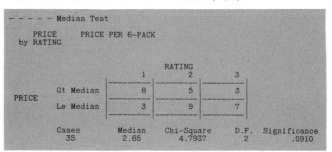

```
- - - - - Median Test
     PRICE       PRICE PER 6-PACK
   by RATING


                                RATING
                           1         2         3
                       ---------------------------
           Gt Median   |    8    |    5    |   3   |
   PRICE               ---------------------------
           Le Median   |    3    |    9    |   7   |
                       ---------------------------

           Cases        Median      Chi-Square      D.F.    Significance
            35           2.65         4.7937          2         .0910
```

5.20
The Kruskal-Wallis Test

An experiment described earlier in this chapter investigates the effects of three diets on tumor development in rats. The Mann-Whitney test was calculated to examine the different effects of saturated and unsaturated diets. To test for differences between all three diets, an extension of the Mann-Whitney test can be used. This test is known as the *Kruskal-Wallis one-way analysis of variance.*

The procedure for computing the Kruskal-Wallis test is similar to that used in the Mann-Whitney test. All cases from the groups are combined and ranked. Average ranks are assigned in the case of ties. For each group, the ranks are summed, and the Kruskal-Wallis H statistic is computed from these sums. The H statistic has approximately a chi-square distribution under the hypothesis that the three groups have the same distribution.

Figure 5.20 Kruskal-Wallis one-way analysis of variance output

`NPAR TESTS K-W=TUMOR BY DIET(0,2).`

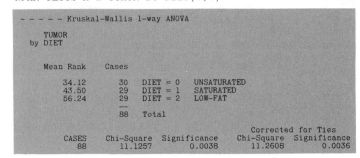

The output in Figure 5.20 shows that the third group, the low-fat-diet group, has the largest average rank. The value of the Kruskal-Wallis statistic (labeled **Chi-Square**) is 11.1257. When the statistic is adjusted for the presence of ties, the value changes to 11.2608 (labeled **Corrected Chi-Square**). The small observed significance level suggests that the development time for a tumor is not the same for all three groups.

5.21
RUNNING
PROCEDURE NPAR
TESTS

You can perform all of the nonparametric tests discussed in this chapter, and several more, with procedure NPAR TESTS. (See Siegel, 1956, for further information about these tests.) In addition to obtaining test statistics, you can request additional statistics, specify missing-value treatments, and use a random subsample of your data for NPAR TESTS. The tests available are summarized in Table 5.21.

Table 5.21 Nonparametric tests available in NPAR TESTS

Data organization	Nominal scale	Ordinal scale
One sample	Chi-square Runs Binomial	Kolmogorov-Smirnov
Two related samples	McNemar	Sign Wilcoxon
k related samples	Cochoran's Q	Friedman Kendall
Two independent samples		Median Mann-Whitney Kolmogorov-Smirnov Wald-Wolfowitz Moses
k independent samples		Median Kruskal-Wallis

NPAR TESTS operates via subcommands, including the OPTIONS and STATISTICS subcommands. The general format for an NPAR TESTS command is

NPAR TESTS *testname*[(*parameters*)]=*varlist*

Each subcommand requests a specific test and lists the variables to be tested. The equals sign is optional. You can use the TO keyword to refer to adjacent variables in the file. The form of the variable list depends on the type of test specified. More than one test may be requested on one NPAR TESTS command.

5.22
One-Sample Tests

The one-sample tests available in NPAR TESTS are the one-sample chi-square test, the Kolmogorov-Smirnov test, the runs test, and the binomial test.

5.23
The One-Sample Chi-Square Test

Use the CHISQUARE subcommand to obtain a one-sample chi-square test. The format is:

NPAR TESTS CHISQUARE=*varlist*[(*lo,hi*)]

The range following the variable list is optional. If it is not specified, each distinct value of the variable named is treated as a separate category. If the range is specified, noninteger values are truncated to integers, resulting in categories with only integer values. Cases with values outside the specified range are excluded from the analysis.

By default, the expected frequencies are assumed to be equal. You can specify other frequencies, however, by using the EXPECTED subcommand, which has the format

EXPECTED=*f1,f2,....,fn*

where *f1* through *fn* are the expected frequencies to be used. You must specify a frequency greater than zero for each category of the variable. The values listed in EXPECTED are treated as proportions rather than actual numbers of cases expected. That is, the values are summed, and each value is then divided by this sum to calculate the proportion of cases expected in the corresponding category. For example, the command

```
NPAR TESTS CHISQUARE=FLOWERS
   /EXPECTED=1,2,2,2,1.
```

specifies 1/8, 2/8, 2/8, 2/8, and 1/8 as the expected proportions for the values of FLOWERS.

The EXPECTED subcommand applies to all variables listed in the preceding CHISQUARE subcommand. If you want to specify different expected frequencies for each variable, use separate CHISQUARE and EXPECTED subcommands for each variable. Several CHISQUARE and EXPECTED subcommands can also be used to test different expected frequencies for the same variable.

The output in Figure 5.13 was produced with the command:

```
NPAR TESTS CHI-SQUARE=DAYOFWK.
```

For each chi-square test, the output consists of the observed and expected numbers of cases in each category, the residual (observed minus expected) for each category, and the chi-square statistic with its degrees of freedom and observed significance level.

5.24
The Kolmogorov-Smirnov One-Sample Test

Use the K-S subcommand to obtain the Kolmogorov-Smirnov test for one sample. The distributions you can test against are the uniform, normal, and Poisson distributions.

The K-S format is

NPAR TESTS K-S(*dis*[*parameters*])=*varlist*

where *dis* is one of the distribution keywords UNIFORM, NORMAL, or POISSON. Each of these keywords has optional parameters which are separated from the keyword and each other by commas:

UNIFORM   *Uniform distribution.* The optional parameters are the minimum and maximum values (in that order). If these are not specified, K-S uses the sample minimum and maximum values.

NORMAL *Normal distribution.* The optional parameters are the mean and standard deviation (in that order). If these are not specified, K-S uses the sample mean and standard deviation.

POISSON *Poisson distribution.* The one optional parameter is the mean. If this is not specified, K-S uses the sample mean. A word of caution about testing against a Poisson distribution: if the mean of the test distribution is large, evaluating the probabilities is a very time-consuming process. If a mean of 100,000 or larger is used, K-S uses a normal approximation to the Poisson distribution.

For example, the command

```
NPAR TESTS K-S(POISSON,5)=HORSKICK.
```

compares the sample distribution of the HORSKICK variable with the Poisson distribution having a mean of 5. The output in Figure 5.12 was produced with the command:

```
NPAR TESTS K-S(NORMAL)=ALCOHOL.
```

The output for the Kolmogorov-Smirnov test includes the distribution used for the test, the most extreme positive, negative, and absolute differences, and the Kolmogorov-Smirnov Z with its observed significance level.

The Kolmogorov-Smirnov test assumes that the parameters of the test distribution have been specified in advance (not calculated from the data). When the parameters are estimated from the sample, the distribution of the test statistic changes. SPSS/PC+ makes no corrections for this.

5.25
The Runs Test

Use subcommand RUNS to obtain the runs test. This subcommand has the general format

NPAR TESTS RUNS(*cutpoint*)=*varlist*

The cutting point dichotomizes the variables in the variable list. Even if a variable is dichotomous to begin with, a cutting point must be specified. For example, a variable that takes only the values 0 and 1 would have 1 for the cutting point, as in the command

```
NPAR TESTS RUNS(1)=SNOW.
```

which produces the output in Figure 5.10. You can specify the observed mean, median, or mode or a value for *cutpoint.*

MEAN *Mean.* All values below the observed mean make up one category; all values greater than or equal to the mean make up the other category.

MEDIAN *Median.* All values below the observed median make up one category; all values greater than or equal to the median make up the other category.

MODE *Mode.* All values below the observed mode make up one category; all values greater than or equal to the mode make up the other category.

value *Specified value.* All values below the specified value make up one category; all values greater than or equal to the specified value make up the other category.

The RUNS output shows the cutting point, the number of runs, the number of cases below the cutting point, the number of cases greater than or equal to the cutting point, and the test statistic Z with its observed significance level.

5.26
The Binomial Test

Use the BINOMIAL subcommand to perform the binomial test. Its format is

NPAR TESTS BINOMIAL[(p)]=*varlist*(*value* or *value1,value2*)

where p is the proportion of cases expected in the *first* category. If p is not specified, a p of 0.5 is used. A two-tailed test is performed only when p is 0.5. When p is any other value, a one-tailed test is performed.

If no values are specified after the variable list, each variable named is assumed to have only two values. If one value follows the variable list, it is used as a cutting point: all cases with values less than or equal to the cutting point go in the first category, and all other cases go in the second category. If two values follow the variable list, all cases with *value1* go in the first category and all cases with *value2* go in the second category. For example, the command

```
NPAR TESTS BINOMIAL=HEADS(0,1).
```

produces the output in Figure 5.11.

The BINOMIAL output shows the value of each category, the number of cases in each category, the test proportion of cases, and the probability of the observed population.

5.27
Tests for Two Related Samples

The McNemar test, the sign test, and the Wilcoxon matched-pairs signed-ranks test are available in NPAR TESTS for paired samples. The subcommands for requesting these tests have the general format

NPAR TESTS *testname=varlist* [WITH *varlist*]

where the keyword WITH and the second variable list are optional, signifying that each variable in the first list is to be paired with each variable in the second list. For example, the command

```
NPAR TESTS SIGN=RATING1 WITH RATING2 RATING3.
```

requests two sign tests, one for RATING1 with RATING2 and one for RATING1 with RATING3.
When only one variable list is specified, each variable in the list is paired with every other variable in the list. For example, the command

```
NPAR TESTS SIGN=RATING1 RATING2 RATING3.
```

produces three sign tests: RATING1 with RATING2, RATING1 with RATING3, and RATING2 with RATING3.

You can also pair variables sequentially by specifying Option 3 on the OPTIONS subcommand.

Option 3 *Sequential pairing of variables for two related samples.*

When Option 3 is requested with a single variable list, the first variable in the list is paired with the second, the second variable with the third, and so on. For example, the command

```
NPAR TESTS SIGN=RATING1 RATING2 RATING3
  /OPTIONS=3.
```

performs two sign tests: one for RATING1 with RATING2 and one for RATING2 with RATING3.

If Option 3 is specified with the keyword WITH and two variable lists, the first variable in the first list before WITH is paired with the first variable in the second list, and so forth. For example, the command

```
NPAR TESTS SIGN=RATING1 RATING2 WITH RATING3 RATING4
  /OPTIONS=3.
```

requests sign tests for RATING1 with RATING3 and RATING2 with RATING4.

5.28
The McNemar Test

The MCNEMAR subcommand requests the McNemar test for two correlated dichotomous variables. Pairs of variables being tested must have the same two values. Variables that are not dichotomous must be recoded before using NPAR TESTS (see *SPSS/PC+ Data Analysis*). If fewer than ten cases have different values for the two variables, the binomial distribution is used to find the observed significance level. The output displayed includes a 2×2 table and the observed significance level. If a chi-square statistic is calculated, it is also displayed.

The format for MCNEMAR is

NPAR TESTS MCNEMAR=*varlist* [WITH *varlist*]

For example, the command

```
NPAR TESTS MCNEMAR=CONTRCT1 CONTRCT2.
```

requests a McNemar test on the 2×2 table for CONTRCT1 and CONTRCT2.

5.29
The Sign Test

The SIGN subcommand requests sign tests for paired variables. The format of SIGN is

NPAR TESTS SIGN=*varlist* [WITH *varlist*]

For example,the output in Figure 5.8 was produced by the command

```
NPAR TESTS SIGN=HSSCALE WITH WSSCALE.
```

If there are more than 25 cases, the observed significance level of the test statistic is based on a normal approximation. If there are 25 or fewer cases, the binomial distribution is used to compute the exact observed significance level.

5.30
The Wilcoxon Matched-Pairs Signed-Ranks Test

The WILCOXON subcommand requests the Wilcoxon test. Its format is

NPAR TESTS WILCOXON=*varlist* [WITH *varlist*]

For example, the output in Figure 5.9 was obtained with the command

```
NPAR TESTS WILCOXON=HSSCALE WITH WSSCALE.
```

The Wilcoxon test output shows the mean rank for each variable, the number of positive, negative, and tied ranks, and the test statistic Z with its observed significance level.

5.31
Tests for *k* Related Samples

Cochran's Q test, the Friedman test, and Kendall's coefficient of concordance W are tests for k related samples that are available in NPAR TESTS. The general format for requesting these tests is

NPAR TESTS *testname*=*varlist*

5.32
Cochran's Q

The COCHRAN subcommand requests Cochran's Q and has the format

NPAR TESTS COCHRAN=*varlist*

The variables to be tested must be dichotomous and coded with the same two values. If they are not, they must be recoded. The output displayed for COCHRAN includes the number of cases in each category for each variable and Cochran's Q with its degrees of freedom and observed significance level.

5.33
The Friedman Test

The Friedman test is requested with the FRIEDMAN subcommand, which has the format

NPAR TESTS FRIEDMAN=*varlist*

For example, the command

```
NPAR TESTS FRIEDMAN=P2DIGIT P3DIGIT P4DIGIT.
```

was used to produce the output in Figure 5.14.

The Friedman test output shows the mean rank for each variable and a chi-square statistic with its degrees of freedom and its observed significance level.

**5.34
Kendall's Coefficient of
Concordance**

The KENDALL subcommand requests Kendall's W and has the format

NPAR TESTS KENDALL=*varlist*

This test assumes that each case is a judge or rater. If you want to treat your variables as judges, you must transpose your data matrix.

The output produced consists of the number of cases, Kendall's W, and a chi-square statistic with its degrees of freedom and observed significance level.

**5.35
Tests for Two Independent
Samples**

NPAR TESTS performs five tests for two independent samples: the two-sample median test, the Mann-Whitney U test, the Kolmogorov-Smirnov two-sample test, the Wald-Wolfowitz runs test, and the Moses test of extreme reactions. The general format for requesting these tests is

NPAR TESTS *testname*=*varlist* BY *variable*(*value1,value2*)

where the variable named after BY is the variable used to group the cases. All cases with *value1* are in the first group and all cases with *value2* are in the second group.

**5.36
The Two-Sample Median Test**

The MEDIAN subcommand requests the two-sample median test. Its format is

NPAR TESTS MEDIAN [(*value*)]=*varlist* BY *variable*(*value1,value2*)

The value in parentheses after MEDIAN is the median to be used for the test. If a value is not specified, the sample median is used. The two values in parentheses following the variable named after BY specify the categories for the grouping variable. A two-sample median test is performed if the first value is greater than the second or if the second value is only one greater than the first. If the second value is more than one greater, a k-sample median test is performed (see Section 5.42). For example, the command

```
NPAR TESTS MEDIAN=SODIUM BY RATING(3,1).
```

was used to produce the output in Figure 5.16.

The Median test output shows a 2×2 table of cases greater than and less than or equal to the median, and the observed significance level. When the number of cases is greater than 30, a chi-square statistic is displayed. When the number of cases is 30 or less, Fisher's exact test (one-tailed) is computed.

**5.37
The Mann-Whitney U Test**

Request the Mann-Whitney test with the M-W subcommand, which has the format

NPAR TESTS M-W=*varlist* BY *variable*(*value1,value2*)

For example, the command

```
NPAR TESTS M-W=TUMOR BY DIET(0,1).
```

was used to produce the output in Figure 5.3.

The output produced by M-W includes the mean rank for each group, the Mann-Whitney U statistic, and the Wilcoxon W. For samples with less than 30 cases, the exact observed significance level (calculated using the algorithm of Dineen and Blakely, 1973) is displayed. For larger samples, a Z statistic with its (approximate) observed significance level is displayed.

**5.38
The Kolmogorov-Smirnov
Two-Sample Test**

The K-S subcommand requests the Kolmogorov-Smirnov two-sample test and has the format

NPAR TESTS K-S=*varlist* BY *variable*(*value1,value2*)

For example, the command

```
NPAR TESTS K-S=ALCOHOL BY RATING(3,1).
```

was used to produce the output in Figure 5.18.

The output shows the number of cases in each group, the most extreme positive, negative, and absolute differences, and the Kolmogorov-Smirnov Z with its observed significance level.

5.39
The Wald-Wolfowitz Test

The Wald-Wolfowitz runs test is obtained with the W-W subcommand, which has the format

NPAR TESTS W-W=*varlist* BY *variable(value1,value2)*

For example, the command

```
NPAR TESTS W-W=CALORIES BY RATING(3,1).
```

was used to produce the output in Figure 5.17.

The output includes the number of cases in each group, the exact number of runs if there are no ties, and the observed significance level. If the sample size is 30 or less, the exact one-tailed observed significance level is calculated. Otherwise, a normal approximation is used to calculate the observed significance level.

5.40
The Moses Test of Extreme Reactions

The MOSES subcommand requests the Moses test of extreme reactions and has the format

NPAR TESTS MOSES[(*n*)]=*varlist* BY *variable(value1,value2)*

where n is the number of cases to be excluded from each end of the (sorted) data. This data trimming is sometimes needed to eliminate distortion due to outliers. If n is not specified, 5% of the cases are trimmed from each end of the range of the control group. *Value1* corresponds to the control group.

The output shows the number of cases in each group, the span of the control group with its observed significance level when all cases are included, and the span of the control group with its significance level after outliers have been removed.

5.41
Tests for *k* Independent Samples

Two tests for k samples are available in NPAR TESTS, the k-sample median test and the Kruskal-Wallis one-way analysis of variance. The general format for requesting these tests is

NPAR TESTS *testname*=*varlist* BY *variable(value1,value2)*

The variable following the BY keyword is used to split the cases into k groups, where *value1* and *value2* specify the minimum and maximum values used to define groups. For example, the command

```
NPAR TESTS MEDIAN=POLRANK BY RACE(1,3).
```

requests that the RACE variable be used to group the data into three categories corresponding to RACE values 1, 2, and 3.

5.42
The *k*-Sample Median Test

The k-sample median test is requested with the MEDIAN subcommand, which has the format

NPAR TESTS MEDIAN [(*value*)] BY *variable(value1,value2)*

The value in parentheses after MEDIAN is the median to be used for the test. If no value is specified, the sample median is used. For a k-sample median test, *value2* must be at least two greater than *value1*. For example, the command

```
NPAR TESTS MEDIAN=SOCATT BY RACE(1,3).
```

requests a three-sample median test for the groups defined by RACE values 1, 2, and 3. But the command

```
NPAR TESTS MEDIAN=SOCATT BY RACE(3,1).
```

requests a two-sample median test for the groups defined by RACE values 1 and 3. The command

```
NPAR TESTS MEDIAN = PRICE BY RATING(1,3).
```

produces the output in Figure 5.19.

The output for the median test includes a $2 \times k$ table and the chi-square test with its degrees of freedom and observed significance level.

5.43
The Kruskal-Wallis One-Way Analysis of Variance

The K-W subcommand requests the Kruskal-Wallis test and has the format

NPAR TESTS K-W=*varlist* BY *variable*(*value1,value2*)

If the first grouping variable is less than the second, every value in the range *value1* to *value2* defines a group. If the first value is greater than the second, two groups are formed, using the two values. For example, the output in Figure 5.20 was obtained with the command

```
NPAR TESTS K-W=TUMOR BY DIET(0,2).
```

The output displayed consists of the mean rank for each group, the number of cases in each group, the chi-square statistic with its observed significance level uncorrected for ties, and the chi-square statistic with its observed significance level corrected for ties.

5.44
Optional Statistics

You can obtain additional summary statistics for all variables named on NPAR TESTS subcommands by specifying Statistics 1 or 2 on the STATISTICS subcommand. All cases with valid values on a variable are used in calculating the statistics for that variable. The following statistics are available:

Statistic 1 *Univariate statistics.* The mean, maximum, minimum, standard deviation, and count are displayed for each variable named on a subcommand.
Statistic 2 *Quartiles and count.* The values corresponding to the 25th, 50th, and 75th percentiles for each variable named on a subcommand are displayed.

5.45
Missing Values

By default, cases with missing values are excluded on a test-by-test basis. That is, cases with missing values for any of the variables used in a particular test are excluded from calculations for that test only. You may request two alternative missing-value treatments with the OPTIONS subcommand.

Option 1 *Include user-missing values.* Cases with user-missing values are included in all tests requested on the command.
Option 2 *Exclude missing values listwise.* Cases missing on any variable named on any subcommand are excluded from all analyses.

5.46
Subsampling

Since many of the NPAR TESTS procedures are based on ranks, cases must be stored in memory. If you do not have enough computer memory to store all the cases, you will need to use Option 4 on the OPTIONS subcommand to select a random subsample of cases for analysis.

Option 4 *Random sampling* if there is insufficient memory.

Because such sampling would invalidate a runs test, this option is ignored when the RUNS subcommand is used.

5.47

Annotated Example   The following SPSS/PC+ commands were used to obtain the output in Figures 5.3
and 5.20.

```
DATA LIST FREE/DIET    TUMOR.
FORMATS DIET(F1.0).
VALUE LABELS DIET 0 'UNSATURATED' 1 'SATURATED' 2 'LOW-FAT'.
BEGIN DATA.
lines of data
END DATA.
NPAR TESTS M-W TUMOR BY DIET(0,1)/
   K-W TUMOR BY DIET(0,2).
FINISH.
```

• The DATA LIST command tells SPSS/PC+ that the two variables DIET and
TUMOR are entered in freefield format.

• The FORMATS command assigns a new format to the variable DIET.

• The VALUE LABELS command assigns descriptive labels to the values of variable
DIET.

• NPAR TESTS requests a Mann-Whitney test and a Kruskal-Wallis test.

Contents

6 Multiple Regression: Procedure REGRESSION

The 1964 Civil Rights Act prohibits discrimination in the workplace based on sex or race. Employers who violate the act, by unfair hiring or advancement, are liable to prosecution. Numerous lawsuits have been filed on behalf of women, blacks, and other groups on these grounds.

The courts have ruled that statistics can be used as *prima facie* evidence of discrimination. Many lawsuits depend heavily on complex statistical analyses, which attempt to demonstrate that similarly qualified individuals are not treated equally (Roberts, 1980). In this chapter, employee records for 474 individuals hired between 1969 and 1971 by a bank engaged in Equal Employment Opportunity litigation are analyzed. A mathematical model is developed that relates beginning salary and salary progression to various employee characteristics such as seniority, education, and previous work experience. One objective is to determine whether sex and race are important predictors of salary.

The technique used to build the model is linear regression analysis, one of the most versatile data analysis procedures. Regression can be used to summarize data as well as to study relations among variables.

6.1
LINEAR REGRESSION

Before examining a model that relates beginning salary to several other variables, consider the relationship between beginning salary and current (as of March 1977) salary. For employees hired during a similar time period, beginning salary should serve as a reasonably good predictor of salary at a later date. Although superstars and underachievers might progress differently from the group as a whole, salary progression should be similar for the others. The scatterplot of beginning salary and current salary produced by the PLOT procedure and shown in Figure 6.1 supports this hypothesis.

A scatterplot may suggest what type of mathematical functions would be appropriate for summarizing the data. A variety of functions are useful in fitting models to data. Parabolas, hyperbolas, polynomials, trigonometric functions, and many more are potential candidates. For the scatterplot in Figure 6.1, current salaries tend to increase linearly with increases in beginning salary. If the plot indicates that a straight line is not a good summary measure of the relationship, you should consider other possibilities, including attempts to transform the data to achieve linearity (see Section 6.27).

Figure 6.1   Scatterplot of beginning and current salaries

```
PLOT VERTICAL=MIN(0) /HORIZONTAL=MIN(0) /VSIZE=35
  /CUTPOINTS=EVERY(3) /SYMBOLS='.+*#@'
  /PLOT=SALNOW WITH SALBEG
```

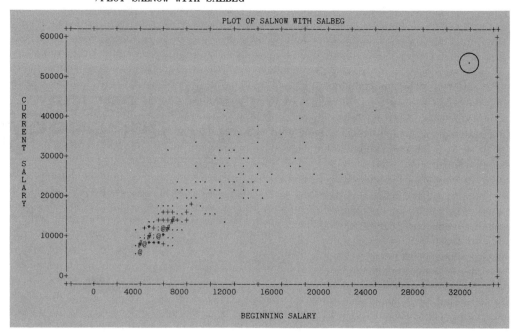

6.2
Outliers

A plot may also indicate the presence of points suspiciously different from the others. Examine such observations, termed *outliers*, carefully to see if they result from errors in gathering, coding, or entering data. The circled point in Figure 6.1 appears to be an outlier. Though neither the value of beginning salary ($6,300) nor the value of current salary ($32,000) is unique, jointly they are unusual.

The treatment of outliers can be difficult. If the point is really incorrect, due to coding or entry problems, you should correct it and rerun the analysis. If there is no apparent explanation for the outlier, consider interactions with other variables as a possible explanation. For example, the outlier may represent an employee who was hired as a low-paid clerical worker while pursuing an MBA degree. After graduation, a rapid rise in position was possible, making education the variable that explains the unusual salary characteristics of the employee.

6.3
Choosing a Regression Line

Since current salary tends to increase linearly with beginning salary, a straight line can be used to summarize the relationship. The equation for the line is

$$\text{predicted current salary} = B_0 + B_1(\text{beginning salary})$$ **Equation 6.3a**

The *slope* (B_1) is the dollar change in the fitted current salary for a dollar change in the beginning salary. The *intercept* (B_0) is the theoretical estimate of current salary if there were a beginning salary of 0.

However, the observed data points do not all fall on a straight line but cluster about it. Many lines can be drawn through the data points; the problem is to select among them. The method of *least squares* results in a line that minimizes the sum of squared vertical distances from the observed data points to the line. Any other line has a larger sum. Figure 6.3a shows the least-squares line superimposed on the salary scatterplot. Several vertical distances from points to the line are also shown.

Figure 6.3a   Regression line for beginning and current salaries

```
PLOT FORMAT=REGRESSION
  /VERTICAL=MIN(0) /HORIZONTAL=MIN(0) /VSIZE 30 /HSIZE 90
  /CUTPOINTS=EVERY(3) /SYMBOLS='.+*#@'
  /PLOT=SALNOW WITH SALBEG
```

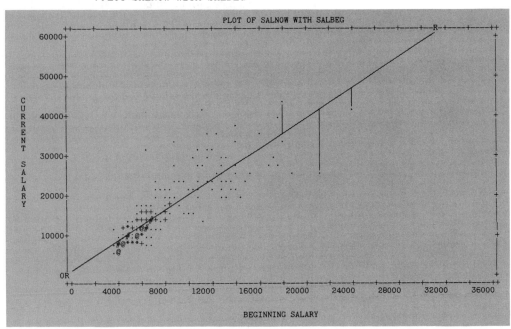

You can use the SPSS/PC+ REGRESSION procedure to calculate the least-squares line. For the data in Figure 6.1, that line is

predicted current salary = 771.28 + 1.91(beginning salary)   **Equation 6.3b**

The slope and intercept values are shown in the column labeled B in the output shown in Figure 6.3b.

Figure 6.3b   Statistics for variables in the equation

```
REGRESSION
  /DEPENDENT=SALNOW
  /METHOD=ENTER SALBEG
```

Variable	B	SE B	Beta	T	Sig T
SALBEG	1.90945	.04741	.88012	40.276	.0000
(Constant)	771.28230	355.47194		2.170	.0305

6.4
The Standardized Regression Coefficient

The *standardized regression coefficient*, labeled Beta in Figure 6.3b, is defined as

$$BETA = B_1 \frac{S_X}{S_Y}$$ **Equation 6.4**

Multiplying the regression coefficient (B_1) by the ratio of the standard deviation of the independent variable (S_X) to the standard deviation of the dependent variable (S_Y) results in a dimensionless coefficient. In fact, the Beta coefficient is the slope of the least-squares line when both X and Y are expressed as Z scores. The Beta coefficient is further discussed in Section 6.38.

6.5
From Samples to Populations

Generally, more is sought in regression analysis than a description of observed data. One usually wishes to draw inferences about the relationship of the variables in the population from which the sample was taken. How are beginning and current salaries related for all employees, not just those included in the sample? To draw inferences about population values based on sample results, the following assumptions are needed:

Normality and Equality of Variance. For any fixed value of the independent variable X, the distribution of the dependent variable Y is normal, with mean $\mu_{Y/X}$ (the mean of Y for a given X) and a constant variance of σ^2 (see Figure 6.5). This assumption specifies that not all employees with the same beginning salary have the same current salary. Instead, there is a normal distribution of current salaries for each beginning salary. Though the distributions have different means, they have the same variance σ^2.

Figure 6.5　Regression assumptions

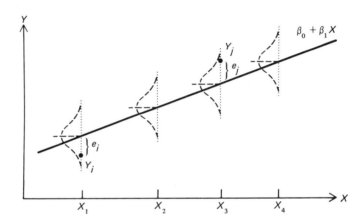

Independence. The Y's are statistically independent of each other. That is, observations are in no way influenced by other observations. For example, observations are *not* independent if they are based on repeated measurements from the same experimental unit. If three observations are taken from each of four families, the twelve observations are not independent.

Linearity. The mean values $\mu_{Y/X}$ all lie on a straight line, which is the population regression line. This line is drawn in Figure 6.5. An alternative way of stating this assumption is that the linear model is correct.

When there is a single independent variable, the model can be summarized by

$$Y_i = \beta_0 + \beta_1 X_i + e_i$$

Equation 6.5

The population parameters (values) for the slope and intercept are denoted by β_1 and β_0. The term e_i, often called an error or disturbance, is the difference between the observed value of Y_i and the subpopulation mean at the point X_i. The e_i are assumed to be normally distributed, independent, random variables with a mean of 0 and variance of σ^2 (see Figure 6.5).

6.6
Estimating Population Parameters

Since β_0 and β_1 are unknown population parameters, they must be estimated from the sample. The least-squares coefficients B_0 and B_1, discussed in Section 6.3, are used to estimate the population parameters.

However, the slope and intercept estimated from a single sample typically differ from the population values and vary from sample to sample. To use these estimates for inference about the population values, the sampling distributions of the two statistics are needed. When the assumptions of linear regression are met, the sampling distributions of B_0 and B_1 are normal with means of β_0 and β_1.

The standard error of B_0 is

$$\sigma_{B_0} = \sigma \sqrt{\frac{1}{N} + \frac{\bar{X}^2}{(N-1)S_X^2}}$$

Equation 6.6a

where S_X^2 is the sample variance of the independent variable. The standard error of B_1 is

$$\sigma_{B_1} = \frac{\sigma}{\sqrt{(N-1)S_X^2}}$$

Equation 6.6b

Since the population variance of the errors, σ^2, is not known, it must also be estimated. The usual estimate of σ^2 is

$$S^2 = \frac{\sum_{i=1}^{N}(Y_i - B_0 - B_1X_i)^2}{N-2}$$

Equation 6.6c

The positive square root of σ^2 is termed the *standard error of the estimate,* or the standard deviation of the residuals. (The reason for this name is discussed in Section 6.15.) The estimated standard errors of the slope and intercept are printed in the third column (labeled SE B) in Figure 6.3b.

6.7
Testing Hypotheses

A frequently tested hypothesis is that there is no linear relationship between X and Y—that the slope of the population regression line is 0. The statistic used to test this hypothesis is

$$t = \frac{B_1}{S_{B_1}}$$

Equation 6.7a

The distribution of the statistic, when the assumptions are met and the hypothesis of no linear relationship is true, is Student's t distribution with $N-2$ degrees of freedom. The statistic for testing the hypothesis that the intercept is 0 is

$$t = \frac{B_0}{S_{B_0}}$$

Equation 6.7b

Its distribution is also Student's t with $N-2$ degrees of freedom.

These t statistics and their two-tailed observed significance levels are displayed in the last two columns of Figure 6.3b. The small observed significance level (less than 0.00005) associated with the slope for the salary data supports the hypothesis that beginning and current salary are linearly related.

6.8
Confidence Intervals

A statistic calculated from a sample provides a point estimate of the unknown parameter. A point estimate can be thought of as the single best guess for the population value. While the estimated value from the sample is typically different from the value of the unknown population parameter, the hope is that it isn't too far away. Based on the sample estimate, it is possible to calculate a range of values that, with a designated likelihood, includes the population value. Such a range is called a *confidence interval*. For example, as shown in Figure 6.8, the 95% confidence interval for β_1, the population slope, is 1.816 to 2.003.

Figure 6.8   Confidence intervals

```
REGRESSION
  /STATISTICS=CI
  /DEPENDENT=SALNOW
  /METHOD=ENTER SALBEG
```

Variable	95% Confdnce Intrvl B	
SALBEG	1.81629	2.00261
(Constant)	72.77921	1469.78540

Ninety-five percent confidence means that, if repeated samples are drawn from a population under the same conditions and 95% confidence intervals are calculated, 95% of the intervals will contain the unknown parameter β_1. Since the parameter value is unknown, it is not possible to determine whether or not a particular interval contains it.

6.9
Goodness of Fit

An important part of any statistical procedure that builds models from data is establishing how well the model actually fits. This topic encompasses the detection of possible violations of the required assumptions in the data being analyzed. Sections 6.10 through 6.16 are limited to the question of how close to the fitted line the observed points fall. Subsequent sections discuss other assumptions and tests for their violation.

6.10
The R^2 Coefficient

A commonly used measure of the goodness of fit of a linear model is R^2, sometimes called the *coefficient of determination.* It can be thought of in a variety of ways. Besides being the square of the correlation coefficient between variables X and Y, it is the square of the correlation coefficient between Y, the observed value of the dependent variable, and $\widehat{Y}$, the predicted value of Y from the fitted line. If for each employee one computes (based on the coefficients in the output in Figure 6.3b) the predicted salary

predicted current salary $= 771.28 + 1.91$(beginning salary)   **Equation 6.10a**

and then calculates the square of the correlation coefficent between predicted current salary and observed current salary, R^2 is obtained. If all the observations fall on the regression line, R^2 is 1. If there is no linear relationship between the dependent and independent variables, R^2 is 0.

Note that R^2 is a measure of the goodness of fit of a particular model and that an R^2 of 0 does not necessarily mean that there is no association between the variables. Instead, it indicates that there is no *linear relationship.*

In the output in Figure 6.10, R^2 is labeled R Square; its square root is called Multiple R. The sample R^2 tends to be an optimistic estimate of how well the model fits the population. The model usually does not fit the population as well as it fits the sample from which it is derived. The statistic *adjusted R^2* attempts to correct R^2 to more closely reflect the goodness of fit of the model in the population. Adjusted R^2 is given by

$$R_a{}^2 = R^2 - \frac{p(1 - R^2)}{N - p - 1}$$ **Equation 6.10b**

where p is the number of independent variables in the equation (1 in the salary example).

Figure 6.10   Summary statistics for the equation

```
REGRESSION VARIABLES
  /DEPENDENT=SALNOW
  /METHOD=ENTER SALBEG
```

```
Multiple R           .88012
R Square             .77461
Adjusted R Square    .77413
Standard Error    3246.14226
```

6.11
Analysis of Variance

To test the hypothesis of no linear relationship between X and Y, several equivalent statistics can be computed. When there is a single independent variable, the hypothesis that the population R^2 is 0 is identical to the hypothesis that the population slope is 0. The test for $R^2_{pop}=0$ is usually obtained from the *analysis of variance* (ANOVA) table (see Figure 6.11a).

Figure 6.11a   Analysis of variance table

```
REGRESSION VARIABLES=SALBEG, SALNOW
  /DEPENDENT=SALNOW
  /METHOD=ENTER SALBEG
```

```
Analysis of Variance
                     DF      Sum of Squares        Mean Square
  Regression          1   17092967800.01931   17092967800.0193
  Residual          472    4973671469.79484     10537439.55465

  F =   1622.11776        Signif F =  .0000
```

The total observed variability in the dependent variable is subdivided into two components—that which is attributable to the regression (labeled Regression) and that which is not (labeled Residual). Consider Figure 6.11b. For a particular point, the distance from Y_i to $\overline{Y}$ (the mean of the Y's) can be subdivided into two parts.

$$Y_i - \overline{Y} = (Y_i - \hat{Y}_i) + (\hat{Y}_i - \overline{Y})$$

Equation 6.11a

Figure 6.11b   Components of variability

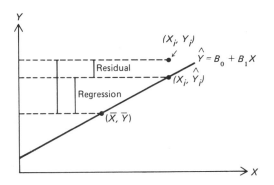

The distance from Y_i, the observed value, to $\hat{Y}_i$, the value predicted by the regression line, or $Y_i - \hat{Y}_i$, is 0 if the regression line passes through the point. It is called the *residual from the regression*. The second component $(\hat{Y}_i - \overline{Y})$ is the distance from the regression line to the mean of the Y's. This distance is "explained" by the regression in that it represents the improvement in the estimate of the dependent variable achieved by the regression. Without the regression, the mean of the dependent variable $(\overline{Y})$ is used as the estimate. It can be shown that

$$\sum_{i=1}^{N} (Y_i - \overline{Y})^2 = \sum_{i=1}^{N} (Y_i - \hat{Y}_i)^2 + \sum_{i=1}^{N} (\hat{Y}_i - \overline{Y})^2 \qquad \text{\textbf{Equation 6.11b}}$$

The first quantity following the equals sign is called the *residual sum of squares* and the second quantity is the *regression sum of squares.* The sum of these is called the *total sum of squares.*

The analysis of variance table displays these two sums of squares under the heading Sum of Squares (Figure 6.11a). The Mean Square for each entry is the Sum of Squares divided by the degrees of freedom (DF). If the regression assumptions are met, the ratio of the mean square regression to the mean square residual is distributed as an F statistic with p and $N-p-1$ degrees of freedom. F serves to test how well the regression model fits the data. If the probability associated with the F statistic is small, the hypothesis that $R^2_{pop}=0$ is rejected. For this example, the F statistic is

$$F = \frac{\text{MEAN SQUARE REGRESSION}}{\text{MEAN SQUARE RESIDUAL}} = 1622 \qquad \text{\textbf{Equation 6.11c}}$$

The observed significance level (SIGNIF F) is less than 0.00005.

The square root of the F value (1622) is 40.28, which is the value of the t statistic for the slope in Figure 6.3b. The square of a t value with k degrees of freedom is an F value with 1 and k degrees of freedom. Therefore, either t or F values can be computed to test that $\beta_i=0$.

Another useful summary statistic is the standard error of the estimate, S, which can also be calculated as the square root of the residual mean square (Section 6.15).

6.12
Another Interpretation of R^2

Partitioning the sum of squares of the dependent variable allows another interpretation of R^2. It is the proportion of the variation in the dependent variable "explained" by the model.

$$R^2 = 1 - \frac{\text{RESIDUAL SUM OF SQUARES}}{\text{TOTAL SUM OF SQUARES}} = 0.775 \qquad \text{\textbf{Equation 6.12a}}$$

Similarly, adjusted R^2 is

$$R^2_a = 1 - \frac{\text{RESIDUAL SUM OF SQUARES}/(N - p - 1)}{\text{TOTAL SUM OF SQUARES}/(N - 1)} \qquad \text{\textbf{Equation 6.12b}}$$

where p is the number of independent variables in the equation (1 in the salary example).

6.13
Predicted Values and Their Standard Errors

By comparing the observed values of the dependent variable to the values predicted by the regression equation, you can learn a good deal about how well a model and the various assumptions fit the data (see the discussion of residuals beginning with Section 6.17). Predicted values are also of interest when the results are used to predict new data. You may wish to predict the mean Y for all cases with a given value of X, denoted X_0, or to predict the value of Y for a single case. For example, you can predict either the mean salary for all employees with a beginning salary of $10,000 or the salary for a particular employee with a beginning salary of $10,000. In both situations, the predicted value

$$\hat{Y}_0 = B_0 + B_1 X_0 = 771 + 1.91 \times 10,000 = 19,871$$ **Equation 6.13**

is the same. What differs is the standard error.

6.14
Predicting Mean Response

The estimated standard error for the predicted mean Y at X_0 is

$$S_{\hat{Y}} = S \sqrt{\frac{1}{N} + \frac{(X_0 - \overline{X})^2}{(N-1)S_X^2}}$$ **Equation 6.14a**

The equation for the standard error shows that the smallest value occurs when X_0 is equal to $\overline{X}$, the mean of X. The larger the distance from the mean, the greater the standard error. Thus, the mean of Y for a given X is better estimated for central values of the observed X's than for outlying values. Figure 6.14a is a plot from the PLOT procedure of the standard errors of predicted mean salaries for different values of beginning salary.

Figure 6.14a   Standard errors for predicted mean responses

```
REGRESSION VARIABLES=SALBEG, SALNOW
   /DEPENDENT=SALNOW
   /METHOD=ENTER SALBEG
   /SAVE=SEPRED(SE)
PLOT CUTPOINTS=EVERY(20) /SYMBOLS='*'
      /PLOT=SE WITH SALBEG.
```

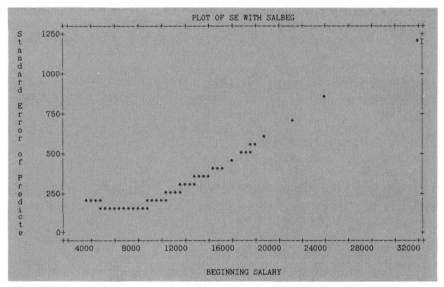

Prediction intervals for the mean predicted salary are calculated in the standard way. The 95% confidence interval at X_0 is

$$\hat{Y} \pm t_{\left(1-\frac{\alpha}{2}, N-2\right)} S_{\hat{Y}}$$ **Equation 6.14b**

Figure 6.14b shows a typical 95% confidence band for predicted mean responses. It is narrowest at the mean of X and increases as the distance from the mean $(X_0 - \overline{X})$ increases.

Figure 6.14b   95% confidence band for mean prediction

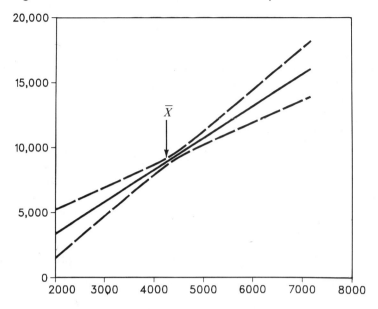

6.15
Predicting a New Value

Although the predicted value for a single new observation at X_0 is the same as the predicted value for the mean at X_0, the standard error is not. The two sources of error when predicting an individual observation are illustrated in Figure 6.15. They are

1   The individual value may differ from the population mean of Y for X_0.
2   The estimate of the population mean at X_0 may differ from the population mean.

Figure 6.15   Sources of error in predicting individual observations

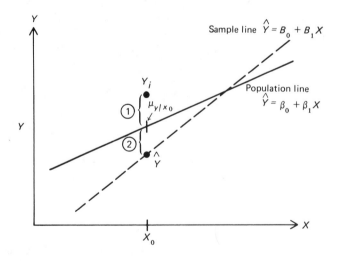

When estimating the mean response, only the second error component is considered. The variance of the individual prediction is the variance of the mean prediction plus the variance of Y_i for a given X. This can be written as

$$S^2_{ind\hat{Y}} = S^2_{\hat{Y}} + S^2 = S^2\left(1 + \frac{1}{N} + \frac{(X_0 - \overline{X})^2}{(N-1)S_X^2}\right)$$

Equation 6.15a

Prediction intervals for the new observation are obtained by substituting S_{indY} for S_Y in the equation for the confidence intervals for the mean given in Section 6.14. If the sample size is large, the terms $1/N$ and

$$\frac{(X_0 - \bar{X})^2}{(N-1)S_X{}^2}$$ Equation 6.15b

are negligible. In that case, the standard error is simply S, which explains the name *standard error of the estimate* for S (see Section 6.6).

6.16
Reading the Casewise Plot

Figure 6.16 shows the output from the beginning and end of a plot of the salary data. The sequence number of the case and an optional labeling variable (SEXRACE) are listed first, followed by the plot of standardized residuals, the observed (SALNOW), predicted (PRED), and residual (RESID) values, and, finally, the standard error of the mean prediction (SEPRED). The variance of an individual prediction can be obtained by adding S^2 to the square of each of the standard error values. You can generate predicted values and the standard errors of the mean responses in the REGRESSION procedure, and you can display both of these values for all cases or for a subset of cases along with a casewise plot.

Figure 6.16   Casewise plot with predicted values and standard errors

```
REGRESSION /WIDTH=132
   /DEPENDENT=SALNOW
   /METHOD=ENTER SALBEG
   /RESIDUALS=ID(SEXRACE)
   /CASEWISE=ALL DEPENDENT PRED RESID SEPRED.
```

```
Casewise Plot of Standardized Residual

*: Selected   M: Missing
                -3.0         0.0         3.0
Case #   SEXRACE  0:.................:...............:0   SALNOW      *PRED      *RESID     *SEPRED
    1      1.00   .              *.              .        16080   16810.6600   -730.6600   167.1489
    2      1.00   .      *       .               .        41400   46598.0758  -5198.0758   828.6655
    3      1.00   .              .    *          .        21960   20247.6695   1712.3305   219.3531
    4      1.00   .              .    *          .        19200   17383.4949   1816.5051   174.0406
    5      1.00   .        *     .               .        28350   33995.7076  -5645.7076   523.9021
    6      1.00   .              .   *           .        27250   25586.4910   1663.5090   329.1520
    7      1.00   .              .   *           .        16080   13946.4854   2133.5146   149.1662
    8      1.00   .              .     *         .        14100   11082.3108   3017.6892   163.3307
    9      1.00   .              .   *           .        12420   10394.9089   2025.0911   171.0096
   10      1.00   .             *.               .        12300   12800.8156   -500.8156   151.0211
   11      1.00   .              .    *          .        15720   12800.8156   2919.1844   151.0211
   12      1.00   .         *    .               .         8880   12227.9807  -3347.9807   153.9241
   ...
   ...
   ...
  470      4.00   .              *               .         9420    9592.9401   -172.9401   181.5927
  471      4.00   .              .*              .         9780    9134.6721    645.3279   188.3196
  472      4.00   .          *   .               .         7680    9249.2391  -1569.2391   186.5956
  473      4.00   .           *  .               .         7380    8561.8372  -1181.8372   197.3294
  474      4.00   .        *     .               .         8340   10738.6099  -2398.6099   166.9964
Case #   SEXRACE  0:.................:...............:0   SALNOW      *PRED      *RESID     *SEPRED
                -3.0         0.0         3.0
```

6.17
Searching for Violations of Assumptions

You usually don't know in advance whether a model such as linear regression is appropriate. Therefore, it is necessary to conduct a search focused on residuals to look for evidence that the necessary assumptions are violated.

6.18
Residuals

In model building, a *residual* is what is left after the model is fit. It is the difference between an observed value and the value predicted by the model.

$$E_i = Y_i - B_0 - B_1 X_i = Y_i - \hat{Y}_i$$ Equation 6.18

In regression analysis, the true errors e_i are assumed to be independent normal values with a mean of 0 and a constant variance of σ^2. If the model is appropriate for the data, the observed residuals E_i, which are estimates of the true errors e_i, should have similar characteristics.

If the intercept term is included in the equation, the mean of the residuals is always 0, so it provides no information about the true mean of the errors. Since the sum of the residuals is constrained to be 0, they are *not* strictly independent. However, if the number of residuals is large when compared to the number of independent variables, the dependency among the residuals can be ignored for practical purposes.

The relative magnitudes of residuals are easier to judge when they are divided by estimates of their standard deviations. The resulting standardized residuals are expressed in standard deviation units above or below the mean. For example, the fact that a particular residual is -5198.1 provides little information. If you know that its standardized form is -3.1, you know not only that the observed value is less than the predicted value but also that the residual is larger than most in absolute value.

Residuals are sometimes adjusted in one of two ways. The *standardized residual* for case i is the residual divided by the square root of the mean square error. Standardized residuals have a mean of 0 and a standard deviation close to 1. The *Studentized residual* is the residual divided by an estimate of its standard deviation that varies from point to point, depending on the distance of X_i from the mean of X. Usually, standardized and Studentized residuals are close in value, but not always. The Studentized residual reflects more precisely differences in the true error variances from point to point.

6.19
Linearity

For the bivariate situation, a scatterplot is a good means for judging how well a straight line fits the data. Another convenient method is to plot the residuals against the predicted values. If the assumptions of linearity and homogeneity of variance are met, there should be no relationship between the predicted and residual values. You should be suspicious of any observable pattern.

For example, fitting a least-squares line to the data in the two left-hand plots in Figure 6.19a yields the residual plots shown on the right. The two residual plots show patterns since straight lines do not fit the data well. Systematic patterns between the predicted values and the residuals suggest possible violations of the linearity assumption. If the assumption was met, the residuals would be randomly distributed in a band about the horizontal straight line through 0, as shown in Figure 6.19b.

Residuals can also be plotted against individual independent variables. Again, if the assumptions are met, you should see a horizontal band of residuals. Consider plotting the residuals against independent variables not in the equation as well. If the residuals are not randomly distributed, you may want to include the variable in the equation for a multiple regression model (see Sections 6.32 through 6.55).

Figure 6.19a   Standardized residuals scatterplots

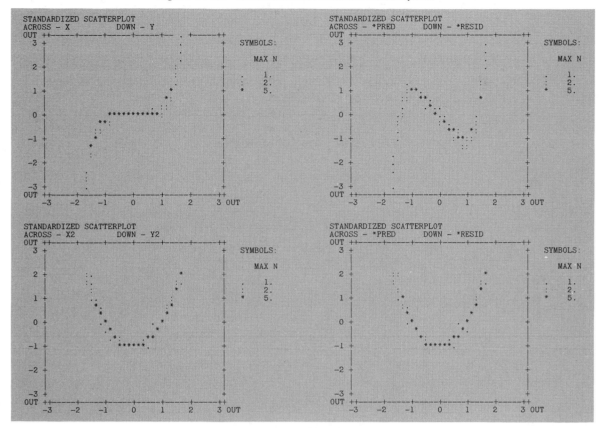

Figure 6.19b   Randomly distributed residuals

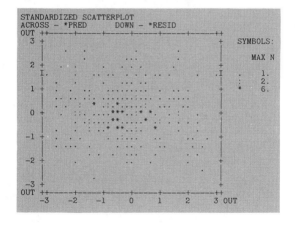

6.20
Equality of Variance

You can also use the previously described plots to check for violations of the equality of variance assumption. If the spread of the residuals increases or decreases with values of the independent variables or with predicted values, you should question the assumption of constant variance of Y for all values of X.

Figure 6.20 is a plot of the Studentized residuals against the predicted values for the salary data. The spread of the residuals increases with the magnitude of the predicted values, suggesting that the variability of current salaries increases with salary level. Thus, the equality of variance assumption appears to be violated.

Figure 6.20   Unequal variance

```
REGRESSION
  /DEPENDENT=SALNOW
  /METHOD=ENTER SALBEG
  /SCATTERPLOT=(*SRESID,*PRED).
```

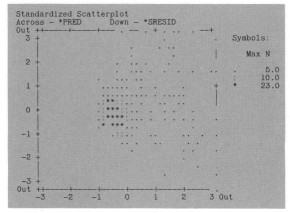

6.21
Independence of Error

Whenever the data are collected and recorded sequentially, you should plot residuals against the sequence variable. Even if time is not considered a variable in the model, it could influence the residuals. For example, suppose you are studying survival time after surgery as a function of complexity of surgery, amount of blood transfused, dosage of medication, and so forth. In addition to these variables, it is also possible that the surgeon's skill increased with each operation and that a patient's survival time is influenced by the number of prior patients treated. The plot of residuals corresponding to the order in which patients received surgery shows a shorter survival time for earlier patients than for later patients (see Figure 6.21). If sequence and the residual are independent, you should not see a discernible pattern.

Figure 6.21   Casewise serial plot

```
CASEWISE PLOT OF STUDENTIZED RESIDUAL

                  -3.0      0.0      3.0      LIFE     *PRED    *RESID   *SRESID
    SEQNUM  TIME  0:........:........:0
        1   78012        .   *    .        .   15.0000  19.5624  -4.5624  -2.2598
        2   78055        .   *    .        .   13.5000  17.8974  -4.3974  -2.1856
        3   78122        .  *     .        .    9.9000  13.8390  -3.9390  -1.9871
        4   78134        .    *   .        .   15.5000  18.5218  -3.0218  -1.4997
        5   78233        .    *   .        .   35.0000  38.2933  -3.2933  -1.7466
        6   78298        .     *  .        .   14.7000  16.6487  -1.9487   -.9720
        7   78344        .      *..        .   34.8000  36.0040  -1.2040   -.6258
        8   79002        .      *.         .   20.8000  20.8111   -.0111   -.0055
        9   79008        .       . *       .   15.9000  14.8796   1.0204    .5123
       10   79039        .       *         .   22.0000  21.6436    .3564    .1762
       11   79101        .       .  *      .   13.7000  11.7578   1.9422    .9910
       12   79129        .       .   *     .   14.2000  11.4456   2.7544   1.4082
       13   79178        .       .   *     .   33.2000  30.3847   2.8153   1.4144
       14   79188        .       .    *    .   26.2000  22.4761   3.7239   1.8401
       15   79189        .       .    *    .   37.4000  33.2984   4.1016   2.0920
      ...
```

The *Durbin-Watson* statistic, a test for sequential correlation of adjacent error terms, is defined as

$$D = \frac{\sum_{t=2}^{N} (E_t - E_{t-1})^2}{\sum_{t=1}^{N} E_t^2}$$

Equation 6.21

The differences between successive residuals tend to be small when error terms are positively correlated and large when error terms are negatively correlated. Thus, small values of D indicate positive correlation and large values of D indicate negative correlation. Consult tables of the D statistic for bounds upon which significance tests can be based (Neter & Wasserman, 1985).

6.22
Normality

The distribution of residuals may not appear to be normal for reasons other than actual nonnormality: misspecification of the model, nonconstant variance, a small number of residuals actually available for analysis, etc. Therefore, you should pursue several lines of investigation. One of the simplest is to construct a histogram of the residuals such as the one shown in Figure 6.22a for the salary data.

Figure 6.22a   Histogram of Studentized residuals

```
REGRESSION
  /DEPENDENT=SALNOW
  /METHOD=ENTER SALBEG
  /RESIDUALS=HISTOGRAM(SRESID).
```

The REGRESSION histogram contains a tally of the observed number of residuals (labeled N) in each interval and the number expected in a normal distribution with the same mean and variance as the residuals (Exp N). The first and last intervals (Out) contain residuals more than 3.16 standard deviations from the mean. Such residuals deserve examination. A histogram of expected N's is superimposed on that of the observed N's. Expected frequencies are indicated by a period. When observed and expected frequencies overlap, a colon is displayed. However, it is unreasonable to expect the observed residuals to be exactly normal—some deviation is expected because of sampling variation. Even if the errors are normally distributed in the population, sample residuals are only approximately normal.

In the histogram in Figure 6.22a, the distribution does not seem normal since there is an exaggerated clustering of residuals toward the center and a straggling tail toward large positive values. Thus, the normality assumption may be violated.

Another way to compare the observed distribution of residuals to that expected under the assumption of normality is to plot the two cumulative distributions against each other for a series of points. If the two distributions are identical, a straight line results. By observing how points scatter about the expected straight line, you can compare the two distributions.

Figure 6.22b is a cumulative probability plot of the salary residuals. Initially, the observed residuals are below the straight line, since there is a smaller number of large negative residuals than expected. Once the greatest concentration of residuals is reached, the observed points are above the line, since the observed cumulative proportion exceeds the expected.

Figure 6.22b   A normal probability (P-P) plot

```
REGRESSION
  /DEPENDENT=SALNOW
  /METHOD=ENTER SALBEG
  /RESIDUALS=HISTOGRAM(SRESID) NORMPROB.
```

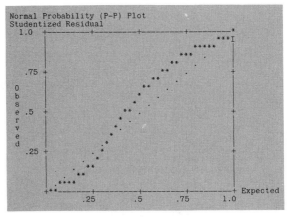

6.23
Locating Outliers

You can spot outliers readily on residual plots since they are cases with very large positive or negative residuals. In the histogram, cases with values greater than $+3.16$ or less than -3.16 appear in the interval labeled Out. In the scatterplots, they appear on the borders of the plot, again labeled Out. Since you usually want more information about outliers, you can use the casewise plotting facility to display identification numbers and a variety of other statistics for cases having residuals beyond a specified cutoff point.

Figure 6.23   Casewise plot of residuals outliers

```
REGRESSION VARIABLES=SALBEG,SALNOW
  /DEPENDENT=SALNOW
  /METHOD=ENTER SALBEG
  /CASEWISE=PLOT (SRESID) DEPENDENT PRED RESID
  /RESIDUALS=ID(SEXRACE).
```

```
Casewise Plot of Studentized Residual

Outliers = 3.      *: Selected   M: Missing

               -6.   -3.  3.    6.
  Case #  SEXRACE  0:.......: ........:0   SALNOW      *PRED       *RESID
      24   1.00    .         ..*      .    28000   17383.4949   10616.5051
      60   1.00    .         ..     *.    32000   12800.8156   19199.1844
      67   1.00    .       * ..      .    26400   37043.1894  -10643.1894
     114   1.00    .         ..*     .    38800   27511.2163   11288.7837
     122   1.00    .      *  ..      .    26700   40869.7266  -14169.7266
     123   1.00    .         ..*     .    36250   24639.4039   11610.5961
     129   1.00    .         ..   *  .    33500   17383.4949   16116.5051
     149   1.00    .         ..     * .   41500   21782.8671   19717.1329
     177   1.00    .         ..*     .    36500   23295.1513   13204.8487

        9 Outliers found.
```

Figure 6.23 lists information for the nine cases with Studentized residuals greater than 3 in absolute value. Only two of these nine employees have current salaries less than those predicted by the model (Cases 67 and 122), while the others have larger salaries. The second column contains identifier information that indicates that all outliers are white males (SEXRACE=1). They all have large salaries, an average of $33,294, while the average for the sample is only $13,767. Thus, there is some evidence that the model may not fit well for the highly paid cases.

6.24
Other Unusual Observations: Mahalanobis' Distance

In Section 6.2, an employee was identified as an outlier because the combination of values for beginning and current salaries was atypical. This case, which is Case 60, shows up in Figure 6.23 since it has a large value for the Studentized residual. Another unusual employee (Case 56) has a beginning salary of $31,992. Since the average beginning salary for the entire sample is only $6,806 and the standard deviation is 3148, the case is eight standard deviations above the mean. But since the Studentized residual is not large, this case does not appear in Figure 6.23.

However, cases that have unusual values for the independent variables can have a substantial impact on the results of analysis and should be identified. One measure of the distance of cases from average values of the independent variables is *Mahalanobis' distance*. In the case of a regression equation with a single independent variable, it is the square of the standardized value of X:

$$D_i = \left(\frac{X_i - \bar{X}}{S_X}\right)^2$$

Equation 6.24

Thus, for Case 56, the Mahalanobis' distance shown in Figure 6.24 is 64 (8^2). When there is more than one independent variable—where Mahalanobis' distance is most valuable—the computations are more complex.

Figure 6.24   Mahalanobis' distances

```
REGRESSION
   /DEPENDENT=SALNOW
   /METHOD=ENTER SALBEG
   /RESIDUALS=OUTLIERS(MAHAL)  ID(SEXRACE).
```

Outliers - Mahalanobis' Distance		
Case #	SEXRACE	*MAHAL
56	1.00	63.99758
2	1.00	29.82579
122	1.00	20.32559
67	1.00	14.99121
132	1.00	12.64145
55	1.00	12.64145
415	2.00	11.84140
5	1.00	11.32255
172	1.00	10.49188
23	1.00	10.46720

6.25
Influential Cases: Deleted Residuals and Cook's Distance

Certain observations in a set of data can have a large influence on estimates of the parameters. Figure 6.25a shows such a point. The regression line obtained for the data is quite different if the point is omitted. However, the residual for the circled point is not particularly large when the case (Case 8) is included in the computations and does not therefore arouse suspicion (see the plot in Figure 6.25b).

Figure 6.25a   Influential observation

```
REGRESSION VARIABLES=X,Y
  /STATISTICS=DEFAULTS CI
  /DEPENDENT=Y /METHOD=ENTER X
  /SCATTERPLOT=(Y,X).
```

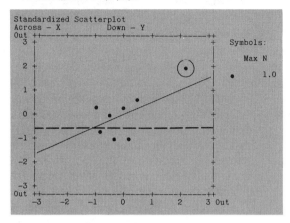

One way to identify an influential case is to compare the residuals for a case when the suspected case is included in the equation and when it is not. The *adjusted predicted value* (ADJPRED) for case i when it is not included in the computation of the regression line is

$$\hat{Y}_i^{(i)} = B_0^{(i)} + B_1^{(i)}X_i$$

Equation 6.25a

where the superscript i indicates that the ith case is excluded. The change in the predicted value when the ith case is deleted (DFFIT) is

$$\hat{Y}_i - \hat{Y}_i^{(i)}$$

Equation 6.25b

The residual calculated for a case when it is not included is called the *deleted residual* (DRESID), computed as

$$Y_i - \hat{Y}_i^{(i)}$$

Equation 6.25c

The deleted residual can be divided by its standard error to produce the *Studentized deleted residual* (SDRESID).

Although the difference between the deleted and ordinary residual for a case is useful as an index of the influence of that case, this measure does not reflect changes in residuals of other observations when the ith case is deleted. *Cook's distance* does consider changes in all residuals when case i is omitted (Cook, 1977). It is defined as

$$C_i = \frac{\sum_{j=1}^{N} (\hat{Y}_j^{(i)} - \hat{Y}_j)^2}{(p + 1)S^2}$$

Equation 6.25d

where p is the number of independent variables.

The casewise plot for the data in Figure 6.25a is shown in Figure 6.25b. The line for Case 8 describes the circled point. It has neither a very large Studentized residual nor a very large Studentized deleted residual. However, the deleted residual is 5.86 ($Y-ADJPRED=12-6.14$), which is somewhat larger than the ordinary residual (1.24). The large Mahalanobis' distance identifies the case as having an X value far from the mean, while the large Cook's D identifies the case as an influential point.

Figure 6.25b Casewise plot to study influential observation

```
REGRESSION /WIDTH 132
   /STATISTICS=DEFAULTS CI
   /DEPENDENT=Y /METHOD=ENTER X
   /CASEWISE=ALL DEPENDENT RESID SRESID DRESID ADJPRED MAHAL COOK
```

```
Casewise Plot of Standardized Residual

*: Selected   M: Missing

         -3.0         0.0          3.0
Case #   0:............:............:0   Y    *RESID   *SRESID  *SDRESID  *ADJPRED   *MAHAL   *COOK D
    1    .            .     *      .  :    7   2.9394   1.4819    1.6990    2.9096   1.0947   .4300
    2    .         *. .            .  :    4   -.5758   -.2780    -.2554    4.7349    .6401   .0107
    3    .            . *          .  :    6    .9091    .4262     .3951    4.9062    .3068   .0184
    4    .      *     .            .  :    3  -2.6061  -1.2000   -1.2566    6.0252    .0947   .1158
    5    .            . *          .  :    7    .8788    .4016     .3717    5.9950    .0038   .0116
    6    .     *      .            .  :    3  -3.6364  -1.6661   -2.0747    7.1791    .0341   .2071
    7    .            .  *         .  :    8    .8485    .3937     .3641    7.0000    .1856   .0138
    8    .            .   *        .  :   12   1.2425   1.1529    1.1929    6.1426   4.6402  2.4687
Case #   0:............:............:0   Y    *RESID   *SRESID  *SDRESID  *ADJPRED   *MAHAL   *COOK D
         -3.0         0.0          3.0
```

The regression coefficients with and without Case 8 are shown in Figures 6.25c and 6.25d. Both $B_0^{(8)}$ and $B_1^{(8)}$ are far removed from B_0 and B_1, since Case 8 is an influential point.

Figure 6.25c Regression results from all cases

```
REGRESSION
   /STATISTICS=DEFAULTS CI
   /DEPENDENT=Y /METHOD=ENTER X.
```

```
------------------------ Variables in the Equation ------------------------

Variable            B        SE B    95% Confdnce Intrvl B      Beta

X               .51514     .21772     -.01759    1.04788       .69476
(Constant)     3.54547    1.41098      .09294    6.99799

----------- in -----------

Variable        T    Sig T

X             2.366  .0558
(Constant)    2.513  .0457
```

Figure 6.25d Regression coefficients without Case 8

```
REGRESSION
   /SELECT=$CASENUM NE 8
   /STATISTICS=DEFAULTS CI
   /DEPENDENT=Y /METHOD=ENTER X
```

```
------------------------ Variables in the Equation ------------------------

Variable            B        SE B    95% Confdnce Intrvl B       Beta

X              .071407    .427380   -1.027192    1.170005      .074513
(Constant)    5.142941   1.911317     .229818   10.056065

----------- in -----------

Variable        T    Sig T

X              .167  .8739
(Constant)    2.691  .0433

End Block Number   1   All requested variables entered.
```

You can examine the change in the regression coefficients when a case is deleted from the analysis by looking at the intercept and X values for DFBETA on the casewise plot. For Case 8 in Figure 6.25e, you see that the change in the intercept is −1.5975 and the change in slope (**X**) is 0.4437.

Figure 6.25e   Diagnostic statistics for influential observations

```
REGRESSION
   /DEPENDENT=Y /METHOD=ENTER X
   /CASEWISE=ALL DEPENDENT DFBETA.
```

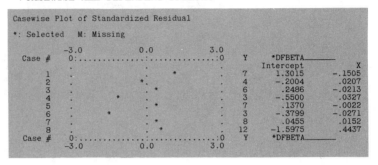

6.26
When Assumptions Appear To Be Violated

When evidence of violation of assumptions appears, you can pursue one of two strategies. You can either formulate an alternative model, such as weighted least squares, or you can transform the variables so that the current model will be more adequate. For example, taking logs, square roots, or reciprocals can stabilize the variance, achieve normality, or linearize a relationship.

6.27
Coaxing a Nonlinear Relationship to Linearity

To try to achieve linearity, you can transform either the dependent or independent variables, or both. If you alter the scale of independent variables, linearity can be achieved without any effect on the distribution of the dependent variable. Thus, if the dependent variable is normally distributed with constant variance for each value of X, it remains so.

When you transform the dependent variable, its distribution is changed. This new distribution must then satisfy the assumptions of the analysis. For example, if logs of the values of the dependent variable are taken, log Y—not the original Y—must be normally distributed with constant variance.

The choice of transformations depends on several considerations. If the form of the true model governing the relationship is known, it should dictate the choice. For instance, if it is known that $\hat{Y}=AC^X$ is an adequate model, taking logs of both sides of the equation results in

$$\log \hat{Y}_i = (\log A) + (\log C) X_i$$
$$\quad\quad [B_0] \quad\quad\quad [B_1]$$

Equation 6.27

Thus, log Y is linearly related to X.

If the true model is not known, you should choose the transformation by examining the plotted data. Frequently, a relationship appears nearly linear for part of the data but is curved for the rest. The first plot in Figure 6.27 is an example. Taking the log of the dependent variable results in the second plot—an improved linear fit.

Other transformations that may diminish curvature are the square root of Y and $-1/Y$. The choice depends, to a certain extent, on the severity of the problem.

Figure 6.27   A transformed relationship

```
REGRESSION
  /DEPENDENT=Y  /ENTER=X
  /SCATTERPLOT=(Y,X)
  /DEPENDENT=LOGY  /ENTER=X
  /SCATTERPLOT=(LOGY,X)
```

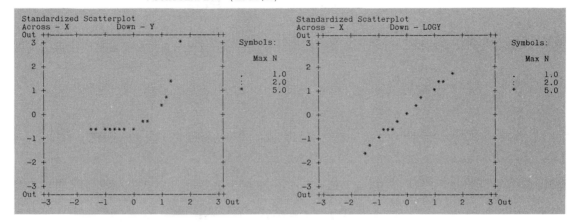

6.28
Coping with Skewness

When the distribution of residuals is positively skewed, the log transformation of the dependent variable is often helpful. For negatively skewed distributions, the square transformation is common. It should be noted that the F tests used in regression hypothesis testing are usually quite insensitive to moderate departures from normality.

6.29
Stabilizing the Variance

If the variance of the residuals is not constant, you can try a variety of remedial measures:

• When the variance is proportional to the mean of Y for a given X, use the square root of Y if all Y_i are positive.

• When the standard deviation is proportional to the mean, try the logarithmic transformation.

• When the standard deviation is proportional to the square of the mean, use the reciprocal of Y.

• When Y is a proportion or rate, the arc sine transformation may stabilize the variance.

6.30
Transforming the Salary Data

The assumptions of constant variance and normality appear to be violated with the salary data (see Figures 6.20 and 6.22a). A regression equation using logs of beginning and current salary was developed to obtain a better fit to the assumptions. Figure 6.30a is a scatterplot of Studentized residuals against predicted values when logs of both variables are used in the regression equation.

Figure 6.30a   Scatterplot of transformed salary data

```
COMPUTE LOGBEG=LG10(SALBEG)
COMPUTE LOGNOW=LG10(SALNOW)
REGRESSION
  /DEPENDENT=LOGNOW
  /METHOD=ENTER LOGBEG
  /SCATTERPLOT=(*SRESID,*PRED)
```

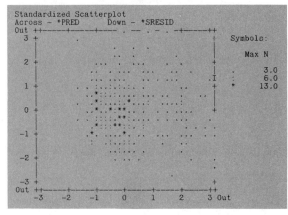

Compare Figures 6.20 and 6.30a and note the improvement in the behavior of the residuals. The spread no longer increases with increasing salary level. Also compare Figures 6.22a and 6.30b and note that the distribution in Figure 6.30b is nearly normal.

Figure 6.30b   Histogram of transformed salary data

```
COMPUTE LOGBEG=LG10(SALBEG)
COMPUTE LOGNOW=LG10(SALNOW)
REGRESSION
  /DEPENDENT=LOGNOW
  /METHOD=ENTER LOGBEG
  /RESIDUALS=HISTOGRAM(SRESID)
```

```
Histogram - Studentized Residual

 N Exp N        (* = 1 Cases,    . : = Normal Curve)
 3   .37    Out ***
 1   .73   3.00 :
 3  1.85   2.67 *:*
 4  4.23   2.33 ***:
10  8.65   2.00 ********:*
14 15.85   1.67 **************
21 26.01   1.33 *********************
31 38.23   1.00 *******************************
48 50.34    .67 ***********************************************.
55 59.38    .33 *******************************************************:****
63 62.74   0.0 ***************************************************************:
64 59.38   -.33 *************************************************************:****
62 50.34   -.67 ***********************************************************.************
44 38.23  -1.00 *********************************************:******
28 26.01  -1.33 ****************************:**
14 15.85  -1.67 **************.
 7  8.65  -2.00 *******.
 1  4.23  -2.33 *.
 1  1.85  -2.67 *.
 0   .73  -3.00 .
 0   .37    Out
```

For the transformed data, the multiple R increases slightly to 0.8864, and the outlier plot contains only four cases (compare with Figures 6.10 and 6.23). Thus, the transformation appears to have resulted in a better model.

6.31
A Final Comment on Assumptions

Rarely are assumptions not violated in one way or another in regression analysis and other statistical procedures. However, this is not a justification for ignoring the assumptions. Cranking out regressions with little thought to possible departures from the necessary assumptions can lead to problems in interpreting and applying results. Significance levels, confidence intervals, and other results are sensitive to certain types of violations and cannot be interpreted in the usual fashion if serious departures exist.

By carefully examining residuals and, if need be, using transformations or other methods of analysis, you are in a much better position to pursue analyses that solve the problems you are investigating. Even if everything isn't perfect, you can at least knowledgeably gauge the possible extent of difficulties.

6.32
MULTIPLE REGRESSION MODELS

Beginning salary seems to be a good predictor of current salary, given the evidence shown above. Nearly 80% ($R^2 = 0.77$ from Figure 6.10) of the observed variability in current salaries can be explained by beginning salary levels. But how do variables such as education level, years of experience, race, and sex affect the salary level at which one enters the company?

6.33
Predictors of Beginning Salary

Multiple linear regression extends bivariate regression by incorporating multiple independent variables. The model can be expressed as:

$$Y_i = \beta_0 + \beta_1 X_{1i} + \beta_2 X_{2i} + \ldots + \beta_p X_{pi} + e_i$$

Equation 6.33

The notation X_{pi} indicates the value of the pth independent variable for case i. Again, the β terms are unknown parameters and the e_i terms are independent random variables that are normally distributed with mean 0 and constant variance σ^2. The model assumes that there is a normal distribution of the dependent variable for every combination of the values of the independent variables in the model. For example, if child's height is the dependent variable and age and maternal height are the independent variables, it is assumed that for every combination of age and maternal height there is a normal distribution of children's heights and, though the means of these distributions may differ, all have the same variance.

6.34
The Correlation Matrix

One of the first steps in calculating an equation with several independent variables is to calculate a correlation matrix for all variables, as shown in Figure 6.34. The variables are the log of beginning salary, years of education, sex, years of work experience, race, and age in years. Variables sex and race are represented by *indicator variables,* that is, variables coded as 0 or 1. SEX is coded 1 for female and 0 for male, and MINORITY is coded 1 for nonwhite and 0 for white.

Figure 6.34   The correlation matrix

```
COMPUTE LOGBEG=LG10(SALBEG)
REGRESSION
  /DESCRIPTIVES=CORR
  /VARIABLES=LOGBEG,EDLEVEL,SEX,WORK,MINORITY,AGE
  /DEPENDENT=LOGBEG
  /METHOD=ENTER EDLEVEL TO AGE
```

	LOGBEG	EDLEVEL	SEX	WORK	MINORITY	AGE
LOGBEG	1.000	.686	-.548	.040	-.173	-.048
EDLEVEL	.686	1.000	-.356	-.252	-.133	-.281
SEX	-.548	-.356	1.000	-.165	-.076	.052
WORK	.040	-.252	-.165	1.000	.145	.804
MINORITY	-.173	-.133	-.076	.145	1.000	.111
AGE	-.048	-.281	.052	.804	.111	1.000

The matrix shows the correlations between the dependent variable (LOGBEG) and each independent variable, as well as the correlations between the independent variables. Particularly note any large intercorrelations between the independent variables, since such correlations can substantially affect the results of multiple regression analysis.

**6.35
Correlation Matrices and
Missing Data**

For a variety of reasons, data files frequently contain incomplete observations. Respondents in surveys scrawl illegible responses or refuse to answer certain questions. Laboratory animals die before experiments are completed. Patients fail to keep scheduled clinic appointments. Thus, before computing the correlation matrix, you must usually decide what to do with cases that have missing values for some of the variables.

Before even considering possible strategies, you should determine whether there is evidence that the missing-value pattern is not random. That is, are there reasons to believe that missing values for a variable are related to the values of that variable or other variables? For example, people with low incomes may be less willing to report their financial status than more affluent people. This may be even more pronounced for people who are poor but highly educated.

One simple method of exploring such possibilities is to subdivide the data into two groups—those observations with missing data on a variable and those with complete data—and examine the distributions of the other variables in the file across these two groups. The SPSS/PC+ procedures CROSSTABS and T-TEST are particularly useful for this. For a discussion of more sophisticated methods for detecting nonrandomness, see Frane (1976).

If it appears that the data are not missing randomly, use great caution in attempting to analyze the data. It may be that no satisfactory analysis is possible, especially if there are only a few cases.

If you are satisfied that the missing data are random, several strategies are available. First, if the same few variables are missing for most cases, consider excluding those variables from the analysis. Since this luxury is not usually available, you can alternatively keep all variables but eliminate the cases with missing values on any of them. This is termed *listwise* missing-value treatment since a case is eliminated if it has a missing value on any variable in the list.

If many cases have missing data for some variables, listwise missing-value treatment may eliminate too many cases and leave you with a very small sample. One common technique is to calculate the correlation coefficient between a pair of variables based on all cases with complete information for the two variables, regardless of whether the cases have missing data on any other variable. For example, if a case has values only for variables 1, 3, and 5, it is used only in computations involving variable pairs 1 and 3, 1 and 5, and 3 and 5. This is *pairwise* missing-value treatment.

Several problems can arise with pairwise matrices, one of which is inconsistency. There are some relationships between coefficients that are impossible but may occur when different cases are used to estimate different coefficients. For example, if age and weight and age and height have a high positive correlation, it is impossible in the same sample for height and weight to have a high negative correlation. However, if the same cases are not used to estimate all three coefficients, such an anomaly can occur.

Another problem with pairwise matrices is that no single sample size can be obtained since each coefficient may be based on a different number of cases. In addition, significance levels obtained from analyses based on pairwise matrices must be viewed with caution, since little is known about hypothesis testing in such situations.

Missing-value problems should not be treated lightly. You should always select a missing-value treatment based on careful examination of the data and not leave the choices up to system defaults. In this example, complete information is available for all cases, so missing values are not a problem.

6.36
Partial Regression Coefficients

The summary output when all independent variables are included in the multiple regression equation is shown in Figure 6.36a. The F test associated with the analysis of variance table is a test of the null hypothesis that

$$\beta_1=\beta_2=\beta_3=\beta_4=\beta_5=0 \qquad \text{Equation 6.36a}$$

In other words, it is a test of whether there is a linear relationship between the dependent variable and the entire set of independent variables.

Figure 6.36a   Statistics for the equation and analysis of variance table

```
COMPUTE LOGBEG=LG10(SALBEG)
REGRESSION VARIABLES=SALBEG LOGBEG EDLEVEL SEX WORK MINORITY AGE
   /DEPENDENT=LOGBEG
   /METHOD=ENTER EDLEVEL TO AGE.
```

```
Multiple R            .78420
R Square              .61498
Adjusted R Square     .61086
Standard Error        .09559

Analysis of Variance
                   DF      Sum of Squares     Mean Square
Regression          5             6.83039         1.36608
Residual          468             4.27638          .00914

F =      149.50125      Signif F = 0.0
```

The statistics for the independent variables in Figure 6.36b are parallel to those obtained in regression with a single independent variable (see Figure 6.3b). In multiple regression, the coefficients labeled B are called *partial regression coefficients* since the coefficient for a particular variable is adjusted for other independent variables in the equation. The equation that relates the predicted log of beginning salary to the independent variables is

$$LOGBEG = 3.3853 + 0.00102(AGE) \qquad \text{Equation 6.36b}$$
$$- 0.10358(SEX) - 0.05237(MINORITY)$$
$$+ 0.03144(EDLEVEL) + 0.00161(WORK)$$

Since the dependent variable is in log units, the coefficients can be approximately interpreted in percentage terms. For example, the coefficient of -0.104 for the SEX variable when females are coded as 1 indicates that female salaries are estimated to be about 10% less than male salaries, after statistical adjustment for age, education, work history, and minority status.

Figure 6.36b   Statistics for variables in the equation

```
COMPUTE LOGBEG=LG10(SALBEG)
REGRESSION VARIABLES=SALBEG LOGBEG EDLEVEL SEX WORK MINORITY AGE
   /DEPENDENT=LOGBEG
   /METHOD=ENTER EDLEVEL TO AGE.
```

Variable	B	SE B	Beta	T	Sig T
AGE	1.015396E-03	6.61324E-04	.07811	1.535	.1254
SEX	-.10358	.01032	-.33699	-10.038	.0000
MINORITY	-.05237	.01084	-.14157	-4.832	.0000
EDLEVEL	.03144	1.74805E-03	.59195	17.988	.0000
WORK	1.607508E-03	9.24066E-04	.09143	1.740	.0826
(Constant)	3.38530	.03323		101.866	.0000

6.37
Determining Important Variables

In multiple regression, one sometimes wants to assign relative importance to each independent variable. For example, you might want to know whether education is more important in predicting beginning salary than previous work experience. There are two possible answers, depending on which of the following questions is asked:

- How important are education and work experience when each one is used alone to predict beginning salary?
- How important are education and work experience when they are used to predict beginning salary along with other independent variables in the regression equation?

The first question is answered by looking at the correlation coefficients between salary and the independent variables. The larger the absolute value of the correlation coefficient, the stronger the linear association. Figure 6.34 shows that education correlates more highly with the log of salary than does previous work experience (0.686 and 0.040, respectively). Thus, you would assign more importance to education as a predictor of salary.

The answer to the second question is considerably more complicated. When the independent variables are correlated among themselves, the unique contribution of each is difficult to assess. Any statement about an independent variable is contingent upon the other variables in the equation. For example, the regression coefficient *(B)* for work experience is 0.0007 when it is the sole independent variable in the equation, compared to 0.00161 when the other four independent variables are also in the equation. The second coefficient is more than twice the size of the first.

6.38
Beta Coefficients

It is also inappropriate to interpret the *B*'s as indicators of the relative importance of variables. The actual magnitude of the coefficients depends on the units in which the variables are measured. Only if all independent variables are measured in the same units—years, for example—are their coefficients directly comparable. When variables differ substantially in units of measurement, the sheer magnitude of their coefficients does not reveal anything about relative importance.

One way to make regression coefficients somewhat more comparable is to calculate *Beta* weights, which are the coefficients of the independent variables when all variables are expressed in standardized (*Z*-score) form (see Figure 6.36b). The Beta coefficients can be calculated directly from the regression coefficients using

$$BETA_k = B_k\left(\frac{S_k}{S_Y}\right) \qquad \text{Equation 6.38}$$

where S_k is the standard deviation of the kth independent variable.

However, the values of the Beta coefficients, like the *B*'s, are contingent on the other independent variables in the equation. They are also affected by the correlations of the independent variables and do not in any absolute sense reflect the importance of the various independent variables.

6.39
Part and Partial Coefficients

Another way of assessing the relative importance of independent variables is to consider the increase in R^2 when a variable is entered into an equation that already contains the other independent variables. This increase is

$$R^2_{change} = R^2 - R^2_{(i)} \qquad \text{Equation 6.39a}$$

where $R^2_{(i)}$ is the square of the multiple correlation coefficent when all independent variables except the ith are in the equation. A large change in R^2 indicates that a variable provides unique information about the dependent variable that is not available from the other independent variables in the equation. The signed square root of the increase is called the *part correlation coefficient*. It is the correlation between Y and X_i when the linear effects of the other independent variables have been removed from X_i. If all independent variables are uncorrelated, the change in R^2 when a variable is entered into the equation is simply the square of the correlation coefficient between that variable and the dependent variable.

The output in Figure 6.39 shows that the addition of years of education to an equation that contains the other four independent variables results in a change in R^2 of 0.266 (.51593²). The square of the part coefficient tells only how much R^2 increases when a variable is added to the regression equation. It does not indicate what proportion of the unexplained variation this increase constitutes. If most of the variation had been explained by the other variables, a small part correlation is all that is possible for the remaining variable. It may therefore be difficult to compare part coefficients.

Figure 6.39 Zero-order, part, and partial correlation coefficients

```
COMPUTE LOGBEG=LG10(SALBEG)
REGRESSION VARIABLES=LOGBEG,EDLEVEL,SEX,WORK,MINORITY,AGE
  /STATISTICS=R CHA BCOV ZPP F
  /DEPENDENT=LOGBEG
  /METHOD=ENTER AGE /ENTER SEX /ENTER MINORITY /ENTER WORK /ENTER
EDLEVEL
```

```
Variable(s) Entered on Step Number
  5..    EDLEVEL   EDUCATIONAL LEVEL


Multiple R            .78420
R Square              .61498        R Square Change      .26619
Adjusted R Square     .61086        F Change         323.55404
Standard Error        .09559        Signif F Change      .0000

F =      149.50125      Signif F = 0.0

--------------- Variables in the Equation ---------------

Variable     Correl Part Cor  Partial        F   Sig F

AGE         -.04780   .04404   .07080     2.357   .1254
SEX         -.54802  -.28792  -.42090   100.761   .0000
MINORITY    -.17284  -.13860  -.21799    23.349   .0000
WORK         .03994   .04990   .08015     3.026   .0826
EDLEVEL      .68572   .51593   .63934   323.554   .0000
(Constant)                            10376.613   .0000
```

A coefficient that measures the proportional reduction in variation is

$$Pr_i^2 = \frac{R^2 - R^2_{(i)}}{1 - R^2_{(i)}}$$

Equation 6.39b

The numerator is the square of the part coefficient; the denominator is the proportion of unexplained variation when all but the ith variable are in the equation. The signed square root of Pr_i^2 is the *partial correlation coefficient*. It can be interpreted as the correlation between the ith independent variable and the dependent variable when the linear effects of the other independent variables have been removed from both X_i and Y. Since the denominator of Pr_i^2 is always less than or equal to 1, the part correlation coefficient is never larger in absolute value than the partial correlation coefficient.

Plots of the residuals of Y and X_i, when the linear effects of the other independent variables have been removed, are a useful diagnostic aid. They are discussed in Section 6.49.

6.40
Building a Model

Our selection of the five variables to predict beginning salary has been arbitrary to some extent. It is unlikely that all relevant variables have been identified and measured. Instead, some relevant variables have no doubt been excluded, while others that were included may not be very important determinants of salary level. This is not unusual; one must try to build a model from available data, as voluminous or scanty as the data may be. Before considering several formal procedures for model building, we will examine some of the consequences of adding and deleting variables from regression equations. The REGRESSION statistics for variables not in the equation are also described.

6.41
Adding and Deleting Variables

The first step in Figure 6.41 shows the equation and summary statistics when years of education is the sole independent variable and log of beginning salary is the dependent variable. Consider the second step in the same figure, when another variable, sex, is added. The value displayed as R Square Change in the second step is the change in R^2 when sex is added. R^2 for education alone is 0.47021, so R^2_{change} is 0.57598−0.47021, or 0.10577.

Figure 6.41 Adding a variable to the equation

```
COMPUTE LOGBEG=LG10(SALBEG)
REGRESSION VARIABLES=LOGBEG,EDLEVEL,SEX
   /STATISTICS=DEFAULTS CHANGE
   /DEPENDENT=LOGBEG
   /METHOD=ENTER EDLEVEL /ENTER SEX.
```

```
Variable(s) Entered on Step Number
   1..    EDLEVEL   EDUCATIONAL LEVEL

Multiple R            .68572
R Square              .47021        R Square Change      .47021
Adjusted R Square     .46909        F Change          418.92011
Standard Error        .11165        Signif F Change       .0000

--------------- Variables in the Equation ---------------

Variable             B          SE B          Beta         T    Sig T

EDLEVEL         .03642 1.77959E-03           .68572    20.468   .0000
(Constant)     3.31001      .02455                    134.821   .0000

Variable(s) Entered on Step Number
   2..    SEX       SEX OF EMPLOYEE

Multiple R            .75893
R Square              .57598        R Square Change      .10577
Adjusted R Square     .57418        F Change          117.48552
Standard Error        .09999        Signif F Change       .0000

--------------- Variables in the Equation ---------------

Variable             B          SE B          Beta         T    Sig T

EDLEVEL         .02984 1.70549E-03           .56183    17.498   .0000
SEX            -.10697 9.86858E-03          -.34802   -10.839   .0000
(Constant)     3.44754      .02539                    135.806   .0000
```

The null hypothesis that the true population value for the change in R^2 is 0 can be tested using

$$F_{change} = \frac{R^2_{change}(N - p - 1)}{q(1 - R^2)} = \frac{(0.1058)(474-2-1)}{1(1-0.5760)} = 117.48$$ **Equation 6.41**

where N is the number of cases in the equation, p is the total number of independent variables in the equation, and q is the number of variables entered at this step. Sometimes, this is referred to as a *partial F test*. Under the hypothesis that the true change is 0, the significance of the value labeled F Change can be obtained from the F distribution with q and $N-p-1$ degrees of freedom.

The hypothesis that the real change in R^2 is 0 can also be formulated in terms of the β parameters. When only the ith variable is added in a step, the hypothesis that the change in R^2 is 0 is equivalent to the hypothesis that β_i is 0. The F value printed for the change in R^2 is the square of the t value displayed for the test of the coefficient, as shown in Figure 6.41. For example, the t value for sex from Figure 6.41 is -10.839. This value squared is 117.48, the value displayed for F Change.

When q independent variables are entered in a single step, the test that R^2 is 0 is equivalent to the simultaneous test that the coefficients of all q variables are 0. For example, if sex and age were added in the same step to the regression equation that contains education, the F test for R^2 change would be the same as the F test which tests the hypothesis that $\beta_{sex}=\beta_{age}=0$.

Entering sex into the equation with education has effects in addition to changing R^2. For example, note the decrease in magnitude of the regression coefficient for education from Step 1 to Step 2 (from 0.03642 to 0.02984) in Figure 6.41. This is attributable to the correlation between sex and level of education.

When highly intercorrelated independent variables are included in a regression equation, results may appear anomalous. The overall regression may be significant while none of the individual coefficients are significant. The signs of the regression coefficients may be counterintuitive. High correlations between independent variables inflate the variances of the estimates, making individual coefficients quite unreliable without adding much to the overall fit of the model. The problem of linear relationships between independent variables is discussed further in Section 6.51.

6.42
Statistics for Variables Not in the Equation

When you have independent variables that have not been entered into the equation, you can examine what would happen if they were entered at the next step. Statistics describing these variables are shown in Figure 6.42. The column labeled Beta In is the standardized regression coefficient that would result if the variable were entered into the equation at the next step. The F test and level of significance are for the hypothesis that the coefficient is 0. (Remember that the partial F test and the t test for the hypothesis that a coefficient is 0 are equivalent.) The partial correlation coefficient with the dependent variable adjusts for the variables already in the equation.

Figure 6.42   Coefficients for variables not in the equation

```
COMPUTE LOGBEG=LG10(SALBEG)
REGRESSION VARIABLES=LOGBEG,EDLEVEL,SEX,WORK,MINORITY,AGE
 /STATISTICS=OUTS F
 /DEPENDENT=LOGBEG
 /METHOD=FORWARD.
```

————— Variables not in the Equation —————					
Variable	Beta In	Partial	Min Toler	F	Sig F
WORK	.14425	.20567	.77382	20.759	.0000
MINORITY	-.12902	-.19464	.84758	18.507	.0000
AGE	.13942	.20519	.80425	20.659	.0000

From statistics calculated for variables not in the equation, you can decide what variable should be entered next. This process is detailed in Section 6.45.

6.43
The "Optimal" Number of Independent Variables

Having seen what happens when sex is added to the equation containing education (Figure 6.41), consider now what happens when the remaining three independent variables are entered one at a time in no particular order. Summary output is shown in Figure 6.43. Step 5 shows the statistics for the equation with all independent variables entered. Step 3 describes the model with education, sex, and work experience as the independent variables.

Figure 6.43 All independent variables in the equation

```
COMPUTE LOGBEG=LG10(SALBEG)
REGRESSION /WIDTH 132
  /VARIABLES=LOGBEG,EDLEVEL,SEX,WORK,AGE,MINORITY
  /STATISTICS=HISTORY F
  /DEPENDENT=LOGBEG
  /METHOD=ENTER EDLEVEL /ENTER SEX /ENTER WORK /ENTER AGE
  /ENTER MINORITY.
```

Step	MultR	Rsq	AdjRsq	F(Eqn)	SigF	RsqCh	FCh	SigCh		Variable	BetaIn	Correl
1	.6857	.4702	.4691	418.920	.000	.4702	418.920	.000	In:	EDLEVEL	.6857	.6857
2	.7589	.5760	.5742	319.896	0.0	.1058	117.486	.000	In:	SEX	-.3480	-.5480
3	.7707	.5939	.5913	229.130	0.0	.0179	20.759	.000	In:	WORK	.1442	.0399
4	.7830	.6130	.6097	185.750	0.0	.0191	23.176	.000	In:	MINORITY	-.1412	-.1728
5	.7842	.6150	.6109	149.501	0.0	.0019	2.357	.125	In:	AGE	.0781	-.0478

Examination of Figure 6.43 shows that R^2 never decreases as independent variables are added. This is always true in regression analysis. However, this does not necessarily mean that the equation with more variables better fits the population. As the number of parameters estimated from the sample increases, so does the goodness of fit to the sample as measured by R^2. For example, if a sample contains six cases, a regression equation with six parameters fits the sample exactly, even though there may be no true statistical relationship at all between the dependent variable and the independent variables.

As indicated in Section 6.10, the sample R^2 in general tends to overestimate the population value of R^2. Adjusted R^2 attempts to correct the optimistic bias of the sample R^2. Adjusted R^2 does not necessarily increase as additional variables are added to an equation and is the preferred measure of goodness of fit because it is not subject to the inflationary bias of unadjusted R^2. This statistic is shown in the column labeled **AdjRsq** in the output.

Although adding independent variables increases R^2, it does not necessarily decrease the standard error of the estimate. Each time a variable is added to the equation, a degree of freedom is lost from the residual sum of squares and one is gained for the regression sum of squares. The standard error may increase when the decrease in the residual sum of squares is very slight and not sufficient to make up for the loss of a degree of freedom for the residual sum of squares. The F value for the test of the overall regression decreases when the regression sum of squares does not increase as fast as the degrees of freedom for the regression.

Including a large number of independent variables in a regression model is never a good strategy, unless there are strong, previous reasons to suggest that they all should be included. The observed increase in R^2 does not necessarily reflect a better fit of the model in the population. Including irrelevant variables increases the standard errors of all estimates without improving prediction. A model with many variables is often difficult to interpret.

On the other hand, it is important not to exclude potentially relevant independent variables. The following sections describe various procedures for selecting variables to be included in a regression model. The goal is to build a concise model that makes good prediction possible.

6.44
Additional Statistics for Comparing Models

In addition to R^2 and adjusted R^2, many other criteria have been suggested for comparing models and selecting among them (Judge et al., 1985). One of the most commonly used alternatives to R^2 is called Mallow's C_p, which measures the standardized total mean squared error of prediction for the observed data. It is defined as

$$C_p = \frac{SSE}{\hat{\sigma}^2} + 2p - N$$

Equation 6.44a

where σ^2 is an estimate of σ^2 usually obtained from the full set of variables, SSE is the error sum of squares from a model with p coefficients, including the constant, and N is the sample size.

The first part of Mallow's C_p is called the "variance" component, the second the bias component. Subsets of variables that produce values close to p are considered good. Graphical methods for evaluation of models based on C_p are discussed in Daniel and Wood (1980) and Draper and Smith (1981).

Amemiya's prediction criteria PC, is akin to adjusted R^2 with a higher penalty for adding variables. It is defined as

$$PC = \frac{N+p}{N-p}(1-R^2)$$ **Equation 6.44b**

Aikake's information criterion is based on an information measure of model selection. It is computed as

$$AIC = N\,ln\left(\frac{SSE}{N}\right) + 2p$$ **Equation 6.44c**

The Schwarz Bayesian criterion is

$$SBC = N\,ln\left(\frac{SSE}{N}\right) + p\,ln(N)$$ **Equation 6.44d**

Detailed discussions of these criteria can be found in Judge et al. (1985).

6.45
Procedures for Selecting Variables

You can construct a variety of regression models from the same set of variables. For instance, you can build seven different equations from three independent variables: three with only one independent variable, three with two independent variables, and one with all three. As the number of variables increases, so does the number of potential models (ten independent variables yield 1,023 models).

Although there are procedures for computing all possible regression equations, several other methods do not require as much computation and are more frequently used. Among these procedures are forward selection, backward elimination, and stepwise regression. None of these variable selection procedures is "best" in any absolute sense; they merely identify subsets of variables that, for the sample, are good predictors of the dependent variable.

6.46
Forward Selection

In *forward selection*, the first variable considered for entry into the equation is the one with the largest positive or negative correlation with the dependent variable. The F test for the hypothesis that the coefficient of the entered variable is 0 is then calculated. To determine whether this variable (and each succeeding variable) is entered, the F value is compared to an established criterion. You can specify one of two criteria in SPSS/PC+. One criterion is the minimum value of the F statistic that a variable must achieve in order to enter, called *F-to-enter* (keyword FIN), with a default value of 3.84. The other criterion you can specify is the probability associated with the F statistic, called *probability of F-to-enter* (keyword PIN), with a default of 0.05. In this case, a variable enters into the equation only if the probability associated with the F test is less than or equal to the default 0.05 or the value you specify. By default, the probability of F-to-enter is the criterion used.

These two criteria are not necessarily equivalent. As variables are added to the equation, the degrees of freedom associated with the residual sum of squares decrease while the regression degrees of freedom increase. Thus, a fixed F value has different significance levels depending on the number of variables currently in the equation. For large samples, the differences are negligible.

The actual significance level associated with the *F*-to-enter statistic is not the one usually obtained from the *F* distribution, since many variables are being examined and the largest *F* value is selected. Unfortunately, the true significance level is difficult to compute since it depends not only on the number of cases and variables but also on the correlations between independent variables.

If the first variable selected for entry meets the criterion for inclusion, forward selection continues. Otherwise, the procedure terminates with no variables in the equation. Once one variable is entered, the statistics for variables not in the equation are used to select the next one. The partial correlations between the dependent variable and each of the independent variables not in the equation, adjusted for the independent variables in the equation, are examined. The variable with the largest partial correlation is the next candidate. Choosing the variable with the largest partial correlation in absolute value is equivalent to selecting the variable with the largest *F* value.

If the criterion is met, the variable is entered into the equation and the procedure is repeated. The procedure stops when there are no other variables that meet the entry criterion.

To include a specific number of independent variables in the equation, you can specify the number of steps and SPSS/PC+ selects only the first *n* variables that meet entry requirements. Another criterion that is always checked before a variable is entered is the tolerance, which is discussed in Section 6.51.

Figure 6.46a shows output generated from a forward-selection procedure using the salary data. The default entry criterion is PIN=0.05. In the first step, education (variable EDLEVEL) is entered since it has the highest correlation with beginning salary. The significance level associated with education is less than 0.0005, so it certainly meets the criterion for entry.

Figure 6.46a Summary statistics for forward selection

```
COMPUTE LOGBEG=LG10(SALBEG)
REGRESSION /WIDTH 132
    /VARIABLES=LOGBEG,EDLEVEL,SEX,WORK,MINORITY,AGE
    /STATISTICS=HISTORY F
    /DEPENDENT=LOGBEG
    /METHOD=FORWARD.
```

Step	MultR	Rsq	AdjRsq	F(Eqn)	SigF	RsqCh	FCh	SigCh		Variable	BetaIn	Correl
1	.6857	.4702	.4691	418.920	.000	.4702	418.920	.000	In:	EDLEVEL	.6857	.6857
2	.7589	.5760	.5742	319.896	0.0	.1058	117.486	.000	In:	SEX	-.3480	-.5480
3	.7707	.5939	.5913	229.130	0.0	.0179	20.759	.000	In:	WORK	.1442	.0399
4	.7830	.6130	.6097	185.750	0.0	.0191	23.176	.000	In:	MINORITY	-.1412	-.1728

To see how the next variable, SEX, was selected, look at the statistics shown in Figure 6.46b for variables not in the equation when only EDLEVEL is in the equation. The variable with the largest partial correlation is SEX. If entered at the next step, it would have an *F* value of approximately 117 for the test that its coefficient is 0. Since the probability associated with the *F* is less than 0.05, variable SEX is entered in the second step.

Once variable SEX enters at Step 2, the statistics for variables not in the equation must be examined (see Figure 6.42). The variable with the largest absolute value for the partial correlation coefficient is now years of work experience. Its *F* value is 20.759 with a probability less than 0.05, so variable WORK is entered in the next step. The same process takes place with variable MINORITY and it is entered, leaving age as the only variable out of the equation. However, as shown in Figure 6.46c, the significance level associated with the age coefficient *F* value is 0.1254, which is too large for entry. Thus, forward selection yields the summary table for the four steps shown in Figure 6.46a.

Figure 6.46b Status of the variables at the first step

```
COMPUTE LOGBEG=LG10(SALBEG)
REGRESSION VARIABLES=LOGBEG,EDLEVEL,SEX,WORK,MINORITY,AGE
  /STATISTICS=F
  /DEPENDENT=LOGBEG
  /METHOD=FORWARD.
```

```
------------------- Variables in the Equation -------------------

Variable              B          SE B       Beta          F    Sig F

EDLEVEL          .03642  1.77959E-03       .68572    418.920   .0000
(Constant)      3.31001       .02455                18176.773  .0000


--------------- Variables not in the Equation ---------------

Variable     Beta In  Partial  Min Toler        F   Sig F

SEX          -.34802  -.44681    .87327   117.486   .0000
WORK          .22747   .30241    .93632    47.408   .0000
MINORITY     -.08318  -.11327    .98234     6.121   .0137
AGE           .15718   .20726    .92113    21.140   .0000
```

Figure 6.46c The last step

```
COMPUTE LOGBEG=LG10(SALBEG)
REGRESSION VARIABLES=LOGBEG,EDLEVEL,SEX,WORK,MINORITY,AGE
  /STATISTICS=F
  /DEPENDENT=LOGBEG
  /METHOD=FORWARD.
```

```
--------------- Variables not in the Equation ---------------

Variable     Beta In  Partial  Min Toler        F   Sig F

AGE           .07811   .07080    .29784     2.357   .1254
```

6.47
Backward Elimination

While forward selection starts with no independent variables in the equation and sequentially enters them, *backward elimination* starts with all variables in the equation and sequentially removes them. Instead of entry criteria, removal criteria are specified.

Two removal criteria are available in SPSS/PC+. The first is the minimum F value (FOUT) that a variable must have in order to remain in the equation. Variables with F values less than this *F-to-remove* are eligible for removal. The second criterion available is the maximum probability of *F*-to-remove (keyword POUT) a variable can have. The default FOUT value is 2.71 and the default POUT value is 0.10. The default criterion is POUT.

Figure 6.47a Backward elimination at the first step

```
COMPUTE LOGBEG=LG10(SALBEG)
REGRESSION /WIDTH 132
  /VARIABLES=LOGBEG,EDLEVEL,SEX,WORK,MINORITY,AGE
  /STATISTICS=COEFF ZPP F
  /DEPENDENT=LOGBEG
  /METHOD=BACKWARD.
```

```
------------------------- Variables in the Equation -------------------------

Variable              B          SE B       Beta   Correl  Part Cor  Partial

AGE          9.829958E-04  6.58814E-04    .075586 -.049770  .042803  .068807
SEX              -.103465       .010323   -.336625 -.548020 -.287522 -.420378
MINORITY         -.052344       .010839   -.141515 -.172836 -.138541 -.217877
EDLEVEL           .031446       .001748    .592008  .685719  .515982  .639324
WORK              .001647  9.20151E-04    .093683  .039940  .051352  .082466
(Constant)       3.386540       .033067


--------------- in ---------------

Variable           F   Sig F

AGE            2.226   .1364
SEX          100.456   .0000
MINORITY      23.323   .0000
EDLEVEL      323.523   .0000
WORK           3.204   .0741
(Constant) 10488.887   .0000
```

Look at the salary example again, this time constructing the model with backward elimination. The output in Figure 6.47a is from the first step, in which all variables are entered into the equation. The variable with the smallest partial correlation coefficient, AGE, is examined first. Since the probability of its F (0.1254) is greater than the default POUT criterion value of 0.10, variable AGE is removed.

Figure 6.47b   Backward elimination at the last step

```
COMPUTE LOGBEG=LG10(SALBEG)
REGRESSION /WIDTH=132
  /VARIABLES=LOGBEG,EDLEVEL,SEX,WORK,MINORITY,AGE
  /STATISTICS=COEFF ZPP F
  /DEPENDENT=LOGBEG
  /METHOD=BACKWARD.
```

```
---------------------- Variables in the Equation ----------------------

Variable                B           SE B         Beta    Correl  Part Cor   Partial

SEX                -.099042      .009901     -.322234  -.548020  -.287333  -.419331
MINORITY           -.052245      .010853     -.141248  -.172836  -.138282  -.216998
EDLEVEL             .031433      .001751      .591755   .685719   .515768   .638270
WORK                .002753  5.45823E-04      .156592   .039940   .144891   .226848
(Constant)         3.411953      .028380


---------- in -----------              ---------- not in ----------

Variable          F    Sig F          Variable          F   Sig F

SEX          100.063   .0000          AGE           2.226   .1364
MINORITY      23.176   .0000
EDLEVEL      322.412   .0000
WORK          25.444   .0000
(Constant) 14454.046   .0000
```

The equation is then recalculated without AGE, producing the statistics shown in Figure 6.47b. The variable with the smallest partial correlation is MINORITY. However, its significance is less than the 0.10 criterion, so backward elimination stops. The equation resulting from backward elimination is the same as the one from forward selection. This is not always the case, however. Forward- and backward-selection procedures can give different results, even with comparable entry and removal criteria.

6.48
Stepwise Selection

Stepwise selection of independent variables is really a combination of backward and forward procedures and is probably the most commonly used method. The first variable is selected in the same manner as in forward selection. If the variable fails to meet entry requirements (either FIN or PIN), the procedure terminates with no independent variables in the equation. If it passes the criterion, the second variable is selected based on the highest partial correlation. If it passes entry criteria, it also enters the equation.

After the first variable is entered, stepwise selection differs from forward selection: the first variable is examined to see whether it should be removed according to the removal criterion (FOUT or POUT) as in backward elimination. In the next step, variables not in the equation are examined for entry. After each step, variables already in the equation are examined for removal. Variables are removed until none remain that meet the removal criterion. To prevent the same variable from being repeatedly entered and removed, PIN must be less than POUT (or FIN greater than FOUT). Variable selection terminates when no more variables meet entry and removal criteria.

In the salary example, stepwise selection with the default criteria results in the same equation produced by both forward selection and backward elimination (see Figure 6.48).

Figure 6.48 Stepwise output

```
COMPUTE LOGBEG=LG10(SALBEG)
REGRESSION VARIABLES=LOGBEG EDLEVEL SEX WORK MINORITY AGE
    /STATISTICS=R COEFF OUTS F
    /DEPENDENT=LOGBEG
    /METHOD=STEPWISE.
```

```
Listwise Deletion of Missing Data

Equation Number 1   Dependent Variable..   LOGBEG

Beginning Block Number  1.  Method: Stepwise


Variable(s) Entered on Step Number
   1..   EDLEVEL   EDUCATIONAL LEVEL


Multiple R          .68572
R Square            .47021
Adjusted R Square   .46909
Standard Error      .11165

F =    418.92011     Signif F =  .0000
```

Variable	B	SE B	Beta	F	Sig F		Variable	Beta In	Partial	Min Toler	F	Sig F

```
----------------- Variables in the Equation -------------------          ------------ Variables not in the Equation -------------

Variable           B        SE B      Beta        F    Sig F      Variable   Beta In  Partial  Min Toler        F   Sig F

EDLEVEL        .03642 1.77959E-03    .68572   418.920  .0000      SEX       -.34802  -.44681    .87327   117.486  .0000
(Constant)    3.31001    .02455             18176.773  .0000      WORK       .22747   .30241    .93632    47.408  .0000
                                                                  MINORITY  -.08318  -.11327    .98234     6.121  .0137
                                                                  AGE        .15718   .20726    .92113    21.140  .0000


             * * * * * * * * * * * * * * * * * *


Variable(s) Entered on Step Number
   2..   SEX      SEX OF EMPLOYEE


Multiple R          .75893
R Square            .57598
Adjusted R Square   .57418
Standard Error      .09999

F =    319.89574     Signif F = 0.0


----------------- Variables in the Equation -------------------          ------------ Variables not in the Equation -------------

Variable           B        SE B      Beta        F    Sig F      Variable   Beta In  Partial  Min Toler        F   Sig F

EDLEVEL        .02984 1.70549E-03    .56183   306.191  .0000      WORK       .14425   .20567    .77382    20.759  .0000
SEX           -.10697 9.86858E-03   -.34802   117.486  .0000      MINORITY  -.12902  -.19464    .84758    18.507  .0000
(Constant)    3.44754    .02539             18443.284  .0000      AGE        .13942   .20519    .80425    20.659  .0000

                                                                 * * * * * * * * * * * * * * * * * * * * *


Variable(s) Entered on Step Number
   3..   WORK     WORK EXPERIENCE


Multiple R          .77066
R Square            .59391
Adjusted R Square   .59132
Standard Error      .09796

F =    229.13001     Signif F = 0.0


----------------- Variables in the Equation -------------------          ------------ Variables not in the Equation -------------

Variable           B             SE B      Beta        F    Sig F      Variable   Beta In  Partial  Min Toler        F   Sig F

EDLEVEL        .03257     1.77493E-03    .61321   336.771  .0000      MINORITY  -.14125  -.21700    .75967    23.176  .0000
SEX           -.09403        .01008     -.30594    87.099  .0000      AGE        .07633   .06754    .29839     2.149  .1433
WORK      2.536163E-03  5.56642E-04    .14425    20.759  .0000
(Constant)    3.38457        .02845             14150.645  .0000     * * * * * * * * * * * * * * * * * * * * *


Variable(s) Entered on Step Number
   4..   MINORITY  MINORITY CLASSIFICATION


Multiple R          .78297
R Square            .61304
Adjusted R Square   .60974
Standard Error      .09573

F =    185.74958     Signif F = 0.0
----------------- Variables in the Equation -------------------          ------------ Variables not in the Equation -------------

Variable           B             SE B      Beta        F    Sig F      Variable   Beta In  Partial  Min Toler        F   Sig F

EDLEVEL        .03143     1.75056E-03    .59176   322.412  .0000      AGE        .07811   .07080    .29784     2.357  .1254
SEX           -.09904     9.90104E-03   -.32223   100.063  .0000
WORK      2.753243E-03  5.45823E-04    .15659    25.444  .0000      End Block Number  1   PIN =     .050 Limits reached.
MINORITY      -.05225        .01085     -.14125    23.176  .0000
(Constant)    3.41195        .02838             14454.046  .0000
```

The three procedures do not always result in the same equation, though you should be encouraged when they do. The model selected by any method should be carefully studied for violations of the assumptions. It is often a good idea to develop several acceptable models and then choose among them based on interpretability, ease of variable acquisition, parsimony, and so forth.

6.49
Checking for Violation of Assumptions

The procedures discussed in Sections 6.17 through 6.22 for checking for violations of assumptions in bivariate regression apply in the multivariate case as well. Residuals should be plotted against predicted values as well as against each independent variable. The distribution of residuals should be examined for normality.

Several additional residual plots may be useful for multivariate models. One of these is the partial regression plot. For the *j*th independent variable, it is obtained by calculating the residuals for the dependent variable when it is predicted from all the independent variables excluding the *j*th and by calculating the residuals for the *j*th independent variable when it is predicted from all of the other independent variables. This removes the linear effect of the other independent variables from both variables. For each case, these two residuals are plotted against each other.

A partial regression plot for educational level for the regression equation that contains work experience, minority, sex, and educational level as the independent variables is shown in Figure 6.49a. (Summary statistics for the regression equation with all independent variables are displayed in the last step of Figure 6.48.)

Figure 6.49a Partial regression plot from PLOT

```
COMPUTE LOGBEG=LG10(SALBEG)
REGRESSION VARIABLES=LOGBEG SEX MINORITY EDLEVEL WORK
  /DEPENDENT=LOGBEG
  /METHOD=ENTER MINORITY SEX WORK
  /SAVE=RESID(RES1)
  /DEPENDENT=EDLEVEL
  /METHOD=ENTER MINORITY SEX WORK
  /SAVE=RESID(RES2).
PLOT FORMAT=REGRESSION /PLOT=RES1 WITH RES2.
```

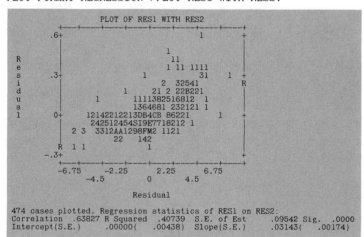

Several characteristics of the partial regression plot make it a particularly valuable diagnostic tool. The slope of the regression line for the two residual variables (0.03143) is equal to the coefficient for the EDLEVEL variable in the multiple regression equation after the last step (Step 4 in Figure 6.48). Thus, by examining the bivariate plot, you can conveniently identify points that are "influential" in the determination of the particular regression coefficient (see Sections 6.23 through 6.25). The correlation coefficient between the two residuals,

0.638, is the partial correlation coefficient discussed in Section 6.39. The residuals from the least-squares line in Figure 6.49a are equal to the residuals from the final multiple regression equation, which includes all the independent variables.

The partial regression plot also helps you assess inadequacies of the selected model and violations of the underlying assumptions. For example, the partial regression plot of educational level does not appear to be linear, suggesting that an additional term, such as years of education squared, might also be included in the model. This violation is much easier to spot using the partial regression plot than the plot of the independent variable against the residual from the equation with all independent variables. Figures 6.49b and 6.49c show the residual scatterplot and partial regression plot produced by the REGRESSION procedure. Note that the nonlinearity is much more apparent in the partial regression plot.

Figure 6.49b   Residual scatterplot from REGRESSION

```
COMPUTE LOGBEG=LG10(SALBEG)
REGRESSION VARIABLES=LOGBEG SEX MINORITY EDLEVEL WORK
  /DEPENDENT=LOGBEG
  /METHOD=STEPWISE
  /SCATTERPLOT=(*RESID,EDLEVEL)
```

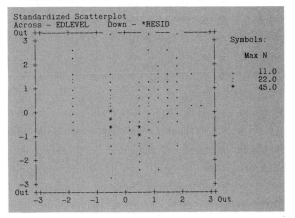

Figure 6.49c   Partial regression plot from REGRESSION

```
COMPUTE LOGBEG=LG10(SALBEG)
REGRESSION VARIABLES=LOGBEG SEX MINORITY EDLEVEL WORK
  /DEPENDENT=LOGBEG
  /METHOD=STEPWISE
  /PARTIALPLOT=EDLEVEL.
```

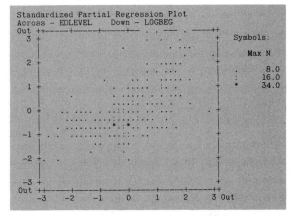

Figure 6.49d contains the summary statistics when the number of years of education squared is included in the multiple regression equation. The multiple R^2 increases from 0.61 (Step 4 in Figure 6.48) to 0.71, a significant improvement.

Figure 6.49d   The regression equation with education squared

```
COMPUTE LOGBEG=LG10(SALBEG)
COMPUTE ED2=EDLEVEL*EDLEVEL
REGRESSION VARIABLES=LOGBEG SEX MINORITY EDLEVEL ED2 WORK
   /DEPENDENT=LOGBEG
   /METHOD=ENTER.
```

```
Variable(s) Entered on Step Number   1..   WORK       WORK EXPERIENCE
                                      2..   MINORITY   MINORITY CLASSIFICATION
                                      3..   SEX        SEX OF EMPLOYEE
                                      4..   EDLEVEL    EDUCATIONAL LEVEL
                                      5..   ED2

Multiple R           .84302       Analysis of Variance
R Square             .71068                          DF    Sum of Squares    Mean Square
Adjusted R Square    .70759       Regression          5           7.89331        1.57866
Standard Error       .08286       Residual          468           3.21345         .00687

                                  F =      229.91286      Signif F = 0.0
```

6.50
Looking for Influential Points

As discussed in Sections 6.23 through 6.25, when building a regression model it is important to identify cases that are influential or that have a disproportionately large effect on the estimated model. We can look for cases that change the values of the regression coefficients and of predicted values, cases that increase the variances of the coefficients, and cases that are poorly fitted by the model.

Among the important influence measures is the leverage (LEVER) of a case. The predicted values of the dependent variable can be expressed as

$$\hat{Y} = H Y$$

Equation 6.50a

The diagonal elements of the H matrix (commonly called the hat matrix) are called leverages. The leverage for a case describes the impact of the observed value of the dependent variable on the prediction of the fitted value. Leverages are important in their own right and as fundamental building blocks for other diagnostic measures. For example, the Mahalanobis' distance for a point is obtained by multiplying the leverage value by $N-1$.

The REGRESSION procedure computes centered leverages (LEVER). They range from $-1/N$ to $(N-1)/N$, where N is the number of observations. The mean value for the centered leverage is p/N, where p is the number of independent variables in the equation. A leverage of $-1/N$ identifies a point with no influence on the fit, while a point with a leverage of $(N-1)/N$ indicates that a degree of freedom has been devoted to fitting the data point. Ideally you would like each observation to exert a roughly equal influence. That is, you want all of the leverages to be near p/N. It is a good idea to examine points with leverage values that exceed $2p/N$.

To see the effect of a case on the estimation of the regression coefficients, you can look at the change in each of the regression coefficients when the case is removed from the analysis. REGRESSION can display or save the actual change in each of the coefficients, including the intercept (DFBETA) and the standardized change (SDBETA).

Figure 6.50a is a plot of SDBETA for the MINORITY variable against a case ID number. Note that, as expected, most of the points cluster in a horizontal band around 0. However, there are a few points far removed from the rest. Belsley et al. (1980) recommend examining SDBETA values that are larger than

$$\frac{2}{\sqrt{N}}$$

Equation 6.50b

Figure 6.50a Plot of SDBETA values for variable MINORITY

```
COMPUTE LOGBEG=LG10(SALBEG).
COMPUTE ED2=EDLEVEL*EDLEVEL.
REGRESSION VARIABLES=LOGBEG SEX MINORITY EDLEVEL ED2 WORK
  /DEPENDENT=LOGBEG /METHOD=ENTER.
  /SAVE SDBETA.
PLOT PLOT=SDB2_1 WITH ID.
```

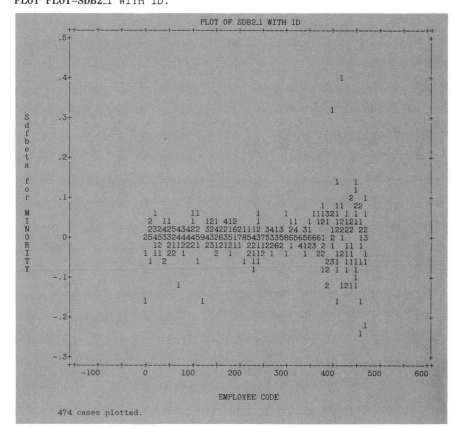

In addition to looking at the change in the regression coefficients when a case is deleted from an analysis, we can look at the change in the predicted value (DFFIT) or at the standardized change (SDFFIT). Cases with large values far removed from the rest should be examined. As a rule of thumb, you may want to look at standardized values larger than

$$\frac{2}{\sqrt{p/N}}$$

Equation 6.50c

Another type of influential observation is one that influences the variance of the estimated regression coefficients. A measure of the impact of an observation on the variance-covariance matrix of the parameter estimates is called the covariance ratio (COVRATIO). It is computed as the ratio of the determinant of the variance-covariance matrix computed without the case to the determinant of the variance-covariance matrix computed with all cases. If this ratio is close to 1, the case leaves the variance-covariance matrix relatively unchanged. Belsley et al. (1980) recommend examining points for which the absolute value of the ratio minus 1 is greater than $3p/N$.

Figure 6.50b is a plot of COVRATIO for the salary example. Note the circled point, which has a COVRATIO substantially smaller than the rest.

Figure 6.50b   Plot of the covariance ratio (COVRATIO)

```
COMPUTE LOGBEG=LG10(SALBEG).
COMPUTE ED2=EDLEVEL*EDLEVEL.
REGRESSION VARIABLES=LOGBEG SEX MINORITY EDLEVEL ED2 WORK
  /DEPENDENT=LOGBEG /METHOD=ENTER
  /SAVE COVRATIO.
PLOT PLOT=COV_1 WITH ID.
```

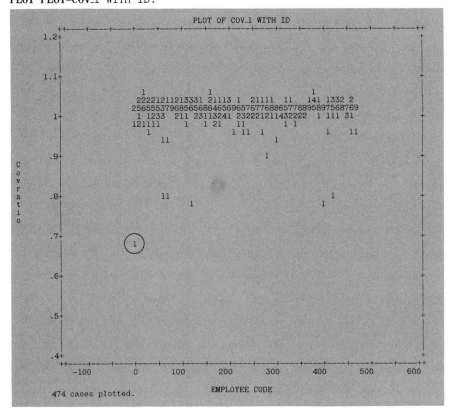

6.51
Measures of Collinearity

Collinearity refers to the situation in which there is a high multiple correlation when one of the independent variables is regressed on the others (i.e., when there is a high correlation between independent variables). The problem with collinear variables is that they provide very similar information, and it is difficult to separate out the effects of the individual variables. Diagnostics are available which allow you to detect the presence of collinear data and to assess the extent to which the collinearity has degraded the estimated parameters.

The tolerance of a variable is a commonly used measure of collinearity. The tolerance (TOL) of variable i is defined as $1-R_i^2$, where R_i is the multiple correlation coefficient when the ith independent variable is predicted from the other independent variables. If the tolerance of a variable is small, it is almost a linear combination of the other independent variables.

The variance inflation factor (VIF) is closely related to the tolerance. In fact, it is defined as the reciprocal of the tolerance. That is, for the ith variable,

$$\text{VIF}_i = 1/(1-R_i^2)$$ **Equation 6.51**

This quantity is called the variance inflation factor since the term is involved in the calculation of the variance of the ith regression coefficient. As the variance inflation factor increases, so does the variance of the regression coefficient.

Figure 6.51 shows the tolerances and VIFs for the variables in the final model. Note the low tolerances and high VIFs for EDLEVEL and ED2 (the square of

EDLEVEL). This is to be expected since there is a relationship between these two variables.

Figure 6.51 Measures of collinearity: tolerance and VIF

```
COMPUTE LOGBEG=LG10(SALBEG).
COMPUTE ED2=EDLEVEL*EDLEVEL.
REGRESSION VARIABLES=LOGBEG SEX MINORITY EDLEVEL ED2 WORK
   /STATISTICS=COEF TOL
   /DEPENDENT=LOGBEG /METHOD=ENTER.
```

```
------------------------- Variables in the Equation -------------------------

Variable            B            SE B       Beta     Tolerance       VIF          T

WORK          .001794   4.78593E-04    .102038      .834367       1.199      3.749
MINORITY     -.038225        .009460   -.103342      .945107       1.058     -4.041
SEX          -.082503        .008671   -.268426      .776799       1.287     -9.515
EDLEVEL      -.089624        .009751  -1.687260      .018345      54.511     -9.191
ED2           .004562   3.63028E-04   2.312237      .018263      54.756     12.567
(Constant)   4.173910        .065417                                        63.804


------ in ------

Variable    Sig T

WORK        .0002
MINORITY    .0001
SEX         .0000
EDLEVEL     .0000
ED2         .0000
(Constant)  .0000
```

Two useful tools for examining the collinearity of a data matrix are the eigenvalues of the scaled, uncentered cross-products matrix and the decomposition of regression variance corresponding to the eigenvalues.

6.52 Eigenvalues and Condition Indexes

We can compare the eigenvalues of the scaled, uncentered cross-products matrix to see if some are much larger than others. If this is the case, the data matrix is said to be "ill-conditioned." If a matrix is ill-conditioned, small changes in the values of the independent or dependent variables may lead to large changes in the solution. The condition index is defined as

$$cond\ index_i = \sqrt{\frac{EIGENVALUE_{max}}{EIGENVALUE_i}}$$

Equation 6.52

There are as many near dependencies among the variables as there are large condition indexes.

Figure 6.52 shows the eigenvalues and condition indexes for the salary example. You can see that the last two eigenvalues are much smaller than the rest. Their condition indexes are 10.29 and 88.22.

Figure 6.52 Measures of collinearity: eigenvalues and condition indexes

```
COMPUTE LOGBEG=LG10(SALBEG).
COMPUTE ED2=EDLEVEL*EDLEVEL.
REGRESSION VARIABLES=LOGBEG SEX MINORITY EDLEVEL ED2 WORK
   /STATISTICS=COLLIN
   /DEPENDENT=LOGBEG /METHOD=ENTER.
```

```
Collinearity Diagnostics

Number  Eigenval    Cond    Variance Proportions
                    Index   Constant      SEX  MINORITY   EDLEVEL      ED2
   1    4.08812     1.000    .00019    .01223   .01375    .00004   .00013
   2     .79928     2.262    .00005    .08212   .65350    .00002   .00009
   3     .59282     2.626    .00001    .37219   .22139    .00003   .00022
   4     .48061     2.917    .00005    .14964   .05421    .00012   .00091
   5     .03864    10.286    .05223    .37811   .04876    .00004   .02337
   6     .00053    88.221    .94746    .00571   .00839    .99975   .97527


           WORK
   1      .01466
   2      .04351
   3      .17437
   4      .51370
   5      .20721
   6      .04655
```

6.53
Variance Proportions

The variances of each of the regression coefficients, including the constant, can be decomposed into a sum of components associated with each of the eigenvalues. If a high proportion of the variance of two or more coefficients is associated with the same eigenvalue, there is evidence for a near dependency.

Consider Figure 6.52 again. Each of the columns after the condition index tells you the proportion of the variance of each of the coefficients associated with each of the eigenvalues. Consider the column for the SEX coefficient. You see that 1.22% of the variance of the coefficient is attributable to the first eigenvalue, 8.2% to the second, and similarly 0.57% to the sixth (the proportions in each column sum to 1).

In this table you're looking for variables with high proportions for the same eigenvalue. For example, looking at the last eigenvalue, you see that it accounts for 95% of the variance of the constant, almost 100% of the variance of EDLEVEL, and 98% of the variance of ED2. This tells you that these three variables are highly dependent. Since the other independent variables have small variance proportions for the sixth eigenvalue, it does not appear that the observed dependencies are affecting their coefficients. (See Belsley et al., 1980, for an extensive discussion of these diagnostics.)

6.54
Interpreting the Equation

The multiple regression equation estimated above suggests several findings. Education appears to be the best predictor of beginning salary, at least among the variables included in this study (Figure 6.47a). The sex of the employee also appears to be important. Women are paid less than men since the sign of the regression coefficient is negative (men are coded 0 and women are coded 1). Years of prior work experience and race are also related to salary, but when education and sex are included in the equation, the effect of experience and race is less striking.

Do these results indicate that there is sex discrimination at the bank? Not necessarily. It is well recognized that all education is not equally profitable. Master's degrees in business administration and political science are treated quite differently in the marketplace. Thus, a possible explanation of the observed results is that women enter areas that are just not very well paid. Although this may suggest inequities in societal evaluation of skills, it does not necessarily imply discrimination at the bank. Further, many other potential job-related skills or qualifications are not included in the model. Also, some of the existing variables, such as age, may make nonlinear as well as linear contributions to the fit. Such contributions can often be approximated by including new variables that are simple functions of the existing one. For example, the age values squared may improve the fit.

6.55
Statistics for Unselected Cases

As previously noted, a model usually fits the sample from which it is derived better than it fits the population. A sometimes useful strategy for obtaining an estimate of how well the model fits the population is to split the sample randomly into two parts. One part is then used to estimate the model, while the remaining cases are reserved for testing the goodness of fit.

It is also sometimes interesting to split the data on some characteristics of the sample. For example, you can develop the salary equation for males alone and then apply it to females to see how well it fits. For example, Figure 6.55 shows histograms of residuals for males (denoted as selected cases) and females (unselected cases). Note that the females' salaries are too large when predicted from the male equation since most of the residuals are negative. The multiple R for the females is 0.45596, which is smaller than the 0.73882 for males (stepwise selection was used).

Figure 6.55 Histograms for males (selected) and females (unselected)

```
COMPUTE LOGBEG=LG10(SALBEG)
COMPUTE ED2=EDLEVEL*EDLEVEL
REGRESSION WIDTH=90
  /SELECT SEX EQ 0
  /VARIABLES=LOGBEG,EDLEVEL,ED2,SEX,WORK,MINORITY,AGE
  /DEPENDENT=LOGBEG
  /METHOD=STEPWISE
  /RESIDUALS=HISTOGRAM.
```

```
Histogram - Standardized Residual
- Selected Cases
 N Exp N      (* = 1 Cases,    . : = Normal Curve)
 3   .20  Out ***
 3   .40  3.00 ***
 0  1.01  2.67 .
 1  2.30  2.33 *.
 2  4.71  2.00 ** .
 5  8.63  1.67 ***** .
11 14.16  1.33 ********** .
19 20.81  1.00 ******************* .
26 27.40   .67 ***************************.
35 32.32   .33 ******************************.***
31 34.15  0.0 ******************************* .
30 32.32  -.33 ****************************** .
42 27.40  -.67 ***************************.****************
31 20.81 -1.00 *******************:*********
10 14.16 -1.33 ********** .
 5  8.63 -1.67 *****
 3  4.71 -2.00 *** .
 0  2.30 -2.33 .
 1  1.01 -2.67 :
 0   .40 -3.00
 0   .20  Out

Histogram - Standardized Residual
- Unselected Cases
 N Exp N      (X = 1 Cases,    . : = Normal Curve)
 0   .17  Out
 0   .33  3.00 .
 0   .84  2.67 .
 0  1.93  2.33 .
 0  3.94  2.00   .
 1  7.22  1.67 X    .
 1 11.85  1.33 X       .
 3 17.42  1.00 XXX        .
 4 22.94   .67 XXXX         .
10 27.06   .33 XXXXXXXXXX          .
14 28.59  0.0 XXXXXXXXXXXXX       .
32 27.06  -.33 XXXXXXXXXXXXXXXXXXXXXXXXXX:XXXXX
32 22.94  -.67 XXXXXXXXXXXXXXXXXXXXXX:XXXXXXXX
52 17.42 -1.00 XXXXXXXXXXXXXXX:XXXXXXXXXXXXXXXXXXXXXXXXXXXXXXXXXXXX
22 11.85 -1.33 XXXXXXXXXX:XXXXXXXXX
13  7.22 -1.67 XXXXX:XXXXX
12  3.94 -2.00 XXX:XXXXXXX
 8  1.93 -2.33 X:XXXXX
 7   .84 -2.67 :XXXXX
 1   .33 -3.00 X
 4   .17  Out XXXX
```

6.56 RUNNING PROCEDURE REGRESSION

The REGRESSION procedure provides five equation-building methods: forward selection, backward elimination, stepwise selection, forced entry, and forced removal. The subcommands for residual analysis help detect influential data points, outliers, and violations of the regression model assumptions.

6.57 Building the Equation

To build a simple regression model, you must specify three required subcommands: a VARIABLES subcommand that names the variables to be analyzed, a DEPENDENT subcommand that indicates the dependent variable, and a METHOD subcommand that names the method to be used. For example, to build the simple bivariate model of beginning salary and current salary discussed earlier in the chapter, specify

```
REGRESSION VARIABLES=SALBEG SALNOW
  /DEPENDENT=SALNOW
  /METHOD=ENTER SALBEG.
```

The beginning (SALBEG) and current (SALNOW) salaries are named, with the latter specified as the dependent variable. The ENTER keyword enters beginning salary into the equation. The output produced from this command is shown in Figures 6.3b, 6.10, and 6.11a.

6.58
VARIABLES Subcommand

The optional VARIABLES subcommand lists all variables to be used in the regression analysis. The order of variables on the VARIABLES subcommand determines the order of variables in the correlation matrix. The keyword TO can be used on the VARIABLES subcommand to imply consecutive variables on the active system file. On subsequent DEPENDENT and METHOD subcommands, the keyword TO refers to the order of variables on the VARIABLES subcommand.

The VARIABLES subcommand is followed by a variable list or either one of the following keywords:

ALL *Include all user-defined variables in the active system file.*

(COLLECT) *Include all variables named on the DEPENDENT and METHOD subcommands.* This is the default if the VARIABLES subcommand is not included.

If you do not include a VARIABLES subcommand or you specify the keyword (COLLECT), the METHOD subcommand(s) must include a variable list. If used, the VARIABLES subcommand must precede the first DEPENDENT and METHOD subcommands, as in:

```
REGRESSION VARIABLES=SALBEG SALNOW LOGBEG
 EDLEVEL SEX WORK MINORITY AGE
  /DEPENDENT=LOGBEG
  /METHOD=ENTER EDLEVEL TO AGE.
```

6.59
DEPENDENT Subcommand

The DEPENDENT subcommand indicates the dependent variable for the regression analysis. The DEPENDENT subcommand is followed by a variable name or variable list. If you specify more than one variable on the DEPENDENT subcommand, SPSS produces a separate equation for each dependent variable specified.

You can specify more than one analysis with multiple DEPENDENT and METHOD subcommands. For example, to run both a bivariate and multivariate analysis in the same REGRESSION procedure, specify

```
REGRESSION VARIABLES=SALBEG SALNOW LOGBEG
 EDLEVEL SEX WORK MINORITY AGE
  /DEPENDENT=SALNOW
  /METHOD=ENTER SALBEG
  /DEPENDENT=LOGBEG
  /METHOD=ENTER EDLEVEL TO AGE.
```

The first DEPENDENT subcommand defines a single equation with SALNOW as the dependent variable, and the METHOD subcommand enters SALBEG into the equation. The second DEPENDENT subcommand defines another equation, with LOGBEG as the dependent variable. The associated METHOD subcommand enters variables EDLEVEL to AGE into the equation. The TO convention for naming consecutive variables used in the second METHOD subcommand refers to the order in which the variables are named on the VARIABLES subcommand, not their order on the active system file. See Figures 6.36a and 6.36b for the output from the second equation.

If you specify more than one variable on the DEPENDENT subcommand, SPSS produces a separate equation for each dependent variable specified.

6.60
METHOD Subcommand

At least one METHOD subcommand must immediately follow each DEPENDENT subcommand, specifying the method to be used in developing the regression equation. The available methods are

FORWARD (varlist) *Forward variable selection.* Variables are entered one at a time based on entry criteria (Section 6.46).

BACKWARD (varlist) *Backward variable elimination.* All variables are entered and then removed one at a time based on removal criteria (Section 6.47).

STEPWISE (varlist)	*Stepwise variable entry and removal.* Variables are examined at each step for entry or removal (Section 6.48).
ENTER (varlist)	*Forced entry.* The variables named are entered in a single step. The default variable list is all independent variables.
REMOVE (varlist)	*Forced removal.* The variables named are removed in a single step. REMOVE must have an accompanying variable list.
TEST (varlist)	*Test indicated subsets of independent variables.* TEST offers an easy way to test a variety of models using R^2 change and its test of significance as the criterion for the "best" model. TEST must have an accompanying variable list.

A variable list is required with the REMOVE and TEST keywords and is optional for the other METHOD keywords. The default variable list for methods FORWARD, BACKWARD, STEPWISE, and ENTER includes all variables named on the VARIABLES subcommand that are not named on the preceding DEPENDENT subcommand. For example, to request the backward-elimination method discussed in Section 6.47, specify

```
REGRESSION VARIABLES=LOGBEG EDLEVEL SEX WORK MINORITY AGE
  /DEPENDENT=LOGBEG
  /METHOD=BACKWARD.
```

The keyword METHOD is optional and may be omitted. For example, the command

```
REGRESSION VARIABLES=LOGBEG EDLEVEL SEX WORK MINORITY AGE
  /DEPENDENT=LOGBEG
  /BACKWARD.
```

produces the same results as the previous example.

You can specify multiple METHOD subcommands. For example, you might want to force one variable into the equation first and then enter the remaining variables in a forward-selection fashion, as in

```
REGRESSION VARIABLES=LOGBEG EDLEVEL SEX WORK MINORITY AGE
  /DEPENDENT=LOGBEG
  /METHOD=ENTER EDLEVEL
  /METHOD=FORWARD SEX TO AGE.
```

6.61 STATISTICS Subcommand

By default, REGRESSION displays the four sets of statistics described for keywords R, ANOVA, COEFF, and OUTS below. These statistics are shown in Figures 6.3b, 6.10, and 6.11a for the bivariate equation, and in Figures 6.36a and 6.36b for the multivariate equation. You can specify exactly which statistics you want displayed by any of the following keywords on the STATISTICS subcommand.

DEFAULTS	R, *ANOVA, COEFF, and OUTS.* These statistics are displayed when the STATISTICS subcommand is omitted or if no keywords are specified on the subcommand. If you specify statistics keywords on a STATISTICS subcommand, the default statistics will not appear unless you specify them explicitly, either individually or with the DEFAULTS keyword.
ALL	*All statistics except* F, *LINE, and END.*
R	*Multiple* R. Displays multiple R, R^2, adjusted R^2, and the standard error. (See Figure 6.10.)
ANOVA	*Analysis of variance table.* Displays degrees of freedom, sums of squares, mean squares, F value for multiple R, and the observed significance level of F. (See Figure 6.11a.)
CHA	*Displays change in R^2 between steps, F value for change in R^2, and significance of F.* (See Figure 6.41.)
BCOV	*Variance-covariance matrix of regression coefficients.* Displays a matrix with covariances below the diagonal, correlations above the diagonal, and variances on the diagonal.
XTX	*Sweep matrix.*

COLLIN *Collinearity diagnostics.* Includes the variance inflation factor (VIF), the eigenvalues of the scaled and uncentered cross-products matrix, condition indices, and variance-decomposition proportions (Belsley et al., 1980).

SELECTION *Aids to selecting set of regressors.* Includes Akaike information criterion (AIK), Amemiya's prediction criterion (PC), Mallow's conditional mean squared error of prediction criterion (Cp), and Schwarz Bayesian criterion (SBC) (Judge et al., 1985).

COEFF *Statistics for variables in the equation.* Displays regression coefficient B, standard error of B, standardized coefficient Beta, t value for B, and two-tailed significance level of t.

OUTS *Statistics for variables not in the equation* that have been named on the VARIABLES subcommand. Statistics are Beta if the variable were entered, t value for Beta, significance level of t, partial correlation with the dependent variable controlling for variables in the equation, and minimum tolerance. (See Figure 6.42.)

ZPP *Zero-order, part, and partial correlation.* (See Figure 6.39.)

CI *Confidence intervals.* Displays the 95% confidence interval for the unstandardized regression coefficient. (See Figure 6.8.)

SES *Approximate standard error of the standardized regression coefficients.* (Meyer and Younger, 1976)

TOL *Tolerance.* Displays tolerance and VIF for variables in the equation and, for variables not in the equation, the tolerance a variable would have if it were the only variable entered next. (See Figure 6.51.)

F F *value for* B *and significance of* F. Displayed instead of t for COEFF and OUTS. (See, for example, Figures 6.46b, 6.46c, 6.47a, and 6.47b.)

LINE *Summary line for each step in step methods.* Displays a single summary line for each step in BACKWARD, FORWARD, or STEPWISE methods and the default or requested statistics at the end of each method block (BACKWARD, FORWARD, STEPWISE, ENTER, REMOVE, or TEST).

HISTORY *Step history.* Displays a summary report with a summary line for each method (ENTER, REMOVE, or TEST, if the equation changes) or step if the method entails steps (FORWARD, BACKWARD, or STEPWISE). If history is the only statistic requested, COEFF is displayed for the final equation. (See Figures 6.43 and 6.46a.)

END *One summary line per step or method block.* Displays a summary line per step for BACKWARD, FORWARD, or STEPWISE, and one summary line per block for ENTER, REMOVE, or TEST, if the equation changes.

The STATISTICS subcommand must appear before the DEPENDENT subcommand that initiates the equation and remains in effect until overridden by another STATISTICS subcommand. For example, to produce the output in Figure 6.8, specify

```
REGRESSION VARIABLES=SALBEG SALNOW
  /STATISTICS=CI
  /DEPENDENT=SALNOW
  /METHOD=ENTER SALBEG.
```

To produce the output for the multivariate example shown in Figure 6.41, specify

```
REGRESSION VARIABLES=LOGBEG EDLEVEL SEX WORK MINORITY AGE
  /STATISTICS=R CHANGE COEFF
  /DEPENDENT=LOGBEG
  /METHOD=ENTER EDLEVEL
  /METHOD=ENTER SEX.
```

**6.62
CRITERIA Subcommand**

You can control the statistical criteria by which REGRESSION chooses variables for entry into or removal from an equation with the CRITERIA subcommand. Place the CRITERIA subcommand after the VARIABLES subcommand and before the DEPENDENT subcommand. A CRITERIA subcommand affects any subsequent DEPENDENT and METHOD subcommands and remains in effect until overridden with another CRITERIA subcommand.

The CRITERIA keywords are

DEFAULTS
PIN(0.05), POUT(0.10), and TOLERANCE(0.0001). These are the defaults if no CRITERIA subcommand is specified. If criteria have been changed, DEFAULTS restores the default values.

PIN(value)
Probability of F-to-enter. Use to override the default value of 0.05.

POUT(value)
Probability of F-to-remove. Use to override the default value of 0.10.

FIN(value)
F-to-enter. The default value is 3.84. FIN and PIN are mutually exclusive.

FOUT(value)
F-to-remove. The default value is 2.71. FOUT overrides the default POUT criteria. If both FOUT and POUT are specified on the same CRITERIA subcommand, only the last one specified will be in effect.

TOLERANCE(value)
Tolerance. The default value is 0.0001. All variables must pass both tolerance and minimum tolerance tests before entering the equation. The minimum tolerance is the smallest tolerance for that variable or any other variable in the equation if the variable is entered.

MAXSTEPS(n)
Maximum number of steps. For the STEPWISE method, the default is twice the number of independent variables. For the FORWARD and BACKWARD methods, the default maximum is the number of variables meeting the PIN and POUT or FIN and FOUT criteria. The MAXSTEPS value applies to the total model. The default value for the total model is the sum of the maximum number of steps over each method in the model.

For example, to change stepwise entry and removal criteria to FIN and FOUT and use their default values of 3.84 and 2.71, respectively, specify

```
REGRESSION VARIABLES=LOGBEG EDLEVEL SEX WORK MINORITY AGE
  /CRITERIA=FIN,FOUT
  /DEPENDENT=LOGBEG
  /METHOD=STEPWISE.
```

6.63 ORIGIN Subcommand

The regression model contains a constant term. You can use the ORIGIN subcommand to suppress this term and obtain regression through the origin. The NOORIGIN subcommand, which is the default, requests that equations include a constant term.

Place the ORIGIN or NOORIGIN subcommand between the VARIABLES subcommand and the DEPENDENT subcommand for the equation. For example,

```
REGRESSION VARIABLES=SALBEG SALNOW,EDLEVEL
  /DEPENDENT=SALNOW
  /METHOD=ENTER SALBEG
  /ORIGIN
  /DEPENDENT=SALBEG
  /METHOD=ENTER EDLEVEL.
```

requests two equations, the first with a constant term (the default) and the second with regression through the origin.

There are no specifications for the ORIGIN and NOORIGIN subcommands. Once specified, the ORIGIN subcommand remains in effect until NOORIGIN is requested.

6.64 SELECT Subcommand

Use the SELECT subcommand to select a subset of cases for computing the regression equation. Only selected cases contribute to the correlation coefficients and to the regression equation. Residuals and predicted values are calculated and reported separately for both selected and unselected cases. The SELECT subcommand can precede or immediately follow the VARIABLES subcommand and is in effect for the entire REGRESSION command. The form of the SELECT subcommand is

```
/SELECT = varname   relation   value
```

The *relation* can be EQ, NE, LT, LE, GT, or GE.

For example, to generate separate residuals histograms for males and females based on the equation developed for males alone (SEX=0) as shown in Figure 6.55, specify

```
REGRESSION SELECT SEX EQ 0
   /VARIABLES=LOGBEG EDLEVEL SEX WORK MINORITY AGE
   /DEPENDENT=LOGBEG
   /METHOD=STEPWISE
   /RESIDUALS=HISTOGRAM.
```

6.65
MISSING Subcommand

Use the MISSING subcommand to specify the treatment of cases with missing values. If the MISSING subcommand is omitted, a case with user- or system-missing values for any variable named on the VARIABLES subcommand is excluded from the computation of the correlation matrix on which all analyses are based. The MISSING subcommand can precede or immediately follow the VARIABLES subcommand and is in effect for the entire REGRESSION command.

The available keywords are

LISTWISE   *Delete cases with missing values listwise.* Only cases with valid values for all variables listed on the VARIABLES subcommand are included in analyses. If INCLUDE is also specified, only cases with system-missing values are deleted listwise. LISTWISE is the default.

PAIRWISE   *Delete cases with missing values pairwise.* Cases with complete data on the pair of variables being correlated are used to compute the correlation coefficient. If INCLUDE is also specified, only cases with system-missing values are deleted pairwise.

MEANSUBSTITUTION   *Replace missing values with the variable mean.* All cases are used for computations, with the mean of a variable substituted for missing observations. If INCLUDE is also specified, user-missing values are included in the computation of the means and only system-missing values are substituted.

INCLUDE   *Include all cases with user-missing values.* Only cases with system-missing values are excluded.

If you specify any combination of LISTWISE, PAIRWISE, and MEANSUBSTITUTION on the same MISSING subcommand, only the last one specified will be in effect. If INCLUDE is also specified, it will also be in effect.

6.66
DESCRIPTIVES Subcommand

You can request a variety of descriptive statistics with the DESCRIPTIVES subcommand. These statistics are displayed for all variables specified on the VARIABLES subcommand, regardless of which variables you specify for computations. Descriptive statistics are based on all valid cases for each variable if you have specified PAIRWISE or MEANSUB on the MISSING subcommand. Otherwise, only cases that are included in the computation of the correlation matrix are used. If you specify the DESCRIPTIVES subcommand without any keywords, the statistics listed for keyword DEFAULTS are displayed. If you name any statistics on DESCRIPTIVES, only those explicity requested are displayed.

The following descriptive statistics are available:

DEFAULTS   *MEAN, STDDEV, and CORR.* This is the default if DESCRIPTIVES is specified without any keywords.

MEAN   *Variable means.*

STDDEV   *Variable standard deviations.*

VARIANCE	*Variable variances.*
CORR	*Correlation matrix.*
SIG	*One-tailed significance levels for the correlation coefficients.*
BADCORR	*Correlation matrix only if some coefficients cannot be computed.*
COV	*Covariance matrix.*
XPROD	*Cross-product deviations from the mean.*
N	*Number of cases used to compute the correlation coefficients.*
ALL	*All descriptive statistics.*

For example, to produce the correlation matrix shown in Figure 6.34, specify

```
REGRESSION DESCRIPTIVES=CORR
  /VARIABLES=LOGBEG EDLEVEL SEX WORK MINORITY AGE
  /DEPENDENT=LOGBEG
  /METHOD=ENTER EDLEVEL TO AGE.
```

6.67
Analyzing Residuals

Once you have built an equation, REGRESSION can calculate a variety of temporary variables containing several types of residuals, predicted values, and related measures. You can use these variables to detect outliers and influential data points and to examine the regression assumptions described in Sections 6.17 through 6.22.

The following temporary variables are available for the analysis of residuals.

PRED	*Unstandardized predicted values.* (See Section 6.13.)
ZPRED	*Standardized predicted values.* (See Section 6.13.)
SEPRED	*Standard errors of the predicted values.* (See Section 6.14.)
RESID	*Unstandardized residuals.* (See Section 6.18.)
ZRESID	*Standardized residuals.* (See Section 6.18.)
SRESID	*Studentized residuals.* (See Section 6.18.)
MAHAL	*Mahalanobis' distance.* (See Section 6.24.)
ADJPRED	*Adjusted predicted values.* (See Section 6.25.)
DRESID	*Deleted residuals.* (See Section 6.25.)
SDRESID	*Studentized deleted residuals.* (See Section 6.25.)
COOK	*Cook's distances.* (See Section 6.25.)
LEVER	*Leverage values.* (See Section 6.49.)
DFBETA	*DFBETA.* The change in the regression coefficient that results from the deletion of the ith case. A DFBETA value is computed for each case for each regression coefficient generated in a model.
SDBETA	*Standardized DFBETA.* An SDBETA value is computed for each case for each regression coefficient generated in a model. (See Belsley et al., 1980.)
DFFIT	*DFFIT.* DFFIT is the change in the predicted value when the ith case is deleted. (See Belsley et al., 1980.)
SDFIT	*Standardized DFFIT.* (See Belsley et al., 1980.)
COVRATIO	*COVRATIO.* Ratio of the determinant of the covariance matrix with the ith case deleted to the determinant of the covariance matrix with all cases included. (See Belsley et al., 1980.)
MCIN	*Lower and upper bounds for the prediction interval of the mean predicted response.* A lower bound LMCIN and an upper bound UMCIN are generated. The default confidence interval is 95%. The interval may be reset with the CIN subcommand. (See Dillon & Goldstein, 1984.)
ICIN	*Lower and upper bounds for the prediction interval for a single observation.* (See Dillon & Goldstein, 1978.) A lowerbound LICIN and an upperbound UICIN are generated. The default confidence interval is 95%. The interval may be reset with the CIN subcommand.

Residuals analysis is specified with four subcommands: RESIDUALS, CASEWISE, PARTIALPLOT, and SCATTERPLOT. You can specify these subcommands in any order, but you cannot specify more than one of each per equation, and they must immediately follow the last METHOD subcommand that completes an equation. The residuals subcommands affect only the equation they follow. Requesting any residuals analysis always produces descriptive statistics on at least four of the temporary variables (PRED, ZPRED, RESID, and ZRESID).

All variables are standardized before plotting. If an unstandardized version of a variable is requested, the standardized version is plotted.

**6.68
RESIDUALS
Subcommand**

Use the RESIDUALS subcommand to obtain the statistics and plots listed below. Specifying the RESIDUALS subcommand without any specifications produces the display described for keyword DEFAULTS. If any keywords are specified on RESIDUALS, *only* the displays for those keywords are produced.

DEFAULTS *HISTOGRAM(ZRESID), NORMPROB(ZRESID), OUTLI-ERS plots(ZRESID), SIZE(SMALL), and DURBIN. These plots are produced if RESIDUALS is specified without any specifications.*

HISTOGRAM(tempvars) *Histogram of standardized temporary variables named. The default temporary variable is ZRESID. Other variables that can be plotted are PRED, RESID, ZPRED, DRESID, AD-JPRED, SRESID, and SDRESID. (See Figure 6.22a.)*

NORMPROB(tempvars) *Normal probability (P-P) plot of standardized values. The default variable is ZRESID. Other variables that can be plotted are PRED, RESID, ZPRED, and DRESID. (See Figure 6.22b.)*

SIZE(plotsize) *Plot sizes. The plot size can be specified as SMALL or LARGE. The default is LARGE if the display width is at least 120 and the page length is at least 55.*

OUTLIERS(tempvars) *The ten most extreme values for the temporary variables named. The default temporary variable is ZRESID. Other variables can be RESID, DRESID, SRESID, SDRESID MAHAL, and COOK. (See Figure 6.24.)*

DURBIN *Durbin-Watson test statistic. (See Section 6.21.)*

ID(varname) *Identification labels for casewise and outlier plots. Cases are labeled with values of the variable named after the ID keyword. By default, the plots are labeled with the sequential case number. ID also labels the CASEWISE list of cases. (See Figures 6.23 and 6.24.)*

POOLED *Pooled plots and statistics when the SELECT subcommand is in effect. All cases in the active file are used. The default is separate reporting of residuals statistics and plots for selected and unselected cases.*

For example, to produce the output shown in Figures 6.22a, 6.22b, and 6.24, specify

```
REGRESSION VARIABLES=SALBEG SALNOW
   /DEPENDENT=SALNOW
   /METHOD=ENTER SALBEG
   /RESIDUALS=HISTOGRAM(SRESID) NORMPROB
             OUTLIERS(MAHAL) ID(SEXRACE) SIZE (SMALL).
```

**6.69
CASEWISE Subcommand**

You can display a casewise plot of one of the temporary variables accompanied by a listing of the values of the dependent and the temporary variables. The plot can be requested for all cases or limited to outliers. Specifying the CASEWISE subcommand without keywords produces the output listed for DEFAULTS.

The following may be specified on the CASEWISE subcommand.

DEFAULTS *OUTLIERS(3), PLOT(ZRESID), DEPENDENT, PRED, and RESID. This is the default if CASEWISE is specified without any keywords.*

OUTLIERS(value)   *Limit plot to outliers greater than or equal to the standardized absolute value of the plotted variable.* The default value is 3. (See Figure 6.23.)

ALL   *Include all cases in the casewise plot.* Produces a plot of all cases, including outliers. The keyword OUTLIERS is ignored when ALL is specified.

PLOT(tempvar)   *Plot the standardized values of the temporary variable named.* The default variable is ZRESID. The other variables that can be plotted are RESID, DRESID, SRESID, and SDRESID. (See Figure 6.23.)

varlist   *List values of the DEPENDENT and temporary variables named.* Any temporary variable, including LEVER, can be listed. The defaults are DEPENDENT (the dependent variable), PRED, and RESID. (See Figures 6.16 and 6.23.)

For example, to produce the casewise plot shown in Figure 6.16, specify

```
REGRESSION VARIABLES=SALBEG SALNOW
  /DEPENDENT=SALNOW
  /METHOD=ENTER SALBEG
  /RESIDUALS=ID(SEXRACE)
  /CASEWISE=ALL DEPENDENT PRED RESID SEPRED.
```

To plot outliers whose absolute values are equal to or greater than 3 based on ZRESID, you need only specify the CASEWISE subcommand. To base the plot on Studentized residuals and label it with an ID variable, as shown in Figure 6.23, specify

```
REGRESSION VARIABLES=SALBEG SALNOW
  /DEPENDENT=SALNOW
  /METHOD=ENTER SALBEG
  /RESIDUALS=ID(SEXRACE)
  /CASEWISE=PLOT(SRESID).
```

If you request more variables than will fit on the page width set either with the SET WIDTH command or the WIDTH subcommand in REGRESSION, your output will be truncated (see Section 6.75).

**6.70
SCATTERPLOT
Subcommand**

Use the SCATTERPLOT subcommand to generate scatterplots for the variables in the equation. You must name at least one pair of variables on the SCATTERPLOT subcommand. Optionally, you can specify the SIZE keyword to control the size of the plots. All scatterplots are standardized.

The specifications for SCATTERPLOT are

(varname,varname)   *The pair of variables to be plotted.* Available variables are PRED, RESID, ZPRED, ZRESID, DRESID, ADJPRED, SRESID, SDRESID, and any variable named on the VARIABLES subcommand. Temporary variables should be preceded by an asterisk on this subcommand.

SIZE(plotsize)   *Plot sizes.* Plot size can be SMALL or LARGE. The default is SMALL.

The first variable named inside the parentheses is plotted on the vertical (Y) axis, and the second is plotted on the horizontal (X) axis. For example, to generate the scatterplot shown in Figure 6.20, specify

```
REGRESSION VARIABLES=SALBEG SALNOW
  /DEPENDENT=SALNOW
  /METHOD=ENTER SALBEG
  /SCATTERPLOT=(*SRESID,*PRED).
```

To produce a scatterplot for SRESID and PRED based on the logarithmic transformation of both the dependent and independent variables, as shown in Figure 6.30a, use the SCATTERPLOT subcommand above along with the following transformation commands:

```
COMPUTE LOGBEG=LG10(SALBEG).
COMPUTE LOGNOW=LG10(SALNOW).
REGRESSION VARIABLES=LOGBEG,LOGNOW
  /DEPENDENT=LOGNOW
  /METHOD=ENTER LOGBEG
  /SCATTERPLOT=(*SRESID,*PRED).
```

To produce more than one scatterplot, simply add pairs of variable names in parentheses, as in

```
/SCATTERPLOT=(*SRESID,*PRED)(SALBEG,*PRED)
```

6.71
PARTIALPLOT
Subcommand

Use the PARTIALPLOT subcommand to generate partial residual plots. Partial residual plots are scatterplots of the residuals of the dependent variable and an independent variable when both variables are regressed on the rest of the independent variables.

If no variable list is given on the PARTIALPLOT subcommand, a partial residual plot is produced for every independent variable in the equation. Plots are displayed in descending order of the standard error of *B*. All plots are standardized.

The specifications on the PARTIALPLOT subcommand are

varlist   *Independent variables to be used in partial residual plot.* At least two independent variables must be in the equation for a partial residual plot to be produced. You can specify the keyword ALL to obtain the default plots for every independent variable in the equation.

SIZE(plotsize) *Plot sizes.* The plot size can be specified as SMALL or LARGE. The default plot size is SMALL.

For example, the following commands produced Figure 6.49a:

```
COMPUTE LOGBEG=LG10(SALBEG).
REGRESSION VARIABLES=LOGBEG SEX MINORITY EDLEVEL WORK
  /DEPENDENT=LOGBEG /METHOD=STEPWISE
  /PARTIALPLOT=EDLEVEL.
```

6.72
SAVE Subcommand

Use the SAVE subcommand to save any or all of the temporary variables described in Section 6.67. The format is the name of the temporary variable followed by a valid variable name in parentheses, as in

```
GET FILE='BANK.SYS'.
REGRESSION VARIABLES=SALBEG, SALNOW
  /DEPENDENT=SALNOW
  /METHOD=ENTER SALBEG
  /SAVE=SEPRED(SE).
PLOT CUTPOINTS=EVERY(20) /SYMBOLS='.'
  /PLOT=SE WITH SALBEG.
```

This example saves the standard errors of the predicted values with variable name SE. Then the PLOT procedure is used to plot the standard errors against the values of the independent variable SALBEG. Figure 6.14a shows the plot.

If you don't specify a new variable name, SPSS generates a new variable name by default.

If you specify DFBETA or SDBETA, the number of new variables saved is equal to the total number of variables in the equation, including the constant. For example, the command

```
REGRESSION DEPENDENT=SALBEG
 /METHOD=ENTER AGE SEX
 /SAVE=DFBETA(DFBVAR).
```

will create and save three new variables with the names DFBVAR0, DFBVAR1, and DFBVAR2.

You can use the keyword FITS to automatically save the temporary variables DFFIT, SDFIT, DFBETA, SDBETA, and COVRATIO, as in:

```
/SAVE=FITS.
```

If you specify FITS, you cannot specify new variable names. SPSS automatically generates new variable names.

6.73
READ and WRITE Subcommands

Procedure REGRESSION can read and write matrix materials, which can be processed more quickly than cases. Use the WRITE subcommand to write matrix materials to a file. You can write default matrix materials or specify the materials you want to write, including variable means, standard deviations, variances, a correlation or covariance matrix, and the number of cases used to compute the correlations or covariances. You can then use the READ subcommand to read the matrix materials into REGRESSION for additional analysis.

The READ subcommand can also read matrix materials written by other procedures, such as CORRELATION, or entered as data in free or fixed format. See Command Reference: Regression—Matrix Materials for complete instructions on using matrix materials with REGRESSION.

6.74
REGWGT Subcommand

The REGWGT subcommand specifies a variable for estimating weighted least-squares models. The only specification on REGWGT is the name of the single variable containing the weights, as in

```
REGRESSION VARIABLES=IQ TO ACHIEVE /REGWGT=WGT1
   /DEPENDENT=VARY /METHOD=ENTER /SAVE=PRED(P) RESID(R).
```

REGWGT remains in effect for all analyses specified on the REGRESSION command. If you specify more than one REGWGT subcommand, only the last one specified will be in effect.

6.75
WIDTH Subcommand

You can use the WIDTH subcommand to control the width of the display produced by the REGRESSION procedure. The default is the width specified on the SET command. The WIDTH subcommand in REGRESSION overrides the width specified on SET.

You can use the WIDTH subcommand to change the appearance of your output. For example, in Figure 6.41 statistics for variables in the equation and variables not in the equation are displayed side by side. In Figure 6.46b, the command

```
REGRESSION WIDTH=80
   /VARIABLES=LOGBEG EDLEVEL SEX WORK MINORITY AGE
   /STATISTICS=F /DEPENDENT=LOGBEG /METHOD=FORWARD.
```

displays the statistics for variables not in the equation below the statistics for variables in the equation.

A smaller page width limits the number of statistics that can be displayed in a summary line and may also cause casewise output to be truncated (see Section 6.69). Specifying a smaller page width may also reduce the size of scatter and normal-probability plots in the residuals output.

6.76
Annotated Example

To produce the stepwise variable selection example discussed in Section 6.48, specify

```
DATA LIST FILE='EMPLOYEE.DAT'
   /  ID 1-4 SALBEG 6-10 SEX 12 TIME 14-15
       AGE 17-20 (2) SALNOW 22-26 EDLEVEL 28-29
       WORK 31-34 (2) JOBCAT MINORITY 36-37.
VAR LABELS   ID 'EMPLOYEE CODE'/
             SALBEG 'BEGINNING SALARY'/
             SEX 'SEX OF EMPLOYEE'/
             TIME 'JOB SENIORITY'/
             AGE 'AGE OF EMPLOYEE'/
             SALNOW 'CURRENT SALARY'/
             EDLEVEL 'EDUCATIONAL LEVEL'/
             WORK 'WORK EXPERIENCE'/
             JOBCAT 'EMPLOYMENT CATEGORY'/
             MINORITY 'MINORITY CLASSIFICATION'.
VALUE LABELS   SEX 0'MALES' 1'FEMALES'/
             JOBCAT 1 'CLERICAL' 2 'OFFICE TRAINEE'
                    3 'SECURITY OFFICER'
                    4 'COLLEGE TRAINEE' 5 'EXEMPT EMPLOYEE'
                    6 'MBA TRAINEE' 7 'TECHNICAL'/
             MINORITY 0 'WHITE' 1 'NONWHITE'.
MISSING VALUES SALBEG,TIME TO EDLEVEL,JOBCAT (0)/SEX,MINORITY (9).
FORMATS   SALBEG SALNOW (COMMA6.0).
COMPUTE LOGBEG=LG10(SALBEG).
COMPUTE LOGNOW=LG10(SALNOW).
REGRESSION VARIABLES=LOGBEG,EDLEVEL,SEX,WORK,MINORITY,AGE/
             STATISTICS=R,COEFF,OUTS,F/
             DEPENDENT=LOGBEG/
             METHOD=STEPWISE.
FINISH.
```

- The DATA LIST command defines the data file and variable names and gives the column locations for each variable.

- The VARIABLE LABELS and VALUE LABELS commands supply descriptive labels for the variables and their values.

- The MISSING VALUES command assigns the value 0 as missing for SALBEG, TIME TO EDLEVEL, and JOBCAT, and the value 9 as missing for SEX and MINORITY.

- The FORMATS command assigns a comma display and write format to the variables SALBEG and SALNOW.

- The COMPUTE commands create the new variables LOGBEG and LOGNOW.

- The REGRESSION command asks for a stepwise regression of the named variables with LOGBEG as the dependent variable. It also asks for the statistics R, COEFF, OUTS, and F.

The output from this example is shown in Figure 6.48.

Contents _____

7 Factor Analysis: Procedure FACTOR

What are creativity, love, and altruism? Unlike variables such as weight, blood pressure, and temperature, they cannot be measured on a scale, sphygmomanometer, or thermometer, in units of pounds, millimeters of mercury, or degrees Fahrenheit. Instead they can be thought of as unifying constructs or labels that characterize responses to related groups of variables. For example, answers of "strongly agree" to items such as he (or she) sends me flowers, listens to my problems, reads my manuscripts, laughs at my jokes, and gazes deeply into my soul, may lead one to conclude that the love "factor" is present. Thus, love is not a single measurable entity but a construct which is derived from measurement of other, directly observable variables. Identification of such underlying dimensions or factors greatly simplifies the description and understanding of complex phenomena, such as social interaction. For example, postulating the existence of something called "love" explains the observed correlations between the responses to numerous and varied situations.

Factor analysis is a statistical technique used to identify a relatively small number of factors that can be used to represent relationships among sets of many interrelated variables. For example, variables such as scores on a battery of aptitude tests may be expressed as a linear combination of factors that represent verbal skills, mathematical aptitude, and perceptual speed. Variables such as consumer ratings of products in a survey can be expressed as a function of factors such as product quality and utility. Factor analysis helps identify these underlying, not directly observable, constructs.

A huge number of variables can be used to describe a community—degree of industrialization, commercial activity, population, mobility, average family income, extent of home ownership, birth rate, and so forth. However, descriptions of what is meant by the term "community" might be greatly simplified if it were possible to identify underlying dimensions, or factors, of communities. This was attempted by Jonassen and Peres (1960), who examined 82 community variables from 88 counties in Ohio. This chapter uses a subset of their variables (shown in Table 7.0) to illustrate the basics of factor analysis.

Table 7.0 Community variables

POPSTABL	population stability
NEWSCIRC	weekly per capita local newspaper circulation
FEMEMPLD	percentage of females 14 years or older in labor force
FARMERS	percentage of farmers and farm managers in labor force
RETAILNG	per capita dollar retail sales
COMMERCL	total per capita commercial activity in dollars
INDUSTZN	industrialization index
HEALTH	health index
CHLDNEGL	total per capita expenditures on county aid to dependent children
COMMEFFC	index of the extent to which a community fosters a high standard of living
DWELGNEW	percentage of dwelling units built recently
MIGRNPOP	index measuring the extent of in- and out-migration
UNEMPLOY	unemployment index
MENTALIL	extent of mental illness

7.1
THE FACTOR
ANALYSIS MODEL

The basic assumption of factor analysis is that underlying dimensions, or factors, can be used to explain complex phenomena. Observed correlations between variables result from their sharing these factors. For example, correlations between test scores might be attributable to such shared factors as general intelligence, abstract reasoning skill, and reading comprehension. The correlations between the community variables might be due to factors like amount of urbanization, the socioeconomic level or welfare of the community, and the population stability. The goal of factor analysis is to identify the not-directly-observable factors based on a set of observable variables.

The mathematical model for factor analysis appears somewhat similar to a multiple regression equation. Each variable is expressed as a linear combination of factors which are not actually observed. For example, the industrialization index might be expressed as

$$\text{INDUSTZN} = a(\text{URBANISM}) + b(\text{WELFARE}) + c(\text{INFLUX}) + U_{\text{INDUSTZN}}$$ **Equation 7.1a**

This equation differs from the usual multiple regression equation in that URBANISM, WELFARE, and INFLUX are not single independent variables. Instead, they are labels for groups of variables that characterize these concepts. These groups of variables constitute the factors. Usually, the factors useful for characterizing a set of variables are not known in advance but are determined by factor analysis.

URBANISM, WELFARE, and INFLUX are called *common factors,* since all variables are expressed as functions of them. The U in Equation 7.1a is called a *unique factor,* since it represents that part of the industrialization index that cannot be explained by the common factors. It is unique to the industrialization index variable.

In general, the model for the ith standardized variable is written as

$$X_i = A_{i1}F_1 + A_{i2}F_2 + \ldots + A_{ik}F_k + U_i$$ **Equation 7.1b**

where the F's are the common factors, the U is the unique factor, and the A's are the constants used to combine the k factors. The unique factors are assumed to be uncorrelated with each other and with the common factors.

The factors are inferred from the observed variables and can be estimated as linear combinations of them. For example, the estimated urbanism factor is expressed as

$$\text{URBANISM} = C_1\,\text{POPSTABL} + C_2\,\text{NEWSCIRC} + \ldots + C_{14}\,\text{MENTALIL}$$ **Equation 7.1c**

While it is possible that all of the variables contribute to the urbanism factor, we hope that only a subset of variables characterizes urbanism, as indicated by their large coefficients. The general expression for the estimate of the jth factor F_j is

$$F_j = \sum_{i=1}^{p} W_{ji}X_i = W_{j1}X_1 + W_{j2}X_2 + \ldots + W_{jp}X_p$$ **Equation 7.1d**

The W_i's are known as factor score coefficients, and p is the number of variables.

7.2
Ingredients of a Good
Factor Analysis Solution

Before examining the mechanics of a factor analysis solution, let's consider the characteristics of a successful factor analysis. One goal is to represent relationships among sets of variables parsimoniously. That is, we would like to explain the observed correlations using as few factors as possible. If many factors are needed, little simplification or summarization occurs. We would also like the factors to be meaningful. A good factor solution is both simple and interpretable. When factors can be interpreted, new insights are possible. For example, if liquor preferences can be explained by such factors as sweetness and regional tastes (Stoetzel, 1960), marketing strategies can reflect this.

7.3
STEPS IN A FACTOR ANALYSIS

Factor analysis usually proceeds in four steps.

- First, the correlation matrix for all variables is computed, as in Figure 7.4a. Variables that do not appear to be related to other variables can be identified from the matrix and associated statistics. The appropriateness of the factor model can also be evaluated. At this step you should also decide what to do with cases that have missing values for some of the variables.
- In the second step, factor extraction—the number of factors necessary to represent the data and the method of calculating them—must be determined. At this step, you also ascertain how well the chosen model fits the data.
- The third step, rotation, focuses on transforming the factors to make them more interpretable.
- At the fourth step, scores for each factor can be computed for each case. These scores can then be used in a variety of other analyses.

7.4
Examining the Correlation Matrix

The correlation matrix for the 14 community variables is shown in Figure 7.4a. Since one of the goals of factor analysis is to obtain "factors" that help explain these correlations, the variables must be related to each other for the factor model to be appropriate. If the correlations between variables are small, it is unlikely that they share common factors. Figure 7.4a shows that almost half the coefficients are greater than 0.3 in absolute value. All variables, except the extent of mental illness, have large correlations with at least one of the other variables in the set.

Figure 7.4a Correlation matrix and matrix input

```
DATA LIST MATRIX FREE
  /POPSTABL NEWSCIRC FEMEMPLD FARMERS RETAILNG COMMERCL INDUSTZN
   HEALTH CHLDNEGL COMMEFFC DWELGNEW MIGRNPOP UNEMPLOY MENTALIL.
N 88.
BEGIN DATA.
1.000
-.175 1.000
rest of matrix
END DATA.
FACTOR READ=COR TRIANGLE
  /VARIABLES=POPSTABL TO MENTALIL
   /PRINT=CORRELATION.
```

```
Correlation Matrix:

            POPSTABL  NEWSCIRC  FEMEMPLD  FARMERS  RETAILNG  COMMERCL  INDUSTZN

POPSTABL    1.00000
NEWSCIRC    -.17500   1.00000
FEMEMPLD    -.27600    .61600   1.00000
FARMERS      .36900   -.62500   -.63700  1.00000
RETAILNG    -.12700    .62400    .73600  -.51900   1.00000
COMMERCL    -.06900    .65200    .58900  -.30600    .72700   1.00000
INDUSTZN    -.10600    .71200    .74200  -.54500    .78500    .91100   1.00000
HEALTH      -.14900   -.03000    .24100  -.06800    .10000    .12300    .12900
CHLDNEGL    -.03900   -.17100   -.58900   .25700   -.55700   -.35700   -.42400
COMMEFFC    -.00500    .10000    .47100  -.21300    .45200    .28700    .35700
DWELGNEW    -.67000    .18800    .41300  -.57900    .16500    .03000    .20300
MIGRNPOP    -.47600   -.08600    .06400  -.19800    .00700   -.06800   -.02400
UNEMPLOY     .13700   -.37300   -.68900   .45000   -.65000   -.42400   -.52800
MENTALIL     .23700    .04600   -.23700   .12100   -.19000   -.05500   -.09500


            HEALTH    CHLDNEGL  COMMEFFC  DWELGNEW  MIGRNPOP  UNEMPLOY  MENTALIL

HEALTH      1.00000
CHLDNEGL    -.40700    1.00000
COMMEFFC     .73200   -.66000    1.00000
DWELGNEW     .29000   -.13800    .31100   1.00000
MIGRNPOP     .08300    .14800    .06700    .50500   1.00000
UNEMPLOY    -.34800    .73300   -.60100  -.26600    .18100   1.00000
MENTALIL    -.27900    .24700   -.32400  -.26600   -.30700    .21700   1.00000
```

Bartlett's test of sphericity can be used to test the hypothesis that the correlation matrix is an identity matrix. That is, all diagonal terms are 1 and all off-diagonal terms are 0. The test requires that the data be a sample from a multivariate normal population. From Figure 7.4b, the value of the test statistic for sphericity (based on a chi-square transformation of the determinant of the correlation matrix) is large and the associated significance level is small, so it appears unlikely that the population correlation matrix is an identity. If the hypothesis that the population correlation matrix is an identity cannot be rejected because the observed significance level is large, you should reconsider the use of the factor model.

Figure 7.4b Test-statistic for sphericity

```
FACTOR READ=CORRELATION TRIANGLE
  /VARIABLES=POPSTABL TO MENTALIL
  /PRINT=CORRELATION  KMO  AIC.
```

```
Kaiser-Meyer-Olkin Measure of Sampling Adequacy =  .76968

Bartlett Test of Sphericity = 946.15313, Significance =      .00000
```

Another indicator of the strength of the relationship among variables is the partial correlation coefficient. If variables share common factors, the partial correlation coefficients between pairs of variables should be small when the linear effects of the other variables are eliminated. The partial correlations are then estimates of the correlations between the unique factors and should be close to zero when the factor analysis assumptions are met. (Recall that the unique factors are assumed to be uncorrelated with each other.)

The negative of the partial correlation coefficient is called the anti-image correlation. The matrix of anti-image correlations is shown in Figure 7.4c. If the proportion of large coefficients is high, you should reconsider the use of the factor model.

Figure 7.4c Anti-image correlation matrix

```
FACTOR READ=CORRELATION TRIANGLE
  /VARIABLES=POPSTABL TO MENTALIL
  /PRINT=CORRELATION  KMO  AIC.
```

```
Anti-Image Correlation Matrix:

          POPSTABL  NEWSCIRC  FEMEMPLD  FARMERS  RETAILNG  COMMERCL  INDUSTZN

POPSTABL   .58174
NEWSCIRC   .01578    .82801
FEMEMPLD   .10076   -.24223    .90896
FARMERS    .03198    .43797   -.00260    .73927
RETAILNG   .14998   -.14295   -.12037    .16426    .86110
COMMERCL   .20138   -.27622    .20714   -.49344   -.19535    .68094
INDUSTZN  -.23815    .08231   -.32790    .41648   -.04602   -.85499    .75581
HEALTH     .26114   -.02839   -.02332    .05845    .38421   -.16150    .08627
CHLDNEGL   .10875   -.24685    .27281   -.03446    .13062    .07043   -.07979
COMMEFFC  -.39878    .05772    .03017   -.16386   -.33700    .09427   -.06742
DWELGNEW   .55010    .04505   -.09493    .33479    .26678    .13831   -.13726
MIGRNPOP   .20693    .22883   -.06689    .11784   -.15886   -.07421    .06501
UNEMPLOY  -.17774   -.05946    .18631   -.12699    .19591   -.01262   -.02503
MENTALIL  -.08437   -.10058    .07770    .03053    .07842   -.02921   -.00056


           HEALTH  CHLDNEGL  COMMEFFC  DWELGNEW  MIGRNPOP  UNEMPLOY  MENTALIL

HEALTH     .59124
CHLDNEGL   .02899    .87023
COMMEFFC  -.70853    .19554    .68836
DWELGNEW   .07480   -.04008   -.30434    .70473
MIGRNPOP   .07460   -.10809   -.14292   -.24074    .61759
UNEMPLOY  -.02904   -.33523    .19240    .02181   -.38208    .87230
MENTALIL   .06821   -.04163    .04728   -.02505    .20487   -.02708    .88390


Measures of sampling adequacy (MSA) are printed on the diagonal.
```

The Kaiser-Meyer-Olkin measure of sampling adequacy is an index for comparing the magnitudes of the observed correlation coefficients to the magnitudes of the partial correlation coefficients. It is computed as

$$\text{KMO} = \frac{\sum_{i \neq j} \sum r_{ij}^2}{\sum_{i \neq j} \sum r_{ij}^2 + \sum_{i \neq j} \sum a_{ij}^2}$$

Equation 7.4a

where r_{ij} is the simple correlation coefficient between variables i and j, and a_{ij} is the partial correlation coefficient between variables i and j. If the sum of the squared partial correlation coefficients between all pairs of variables is small when compared to the sum of the squared correlation coefficients, the KMO measure is close to 1. Small values for the KMO measure indicate that a factor analysis of the variables may not be a good idea, since correlations between pairs of variables cannot be explained by the other variables. Kaiser (1974) characterizes measures in the 0.90's as marvelous, in the 0.80's as meritorious, in the 0.70's as middling, in the 0.60's as mediocre, in the 0.50's as miserable, and below 0.5 as unacceptable. The value of the overall KMO statistic for this example is shown in Figure 7.4b. Since it is close to 0.8, we can comfortably proceed with the factor analysis.

A measure of sampling adequacy can be computed for each individual variable in a similar manner. Instead of including all pairs of variables in the summations, only coefficients involving that variable are included. For the ith variable, the measure of sampling adequacy is

$$\text{MSA}_i = \frac{\sum_{j \neq i} r_{ij}^2}{\sum_{j \neq i} r_{ij}^2 + \sum_{j \neq i} a_{ij}^2}$$

Equation 7.4b

These measures of sampling adequacy are printed on the diagonals of Figure 7.4c. Again, reasonably large values are needed for a good factor analysis. Thus, you might consider eliminating variables with small values for the measure of sampling adequacy.

The squared multiple correlation coefficient between a variable and all other variables is another indication of the strength of the linear association among the variables. These values are shown in the column labeled **Communality** in Figure 7.9a. The extent of mental illness variable has a small multiple R^2, suggesting that it should be eliminated from the set of variables being analyzed. It will be kept in the analysis for illustrative purposes.

7.5
Factor Extraction

The goal of the factor extraction step is to determine the factors. In this example, we will obtain estimates of the initial factors from principal components analysis. Other methods for factor extraction are described in Section 7.10. In principal components analysis, linear combinations of the observed variables are formed. The first principal component is the combination that accounts for the largest amount of variance in the sample. The second principal component accounts for the next largest amount of variance and is uncorrelated with the first. Successive components explain progressively smaller portions of the total sample variance, and all are uncorrelated with each other.

It is possible to compute as many principal components as there are variables. If all principal components are used, each variable can be exactly represented by them, but nothing has been gained since there are as many factors (principal components) as variables. When all factors are included in the solution, all of the variance of each variable is accounted for, and there is no need for a unique factor in the model. The proportion of variance accounted for by the common factors, or the *communality* of a variable, is 1 for all the variables, as shown in Figure 7.5a. In general, principal components analysis is a separate technique from factor analysis. That is, it can be used whenever uncorrelated linear combinations of the observed variables are desired. All it does is transform a set of correlated variables to a set of uncorrelated variables (principal components).

To help us decide how many factors we need to represent the data, it is helpful to examine the percentage of total variance explained by each. The total variance is the sum of the variance of each variable. For simplicity, all variables and factors are expressed in standardized form, with a mean of 0 and a standard deviation of 1. Since there are 14 variables and each is standardized to have a variance of 1, the total variance is 14 in this example.

Figure 7.5a contains the initial statistics for each factor. The total variance explained by each factor is listed in the column labeled Eigenvalue. The next column contains the percentage of the total variance attributable to each factor. For example, the linear combination formed by Factor 2 has a variance of 2.35, which is 16.8% of the total variance of 14. The last column, the cumulative percentage, indicates the percentage of variance attributable to that factor and those that precede it in the table. Note that the factors are arranged in descending order of variance explained. Note also that although variable names and factors are displayed on the same line, there is no correspondence between the two parts of the table. The first two columns provide information about the individual variables, while the last four columns describe the factors. Note that there is no correspondence between the lines in the two halves of the table.

Figure 7.5a   Initial statistics

```
FACTOR READ=CORRELATION TRIANGLE
  /VARIABLES=POPSTABL TO MENTALIL.
```

```
Extraction  1  for Analysis  1. Principal-Components Analysis (PC)

Initial Statistics:

Variable     Communality  *  Factor   Eigenvalue   Pct of Var   Cum Pct
                          *
POPSTABL       1.00000    *    1       5.70658        40.8         40.8
NEWSCIRC       1.00000    *    2       2.35543        16.8         57.6
FEMEMPLD       1.00000    *    3       2.00926        14.4         71.9
FARMERS        1.00000    *    4        .89745         6.4         78.3
RETAILNG       1.00000    *    5        .75847         5.4         83.8
COMMERCL       1.00000    *    6        .53520         3.8         87.6
INDUSTZN       1.00000    *    7        .50886         3.6         91.2
HEALTH         1.00000    *    8        .27607         2.0         93.2
CHLDNEGL       1.00000    *    9        .24511         1.8         94.9
COMMEFFC       1.00000    *   10        .20505         1.5         96.4
DWELGNEW       1.00000    *   11        .19123         1.4         97.8
MIGRNPOP       1.00000    *   12        .16982         1.2         99.0
UNEMPLOY       1.00000    *   13        .10202          .7         99.7
MENTALIL       1.00000    *   14        .03946          .3        100.0
```

Figure 7.5a shows that almost 72% of the total variance is attributable to the first three factors. The remaining eleven factors together account for only 28.1% of the variance. Thus, a model with three factors may be adequate to represent the data.

Several procedures have been proposed for determining the number of factors to use in a model. One criterion suggests that only factors that account for variances greater than 1 (the eigenvalue is greater than 1) should be included. Factors with a variance less than 1 are no better than a single variable, since each variable has a variance of 1. Although this is the default criterion in SPSS/PC+ FACTOR, it is not always a good solution (see Tucker, Koopman, and Linn, 1969).

Figure 7.5b is a plot of the total variance associated with each factor. Typically, the plot shows a distinct break between the steep slope of the large factors and the gradual trailing off of the rest of the factors. This gradual trailing off is called the *scree* (Cattell, 1966) because it resembles the rubble that forms at the foot of a mountain. Experimental evidence indicates that the scree begins at the *k*th factor, where *k* is the true number of factors. From the scree plot, it again appears that a three-factor model should be sufficient for the community example.

Figure 7.5b Scree plot

```
FACTOR READ=CORRELATION TRIANGLE
   /VARIABLES=POPSTABL TO MENTALIL
   /PLOT=EIGEN.
```

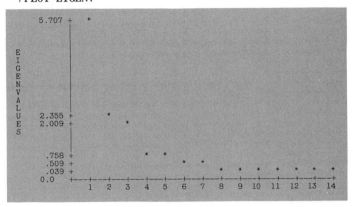

7.6
The Three Factors

Figure 7.6 contains the coefficients that relate the variables to the three factors. The figure shows that the industrialization index can be expressed as

$$INDUSTZN = 0.844F_1 + 0.300F_2 + 0.238F_3$$

Equation 7.6a

Similarly, the health index is

$$HEALTH = 0.383F_1 - 0.327F_2 - 0.635F_3$$

Equation 7.6b

Figure 7.6 Factor matrix

```
FACTOR READ=CORRELATION TRIANGLE
   /VARIABLES=POPSTABL TO MENTALIL.
```

Factor Matrix:

	FACTOR 1	FACTOR 2	FACTOR 3
POPSTABL	-.30247	.68597	-.36451
NEWSCIRC	.67238	.28096	.49779
FEMEMPLD	.89461	.01131	.08063
FARMERS	-.68659	.20002	-.40450
RETAILNG	.85141	.24264	.09351
COMMERCL	.72503	.39394	.19896
INDUSTZN	.84436	.29956	.23775
HEALTH	.38347	-.32718	-.63474
CHLDNEGL	-.67430	-.12139	.52896
COMMEFFC	.63205	-.15540	-.64221
DWELGNEW	.45886	-.73940	.18706
MIGRNPOP	.07894	-.74371	.24335
UNEMPLOY	-.78714	-.09777	.30110
MENTALIL	-.30025	.45463	.27134

Each row of Figure 7.6 contains the coefficients used to express a standardized variable in terms of the factors. These coefficients are called *factor loadings*, since they indicate how much weight is assigned to each factor. Factors with large coefficients (in absolute value) for a variable are closely related to the variable. For example, Factor 1 is the factor with the largest loading for the INDUSTZN variable. The matrix of factor loadings is called the *factor pattern* matrix.

When the estimated factors are uncorrelated with each other (orthogonal), the factor loadings are also the correlations between the factors and the variables. Thus, the correlation between the health index and Factor 1 is 0.383. Similarly, there is a slightly smaller correlation (−0.327) between the health index and Factor 2. The matrix of correlations between variables and factors is called the *factor structure* matrix. When the factors are orthogonal, the factor structure matrix and the factor pattern matrix are equivalent. As shown in Figure 7.6, such a matrix is labeled the factor matrix in SPSS/PC+ output.

7.7
More on the Factor Matrix

There is yet another interpretation of the factor matrix in Figure 7.6. Whether the factors are orthogonal or not, the factor loadings are the standardized regression coefficients in the multiple regression equation, with the original variable as the dependent variable and the factors as the independent variables. If the factors are uncorrelated, the values of the coefficients are not dependent on each other. They represent the unique contribution of each factor, and are the correlations between the factors and the variable.

To judge how well the three-factor model describes the original variables, we can compute the proportion of the variance of each variable explained by the three-factor model. Since the factors are uncorrelated, the total proportion of variance explained is just the sum of the variance proportions explained by each factor.

Consider, for example, the health index. Factor 1 accounts for 14.7% of the variance for this variable. This is obtained by squaring the correlation coefficient for Factor 1 and HEALTH (0.383). Similarly, Factor 3 explains 40.3% $((-0.635)^2)$ of the variance. The total percentage of variance in the health index accounted for by this three-factor model is therefore 65.7% (14.7 + 10.7 + 40.3). The proportion of variance explained by the common factors is called the *communality* of the variable.

The communalities for the variables are shown in Figure 7.7, together with the percentage of variance accounted for by each of the retained factors. This table is labeled **Final Statistics**, since it shows the communalities and factor statistics after the desired number of factors has been extracted. When factors are estimated using the method of principal components, the factor statistics are the same in the tables labeled as initial and final. However, the communalities are different since all of the variances of the variables are not explained when only a subset of factors is retained.

Figure 7.7 Communality of variables

```
FACTOR READ=CORRELATION TRIANGLE
  /VARIABLES=POPSTABL TO MENTALIL.
```

```
Final Statistics:

Variable    Communality  *  Factor   Eigenvalue   Pct of Var   Cum Pct
                         *
POPSTABL       .69491    *    1        5.70658        40.8        40.8
NEWSCIRC       .77882    *    2        2.35543        16.8        57.6
FEMEMPLD       .80696    *    3        2.00926        14.4        71.9
FARMERS        .67503    *
RETAILNG       .79253    *
COMMERCL       .72044    *
INDUSTZN       .85921    *
HEALTH         .65699    *
CHLDNEGL       .74921    *
COMMEFFC       .83607    *
DWELGNEW       .79226    *
MIGRNPOP       .61855    *
UNEMPLOY       .71981    *
MENTALIL       .37047    *
```

Communalities can range from 0 to 1, with 0 indicating that the common factors explain none of the variance, and 1 indicating that all the variance is explained by the common factors. The variance that is not explained by the common factors is attributed to the unique factor and is called the *uniqueness* of the variable.

7.8
The Reproduced Correlation Matrix

One of the basic assumptions of factor analysis is that the observed correlation between variables is due to the sharing of common factors. Therefore, the estimated correlations between the factors and the variables can be used to estimate the correlations between the variables. In general, if factors are orthogonal, the estimated correlation coefficient for variables i and j is

$$r_{ij} = \sum_{f=1}^{k} r_{fi} r_{fj} = r_{1i} r_{1j} + r_{2i} r_{2j} + \ldots r_{ki} r_{kj}$$

Equation 7.8a

where k is the number of common factors, and r_{fi} is the correlation between the fth factor and the ith variable.

From Figure 7.6 and Equation 7.8a, the estimated correlation coefficient for HEALTH and COMMEFFC, based on the three-factor model, is

$$r_{8,10} = (0.38)(0.63) + (-0.33)(-0.16) + (-0.63)(-0.64) = 0.70.$$

Equation 7.8b

Figure 7.4a shows that the observed correlation coefficient between HEALTH and COMMEFFC is 0.73, so the difference between the observed correlation coefficient and that estimated from the model is about -0.03. This difference is called a residual.

The estimated correlation coefficients and the residuals are shown in Figure 7.8. The residuals are listed above the diagonal and the estimated correlation coefficients are below the triangle. The values with asterisks (on the diagonal) are the communalities discussed in Section 7.7.

Figure 7.8   Estimated correlations and residuals

```
FACTOR READ=CORRELATION TRIANGLE
   /VARIABLES=POPSTABL TO MENTALIL
   /PRINT=REPR.
```

```
Reproduced Correlation Matrix:

             POPSTABL    NEWSCIRC    FEMEMPLD    FARMERS    RETAILNG

POPSTABL      .69491*     .01709      .01623     -.12332    -.00183
NEWSCIRC     -.19209      .77882*    -.02883     -.01820    -.06320
FEMEMPLD     -.29223      .64483      .80696*     .00758    -.03597
FARMERS       .49232     -.60680     -.64458      .67503*    .05486
RETAILNG     -.12517      .68720      .77197     -.57386     .79253*
COMMERCL     -.02159      .69721      .66912     -.49948     .73149
INDUSTZN     -.13656      .77024      .77793     -.61598     .81382
HEALTH       -.10906     -.15005      .28818     -.07198     .18775
CHLDNEGL     -.07212     -.22418     -.56196      .22473    -.55410
COMMEFFC     -.06368      .06163      .51190     -.20527     .44037
DWELGNEW     -.71418      .19390      .41722     -.53861     .22876
MIGRNPOP     -.62274     -.03474      .08183     -.30139    -.09049
UNEMPLOY      .06126     -.40684     -.68101      .39909    -.66575
MENTALIL      .30378      .06093     -.24158      .18733    -.11995


             COMMERCL    INDUSTZN    HEALTH      CHLDNEGL   COMMEFFC

POPSTABL     -.04741      .03056     -.03994      .03312     .05868
NEWSCIRC     -.04521     -.05824      .12005      .05318     .03837
FEMEMPLD     -.08012     -.03593     -.04718     -.02704    -.04090
FARMERS       .19348      .07098      .00398      .03227    -.00773
RETAILNG     -.00449     -.02882     -.08775     -.00290     .01163
COMMERCL      .72044*     .13350      .10014      .07447     .01773
INDUSTZN      .77750      .85921*     .05413      .05596     .02256
HEALTH        .02286      .07487      .65699*     .14761     .03114
CHLDNEGL     -.43147     -.47996     -.55461      .74921*    .08703
COMMEFFC      .26927      .33444      .70086     -.74703     .83607*
DWELGNEW      .07863      .21042      .29914     -.12070     .28479
MIGRNPOP     -.18732     -.09828      .11913      .16577     .00918
UNEMPLOY     -.54931     -.62233     -.46098      .70191    -.67569
MENTALIL      .01539     -.05282     -.43612      .29080    -.43468


             DWELGNEW    MIGRNPOP    UNEMPLOY    MENTALIL

POPSTABL      .04418      .14674      .07574     -.06678
NEWSCIRC     -.00590     -.05126      .03384     -.01493
FEMEMPLD     -.00422     -.01783     -.00799      .00458
FARMERS      -.04039      .10339      .05091     -.06633
RETAILNG     -.06376      .09749      .01575     -.07005
COMMERCL     -.04863      .11932      .12531     -.07039
INDUSTZN     -.00742      .07428      .09433     -.04218
HEALTH       -.00914     -.03613      .11298      .15712
CHLDNEGL     -.01730     -.01777      .03109     -.04380
COMMEFFC      .02621      .05782      .07469      .11068
DWELGNEW      .79226*    -.12664     -.03343      .15717
MIGRNPOP      .63164      .61855*     .09715     -.01121
UNEMPLOY     -.23257      .08385      .71981*    -.05659
MENTALIL     -.42317     -.29579      .27359      .37047*


The lower left triangle contains the reproduced correlation matrix;  The
diagonal, communalities; and the upper right triangle, residuals between
the observed correlations and the reproduced correlations.

There are   42 (46.0%) residuals (above diagonal) that are > 0.05
```

Below the matrix is a message indicating how many residuals are greater than 0.05 in absolute value. In the community example, less than half (46%) are greater than 0.05 in absolute value. The magnitudes of the residuals indicate how well the fitted model reproduces the observed correlations. If the residuals are large, the model does not fit the data well and should probably be reconsidered.

7.9
Some Additional Considerations

If a method other than principal components analysis is used to extract the initial factors, there are differences in parts of the factor output. Consider, for example, Figure 7.9a, which contains the initial statistics obtained when the maximum-likelihood algorithm is used.

Figure 7.9a   Maximum-likelihood extractions

```
FACTOR READ=CORRELATION TRIANGLE
  /VARIABLES=POPSTABL TO MENTALIL
  /EXTRACTION=ML.
```

Variable	Communality	*	Factor	Eigenvalue	Pct of Var	Cum Pct
POPSTABL	.62385	*	1	5.70658	40.8	40.8
NEWSCIRC	.71096	*	2	2.35543	16.8	57.6
FEMEMPLD	.77447	*	3	2.00926	14.4	71.9
FARMERS	.74519	*	4	.89745	6.4	78.3
RETAILNG	.79259	*	5	.75847	5.4	83.8
COMMERCL	.90987	*	6	.53520	3.8	87.6
INDUSTZN	.92914	*	7	.50886	3.6	91.2
HEALTH	.66536	*	8	.27607	2.0	93.2
CHLDNEGL	.67987	*	9	.24511	1.8	94.9
COMMEFFC	.79852	*	10	.20505	1.5	96.4
DWELGNEW	.72576	*	11	.19123	1.4	97.8
MIGRNPOP	.50560	*	12	.16982	1.2	99.0
UNEMPLOY	.72549	*	13	.10202	.7	99.7
MENTALIL	.23825	*	14	.03946	.3	100.0

Initial Statistics:

Regardless of the algorithm used, by default the number of factors to be retained is determined by the principal components solution because it is easily obtainable. Thus, most of the output in Figure 7.9a is identical to that displayed in Figure 7.5a. The only exception is the column of communalities. In the principal components solution, all initial communalities are listed as 1's. In all other solutions, the initial estimate of the communality of a variable is the multiple R^2 from the regression equation that predicts that variable from all other variables. These initial communalities are used in the estimation algorithm.

When a method other than principal components analysis is used to estimate the final factor matrix, the percentage of variance explained by each final factor is usually different. Figure 7.9b contains the final statistics from a maximum-likelihood solution. The final three factors extracted explain only 63% of the total variance, as compared to 72% for the first three principal components. The first factor accounts for 35.5% of the total variance, as compared to 40.8% for the first principal component.

Figure 7.9b   Maximum-likelihood final statistics

```
FACTOR READ=CORRELATION TRIANGLE
  /VARIABLES=POPSTABL TO MENTALIL
  /EXTRACTION=ML.
```

Final Statistics:

Variable	Communality	*	Factor	Eigenvalue	Pct of Var	Cum Pct
POPSTABL	.52806	*	1	4.96465	35.5	35.5
NEWSCIRC	.57439	*	2	2.17833	15.6	51.0
FEMEMPLD	.75057	*	3	1.67661	12.0	63.0
FARMERS	.56808	*				
RETAILNG	.72089	*				
COMMERCL	.87128	*				
INDUSTZN	.96817	*				
HEALTH	.33383	*				
CHLDNEGL	.78341	*				
COMMEFFC	.62762	*				
DWELGNEW	.87445	*				
MIGRNPOP	.35074	*				
UNEMPLOY	.70833	*				
MENTALIL	.15977	*				

The proportion of the total variance explained by each factor can be calculated from the factor matrix. The proportion of the total variance explained by Factor 1 is calculated by summing the proportions of variance of each variable attributable to Factor 1. Figure 7.9c, the factor matrix for the maximum-likelihood solution, shows that Factor 1 accounts for $(-0.16)^2$ of the POPSTABL variance, 0.72^2 of the NEWSCIRC variance, 0.81^2 of the FEMEMPLD variance, and so on for the other variables. The total variance attributable to Factor 1 is therefore

Total variance   **Equation 7.9**

$$\begin{aligned} \text{for Factor 1} \ &= (-0.16)^2 + 0.72^2 + 0.81^2 + (-0.59)^2 + 0.83^2 + 0.89^2 \\ &+ 0.97^2 + 0.20^2 + (-0.52)^2 + 0.44^2 + 0.27^2 + (-0.00)^2 \\ &+ (-0.62)^2 + (-0.15)^2 \ = 4.96 \end{aligned}$$

This is the eigenvalue displayed for Factor 1 in Figure 7.9b.

Figure 7.9c   Maximum-likelihood factor matrix

```
FACTOR READ=CORRELATION TRIANGLE
  /VARIABLES=POPSTABL TO MENTALIL
  /EXTRACTION=ML.
```

```
Factor Matrix:

                FACTOR  1     FACTOR  2     FACTOR  3

POPSTABL         -.16474       -.62235       -.33705
NEWSCIRC          .71934       -.04703        .23394
FEMEMPLD          .80703        .27934       -.14573
FARMERS          -.58607       -.43787       -.18130
RETAILNG          .83267        .00538       -.16588
COMMERCL          .88945       -.27142        .08063
INDUSTZN          .97436       -.10452        .08869
HEALTH            .19912        .35743       -.40795
CHLDNEGL         -.51856       -.17816        .69481
COMMEFFC          .44351        .33795       -.56277
DWELGNEW          .27494        .86373        .22983
MIGRNPOP         -.00353        .49141        .33052
UNEMPLOY         -.62354       -.25283        .50558
MENTALIL         -.14756       -.33056        .16948
```

7.10
Methods for Factor Extraction

Several different methods can be used to obtain estimates of the common factors. These methods differ in the criterion used to define "good fit." Principal axis factoring proceeds much as principal components analysis, except that the diagonals of the correlation matrix are replaced by estimates of the communalities. At the first step, squared multiple correlation coefficients can be used as initial estimates of the communalities. Based on these, the requisite number of factors is extracted. The communalities are reestimated from the factor loadings, and factors are again extracted, with the new communality estimates replacing the old. This continues until negligible change occurs in the communality estimates.

The method of unweighted least squares produces, for a fixed number of factors, a factor pattern matrix that minimizes the sum of the squared differences between the observed and reproduced correlation matrices (ignoring the diagonals). The generalized least-squares method minimizes the same criterion; however, correlations are weighted inversely by the uniqueness of the variables. That is, correlations involving variables with high uniqueness are given less weight than correlations involving variables with low uniqueness.

The maximum-likelihood method produces parameter estimates that are the most likely to have produced the observed correlation matrix if the sample is from a multivariate normal distribution. Again, the correlations are weighted by the inverse of the uniqueness of the variables, and an iterative algorithm is employed.

The alpha method considers the variables in a particular analysis to be a sample from the universe of potential variables. It maximizes the alpha reliability of the factors. This differs from the previously described methods, which consider the cases to be a sample from some population and the variables to be fixed. With alpha factor extraction, the eigenvalues can no longer be obtained as the sum of the squared factor loadings and the communalities for each variable are not the sum of the squared loadings on the individual factors. See Harman (1967) and Kim and Mueller (1978) for discussions of the different factor estimation algorithms.

7.11
Goodness of Fit of the Factor Model

When factors are extracted using generalized least squares or maximum-likelihood estimation and it is assumed that the sample is from a multivariate normal population, it is possible to obtain goodness-of-fit tests for the adequacy of a k-factor model. For large sample sizes, the goodness-of-fit statistic tends to be distributed as a chi-squared variate. In most applications, the number of common factors is not known, and the number of factors is increased until a reasonably good fit is obtained—that is, until the observed significance level is no longer small. The statistics obtained in this fashion are not independent and the true significance level is not the same as the observed significance level at each step.

The value of the chi-squared goodness-of-fit statistic is directly proportional to the sample size. The degrees of freedom are a function of only the number of common factors and the number of variables. (For the chi-squared statistic to have positive degrees of freedom, the number of common factors cannot exceed the largest integer satisfying

$$m < 0.5(2p + 1 - \sqrt{8p + 1})$$

Equation 7.11

where m is the number of common factors to be extracted and p is the number of variables). For large sample sizes, the goodness-of-fit test may cause rather small discrepancies in fit to be deemed statistically significant, resulting in a larger number of factors being extracted than is really necessary.

Table 7.11 contains the goodness-of-fit statistics for maximum-likelihood extraction for different numbers of common factors. Using this criterion, six common factors are needed to adequately represent the community data.

Table 7.11 Goodness-of-fit statistics

Number of factors	Chi-square statistic	Iterations required	Significance
3	184.8846	13	0.0000
4	94.1803	8	0.0000
5	61.0836	11	0.0010
6	27.3431	15	0.1985

7.12
Summary of the Extraction Phase

In the factor extraction phase, the number of common factors needed to adequately describe the data is determined. This decision is based on eigenvalues and percentage of the total variance accounted for by different numbers of factors. A plot of the eigenvalues (the scree plot) is also helpful in determining the number of factors.

7.13
The Rotation Phase

Although the factor matrix obtained in the extraction phase indicates the relationship between the factors and the individual variables, it is usually difficult to identify meaningful factors based on this matrix. Often the variables and factors do not appear correlated in any interpretable pattern. Most factors are correlated with many variables. Since one of the goals of factor analysis is to identify factors that are substantively meaningful (in the sense that they summarize sets of closely related variables), the *rotation* phase of factor analysis attempts to transform the initial matrix into one that is easier to interpret.

Consider Figure 7.13a, which is a factor matrix for four hypothetical variables. From the factor loadings, it is difficult to interpret any of the factors, since the variables and factors are intertwined. That is, all factor loadings are quite high, and both factors explain all of the variables.

Figure 7.13a Hypothetical factor matrix

```
FACTOR VARIABLES=V1 V2 V3 V4
  /READ=FACTOR(2)
  /PLOT=ROTATION(1,2).
```

Factor Matrix:

	FACTOR 1	FACTOR 2
V1	.50000	.50000
V2	.50000	-.40000
V3	.70000	.70000
V4	-.60000	.60000

Figure 7.13b Rotated hypothetical factor matrix

Rotated Factor Matrix:

	FACTOR 1	FACTOR 2
V1	.70684	-.01938
V2	.05324	-.63809
V3	.98958	-.02713
V4	.02325	.84821

In the factor matrix in Figure 7.13b, variables V1 and V3 are highly related to Factor 1, while V2 and V4 load highly on Factor 2. By looking at what variables V2 and V4 have in common (such as a measurement of job satisfaction, or a characterization of an anxious personality), we may be able to identify Factor 2. Similar steps can be taken to identify Factor 1. The goal of rotation is to transform complicated matrices like that in Figure 7.13a into simpler ones like that in Figure 7.13b.

Consider Figure 7.13c, which is a plot of variables V1 to V4 using the factor loadings in Figure 7.13a as the coordinates, and Figure 7.13d, which is the corresponding plot for Figure 7.13b. Note that Figure 7.13c would look exactly like Figure 7.13d if the dotted lines were rotated to be the reference axes. When the axes are maintained at right angles, the rotation is called orthogonal. If the axes are not maintained at right angles, the rotation is called oblique. Oblique rotation is discussed in Section 7.16.

Figure 7.13c Prior to rotation

```
FACTOR VARIABLES=V1 V2 V3 V4
  /READ=FACTOR(2)
  /PLOT=ROTATION(1,2)
  /ROTATION=NOROTATE.
```

Horizontal Factor 1   Vertical Factor 2

Symbol	Variable	Coordinates	
1	V1	.500	.500
2	V2	.500	-.400
3	V3	.700	.700
4	V4	-.600	.600

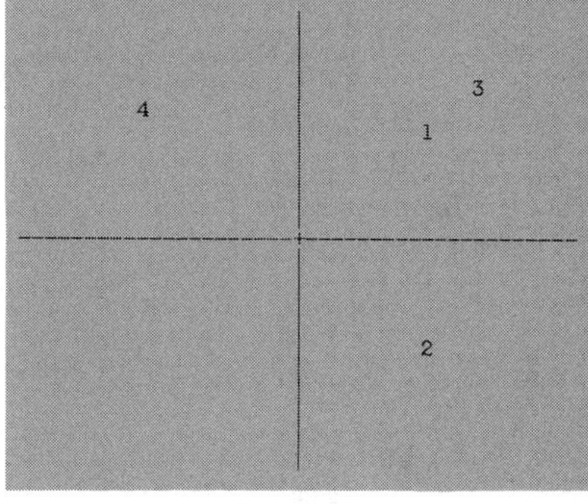

Figure 7.13d   Orthogonal rotation

```
FACTOR VARIABLES=V1 V2 V3 V4
  /READ=FACTOR(2)
  /ROTATION=VARIMAX
  /PLOT=ROTATION(1,2).
```

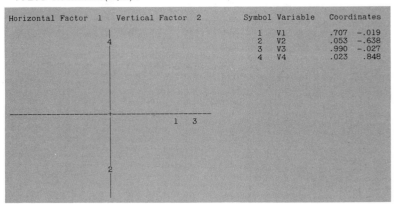

The purpose of rotation is to achieve a simple structure. This means that we would like each factor to have nonzero loadings for only some of the variables. This helps us interpret the factors. We would also like each variable to have nonzero loadings for only a few factors, preferably one. This permits the factors to be differentiated from each other. If several factors have high loadings on the same variables, it is difficult to ascertain how the factors differ.

Rotation does not affect the goodness of fit of a factor solution. That is, although the factor matrix changes, the communalities and the percentage of total variance explained do not change. The percentage of variance accounted for by each of the factors does, however, change. Rotation redistributes the explained variance for the individual factors. Different rotation methods may actually result in the identification of somewhat different factors.

A variety of algorithms are used for orthogonal rotation to a simple structure. The most commonly used method is the *varimax* method, which attempts to minimize the number of variables that have high loadings on a factor. This should enhance the interpretability of the factors.

The *quartimax* method emphasizes simple interpretation of variables, since the solution minimizes the number of factors needed to explain a variable. A quartimax rotation often results in a general factor with high-to-moderate loadings on most variables. This is one of the main shortcomings of the quartimax method.

The *equamax* method is a combination of the varimax method, which simplifies the factors, and the quartimax method, which simplifies variables.

Consider Figure 7.13e, which shows the factor matrices for the community data before rotation and again after a varimax (and quartimax and equamax) orthogonal rotation procedure.

The unrotated factor matrix is difficult to interpret. Many variables have moderate-size correlations with several factors. After rotation, the number of large and small factor loadings increases. Variables are more highly correlated with single factors. Interpretation of the factors also appears possible. For example, the first factor shows string positive correlation with newspaper circulation, percentage of females in the labor force, sales, commercial activity, and the industrialization index. It also shows a strong negative correlation with the number of farmers. Thus, Factor 1 might be interpreted as measuring something like "urbanism." The second factor is positively correlated with health and a high standard of living and negatively correlated with aid to dependent children, unemployment, and mental illness. This factor describes the affluence or welfare of a community. The last factor is associated with the instability or influx of a community. Thus, communities may be fairly well characterized by three factors—urbanism, welfare, and influx.

Figure 7.13e Factor matrices for community data

```
FACTOR READ=CORRELATION TRIANGLE
  /VARIABLES=POPSTABL TO MENTALIL
  /EXTRACT=PC
  /ROTATION=VARIMAX
  /ROTATION=QUARTIMAX
  /ROTATION=EQUAMAX.
```

Factor Matrix: (unrotated)

	FACTOR 1	FACTOR 2	FACTOR 3
POPSTABL	-.30247	.68597	-.36451
NEWSCIRC	.67238	.28096	.49779
FEMEMPLD	.89461	.01131	.08063
FARMERS	-.68659	.20002	-.40450
RETAILNG	.85141	.24264	.09351
COMMERCL	.72503	.39394	.19896
INDUSTZN	.84436	.29956	.23775
HEALTH	.38347	-.32718	-.63474
CHLDNEGL	-.67430	-.12139	.52896
COMMEFFC	.63205	-.15540	-.64221
DWELGNEW	.45886	-.73940	.18706
MIGRNPOP	.07894	-.74371	.24335
UNEMPLOY	-.78714	-.09777	.30110
MENTALIL	-.30025	.45463	.27134

Rotated Factor Matrix: (varimax)

	FACTOR 1	FACTOR 2	FACTOR 3
POPSTABL	-.13553	.00916	-.82247
NEWSCIRC	.86634	-.14256	.08920
FEMEMPLD	.78248	.37620	.23055
FARMERS	-.65736	-.04537	-.49077
RETAILNG	.83993	.29454	.01705
COMMERCL	.83432	.11068	-.11000
INDUSTZN	.91325	.15773	.01730
HEALTH	-.05806	.79424	.15101
CHLDNEGL	-.39791	-.75492	.14486
COMMEFFC	.21186	.88794	.05241
DWELGNEW	.17484	.22931	.84208
MIGRNPOP	-.12119	-.00660	.77706
UNEMPLOY	-.57378	-.62483	.01311
MENTALIL	.03133	-.47460	-.37979

Rotated Factor Matrix: (quartimax)

	FACTOR 1	FACTOR 2	FACTOR 3
POPSTABL	-.14884	.00769	-.82018
NEWSCIRC	.85549	-.20254	.07706
FEMEMPLD	.81105	.32272	.21214
FARMERS	-.66736	-.00515	-.47920
RETAILNG	.85885	.23432	-.00105
COMMERCL	.83802	.04963	-.12529
INDUSTZN	.92229	.09267	.00000
HEALTH	.00097	.79832	.14028
CHLDNEGL	-.44778	-.72272	.16242
COMMEFFC	.27508	.87127	.03590
DWELGNEW	.20527	.22763	.83565
MIGRNPOP	-.10781	.01249	.77896
UNEMPLOY	-.61627	-.58226	.03168
MENTALIL	-.00897	-.48069	-.37326

Rotated Factor Matrix: (equamax)

	FACTOR 1	FACTOR 2	FACTOR 3
POPSTABL	-.12961	.01218	-.82338
NEWSCIRC	.86917	-.12003	.09470
FEMEMPLD	.77037	.39514	.23949
FARMERS	-.65223	-.05898	-.49613
RETAILNG	.83157	.31678	.02580
COMMERCL	.83185	.13387	-.10273
INDUSTZN	.90854	.18199	.02554
HEALTH	-.08047	.79116	.15682
CHLDNEGL	-.37857	-.76645	.13585
COMMEFFC	.18756	.89284	.06103
DWELGNEW	.16236	.22710	.84518
MIGRNPOP	-.12675	-.01613	.77603
UNEMPLOY	-.55688	-.64006	.00379
MENTALIL	.04688	-.47050	-.38327

7.14
Factor Loading Plots

A convenient means of examining the success of an orthogonal rotation is to plot the variables using the factor loadings as coordinates. In Figure 7.14a, the variables are plotted using Factors 1 and 2 after varimax rotation of the two factors. The plotted numbers represent the number of the variable; e.g., 7 represents the seventh variable (INDUSTZN). The coordinates correspond to the factor loadings in Figure 7.13e for the varimax-rotated solution. The coordinates are also listed next to each plot. In Figure 7.14b, the variables are plotted using Factors 1 and 2 before rotation.

Figure 7.14a Varimax-rotated solution

```
FACTOR READ=CORRELATION TRIANGLE
   /VARIABLES=POPSTABL TO MENTALIL
   /ROTATION=VARIMAX
   /PLOT=ROTATION(1,2).
```

Symbol	Variable	Coordinates	
1	POPSTABL	-.136	.009
2	NEWSCIRC	.866	-.143
3	FEMEMPLD	.782	.376
4	FARMERS	-.657	-.045
5	RETAILNG	.840	.295
6	COMMERCL	.834	.111
7	INDUSTZN	.913	.158
8	HEALTH	-.058	.794
9	CHLDNEGL	-.398	-.755
10	COMMEFFC	.212	.888
11	DWELGNEW	.175	.229
12	MIGRNPOP	-.121	-.007
13	UNEMPLOY	-.574	-.625
14	MENTALIL	.031	-.475

Figure 7.14b Unrotated solution

```
FACTOR READ=CORRELATION TRIANGLE
   /VARIABLES=POPSTABL TO MENTALIL
   /ROTATION=NOROTATE
   /PLOT=ROTATION(1,2).
```

Symbol	Variable	Coordinates	
1	POPSTABL	-.302	.686
2	NEWSCIRC	.672	.281
3	FEMEMPLD	.895	.011
4	FARMERS	-.687	.200
5	RETAILNG	.851	.243
6	COMMERCL	.725	.394
7	INDUSTZN	.844	.300
8	HEALTH	.383	-.327
9	CHLDNEGL	-.674	-.121
10	COMMEFFC	.632	-.155
11	DWELGNEW	.459	-.739
12	MIGRNPOP	.079	-.744
13	UNEMPLOY	-.787	-.098
14	MENTALIL	-.300	.455

If a rotation has achieved a simple structure, clusters of variables should occur near the ends of the axes and at their intersection. Variables at the end of an axis are those that have high loadings on only that factor. Variables near the origin of the plot have small loadings on both factors. Variables that are not near the axes are explained by both factors. If a simple structure has been achieved, there should be few, if any, variables with large loadings on more than one factor.

7.15
Interpreting the Factors

To identify the factors, it is necessary to group the variables that have large loadings for the same factors. Plots of the loadings, as discussed in Section 7.14, are one way of determining the clusters of variables. Another convenient strategy is to sort the factor pattern matrix so that variables with high loadings on the same factor appear together, as shown in Figure 7.15a. Small factor loadings can be omitted from such a table. In Figure 7.15b, no loadings less than 0.5 in absolute value are displayed. Note that the mental illness variable, as expected, does not correlate highly with any of the factors.

Figure 7.15a Sorted loadings

```
FACTOR READ=CORRELATION TRIANGLE
  /VARIABLES=POPSTABL TO MENTALIL
  /FORMAT=SORT
  /ROTATION=VARIMAX.
```

Rotated Factor Matrix:

	FACTOR 1	FACTOR 2	FACTOR 3
INDUSTZN	.91325	.15773	.01730
NEWSCIRC	.86634	-.14256	.08920
RETAILNG	.83993	.29454	.01705
COMMERCL	.83432	.11068	-.11000
FEMEMPLD	.78248	.37620	.23055
FARMERS	-.65736	-.04537	-.49077
COMMEFFC	.21186	.88794	.05241
HEALTH	-.05806	.79424	.15101
CHLDNEGL	-.39791	-.75492	.14486
UNEMPLOY	-.57378	-.62483	.01311
MENTALIL	.03133	-.47460	-.37979
DWELGNEW	.17484	.22931	.84208
POPSTABL	-.13553	.00916	-.82247
MIGRNPOP	-.12119	-.00660	.77706

Figure 7.15b Sorted and blanked loadings

```
FACTOR READ=CORRELATION TRIANGLE
  /VARIABLES=POPSTABL TO MENTALIL
  /FORMAT=SORT BLANK(.5)
  /ROTATION=VARIMAX.
```

Rotated Factor Matrix:

	FACTOR 1	FACTOR 2	FACTOR 3
INDUSTZN	.91325		
NEWSCIRC	.86634		
RETAILNG	.83993		
COMMERCL	.83432		
FEMEMPLD	.78248		
FARMERS	-.65736		
COMMEFFC		.88794	
HEALTH		.79424	
CHLDNEGL		-.75492	
UNEMPLOY	-.57378	-.62483	
MENTALIL			
DWELGNEW			.84208
POPSTABL			-.82247
MIGRNPOP			.77706

7.16
Oblique Rotation

Orthogonal rotation results in factors that are uncorrelated. Although this is an appealing property, sometimes allowing for correlations among factors simplifies the factor pattern matrix. Consider Figure 7.16a, which is a plot of the factor loadings for six variables. Note that if the axes went through the points (the solid line), a simpler factor pattern matrix would result than with an orthogonal rotation (the dotted lines). Factor pattern matrices for both rotations are shown in Figure 7.16b.

Figure 7.16a Plot of factor loadings

```
Horizontal Factor  1   Vertical Factor  2        Symbol Variable    Coordinates

                                                    1     X1        .766   -.232
                                  o                 2     X2        .670   -.203
                            |                       3     X3        .574   -.174
                            |                       4     X4        .454    .533
                        4                           5     X5        .389    .457
                      5                              6     X6        .324    .381
                      6
               |
     ----------+-----------------------------
               |
               |       3
               |     2  1
               |
               |
               |
```

Figure 7.16b Rotated varimax and oblique factor loadings

```
Rotated Factor Matrix: (varimax)

                 FACTOR   1      FACTOR   2

X1                 .78313         .16345
X2                 .68523         .14302
X3                 .58734         .12259
X4                 .14302         .68523
X5                 .12259         .58734
X6                 .10215         .48945


Pattern Matrix: (oblique)

                 FACTOR   1      FACTOR   2

X1                 .80000         .00000
X2                 .70000        -.00000
X3                 .60000        -.00000
X4                 .00000         .70000
X5                -.00000         .60000
X6                -.00000         .50000
```

There are several reasons why oblique rotation has come into favor. It is unlikely that influences in nature are uncorrelated. And even if they are uncorrelated in the population, they need not be so in the sample. Thus, oblique rotations have often been found to yield substantively meaningful factors.

7.17
Factor Pattern and Structure Matrices

Oblique rotation preserves the communalities of the variables, as does orthogonal rotation. When oblique rotation is used, however, the factor loadings and factor variable correlations are no longer identical. The factor loadings are still partial regression coefficients, but since the factors are correlated, they are no longer equal to the simple factor variable correlations. (Remember that the regression coefficients depend on the interrelationships of the independent variables when these are correlated.) Therefore, separate factor loading and factor structure matrices are displayed as part of the output.

7.18
Algorithm for Oblique Rotation

The method for oblique rotation available in SPSS/PC+ is called OBLIMIN. A parameter called δ (delta) controls the extent of obliqueness. When δ is zero, the factors are most oblique. For negative values of δ, the factors become less oblique as δ becomes more negative. Harman (1967) recommends that δ be either zero or negative.

The factor loadings for the communities data after an oblique rotation are shown in the factor pattern matrix in Figure 7.18a. The loadings are no longer constrained to a range from -1 to $+1$. The correlations between the factors and variables are shown in Figure 7.18b, the factor structure matrix.

Figure 7.18a   Factor pattern matrix

```
FACTOR READ=CORRELATION TRIANGLE
    /VARIABLES=POPSTABL TO MENTALIL
    /FORMAT=SORT
    /ROTATION=OBLIMIN.
```

```
Pattern Matrix:

                   FACTOR  1       FACTOR  2       FACTOR  3

    INDUSTZN        .91577          .02882         -.04731
    NEWSCIRC        .90594         -.06987          .26053
    COMMERCL        .84325          .15024         -.01504
    RETAILNG        .82253          .03760         -.19782
    FEMEMPLD        .74906         -.17274         -.27862
    FARMERS        -.65969          .46636         -.06041

    POPSTABL       -.12570          .82380         -.06787
    DWELGNEW        .13426         -.82258         -.17248
    MIGRNPOP       -.13720         -.78724          .03070

    COMMEFFC        .09940          .02770         -.88775
    HEALTH         -.16689         -.08909         -.81993
    CHLDNEGL       -.31128         -.22218          .73693
    UNEMPLOY       -.50651         -.08531          .57387
    MENTALIL        .10140          .34462          .47495
```

Figure 7.18b   Factor structure matrix

```
Structure Matrix:

                   FACTOR  1       FACTOR  2       FACTOR  3

    INDUSTZN        .92553         -.04717         -.27457
    RETAILNG        .86963         -.05222         -.40031
    NEWSCIRC        .84545         -.10235          .02205
    COMMERCL        .83566          .08423         -.20712
    FEMEMPLD        .83252         -.26822         -.49178
    FARMERS        -.67979          .50798          .17096

    DWELGNEW        .24017         -.85671         -.32064
    POPSTABL       -.17101          .82390          .07829
    MIGRNPOP       -.08527         -.77258         -.04400

    COMMEFFC        .32149         -.10314         -.90901
    HEALTH          .04692         -.19032         -.79016
    CHLDNEGL       -.48053         -.09623          .78468
    UNEMPLOY       -.64496          .03280          .68993
    MENTALIL       -.04466          .40290          .49721
```

The correlation matrix for the factors is in Figure 7.18c. Note that there are small correlations between all three factors. In the case of an orthogonal rotation, the factor correlation matrix is an identity matrix: that is, there are 1's on the diagonal and 0's elsewhere.

Figure 7.18c   Factor correlation matrix

```
Factor Correlation Matrix:

                   FACTOR  1       FACTOR  2       FACTOR  3

    FACTOR  1      1.00000
    FACTOR  2      -.07580         1.00000
    FACTOR  3      -.25253          .13890         1.00000
```

The oblique rotation resulted in the same grouping of variables as did the orthogonal rotation. The interpretation of the factors does not change based on it.

7.19
Factor Scores

Since one of the goals of factor analysis is to reduce a large number of variables to a smaller number of factors, it is often desirable to estimate factor scores for each case. The factor scores can be used in subsequent analyses to represent the values of the factors. Plots of factor scores for pairs of factors are useful for detecting unusual observations.

Recall from Section 7.1 that a factor can be estimated as a linear combination of the original variables. That is, for case k, the score for the jth factor is estimated as

$$\hat{F}_{jk} = \sum_{i=1}^{p} W_{ji} X_{ik}$$

Equation 7.19a

where X_{ik} is the standardized value of the *i*th variable for case *k* and W_{ji} is the factor score coefficient for the *j*th factor and the *i*th variable. Except for principal components analysis, exact factor scores cannot be obtained. Estimates are obtained instead.

There are several methods for estimating factor score coefficients. Each has different properties and results in different scores (see Tucker, 1971, and Harman, 1967). The three methods available in SPSS/PC+ FACTOR (Anderson-Rubin, regression, and Bartlett) all result in scores with a mean of 0. The Anderson-Rubin method always produces uncorrelated scores with a standard deviation of 1, even when the original factors are estimated to be correlated. The regression factor scores (the default) have a variance equal to the squared multiple correlation between the estimated factor scores and the true factor values. (These are shown on the diagonal in Figure 7.19b.) Regression method factor scores can be correlated even when factors are assumed to be orthogonal. If principal components extraction is used, all three methods result in the same factor scores, which are no longer estimated but are exact.

Figure 7.19a contains the factor score coefficients used to calculate regression method factor scores for the community data. The correlation matrix for the estimated scores is shown in Figure 7.19b.

Figure 7.19a   Factor coefficient matrix

```
FACTOR READ=CORRELATION TRIANGLE
  /VARIABLES=POPSTABL TO MENTALIL
  /PRINT=FSCORES
  /EXTRACTION=ML
  /ROTATION=VARIMAX.
```

```
Factor Score Coefficient Matrix:

                FACTOR  1      FACTOR  2      FACTOR  3

POPSTABL        -.00150         .03191        -.15843
NEWSCIRC         .05487        -.06095         .03524
FEMEMPLD         .01729         .14014         .05328
FARMERS         -.01797         .00113        -.11462
RETAILNG         .03728         .09460        -.03577
COMMERCL         .20579        -.11667        -.10723
INDUSTZN         .77285        -.27024         .00882
HEALTH          -.02786         .09971        -.00161
CHLDNEGL         .08404        -.44657         .16521
COMMEFFC        -.05030         .23211        -.03623
DWELGNEW        -.05117         .07034         .68792
MIGRNPOP         .00029        -.03198         .09778
UNEMPLOY         .03856        -.26435         .05378
MENTALIL         .01264        -.04224        -.01691
```

Figure 7.19b   Covariance matrix for estimated regression factor scores

```
FACTOR READ=CORRELATION TRIANGLE
  /VARIABLES=POPSTABL TO MENTALIL
  /PRINT=FSCORES
  /EXTRACTION=ML
  /ROTATION=VARIMAX.
```

```
Covariance Matrix for Estimated Regression Factor Scores:

                FACTOR  1      FACTOR  2      FACTOR  3

FACTOR  1        .96763
FACTOR  2        .03294         .87641
FACTOR  3        .00042         .02544         .89452
```

To see how factor scores are calculated, consider Table 7.19, which contains standardized values for the original 14 variables for 5 counties, and factor score values for the three factors. For each factor, the factor scores are obtained by multiplying the standardized values by the corresponding factor score coefficients. Thus, for Adams County the value for Factor 1 is -1.328.

$-.00150 \times -.36 + .05487 \times -.93 + .01729 \times -1.06 + \dots$ **Equation 7.19b**
$+ .01264 \times -.76 = -1.328$

Table 7.19 Standardized values and factor scores

County

Variable	Adams	Butler	Crawford	Cuyahoga	Hamilton
POPSTABL	−0.36	−1.49	2.44	−0.13	−0.30
NEWSCIRC	−0.93	0.39	−0.26	2.04	1.17
FEMEMPLD	−1.06	0.41	0.24	1.30	1.03
FARMERS	2.20	−0.67	0.01	−0.93	−0.90
RETAILNG	−1.41	0.49	0.58	1.15	1.07
COMMERCL	−0.89	−0.30	−0.07	1.58	2.02
INDUSTZN	−1.14	−0.11	0.03	1.53	1.85
HEALTH	−0.25	−0.56	−1.32	−0.36	−1.17
CHLDNEGL	−1.26	0.79	−0.61	0.63	0.99
COMMEFFC	−0.20	0.78	−0.87	−0.78	−1.66
DWELGNEW	−0.52	0.52	−1.09	−0.01	−0.22
MIGRNPOP	−0.98	0.16	−0.60	0.63	1.13
UNEMPLOY	−0.75	−0.36	−0.44	1.56	0.76
MENTALIL	−0.76	−0.77	−0.46	−0.14	0.61

Factor	Scores				
Factor 1	−1.328	−0.089	0.083	1.862	2.233
Factor 2	0.897	0.027	0.197	−1.362	−1.79
Factor 3	−0.830	0.831	−1.290	0.342	0.226

7.20
RUNNING PROCEDURE FACTOR

A variety of extraction and rotation techniques are available in the SPSS/PC+ FACTOR procedure. The extraction methods available include principal components analysis (Section 7.5) and the maximum-likelihood factor method (Section 7.9). The factor rotation methods are varimax, equamax, quartimax, and oblimin.

You can also request scree plots and factor loading plots to help in selecting and interpreting factors. FACTOR will accept a correlation matrix or a factor loading matrix as input, as well as the original values of your variables for cases.

7.21
Global and Analysis Block Subcommands

There are two main types of FACTOR subcommands: global and analysis block. Global subcommands are specified once and are in effect for the entire FACTOR procedure. Analysis block subcommands apply only to the ANALYSIS subcommand that precedes them. Within an analysis block, there are extraction and rotation phase subcommands.

The global subcommands are VARIABLES, MISSING, and WIDTH. The VARIABLES subcommand identifies the subset of variables from the active file available for analysis by FACTOR. The MISSING subcommand provides several alternative missing-value treatments. WIDTH controls the width of the display.

An analysis block begins with an ANALYSIS subcommand, which names a subset of variables from the list specified on the VARIABLES subcommand. If you omit the ANALYSIS subcommand, all variables named on the VARIABLES subcommand are used.

Analysis block subcommands include EXTRACTION, ROTATION, CRITERIA, SAVE, etc. You also can tailor the statistics displayed for an analysis block by specifying the PRINT subcommand to request optional statistics, the FORMAT subcommand to reformat factor loading and structure matrices, and the PLOT subcommand to obtain scree plots and factor loading plots.

The extraction phase is initiated with the EXTRACTION subcommand. (A principal components analysis is performed if there is no EXTRACTION subcommand.) The CRITERIA subcommand controls the number of factors selected in subsequent extractions, and the DIAGONAL subcommand supplies initial diagonal values for principal axis factoring.

B

Statistics Guide

The rotation phase is initiated with the ROTATION subcommand, which specifies the rotation method to use. The default varimax rotation is obtained if you omit both EXTRACTION and ROTATION. No rotation occurs if EXTRACTION is specified without ROTATION. The CRITERIA subcommand controls subsequent rotation, as well as extraction, criteria.

Optional subcommands are available to write and read matrices for FACTOR (see Figure 7.4a for an example of matrix input).

7.22
Subcommand Order

The global subcommands VARIABLES and MISSING must be the first specifications. The remaining subcommands can appear in any logical order.

Within an analysis block, the placement of CRITERIA is important, as it affects all extractions and rotations that follow. Once specified, a CRITERIA subcommand is in effect for the remainder of the FACTOR procedure. However, you can specify more than one CRITERIA subcommand.

7.23
Specifying the Variables

The VARIABLES subcommand lists the variables to analyze. If you do not specify a subsequent EXTRACTION or ROTATION subcommand, the default principal components analysis with varimax rotation is produced:

```
FACTOR VARIABLES=POPSTABL NEWSCIRC FEMEMPLD FARMERS
    RETAILNG COMMERCL INDUSTZN HEALTH CHLDNEGL COMMEFFC
    DWELGNEW MIGRNPOP UNEMPLOY MENTALIL.
```

If the variables exist in that order on the active file, the command

```
FACTOR VARIABLES=POPSTABL TO MENTALIL.
```

produces the output shown in Figures 7.5a, 7.6, and 7.7.

VARIABLES is the only required subcommand and must be placed before all other subcommands except MISSING and WIDTH. Only variables named on the VARIABLES subcommand can be referred to in subsequent subcommands. You can specify only one VARIABLES subcommand on a FACTOR command.

7.24
Missing Values

FACTOR results are based on the correlation matrix for the variables listed on the VARIABLES subcommand. Use the MISSING subcommand to specify the missing-value treatment for this matrix. If you omit the MISSING subcommand, or include it with no specifications, missing values are deleted listwise.

LISTWISE *Delete missing values listwise.* Only cases with valid values on all variables on the VARIABLES subcommand are used. This is the default.

PAIRWISE *Delete missing values pairwise.* Cases with complete data on each pair of variables correlated are used.

MEANSUB *Replace missing values with the variable mean.* This includes both user-missing and system-missing values.

INCLUDE *Include missing values.* Cases with user-missing values are treated as valid observations. System-missing values are excluded from analysis.

DEFAULT *Same as LISTWISE.*

For example, the command

```
FACTOR VARIABLES=IQ GPA TESTSCOR STRESS SAT PSYCHTST
    /MISSING=PAIRWISE.
```

requests a default analysis that uses pairwise missing-value treatment in calculating the correlation matrix.

You can specify only one MISSING subcommand per FACTOR command. The MISSING subcommand must be placed before all other subcommands except VARIABLES and WIDTH. MISSING is ignored with matrix input.

7.25
Specifying Output Width

The WIDTH subcommand controls the display width for factor output. For example, the subcommand

```
/WIDTH=80
```

requests output that is 80 characters wide. The value on WIDTH must be an integer. This value overrides the one specified on the SET command. You can specify only one WIDTH subcommand per FACTOR command. The WIDTH subcommand can be placed anywhere.

7.26
Specifying Analyses

The ANALYSIS subcommand allows you to perform analyses on subsets of variables named on the VARIABLES subcommand. For example, the command

```
FACTOR VARIABLES=POPSTABL TO MENTALIL
  /ANALYSIS=FEMEMPLD FARMERS INDUSTZN HEALTH CHILDNEGL DWELGNEW
  /ANALYSIS=POPSTABL NEWSCIRC FEMEMPLD COMMERCL UNEMPLOY MENTALIL.
```

requests two default principal components analyses. The first uses variables FEMEMPLD, FARMERS, INDUSTZN, HEALTH, CHLDNEGL, and DWELGNEW, and the second uses variables POPSTABL, NEWSCIRC, FEMEMPLD, COMMERCL, UNEMPLOY, and MENTALIL.

If you do not include the ANALYSIS subcommand, FACTOR uses all of the variables listed on the VARIABLES subcommand for the analysis.

The TO keyword in a variable list on the ANALYSIS subcommand refers to the order of variables on the VARIABLES subcommand, not to their order in the file. Otherwise, the usual SPSS/PC+ conventions for variable lists are followed. You can use the keyword ALL to refer to all of the variables listed on the VARIABLES subcommand.

If you follow the VARIABLES subcommand with another analysis block subcommand prior to the ANALYSIS subcommand, you implicitly initiate an analysis block. For example, the command

```
FACTOR VARIABLES=POPSTABL TO MENTALIL
  /PRINT=DEFAULTS CORRELATIONS
  /ANALYSIS=FEMEMPLD FARMERS INDUSTZN HEALTH CHILDNEGL DWELGNEW
  /ANALYSIS=POPSTABL NEWSCIRC FEMEMPLD COMMERCL UNEMPLOY MENTALIL.
```

requests three analyses. The first uses all variables and prints the correlation matrix along with the defaults, and the second and third use different subsets of the variable list and print only the defaults.

7.27
Specifying the Extraction Method

To specify the extraction method, use the EXTRACTION subcommand with one of the keywords shown below.

PC | *Principal components analysis.* This is the default.
PAF | *Principal axis factoring.*
ML | *Maximum likelihood.*
ALPHA | *Alpha factoring.*
IMAGE | *Image factoring.*
ULS | *Unweighted least squares.*
GLS | *Generalized least squares.*
PA1 | *Same as PC.*
PA2 | *Same as PAF.*
DEFAULT | *Same as PC.*

You can specify more than one EXTRACTION subcommand. For example, the command

```
FACTOR VARIABLES=IQ GPA TESTSCOR STRESS SAT PSYCHTST
  /EXTRACTION=ML
  /EXTRACTION=PC.
```

produces output based on two extraction methods—maximum likelihood and principal components. You can specify multiple EXTRACTION subcommands in each analysis block to produce output for different extraction methods for subsets of variables named on the VARIABLES subcommand.

If you use the EXTRACTION subcommand without a subsequent ROTATION subcommand, the factor pattern matrix is not rotated (see Section 7.30).

7.28
Specifying Diagonal Values

Use the DIAGONAL subcommand to specify initial diagonal values in conjunction with principal axis factoring (EXTRACTION=PAF). You can specify any one of the following:

value list *Diagonal values.* User-supplied diagonal values are used only for principal axis factoring.

DEFAULT *1's on the diagonal for principal components or initial communality estimates on the diagonal for factor methods.*

You must supply the same number of diagonal values as there are variables in the analysis. For example, the command

```
FACTOR VARIABLES=IQ GPA TESTSCOR SAT EDYEARS
  /DIAGONAL=.55 .45 .35 .40 .50
  /EXTRACTION=PAF.
```

assigns five diagonal values for the specified principal axis factoring. You can use the prefix *n* and an asterisk to indicate replicated values. For example, 5*0.80 is the same as specifying 0.80 five times.

7.29
Specifying Extraction and Rotation Criteria

Use CRITERIA to control criteria for extractions and rotations that follow the subcommand.

FACTORS(nf) *Number of factors extracted.* The default is the number of eigenvalues greater than MINEIGEN (see below).

MINEIGEN(eg) *Minimum eigenvalue used to control the number of factors.* The default value is 1.

ITERATE(ni) *Number of iterations for the factor solution.* The default value is 25.

ECONVERGE(e1) *Convergence criterion for extraction.* The default value is 0.001.

RCONVERGE(e2) *Convergence criterion for rotation.* The default value is 0.0001.

KAISER *Kaiser normalization in rotation.* This is the default.

NOKAISER *No Kaiser normalization.*

DELTA(d) *Value of delta for direct oblimin rotation.* The default value is 0.

DEFAULT *Use default values for all criteria.*

Once specified, criteria stay in effect for the procedure until explicitly overridden. For example, the command

```
FACTOR VARIABLES=IQ GPA TESTSCOR STRESS SAT PSYCHTST
  /CRITERIA=FACTORS(2)
  /ANALYSIS=ALL
  /CRITERIA=DEFAULT.
```

produces two factor analyses for the same set of variables. The first analysis limits the number of factors extracted to 2, and the second extracts all factors whose eigenvalue is greater than 1.

7.30
Rotating Factors

Four rotation methods are available in FACTOR: varimax, equamax, quartimax, and oblimin (see Section 7.13). When both the EXTRACTION and ROTATION subcommands are omitted, the factors are rotated using the varimax method. However, if EXTRACTION is specified but ROTATION is not, the factors are not rotated. To specify a rotation method other than these defaults, use the ROTATION subcommand.

VARIMAX	*Varimax rotation.* This is the default if both EXTRACTION and ROTATION are omitted.
EQUAMAX	*Equamax rotation.*
QUARTIMAX	*Quartimax rotation.*
OBLIMIN	*Direct oblimin rotation.*
NOROTATE	*No rotation.* This is the default if EXTRACTION is specified but ROTATION is not.
DEFAULT	*Same as VARIMAX.*

OBLIMIN uses a default delta value of 0. Use the CRITERIA subcommand to change this default (see Section 7.29).

To obtain a factor loading plot based on unrotated factors, use the PLOT subcommand (see Section 7.33) and specify NOROTATE in the ROTATION subcommand, as in

```
FACTOR VARIABLES=IQ GPA TESTSCOR STRESS SAT PSYCHTST
  /PLOT=EIGEN ROTATION(1,2)
  /ROTATION=NOROTATE.
```

You can specify more than one rotation for a given extraction by using multiple ROTATION subcommands. See Section 7.29 for information on controlling rotation criteria.

7.31
Optional Statistics

By default, the statistics listed below under INITIAL, EXTRACTION, and ROTATION are printed. Use the PRINT subcommand to request additional statistics. If you specify PRINT, only those statistics explicity named are displayed. You can use only one PRINT subcommand for each analysis block.

UNIVARIATE	*Numbers of valid observations, means, and standard deviations for the variables named on the ANALYSIS subcommand.*
INITIAL	*Initial communalities, eigenvalues, and percentage of variance explained.* (See Sections 7.5 and 7.7.)
CORRELATION	*Correlation matrix for the variables named on the ANALYSIS subcommand.*
SIG	*Significance levels of correlations.* These are one-tailed probabilities.
DET	*The determinant of the correlation matrix.*
INV	*The inverse of the correlation matrix.*
AIC	*The anti-image covariance and correlation matrices.*
KMO	*The Kaiser-Meyer-Olkin measure of sampling adequacy and Bartlett's test of sphericity.* (See Section 7.4.)
EXTRACTION	*Communalities, eigenvalues, and rotated factor loadings.* (See Sections 7.5 through 7.10.)
REPR	*Reproduced correlations and their residuals.* (See Section 7.8.)
ROTATION	*Rotated factor pattern and structure matrices, factor transformation matrix, and factor correlation matrix.* (See Section 7.13.)
FSCORE	*The factor score coefficient matrix.* By default, this is based on a regression solution.
DEFAULT	*INITIAL, EXTRACTION, and ROTATION statistics.* If you use the EXTRACTION subcommand without a subsequent ROTATION subcommand, only the statistics specified by INITIAL and EXTRACTION are displayed by default.
ALL	*All available statistics.*

For example,

```
FACTOR VARIABLES=POPSTABL TO MENTALIL
  /PRINT=REPR.
```

produced the output in Figure 7.8.

7.32
Sorting the Factor Pattern Matrix

Use the FORMAT subcommand to reformat the display of the factor loading and structure matrices to help you interpret the factors (see Section 7.15). You can use only one FORMAT subcommand per analysis block. The following keywords may be specified on FORMAT:

SORT   *Order the factor loadings by magnitude.*
BLANK(n) *Suppress coefficients lower in absolute value than* n.
DEFAULT   *Turn off blanking and sorting.*

For example, the command

```
FACTOR VARIABLES=POPSTABL TO MENTALIL
  /FORMAT=SORT BLANK(.5).
```

produced the output in Figure 7.15b.

7.33
Obtaining Plots

To obtain a scree plot (Section 7.5) or a factor loading plot (Section 7.14), use the PLOT subcommand with the following keywords:

EIGEN   *Scree plot.* Plots the eigenvalues in descending order.
ROTATION(n1 n2) *Factor loading plot.* The specifications $n1$ and $n2$ refer to the factors used as the axes. Several pairs of factors in parentheses can be specified on one ROTATION specification. A plot is displayed for each pair of factor numbers enclosed in parentheses.

You can specify only one PLOT subcommand per analysis block. Plots are based on rotated factors. To get an unrotated factor plot, you must explicitly specify NOROTATE on the ROTATION subcommand (see Section 7.30).

The plots in Figures 7.5b and 7.14a can be augmented with two additional factor plots by specifying

```
FACTOR VARIABLES=POPSTABL TO MENTALIL
  /PLOT=EIGEN ROTATION(1 2)(1 3)(2 3).
```

7.34
Saving Factor Scores

Use the SAVE subcommand to compute and save factor scores on the active file. (Factor scores cannot be produced from matrix input.) The specifications on the SAVE subcommand include the method for calculating factor scores, how many factor scores to calculate, and a *rootname* to be used in naming the factor scores.

First, choose one of the following method keywords (see Section 7.19):

REG   *The regression method.* This is the default.
BART   *The Bartlett method.*
AR   *The Anderson-Rubin method.*
DEFAULT *Same as REG.*

Next, specify within parentheses the number of desired factor scores and a rootname up to seven characters long to be used in naming the scores. The maximum number of scores equals the order of the factor solution. You can use keyword ALL to calculate factor scores for all extracted factors.

FACTOR uses the rootname to name the factor scores sequentially, as in root1, root2, root3, etc. If you are calculating factor scores for a many-factor solution, make sure that the rootname is short enough to accommodate the number of the highest-order factor score variable. When FACTOR saves the variables on the active file, it automatically supplies a variable label indicating the method used to calculate it, its positional order, and the analysis number.

For example, the following FACTOR command saves factor scores for a study of abortion items:

```
FACTOR VARIABLES=ABDEFECT TO ABSINGLE
  /MISSING=MEANSUB
  /CRITERIA=FACTORS(2)
  /EXTRACTION=ULS
  /ROTATION=VARIMAX
  /SAVE=AR (ALL FSULS).
```

FACTOR calculates two factor scores named FSULS1 and FSULS2 using the Anderson-Rubin method and saves them on the active file.

You can use multiple SAVE subcommands for an extraction. For example,

```
FACTOR VARIABLES=ABDEFECT TO ABSINGLE
  /MISSING=MEANSUB
  /EXTRACTION=ULS
  /ROTATION=VARIMAX
  /SAVE=AR (ALL FSULS)
  /SAVE=BART (ALL BFAC).
```

saves two sets of factor scores. The first set is computed using the Anderson-Rubin method and the second is computed using the Bartlett method.

7.35
Reading and Writing Matrices

You can read either the correlation matrix or factor loadings into FACTOR by specifying *one* of the following keywords on the READ subcommand.

CORRELATION *Read the correlation matrix. This is the default.*
FACTOR(nf) *Read the factor matrix. nf indicates the number of factors in the analysis.*
DEFAULT *Same as CORRELATION.*

You can enter a correlation matrix in lower-triangular form if it contains a diagonal of *1*'s by specifying the keyword TRIANGLE following the keyword CORRELATION on the READ subcommand, as in

```
/READ=CORRELATION TRIANGLE
```

When you read a correlation or factor loading matrix with FACTOR, you must first specify a DATA LIST MATRIX command that points to the file containing the matrix materials and names the variables that will be read. If you supply an N command, FACTOR is able to calculate significance levels for the extraction techniques that use chi-square as a test statistic for the adequacy of the model and Bartlett's test of sphericity, which is available with the KMO keyword on the PRINT subcommand.

When FACTOR reads correlation matrices written by other procedures such as CORRELATION, it skips the record or matrix of n's and prints a message for each line of the matrix of n's.

The following SPSS/PC+ commands read a correlation matrix from an external file:

```
DATA LIST MATRIX FILE='file name' / X1 TO X10.
FACTOR READ/VARIABLES=X1 TO X10.
```

Use the WRITE subcommand with one of the following keywords to write the correlation matrix or the factor loadings to a specified file:

CORRELATION *Write the correlation matrix. This is the default.*
FACTOR *Write the factor matrix.*
DEFAULT *Same as CORRELATION.*

The matrix is written to the results file specified on the SET command (by default, SPSS.PRC).

7.36
Annotated Example   The following SPSS/PC+ commands produce the output in Figures 7.4a, 7.5a, 7.7, 7.8, 7.15a, and 7.19a:

```
DATA LIST MATRIX FREE
   /POPSTABL NEWSCIRC FEMEMPLD FARMERS RETAILNG COMMERCL INDUSTZN
   HEALTH CHLDNEGL COMMEFFC DWELGNEW MIGRNPOP UNEMPLOY MENTALIL.
N 88.
BEGIN DATA.
1.000
-.175 1.000
-.276  .616 1.000
 .369 -.625 -.637 1.000
-.127  .624  .736 -.519 1.000
-.069  .652  .589 -.306  .727 1.000
-.106  .712  .742 -.545  .785  .911 1.000
-.149 -.030  .241 -.068  .100  .123  .129 1.000
-.039 -.171 -.589  .257 -.557 -.357 -.424 -.407 1.000
-.005  .100  .471 -.213  .452  .287  .357  .732 -.660 1.000
-.670  .188  .413 -.579  .165  .030  .203  .290 -.138  .311 1.000
-.476 -.086  .064 -.198  .007 -.068 -.024  .083  .148  .067  .505
1.000
 .137 -.373 -.689  .450 -.650 -.424 -.528 -.348  .733 -.601 -.266  .181
1.000
 .237  .046 -.237  .121 -.190 -.055 -.095 -.279  .247 -.324 -.266 -.307
 .217
1.000
END DATA.
FACTOR READ=COR TRIANGLE
   /VARIABLES=POPSTABL TO MENTALIL
   /PRINT=ALL
   /FORMAT=SORT
   /ROTATION=VARIMAX/
   /ROTATION=OBLIMIN.
FINISH.
```

- The DATA LIST command indicates the variable names used in the analysis and tells SPSS/PC+ that the data are input as a matrix.
- The N command tells SPSS/PC+ upon how many cases the matrix is based.
- The READ subcommand on the FACTOR command reads a correlation matrix in lower-triangular form (the keyword TRIANGLE).
- The VARIABLES subcommand indicates which variables can be included on subsequent subcommands.
- The PRINT subcommand specifies all possible factor results.
- The FORMAT subcommand requests that the factor loadings be ordered by magnitude.
- The first ROTATION subcommand produces an orthogonal varimax rotation. The second ROTATION subcommand requests an oblique oblimin rotation.

Contents _____

8 Cluster Analysis: Procedure CLUSTER

Despite the old adage that opposites attract, it appears instead that likes cluster together. Birds of a feather, yuppies, and many other animate and inanimate objects that share similar characteristics are found together. By studying such clusters, one can determine the characteristics the objects share, as well as those in which they differ. In statistics, the search for relatively homogeneous groups of objects is called *cluster analysis.*

In biology, cluster analysis is used to classify animals and plants. This is called numerical taxonomy. In medicine, cluster analysis is used to identify diseases and their stages. For example, by examining patients who are diagnosed as depressed, one finds that there are several distinct subgroups of patients with different types of depression. In marketing, cluster analysis is used to identify persons with similar buying habits. By examining their characteristics, one may be able to target future marketing strategies more efficiently. See Romesburg (1984) for more examples of the use of cluster analysis.

Although both cluster analysis and discriminant analysis classify objects or cases into categories, discriminant analysis requires you to know group membership for the cases used to derive the classification rule. For example, if you are interested in distinguishing among several disease groups, cases with known diagnoses must be available. Then, based on cases whose group membership is known, discriminant analysis derives a rule for allocating undiagnosed patients. In cluster analysis, group membership for all cases is unknown. In fact, even the number of groups is often unknown. The goal of cluster analysis is to identify homogeneous groups or clusters.

In this chapter the fundamentals of cluster analysis are illustrated using a subset of data presented in a Consumer Reports (1983) survey of beer. Each of 20 beers is characterized in terms of cost per 12 ounces, alcohol content, sodium content, and the number of calories per 12-ounce serving. From these variables is it possible to identify several distinct subgroups of beer?

8.1
BASIC STEPS

As in other statistical procedures, a number of decisions must be made before one embarks on the actual analysis. Which variables will serve as the basis for cluster formation? How will the distance between cases be measured? What criteria will be used for combining cases into clusters?

Selecting the variables to include in an analysis is always crucial. If important variables are excluded, poor or misleading findings may result. For example, in a regression analysis of salary, if variables such as education and experience are not included, the results may be questionable. In cluster analysis, the initial choice of variables determines the characteristics that can be used to identify subgroups. If one is interested in clustering schools within a city and does not include variables like the number of students or the number of teachers, size is automatically excluded as a criterion for establishing clusters. By excluding all measures of taste or quality from the beer data, only physical characteristics and price will determine which beers are deemed similar.

8.2
How Alike are the Cases?

The concepts of distance and similarity are basic to many statistical techniques. Distance is a measure of how far apart two objects are, and similarity measures closeness. Distance measures are small and similarity measures are large for cases that are similar. In cluster analysis, these concepts are especially important, since cases are grouped on the basis of their "nearness." There are many different definitions of distance and similarity. Selection of a distance measure should be based both on the properties of the measure and on the algorithm for cluster formation. See Section 8.11 for further discussion of distance measures.

To see how a simple distance measure is computed, consider Table 8.2a, which shows the values of calories and cost for two of the beers. There is a 13-calorie and 5-cent difference between the two beers. This information can be combined into a single index or distance measure in many different ways. A commonly used index is the squared *Euclidean distance,* which is the sum of the squared differences over all of the variables. In this example, the squared Euclidean distance is 13^2+5^2, or 194.

Table 8.2a   Values of calories and cost for two beers

	Calories	Cost
Budweiser	144	43
Lowenbrau	157	48

The squared Euclidean distance has the disadvantage that it depends on the units of measurement for the variables. For example, if the cost were given as pennies per ounce instead of per twelve ounces, the distance measure would change. Another disadvantage is that when variables are measured on different scales, as in this example, variables that are measured in larger numbers will contribute more to the distance than variables that are recorded in smaller numbers. For example, the 13-calorie difference contributes much more to the distance score than does the 5-cent difference in cost.

One means of circumventing this problem is to express all variables in standardized form. That is, all variables have a mean of 0 and a standard deviation of 1. This is not always the best strategy, however, since the variability of a particular measure can provide useful information (see Sneath and Sokal, 1973).

Table 8.2b shows the Z scores for calories and cost for Budweiser and Lowenbrau based on the means and standard deviations for all twenty beers. The squared Euclidean distance based on the standardized variables is $(0.38-0.81)^2+(-0.46-(-0.11))^2$, or 0.307. The differences in calories and cost are now weighted equally.

Table 8.2b   Z scores for the calories and cost variables

	Calories	Cost
Budweiser	0.38	-0.46
Lowenbrau	0.81	-0.11

8.3
Forming Clusters

Just as there are many methods for calculating distances between objects, there are many methods for combining objects into clusters. A commonly used method for forming clusters is hierarchical cluster analysis, using one of two methods: agglomerative, or divisive. In *agglomerative* hierarchical clustering, clusters are formed by grouping cases into bigger and bigger clusters until all cases are members of a single cluster. *Divisive* hierarchical clustering starts out with all cases grouped into a single cluster and splits clusters until there are as many clusters as there are cases. For a discussion of nonhierarchical clustering methods, see Everitt (1980).

8.4
Agglomerative Clustering

Before discussing the rules for forming clusters, consider what happens during the steps of agglomerative hierarchical cluster analysis. At the first step all cases are considered separate clusters: there are as many clusters as there are cases. At the second step, two of the cases are combined into a single cluster. At the third step, either a third case is added to the cluster already containing two cases, or two additional cases are merged into a new cluster. At every step, either individual cases are added to clusters or already existing clusters are combined. Once a cluster is formed, it cannot be split; it can only be combined with other clusters. Thus, hierarchical clustering methods do not allow cases to separate from clusters to which they have been allocated. For example, if two beers are deemed members of the same cluster at the first step, they will always be members of the same cluster, although they may be combined with additional cases at a later step.

8.5
Criteria for Combining Clusters

There are many criteria for deciding which cases or clusters should be combined at each step. All of these criteria are based on a matrix of either distances or similarities between pairs of cases. One of the simplest methods is *single linkage*, sometimes called "nearest neighbor." The first two cases combined are those that have the smallest distance (or largest similarity) between them. The distance between the new cluster and individual cases is then computed as the minimum distance between an individual case and a case in the cluster. The distances between cases that have not been joined do not change. At every step, the distance between two clusters is the distance between their two closest points.

Another commonly used method is called *complete linkage*, or the "furthest neighbor" technique. In this method, the distance between two clusters is calculated as the distance between their two furthest points. Other methods for combining clusters available in SPSS/PC+ are described in Section 8.11.

8.6
PERFORMING A CLUSTER ANALYSIS

Before considering other distance measures and methods of combining clusters, consider Figure 8.6a, which contains the matrix of squared Euclidean distance coefficients for all possible pairs of the 20 beers, based on standardized calories, sodium, alcohol, and cost. The standardized values were computed by procedure DESCRIPTIVES. The listing of the original and standardized values for these variables is shown in Figure 8.6b.

Figure 8.6a   The squared Euclidean distance coefficient matrix

```
SET WIDTH=WIDE.
DATA LIST
  /ID 1-2 RATING 3 BEER 4-24 (A) ORIGIN 25 AVAIL 26
    PRICE 27-30 COST 31-34 CALORIES 35-37 SODIUM 38-39
    ALCOHOL 40-42 CLASS 43 LIGHT 44.
FORMATS PRICE COST (F4.2) ALCOHOL (F3.1).
MISSING VALUES CLASS(0).
BEGIN DATA.
lines of data
END DATA.
DESCRIPTIVES CALORIES SODIUM ALCOHOL COST
  /OPTIONS=3.
FORMATS ZCALORIE ZSODIUM ZALCOHOL ZCOST (F8.6).
CLUSTER ZCALORIE ZSODIUM ZALCOHOL ZCOST
  /PRINT=DISTANCE
  /METHOD=COMPLETE.
```

Squared Euclidean Dissimilarity Coefficient Matrix

Case	1	2	3	4	5	6	7	8
2	.4922							
3	.3749	.5297						
4	7.0040	8.2298	4.8424					
5	6.1889	7.0897	4.4835	.8700				
6	2.5848	1.6534	3.7263	17.0154	15.2734			
7	4.0720	1.8735	3.1573	12.1251	11.5371	3.1061		
8	3.3568	1.5561	3.6380	14.8000	12.0038	1.3526	2.0742	
9	3.0662	5.4473	4.9962	11.4721	9.5339	7.4577	13.3723	9.6850
10	3.9181	6.8702	5.8179	11.5391	10.0663	8.9551	15.7993	11.5019
11	.2474	.3160	.7568	8.4698	6.8353	1.8432	3.6498	1.9953
12	2.5940	4.1442	4.4322	12.1519	9.1534	5.4981	11.2604	6.4385
13	1.1281	2.8432	1.7663	5.9995	4.9519	6.0530	9.0610	6.8673
14	5.6782	5.3399	4.2859	4.2382	1.6427	11.5628	8.6397	7.0724
15	8.3245	10.1947	6.6075	.7483	.6064	19.5528	16.0117	16.9620
16	16.4081	19.7255	20.8463	33.3380	28.0650	17.6015	32.1339	20.5466
17	.5952	.6788	1.4051	10.0509	7.9746	1.6159	4.3782	1.8230
18	1.9394	.6307	2.1757	11.9216	9.5828	1.2688	1.7169	.3092
19	13.1887	17.6915	16.7104	23.2048	19.8574	19.0673	30.9530	22.3479
20	4.4010	7.4360	6.2635	10.8241	9.1372	10.4511	16.4825	12.7426

Case	9	10	11	12	13	14	15	16
10	.9349							
11	3.4745	4.5082						
12	.6999	1.5600	2.2375					
13	1.6931	1.3437	1.6100	1.6536				
14	10.2578	10.9762	5.1046	7.8646	5.4275			
15	10.2201	10.3631	9.6179	10.9556	5.9694	4.1024		
16	8.6771	6.9127	15.2083	7.1851	12.2231	24.6793	29.7992	
17	3.3828	4.2251	.1147	1.8315	1.7851	5.6395	10.9812	13.1806
18	7.3607	9.4595	1.0094	4.9491	5.0762	5.9553	13.7962	20.0105
19	4.6046	3.0565	13.4011	5.3477	7.9175	20.5149	19.3851	2.8209
20	.3069	.7793	5.1340	1.5271	1.9902	10.8954	9.0403	9.0418

Case	17	18	19
18	1.0802		
19	12.3170	20.1156	
20	5.1327	10.0114	3.6382

Figure 8.6b   Original and standardized values for the 20 beers from procedure LIST

```
DESCRIPTIVES CALORIES SODIUM ALCOHOL COST
  /OPTIONS=3.
FORMATS ZCALORIE ZSODIUM ZALCOHOL ZCOST (F5.2).
LIST VAR=ID BEER CALORIES SODIUM ALCOHOL
          COST ZCALORIE ZSODIUM ZALCOHOL ZCOST.
```

ID	BEER	CALORIES	SODIUM	ALCOHOL	COST	ZCALORIE	ZSODIUM	ZALCOHOL	ZCOST
1	BUDWEISER	144	15	4.7	.43	.38	.01	.34	-.46
2	SCHLITZ	151	19	4.9	.43	.61	.62	.61	-.46
3	LOWENBRAU	157	15	4.9	.48	.81	.01	.61	-.11
4	KRONENBOURG	170	7	5.2	.73	1.24	-1.21	1.00	1.62
5	HEINEKEN	152	11	5.0	.77	.65	-.60	.74	1.90
6	OLD MILWAUKEE	145	23	4.6	.28	.42	1.22	.21	-1.51
7	AUGSBERGER	175	24	5.5	.40	1.41	1.38	1.40	-.67
8	STROHS BOHEMIAN STYLE	149	27	4.7	.42	.55	1.83	.34	-.53
9	MILLER LITE	99	10	4.3	.43	-1.10	-.75	-.18	-.46
10	BUDWEISER LIGHT	113	8	3.7	.44	-.64	-1.06	-.97	-.39
11	COORS	140	18	4.6	.44	.25	.46	.21	-.39
12	COORS LIGHT	102	15	4.1	.46	-1.00	.01	-.45	-.25
13	MICHELOB LIGHT	135	11	4.2	.50	.09	-.60	-.32	.02
14	BECKS	150	19	4.7	.76	.58	.62	.34	1.83
15	KIRIN	149	6	5.0	.79	.55	-1.36	.74	2.04
16	PABST EXTRA LIGHT	68	15	2.3	.38	-2.13	.01	-2.82	-.81
17	HAMMS	136	19	4.4	.43	.12	.62	-.05	-.46
18	HEILEMANS OLD STYLE	144	24	4.9	.43	.38	1.38	.61	-.46
19	OLYMPIA GOLD LIGHT	72	6	2.9	.46	-2.00	-1.36	-2.03	-.25
20	SCHLITZ LIGHT	97	7	4.2	.47	-1.17	-1.21	-.32	-.18

Number of cases read =   20   Number of cases listed =   20

The first entry in Figure 8.6a is the distance between Case 1 and Case 2, Budweiser and Schlitz. This can be calculated from the standardized values in Figure 8.6b as

$$D^2=(0.38-0.61)^2+(0.01-0.62)^2+(0.34-0.61)^2+(-0.46-(-0.46))^2 \\ =0.49 \qquad \textbf{Equation 8.6}$$

Since the distance between pairs of cases is symmetric (that is, the distance between Case 3 and Case 4 is the same as the distance between Case 4 and Case 3), only the lower half of the distance matrix is displayed.

8.7 Icicle Plots

Once the distance matrix has been calculated, the actual formation of clusters can commence. Figure 8.7a summarizes a cluster analysis that uses the complete linkage method. This type of figure is sometimes called a vertical icicle plot because it resembles a row of icicles hanging from eaves.

Figure 8.7a Vertical icicle plot for the 20 beers

```
CLUSTER ZCALORIE ZSODIUM ZALCOHOL ZCOST
  /ID=BEER
  /METHOD=COMPLETE/
  /PLOT=VICICLE.
```

```
Vertical Icicle Plot using Complete Linkage

   (Down) Number of Clusters  (Across) Case Label and number

    O  P  M  C  B  S  M  B  K  H  K  A  H  S  O  H  C  S  L  B
    L  A  I  O  U  C  I  E  I  E  R  U  E  T  L  A  O  C  O  U
    Y  B  C  O  D  H  L  C  R  I  O  G  I  R  D  M  O  H  W  D
    M  S  H  R  W  L  L  K  I  N  N  S  L  O     M  R  L  E  W
    P  T  E  S  E  I  E  S  N  E  E  B  E  H  M  S  S  I  N  E
    I     L     I  T  R        K  N  E  M  S  I        T  B  I
    A  E  O  L  S  Z           E  B  R  A     L        Z  R  S
       X  B  I  E     L        N  O  G  N  B  W           A  E
    G  T     G  R  L  I           U  E  S  O  A           U  R
    O  R  L  H     I  T           R  R     H  U
    L  A  I  T  L  G  E           G     O  E  K
    D     G     I  H                    L  M  E
       L  H     G  T                    D  I  E
    L  I  T     H                          A
    I  G        T                       S  N
    G  H                                T
    H  T                                Y  S
    T                                   L  T
                                        E  Y
                                           L

    1  1  1  1  1  2     1  1           1        1  1
    9  6  3  2  0  0  9  4  5  5  4  7  8  8  6  7  1  2  3  1
 1 +XXXXXXXXXXXXXXXXXXXXXXXXXXXXXXXXXXXXXXXXXXXXXXXXXXXXXXXXXX
 2 +XXXX  XXXXXXXXXXXXXXXXXXXXXXXXXXXXXXXXXXXXXXXXXXXXXXXXXXXX
 3 +XXXX  XXXXXXXXXXXXXXXXXXXXXXXXX  XXXXXXXXXXXXXXXXXXXXXXXXX
 4 +XXXX  XXXXXXXXXXXXX  XXXXXXXXXX  XXXXXXXXXXXXXXXXXXXXXXXXX
 5 +XXXX  XXXXXXXXXXXXX  XXXXXXXXXX  XXXXXXXXXX  XXXXXXXXXXXXX
 6 +XXXX  XXXXXXXXXXXXX  X  XXXXXXX  XXXXXXXXXX  XXXXXXXXXXXXX
 7 +XXXX  XXXXXXXXXXXXX  X  XXXXXXX  X  XXXXXXX  XXXXXXXXXXXXX
 8 +X  X  XXXXXXXXXXXXX  X  XXXXXXX  X  XXXXXXX  XXXXXXXXXXXXX
 9 +X  X  X  XXXXXXXXXX  X  XXXXXXX  X  XXXXXXX  XXXXXXXXXXXXX
10 +X  X  X  X  XXXXXXX  X  XXXXXXX  X  XXXXXXX  XXXXXXXXXXXXX
11 +X  X  X  X  XXXXXXX  X  XXXXXXX  X  XXXXXXX  XXXX  XXXXXXX
12 +X  X  X  X  XXXXXXX  X  XXXXXXX  X  XXXX  X  XXXX  XXXXXXX
13 +X  X  X  X  X  XXXX  X  XXXXXXX  X  XXXX  X  XXXX  XXXXXXX
14 +X  X  X  X  X  XXXX  X  XXXX  X  X  XXXX  X  XXXX  XXXXXXX
15 +X  X  X  X  X  XXXX  X  X  X  X  X  XXXX  X  XXXX  XXXXXXX
16 +X  X  X  X  X  XXXX  X  X  X  X  X  XXXX  X  XXXX  X  XXXX
17 +X  X  X  X  X  XXXX  X  X  X  X  X  XXXX  X  XXXX  X  X  X
18 +X  X  X  X  X  XXXX  X  X  X  X  X  X  X  X  XXXX  X  X  X
19 +X  X  X  X  X  X  X  X  X  X  X  X  X  X  X  XXXX  X  X  X
```

The columns of Figure 8.7a correspond to the objects being clustered. They are identified both by a sequential number ranging from 1 to the number of cases and, when possible, by the labels of the objects. Thus, the first column corresponds to beer number 19, Olympia Gold Light, while the last column corresponds to the first beer in the file, Budweiser. In order to follow the sequence of steps in the cluster analysis, the figure is read from bottom to top.

As previously described, all cases are considered initially as individual clusters. Since there are 20 beers in this example, there are 20 clusters. At the first step the two "closest" cases are combined into a single cluster, resulting in 19 clusters. The bottom line of Figure 8.7a shows these 19 clusters. Each case is represented by a single X separated by blanks. The two cases that have been merged into a single cluster, Coors and Hamm's, do not have blanks separating them. Instead, they are represented by consecutive X's. The row labeled 18 in Figure 8.7a corresponds to the solution at the next step, when 18 clusters are present. At this step Miller Lite and Schlitz Light are merged into a single cluster. Thus, at this point there are 18 clusters, 16 consisting of individual beers and 2 consisting of pairs of beers. At each subsequent step an additional cluster is formed by joining either a case to an already existing multicase cluster, two separate cases into a single cluster, or two multicase clusters.

For example, the row labeled 5 in Figure 8.7a corresponds to a solution that has five clusters. Beers 19 and 16, the very light beers, form one cluster; beers 13, 12, 10, 20, and 9 form the next. These beers, Michelob Light, Coors Light, Budweiser Light, Schlitz Light, and Miller Light, are all light beers, but not as light as the two in the first cluster. The third cluster consists of Beck's, Kirin, Heineken, and Kronenbourg. These are all imported beers. Although no variable in this example explicitly indicates whether beers are domestic or imported, the cost variable (see Figure 8.6b) causes the imported beers to cluster together since they are quite a bit more expensive than the domestic ones. A fourth cluster consists of Augsburger, Heileman's Old Style, Stroh's Bohemian Style, and Old Milwaukee. Inspection of Figure 8.7b shows that all of these beers are distinguished by high sodium content. The last cluster consists of five beers: Hamm's, Coors, Schlitz, Lowenbrau, and Budweiser. These beers share the distinction of being average. That is, they are neither particulary high nor particularly low on the variables measured. Note from Figure 8.7b that, based on the standard deviations, beers in the same cluster, when compared to all beers, are more homogeneous on the variables measured.

Figure 8.7b Cluster characteristics (table from SPSS/PC+ TABLES)

```
CLUSTER ZCALORIE ZSODIUM ZALCOHOL ZCOST
  /ID=BEER
  /METHOD=COMPLETE(CLUSMEM)
  /SAVE=CLUSTER(5).
VALUE LABELS CLUSMEM5 1 'AVERAGE' 2 'EXPENSIVE' 3 'HIGH NA'
   4 'LIGHT' 5 'VERY LIGHT'.
TABLES OBSERVATION=COST CALORIES ALCOHOL SODIUM
  /FTOTAL=TOTAL
  /FORMAT=CWIDTH(10,9)
  /TABLE=CLUSMEM5+TOTAL BY CALORIES+COST+ALCOHOL+SODIUM
  /STATISTICS=MEAN STDDEV.
```

	CALORIES PER 12 FLUID OUNCES		COST PER 12 FLUID OUNCES		ALCOHOL BY VOLUME (IN %)		SODIUM PER 12 FLUID OUNCES IN MG	
	Mean	Standard Deviation	Mean	Standard Deviation	Mean	Standard Deviation	Mean	Standard Deviation
CLUSMEM5								
1	146	8	.44	.02	4.7	.2	17	2
2	155	10	.76	.03	5.0	.2	11	6
3	153	15	.38	.07	4.9	.4	25	2
4	109	16	.46	.03	4.1	.2	10	3
5	70	3	.42	.06	2.6	.4	11	6
TOTAL	132	30	.50	.14	4.4	.8	15	7

Cluster formation continues in Figure 8.7a until all cases are merged into a single cluster, as shown in the first row. Thus, all steps of the cluster analysis are displayed in Figure 8.7a. If we were clustering people instead of beers, the last row would be individual persons, higher up they would perhaps merge into families, these into neighborhoods, and so forth. Often there is not one single, meaningful cluster solution, but many, depending on what is of interest.

8.8
The Agglomeration Schedule

The results of the cluster analysis are summarized in the *agglomeration schedule* in Figure 8.8, which contains the number of cases or clusters being combined at each stage. The first line is Stage 1, the 19-cluster solution. Beers 11 and 17 are combined at this stage, as shown in the columns labeled **Clusters Combined.** The squared Euclidean distance between these two beers is displayed in the column labeled **Coefficient.** Since this is the first step, this coefficient is identical to the distance measure in Figure 8.6a for Cases 11 and 17. The last column indicates at which stage another case or cluster is combined with this one. For example, at the tenth stage, Case 1 is merged with Cases 11 and 17 into a single cluster. The column entitled **Stage Cluster 1st Appears** indicates at which stage a cluster is first formed. For example, the entry of 4 at Stage 5 indicates that Case 1 was first involved in a merge in the previous step (Stage 4). From the line for Stage 4, you can see that, at this point, Case 1 was involved in a merge with Case 3. From the last column of Stage 5 we see that the new cluster (Cases 1, 2, and 3) is next involved in a merge at Stage 10, where the cases combine with Cases 11 and 17.

Figure 8.8   Agglomeration schedule using complete linkage

```
CLUSTER ZCALORIE ZSODIUM ZALCOHOL ZCOST
   /ID=BEER
   /PRINT=SCHEDULE
   /METHOD=COMPLETE.
```

Agglomeration Schedule using Complete Linkage

Stage	Clusters Combined Cluster 1	Cluster 2	Coefficient	Stage Cluster 1st Appears Cluster 1	Cluster 2	Next Stage
1	11	17	.114695	0	0	10
2	9	20	.306903	0	0	8
3	8	18	.309227	0	0	9
4	1	3	.374859	0	0	5
5	1	2	.529696	4	0	10
6	5	15	.606378	0	0	7
7	4	5	.870016	0	6	15
8	9	10	.934909	2	0	11
9	6	8	1.352617	0	3	14
10	1	11	1.405148	5	1	16
11	9	12	1.559987	8	0	12
12	9	13	1.990205	11	0	17
13	16	19	2.820896	0	0	19
14	6	7	3.106108	9	0	16
15	4	14	4.238164	7	0	17
16	1	6	4.378198	10	14	18
17	4	9	12.151937	15	12	18
18	1	4	19.552841	16	17	19
19	1	16	33.338028	18	13	0

The information in Figure 8.8 that is not available in the icicle plot is the value of the distance between the two most dissimilar points of the clusters being combined at each stage. By examining these values, you can get an idea of how unlike the clusters being combined are. Small coefficients indicate that fairly homogeneous clusters are being merged. Large coefficients indicate that clusters containing quite dissimilar members are being combined. The actual value depends on the clustering method and the distance measure used.

These coefficients can also be used for guidance in deciding how many clusters are needed to represent the data. One usually wishes to stop agglomeration as soon as the increase between two adjacent steps becomes large. For example, in Figure 8.8 there is a fairly large increase in the value of the distance measure from a four-cluster to a three-cluster solution (Stages 16 and 17).

8.9
The Dendrogram

Another way of visually representing the steps in a hierarchical clustering solution is with a display called a *dendrogram*. The dendrogram shows the clusters being combined and the values of the coefficients at each step. The dendrogram produced by the SPSS/PC+ CLUSTER procedure does not plot actual distances but rescales them to numbers between 0 and 25. Thus, the ratio of the distances between steps is preserved. The scale displayed at the top of the figure does not correspond to actual distance values.

To understand how a dendrogram is constructed, consider a simple four-beer example. Figure 8.9a contains the icicle plot for the clustering of Kirin, Beck's, Old Milwaukee, and Budweiser. From the icicle plot, you can see that at the first step Budweiser and Old Milwaukee are combined, at the second step Beck's and Kirin are merged, and all four beers are merged into a single cluster at the last step.

Figure 8.9a   Vertical icicle plot for the four-beer example

```
CLUSTER ZCALORIE ZSODIUM ZALCOHOL ZCOST
  /ID=BEER
  /METHOD=COMPLETE
  /PLOT=VICICLE.
```

```
Vertical Icicle Plot using Complete Linkage

   (Down) Number of Clusters  (Across) Case Label and number

         K  B  O  B
         I  E  L  U
         R  C  D  D
         I  K     W
         N  S  M  E
               I  I
               L  S
               W  E
               A  R
               U
               K
               E
               E


         4  3  2  1
      1 +XXXXXXXXXX
      2 +XXXX  XXXX
      3 +X  X  XXXX
```

The distances at which the beers are combined are shown in the agglomeration schedule in Figure 8.9b. From this schedule, we see that the distance between Budweiser and Old Milwaukee is 2.017 when they are combined. Similarly, when Beck's and Kirin are combined, their distance is 6.323. Since the method of complete linkage is used, the distance coefficient displayed for the last stage is the largest distance between a member of the Budweiser-Milwaukee cluster and a member of the Beck's-Kirin cluster. This distance is 16.789.

Figure 8.9b   Agglomeration schedule for the four-beer example

```
CLUSTER ZCALORIE ZSODIUM ZALCOHOL ZCOST
  /ID=BEER
  /PRINT=SCHEDULE
  /METHOD=COMPLETE.
```

Agglomeration Schedule using Complete Linkage

Stage	Clusters Combined Cluster 1	Cluster 2	Coefficient	Stage Cluster 1st Appears Cluster 1	Cluster 2	Next Stage
1	1	2	2.017018	0	0	3
2	3	4	6.323439	0	0	3
3	1	3	16.789215	1	2	0

The information in Figure 8.9b is displayed in the dendrogram in Figure 8.9c, which is read from left to right. Vertical lines denote joined clusters. The position of the line on the scale indicates the distance at which clusters were joined. Since the distances are rescaled to fall in the range of 1 to 25, the largest distance, 16.8, corresponds to the value of 25. The smallest distance, 2.017, corresponds to the value 1. Thus, the second distance (6.32) corresponds to a value of about 8. Note that the ratio of the rescaled distances is, after the first, the same as the ratios of the original distances.

The first two clusters that are joined are Budweiser and Old Milwaukee. They are connected by a line that is 1 unit from the origin since this is the rescaled distance between these points. When Beck's and Kirin are joined, the line that connects them is 8 units from the origin. Similarly, when these two clusters are merged into a single cluster, the line that connects them is 25 units from the origin. Thus, the dendrogram indicates not only which clusters are joined but also the distance at which they are joined.

Figure 8.9c   Dendrogram for the four-beer example

```
CLUSTER ZCALORIE ZSODIUM ZALCOHOL ZCOST
  /ID=BEER
  /METHOD=COMPLETE
  /PLOT=DENDROGRAM.
```

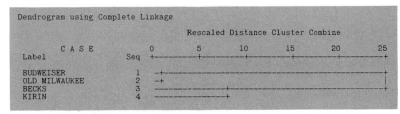

Figure 8.9d contains the dendrogram for the complete 20-beer example. Since many of the distances at the beginning stages are similar in magnitude, one cannot tell the sequence in which some of the early clusters are formed. However, at the last three stages the distances at which clusters are being combined are fairly large. Looking at the dendrogram, it appears that the five-cluster solution (very light beers, light beers, imported beers, high-sodium beers, and "average" beers) may be appropriate since it is easily interpretable and occurs before the distances at which clusters are combined become too large.

Figure 8.9d   Dendrogram using complete linkage for the 20 beers

```
CLUSTER ZCALORIE ZSODIUM ZALCOHOL ZCOST
   /ID=BEER
   /METHOD=COMPLETE
   /PLOT=DENDROGRAM.
```

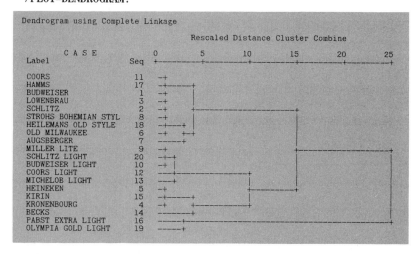

8.10
Some Additional Displays and Modifications

The agglomeration schedule, the icicle plot, and the dendrogram illustrate the results produced by a hierarchical clustering solution. Several variations of these plots may also be useful. For example, when there are many cases, the initial steps of the cluster analysis may not be of particular interest. You might wany to display solutions for only certain numbers of clusters. Or you might want to see the results at every kth step. Figure 8.10a contains the icicle plot of results at every fifth step.

Figure 8.10a   Icicle plot with results at every fifth step

```
CLUSTER ZCALORIE ZSODIUM ZALCOHOL ZCOST
   /ID=BEER
   /METHOD=COMPLETE
   /PLOT=VICICLE(1,19,5).
```

When there are many cases, all of them may not fit across the top of a single page. In this situation it may be useful to turn the icicle plot on its side. This is called a horizontal icicle plot. Figure 8.10b contains the horizontal icicle plot corresponding to Figure 8.7a.

Figure 8.10b   Horizontal icicle plot

```
CLUSTER ZCALORIE ZSODIUM ZALCOHOL ZCOST
  /ID=BEER
  /METHOD=COMPLETE
  /PLOT=HICICLE.
```

```
Horizontal Icicle Plot Using Complete Linkage

                                  Number of Clusters

                                       1111111111
              C A S E           1234567890123456789
    Label                 Seq  +++++++++++++++++++

OLYMPIA GOLD LIGHT        19   XXXXXXXXXXXXXXXXXXX
                               XXXXXXX
                               XXXXXX
PABST EXTRA LIGHT         16   XXXXXXXXXXXXXXXXXXX
                               X
                               X
MICHELOB LIGHT            13   XXXXXXXXXXXXXXXXXXX
                               XXXXXXXX
                               XXXXXXXX
COORS LIGHT               12   XXXXXXXXXXXXXXXXXXX
                               XXXXXXXXX
                               XXXXXXXXX
BUDWEISER LIGHT           10   XXXXXXXXXXXXXXXXXXX
                               XXXXXXXXXXXX
                               XXXXXXXXXXXX
SCHLITZ LIGHT             20   XXXXXXXXXXXXXXXXXXX
                               XXXXXXXXXXXXXXXXX
                               XXXXXXXXXXXXXXXXX
MILLER LITE                9   XXXXXXXXXXXXXXXXXXX
                               XXX
                               XXX
BECKS                     14   XXXXXXXXXXXXXXXXXXX
                               XXXXX
                               XXXXX
KIRIN                     15   XXXXXXXXXXXXXXXXXXX
                               XXXXXXXXXXXXX
                               XXXXXXXXXXXXX
HEINEKEN                   5   XXXXXXXXXXXXXXXXXXX
                               XXXXXXXXXXXXX
                               XXXXXXXXXXXXX
KRONENBOURG                4   XXXXXXXXXXXXXXXXXXX
                               XX
                               XX
AUGSBERGER                 7   XXXXXXXXXXXXXXXXXXX
                               XXXXXX
                               XXXXXX
HEILEMANS OLD STYLE       18   XXXXXXXXXXXXXXXXXXX
                               XXXXXXXXXXXXXXXX
                               XXXXXXXXXXXXXXXX
STROHS BOHEMIAN STYL       8   XXXXXXXXXXXXXXXXXXX
                               XXXXXXXXXXX
                               XXXXXXXXXXX
OLD MILWAUKEE              6   XXXXXXXXXXXXXXXXXXX
                               XXXX
                               XXXX
HAMMS                     17   XXXXXXXXXXXXXXXXXXX
                               XXXXXXXXXXXXXXXXX
                               XXXXXXXXXXXXXXXXX
COORS                     11   XXXXXXXXXXXXXXXXXXX
                               XXXXXXXXXX
                               XXXXXXXXXX
SCHLITZ                    2   XXXXXXXXXXXXXXXXXXX
                               XXXXXXXXXXXXXX
                               XXXXXXXXXXXXXX
LOWENBRAU                  3   XXXXXXXXXXXXXXXXXXX
                               XXXXXXXXXXXXXX
                               XXXXXXXXXXXXXX
BUDWEISER                  1   XXXXXXXXXXXXXXXXXXX
```

Although the composition of clusters at any stage can be discerned from the icicle plots, it is often helpful to display the information in tabular form. Figure 8.10c contains the cluster memberships for the cases at different stages of the solution. From Figure 8.10c, you can easily tell which clusters cases belong to in the two- to five-cluster solutions.

Figure 8.10c Cluster membership at different stages

```
CLUSTER ZCALORIE ZSODIUM ZALCOHOL ZCOST
  /ID=BEER
  /PRINT=CLUSTER(2,5)
  /METHOD=COMPLETE.
```

```
Cluster Membership of Cases using Complete Linkage

                                    Number of Clusters

   Label                 Case     5     4     3     2

   BUDWEISER               1       1     1     1     1
   SCHLITZ                 2       1     1     1     1
   LOWENBRAU               3       1     1     1     1
   KRONENBOURG             4       2     2     2     1
   HEINEKEN                5       2     2     2     1
   OLD MILWAUKEE           6       3     1     1     1
   AUGSBERGER              7       3     1     1     1
   STROHS BOHEMIAN STYL    8       3     1     1     1
   MILLER LITE             9       4     3     2     1
   BUDWEISER LIGHT        10       4     3     2     1
   COORS                  11       1     1     1     1
   COORS LIGHT            12       4     3     2     1
   MICHELOB LIGHT         13       4     3     2     1
   BECKS                  14       2     2     2     1
   KIRIN                  15       2     2     2     1
   PABST EXTRA LIGHT      16       5     4     3     2
   HAMMS                  17       1     1     1     1
   HEILEMANS OLD STYLE    18       3     1     1     1
   OLYMPIA GOLD LIGHT     19       5     4     3     2
   SCHLITZ LIGHT          20       4     3     2     1
```

8.11
More on Calculating Distances and Similarities

There are many methods for estimating the distance or similarity between two cases. But even before these measures are computed, you must decide whether the variables need to be rescaled. When the variables have different scales, such as cents and calories, and they are not standardized, any distance measure will reflect primarily the contributions of variables measured in the large units. For example, the beer data variables were standardized prior to cluster analysis to have a mean of 0 and a standard deviation of 1. Besides standardization to Z-scores, variables can be standardized by dividing by just the standard deviation, the range, the mean, or the maximum. See Romesburg (1984) or Anderberg (1973) for further discussion.

Based on the transformed data, it is possible to calculate many different types of distance and similarity measures. Different distance and similarity measures weight data characteristics differently. The choice among the measures should be based on which differences or similarities in the data are important for a particular application. For example, if one is clustering animal bones, what may matter is not the actual differences in bone size but relationships among the dimensions, since we know that even animals of the same species differ in size. Bones with the same relationship between length and diameter should be judged as similar, regardless of their absolute magnitudes. See Romesburg (1984) for further discussion.

The most commonly used distance measure, the squared Euclidean distance, has been discussed previously. Sometimes its square root, the Euclidean distance, is also used. A distance measure that is based on the absolute values of differences is the *city-block* or *Manhattan* distance. For two cases it is just the sum of the absolute differences of the values for all variables. Since the differences are not squared, large differences are not weighted as heavily as in the squared Euclidean distances. The *Chebychev* distance defines the distance between two cases as the maximum absolute difference in the values over all variables. Thus, it ignores much of the available information.

8.12
Methods for Combining Clusters

Many methods can be used to decide which cases or clusters should be combined at each step. In general, clustering methods fall into three groups: linkage methods, error sums of squares or variance methods, and centroid methods. All are based on either a matrix of distances or a matrix of similarities between pairs of cases. The methods differ in how they estimate distances between clusters at successive steps. Since the merging of clusters at each step depends on the distance measure, different distance measures can result in different cluster solutions for the same clustering method. See Milligan (1980) for comparisons of the performance of some of the different clustering methods.

One of the simplest methods for joining clusters is *single linkage,* sometimes called "nearest neighbor." The first two cases combined are those with the smallest distance, or greatest similarity, between them. The distance between the new cluster and individual cases is then computed as the minimum distance between an individual case and a case in the cluster. The distances between cases that have not been joined do not change. At every step the distance between two clusters is taken to be the distance between their two closest points.

Another commonly used method is called *complete linkage,* or the "furthest neighbor" technique. In this method the distance between two clusters is calculated as the distance between their two furthest points.

The *average linkage between groups method,* often called UPGMA (unweighted pair-group method using arithmetic averages), defines the distance between two clusters as the average of the distances between all pairs of cases in which one member of the pair is from each of the clusters. For example, if Cases 1 and 2 form cluster A and Cases 3, 4, and 5 form cluster B, the distance between clusters A and B is taken to be the average of the distances between the following pairs of cases: (1,3) (1,4) (1,5) (2,3) (2,4) (2,5). This differs from the linkage methods in that it uses information about all pairs of distances, not just the nearest or the furthest. For this reason it is usually preferred to the single and complete linkage methods for cluster analysis.

The UPGMA method considers only distances between pairs of cases in different clusters. A variant of it, *the average linkage within groups,* combines clusters so that the average distance between all cases in the resulting cluster is as small as possible. Thus, the distance between two clusters is taken to be the average of the distances between all possible pairs of cases in the resulting cluster.

Another frequently used method for cluster formation is *Ward's method.* For each cluster the means for all variables are calculated. Then for each case the squared Euclidean distance to the cluster means is calculated. These distances are summed for all of the cases. At each step, the two clusters that merge are those that result in the smallest increase in the overall sum of the squared within-cluster distances.

The *centroid method* calculates the distance between two clusters as the distance between their means for all of the variables. One disadvantage of the centroid method is that the distance at which clusters are combined can actually decrease from one step to the next. Since clusters merged at later stages are more dissimilar than those merged at early stages, this is an undesirable property.

In the centroid method, the centroid of a merged cluster is a weighted combination of the centroids of the two individual clusters, where the weights are proportional to the sizes of the clusters. In the *median method,* the two clusters being combined are weighted equally in the computation of the centroid, regardless of the number of cases in each. This allows small groups to have equal effect on the characterization of larger clusters into which they are merged. Squared Euclidean distances should be used with both centroid and median methods.

Some of the above methods, such as single and complete linkage and the average distances between and within clusters, can be used with similarity or distance measures. Other methods require particular types of distance measures. In particular, the median, centroid, and Ward's methods should use squared Euclidean distances. When similarity measures are used, the criteria for combining is reversed. That is, clusters with large similarity-based measures are merged.

8.13
Clustering Variables

In the previous example, the units used for cluster analysis were individual cases (the different brands of beer). Cluster analysis can also be used to find homogeneous groups of variables. For example, consider the 14 community variables described in Chapter 7. We could use cluster analysis to group the 88 counties included in the study and then examine the resulting clusters to establish the characteristics they share. Another approach is to cluster the 14 variables used to describe the communities. In this case, the unit used for analysis is the variable. The distance or similarity measures are computed for all pairs of variables.

Figure 8.13 contains the results of clustering the community variables using the absolute value of the correlation coefficient as a measure of similarity. The absolute value of the coefficient is used since it is a measure of the strength of the relationship. The sign indicates only the direction. If you want clusters for positively correlated variables only, the sign of the coefficient should be maintained.

Figure 8.13   Cluster analysis of the community variables

```
* CLUSTERING THE COMMUNITY VARIABLES USING THE ABSOLUTE VALUE OF
  THE CORRELATION COEFFICIENT AS A MEASURE OF SIMILARITY.
SET DISK=ON.
DATA LIST MATRIX FREE /
    POPSTABL NEWSCIRC FEMEMPLD FARMERS RETAILNG
    COMMERCL INDUSTZN HEALTH CHLDNEGL COMMEFFC
    DWELGNEW MIGRNPOP UNEMPLOY MENTALIL.
N 88.
BEGIN DATA.
1.000
 .175 1.000
 .276  .616 1.000
 .369  .625  .637 1.000
 .127  .624  .736  .519 1.000
 .069  .652  .589  .306  .727 1.000
 .106  .712  .742  .545  .785  .911 1.000
 .149  .030  .241  .068  .100  .123  .129 1.000
 .039  .171  .589  .257  .557  .357  .424  .407 1.000
 .005  .100  .471  .213  .452  .287  .357  .732  .660 1.000
 .670  .188  .413  .579  .165  .030  .203  .290  .138  .311 1.000
 .476  .086  .064  .198  .007  .068  .024  .083  .148  .067  .505
1.000
 .137  .373  .689  .450  .650  .424  .528  .348  .733  .601  .266  .181
1.000
 .237  .046  .237  .121  .190  .055  .095  .279  .247  .324  .266  .307
.217
1.000
END DATA.
CLUSTER POPSTABL TO MENTALIL
   /READ=TRIANGLE SIMILAR.
FINISH.
```

The clustering procedure is the same whether variables or cases are clustered. It starts out with as many clusters as there are variables. At each successive step, variables or clusters of variables are merged, as shown in the icicle plot in Figure 8.13.

Consider the four-cluster solution. The HEALTH, COMMEFFC, CHLDNEGL, and UNEMPLOY variables form one cluster, the FARMERS, INDUSTZN, COMMERCL, RETAILNG, FEMEMPLD, and NEWSCIRC variables form the second cluster, MENTALIL is a cluster by itself, and the fourth cluster is MIGRNPOP, DWELGNEW, and POPSTABL.

For readers of Chapter 7, this solution should appear familiar. The groupings of the variables are exactly those established by the factor analysis. The first cluster is the WELFARE factor, the second the URBANISM, and the fourth INFLUX. In both cases the extent of mental illness does not appear to be related to the remainder of the variables.

This is not a chance occurrence. Although factor analysis has an underlying theoretical model and cluster analysis is much more ad hoc, both identify related groups of variables. However, factor analysis allows variables to be either positively or negatively related to a factor. Cluster analysis can be restricted to search only for positive associations between variables. Thus, if the absolute values of the correlation coefficients are not taken, variables that correlate negatively with a factor do not appear in the same cluster with variables that correlate positively. For example, the FARMERS variable would not appear with the other urbanism variables. Factor analysis and cluster analysis need not always arrive at the same variable groupings, but it is comforting when they do.

8.14 RUNNING PROCEDURE CLUSTER

Use the CLUSTER procedure to obtain hierarchical clusters for cases when the number of cases is not too large. Variables can also be clustered if the data are in the appropriate format (for example, if you have a correlation matrix or some other measure of distance). CLUSTER provides several measures of dissimilarity and allows you to specify missing-value treatment. A matrix of similarity or dissimilarity coefficients can be entered and used to cluster cases or variables.

8.15 Specifying the Variables

The first specification on CLUSTER is a list of variables to use in computing similarities or distances between cases, as in

```
CLUSTER ZCALORIE ZSODIUM ZALCOHOL ZCOST.
```

The variable list is the only required specification and must precede any optional subcommands. When a matrix is read, the variable list identifies the variables represented in the similarity or distance matrix. These variables are then clustered.

8.16 Selecting the Clustering Method

The METHOD subcommand specifies the clustering method. If you do not specify a method, CLUSTER uses the average-linkage between-groups method (see Section 8.12). You can use more than one method on a single matrix.

BAVERAGE *Average linkage between groups (UPGMA). This is the default.*
WAVERAGE *Average linkage within groups.*
SINGLE *Single linkage or nearest neighbor.*
COMPLETE *Complete linkage or furthest neighbor.*
CENTROID *Centroid clustering (UPGMA).* Square Euclidean distances are commonly used with this method.
MEDIAN *Median clustering (WPGMC).* Squared Euclidean distances are commonly used with this method.

WARD   *Ward's method.* Squared Euclidean distances are commonly used with this method.

DEFAULT   *Same as BAVERAGE.*

For example, the command

```
CLUSTER ZCALORIE ZSODIUM ZALCOHOL ZCOST
  /METHOD=SINGLE COMPLETE.
```

requests clustering with both the single and complete methods.

8.17
Specifying the Distance Measure

Use the MEASURE subcommand to specify the distance measure to use for clustering cases (see Section 8.2 and 8.11). If you omit MEASURE, CLUSTER uses squared Euclidean distances. You can specify only one distance measure.

MEASURE has the following keywords:

SEUCLID   *Squared Euclidean distances.* This is the default. This is the measure commonly used with the centroid, median, and Ward's methods of clustering. The distance between two cases is the sum of the squared differences in values for each variable:

$$\text{Distance}(X, Y) = \sum_i (X_i - Y_i)^2$$

EUCLID   *Euclidean distances.* The distance between two cases is the square root of the sum of the squared differences in values for each variable:

$$\text{Distance}(X, Y) = \sqrt{\sum_i (X_i - Y_i)^2}$$

COSINE   *Cosine of vectors of variables.* This is a pattern similarity measure:

$$\text{Similarity}(X, Y) = \frac{\sum_i (X_i Y_i)}{\sqrt{\sum_i (X_i^2) \sum_i (Y_i^2)}}$$

BLOCK   *City-block or Manhattan distances.* The distance between two cases is the sum of the absolute differences in values for each variable:

$$\text{Distance}(X, Y) = \sum_i |X_i - Y_i|$$

CHEBYCHEV   *Chebychev distance metric.* The distance between two cases is the maximum absolute difference in values for any variable:

$$\text{Distance}(X, Y) = MAX_i |X_i - Y_i|$$

POWER(p,r)   *Distances in an absolute power metric.* The distance between two cases is the *r*th root of the sum of the absolute differences to the *p*th power in values on each variable:

$$\text{Distance}(X, Y) = \left(\sum_i |X_i - Y_i|^p \right)^{1/r}$$

Appropriate selection of integer parameters *p* and *r* yields Euclidean, squared Euclidean, Minkowski, city-block, minimum, maximum, and many other distance metrics.

DEFAULT   *Same as SEUCLID.*

8.18
Specifying Output

CLUSTER automatically displays the clustering method, the similarity or distance measure used for clustering, and the number of cases. The following additional output is controlled by the PRINT subcommand:

SCHEDULE   *Agglomeration schedule.* Display the order in which and distances at which clusters combine to form new clusters, as well as the last cluster level at which a case (or variable) joined the cluster (see Figures 8.8 and 8.9b). The agglomeration schedule is displayed by default if you do not specify PRINT, or if you specify PRINT without any keywords. If you specify any other keywords on PRINT, you must request SCHEDULE explicitly.

CLUSTER(min,max)   *Cluster membership. Min* and *max* specify the minimum and maximum numbers of clusters in the cluster solutions. For each case, CLUSTER displays an identifying label and values indicating which cluster the case belongs to in a given cluster solution (see Figure 8.10c). For example, PRINT=CLUSTER(3,5) displays the clusters to which each case belongs when three, four, and five clusters are produced. Cases are identified by case number plus the value of any string variable specified on the ID subcommand (see Section 8.20).

DISTANCE   *Matrix of distances or similarities between items.* The type of matrix produced (similarities or dissimilarities) depends upon the measure selected. With a large number of clustered cases, DISTANCE uses considerable computer processing time.

DEFAULT   *Same as SCHEDULE.*

NONE   *None of the above.* Use PRINT=NONE when you want to suppress all display output, such as when you are using SAVE.

8.19
Requesting Plots

CLUSTER produces the vertical icicle plot by default. Use the PLOT subcommand to obtain a horizontal icicle plot or a dendrogram. When you specify PLOT, only the requested plots are produced.

VICICLE[(min,max,inc)]   *Vertical icicle plot. Min* and *max* specify the minimum and maximum numbers of cluster solutions to plot, and *inc* specifies the increment to use between cluster levels. Min, max, and inc must be integers. By default, the increment is 1 and all cluster solutions are plotted. For example, PLOT = VICICLE (2,10,2) plots cluster solutions with two, four, six, eight, and ten clusters. VICICLE is the default. (See Figures 8.7a, 8.9a, and 8.10a.)

HICICLE[(min,max,inc)]   *Horizontal icicle plot.* Has the same specifications as VICICLE. (See Figure 8.10b.)

DENDROGRAM   *Dendrogram.* The dendrogram is scaled by joining the distances of the clusters. (See Figures 8.9c and 8.9d.)

NONE   *No plots.*

If there is insufficient memory to plot a dendrogram or icicle plot, CLUSTER performs the cluster analysis, skips the plot, and displays an error message. To obtain a plot when this occurs, specify an increment for VICICLE or HICICLE.

8.20
Identifying Cases

By default, CLUSTER identifies cases by case number. Name a string variable on the ID subcommand to identify cases with string values. For example, the subcommand

    /ID=BEER

produces the beer-name labels in Figures 8.7a, 8.9a, 8.9c, 8.9d, 8.10a, 8.10b, and 8.10c.

8.21
Missing Values

CLUSTER uses listwise deletion as the default missing-value treatment. A case with missing values for any clustering variable is excluded from the analysis. Use the MISSING subcommand to treat user-defined missing values as valid.

LISTWISE *Delete cases with missing values listwise.* This is the default.
INCLUDE *Include user-missing values.*
DEFAULT *Same as LISTWISE.*

Cases with system-missing values for clustering variables are never included in the analysis.

8.22
Matrix Materials

The CLUSTER procedure can read and write similarity and distance matrices. Use the READ subcommand to read a matrix (such as a correlation matrix created by CORRELATION). This allows you to cluster variables or cases using a distance measure not available in CLUSTER. Three keywords indicate the type of matrix to read:

SIMILAR *Matrix of similarity values.* By default, CLUSTER assumes that a dissimilarity or distance matrix is read.
TRIANGLE *Matrix in lower-triangular form.* By default, CLUSTER assumes that a square matrix is read.
LOWER *Matrix in lower-subdiagonal form.* The matrix is in lower-triangular form but without the diagonal elements.

It may be necessary to use more than one of the above keywords to correctly indicate the type of matrix being read. For example, since CLUSTER assumes a square matrix is read, if you have a similarity matrix which is in lower-triangular form, you would have to specify

```
/READ=TRIANGLE SIMILAR
```

as shown in Figure 8.13. Only one similarity or distance matrix can be read in a single procedure.

The WRITE subcommand saves a computed similarity or distance matrix in a file named on the PROCEDURE OUTPUT command. The optional DISTANCE keyword indicates that the saved matrix is a distance matrix.

DISTANCE *Write a distance matrix.* This is the default.

8.23
Saving Cluster Memberships

You can use the SAVE subcommand to save cluster memberships at specified cluster levels as new variables on the active file. You must specify a rootname on the METHOD subcommand for each cluster method for which you wish to save cluster membership, as in

```
CLUSTER A B C
  /METHOD=BAVERAGE(CLUSMEM)
  /SAVE=CLUSTERS(3,5).
```

This command saves each case's cluster memberships for the three-, four-, and five-cluster solutions. The names for the new variables are CLUSMEM5, CLUSMEM4, and CLUSMEM3, and they will appear on the active file in that order. CLUSTER prints the names of variables it adds to the active file.

8.24
Annotated Example

The following commands produce the output in Figures 8.6a, 8.7a, 8.8, 8.9d, 8.10b, and 8.10c.

```
SET WIDTH=WIDE.
DATA LIST
  /ID 1-2 RATING 3 BEER 4-24 (A) ORIGIN 25 AVAIL 26
    PRICE 27-30 COST 31-34 CALORIES 35-37 SODIUM 38-39
    ALCOHOL 40-42 CLASS 43 LIGHT 44.
FORMATS PRICE COST (F4.2) ALCOHOL (F3.1).
MISSING VALUES CLASS(0).
BEGIN DATA.
lines of data
END DATA.
DESCRIPTIVES CALORIES SODIUM ALCOHOL COST
  /OPTIONS=3.
FORMATS ZCALORIE ZSODIUM ZALCOHOL ZCOST (F8.6).
CLUSTER ZCALORIE ZSODIUM ZALCOHOL ZCOST
  /ID=BEER
  /PRINT=CLUSTER(2,5) DISTANCE SCHEDULE
  /METHOD=COMPLETE
  /PLOT=HICICLE VICICLE DENDOGRAM.
FINISH.
```

- The SET command tells SPSS/PC+ to change the width to 132 characters.
- The DATA LIST gives the variable names and column locations for the variables in the analysis.
- The FORMATS command assigns display and write formats to the variables PRICE, COST, and ALCOHOL.
- The MISSING VALUES command assigns the value 0 user-missing status for the variable CLASS.
- The DESCRIPTIVES command adds the Z scores for CALORIES, SODIUM, ALCOHOL, and COST to the active file so they can be used by procedure CLUSTER.
- The FORMATS command assigns print and write formats for the new variables ZCALORIE, ZSODIUM, ZALCOHOL, and ZCOST.
- The CLUSTER command requests a cluster analysis of the standardized values for calories, sodium content, alcohol content, and cost.
- The ID subcommand requests that the values for the string variable BEER be used to identify cases.
- The PRINT command gives the values 2 and 5 as the minimum and maximum numbers of clusters in the cluster membership display. It also requests that a matrix of distances between items and an agglomeration schedule be displayed.
- The METHOD subcommand asks for complete linkage.
- The PLOT subcommand requests a horizontal icicle plot and a dendrogram in addition to the vertical icicle plot.

B

Statistics Guide

Contents

9 Cluster Analysis for Large Files: Procedure QUICK CLUSTER

Chapter 8 discusses the basics of cluster analysis and describes a commonly used method for cluster formation—agglomerative hierarchical clustering. This is but one of many methods available for cluster formation. For a particular problem, selection of a method to use depends not only on the characteristics of the various methods but also on the data set to be analyzed. For example, when the number of cases is large, algorithms that require many computations or storage of all cases in a computer's "memory" may pose difficulties in terms of either time required to perform the computations or available memory.

This chapter describes the QUICK CLUSTER procedure, which can be used to cluster large numbers of cases efficiently without requiring substantial computer resources. Unlike the CLUSTER procedure, which results in a series of solutions corresponding to different numbers of clusters, the QUICK CLUSTER procedure produces only one solution for the number of clusters requested. The number of clusters must be specified by the user.

9.1
THE METHOD

The algorithm used for determining cluster membership in the QUICK CLUSTER procedure is based on nearest centroid sorting (Anderberg, 1973). That is, a case is assigned to the cluster for which the distance between the case and the center of the cluster (centroid) is smallest. The actual mechanics of the procedure depend on the information available. If the cluster centers are known, they can be specified, and case assignment is based on them. Otherwise, cluster centers are estimated from the data.

9.2
Classification When Cluster Centers Are Known

Consider the beer data described in Chapter 8. Using the CLUSTER procedure, we identified five interpretable clusters. If there are additional beers that we want to classify into one of these five clusters, we can use the QUICK CLUSTER procedure as a quick and efficient means of doing so. Each of the new beers is assigned to the cluster to whose center it is closest. For each cluster, the center is just the mean of the four variables for cases in the cluster. These values, standardized, are shown in Figure 9.2a. (The unstandardized values are shown in Chapter 8.)

Figure 9.2a   Standardized values for the 5 clusters from TABLES

```
TABLES OBSERVATION=ZCOST ZCALORIE ZSODIUM ZALCOHOL
    /FTOTAL=TOTAL
    /FORMAT=CWIDTH(10,9)
    /TABLE=CLUSMEM5+TOTAL BY ZCALORIE+ZCOST+ZALCOHOL+ZSODIUM
    /STATISTICS=MEAN STDDEV COUNT.
```

	ZCALORIE			ZCOST			ZALCOHOL			ZSODIUM		
	Mean	Standard Deviation	Count	Mean	Standard Deviation	Count	Mean	Standard Deviation	Count	Mean	Standard Deviation	Count
CLUSMEM5												
AVERAGE	.44	.28	5	-.38	.15	5	.34	.28	5	.34	.31	5
EXPENSIVE	.76	.33	4	1.85	.17	4	.70	.27	4	-.64	.90	4
HIGH NA	.69	.48	4	-.79	.48	4	.64	.53	4	1.45	.26	4
LIGHT	-.77	.52	5	-.25	.19	5	-.45	.31	5	-.72	.47	5
VERY LIGHT	-2.06	.09	2	-.53	.39	2	-2.42	.56	2	-.68	.97	2
TOTAL	-.00	1.00	20	.00	1.00	20	-.00	1.00	20	.00	1.00	20

The centers of the five original clusters are called **Classification Cluster Centers,** since they will be used to assign cases to clusters. These values are shown in Figure 9.2b from procedure QUICK CLUSTER.

Figure 9.2b   Classification cluster centers

```
COMPUTE ZCALORIE=(CALORIES-132.4)/30.26.
COMPUTE ZCOST=(COST-49.65)/14.38.
COMPUTE ZALCOHOL=(ALCOHOL-4.44)/.76.
COMPUTE ZSODIUM=(SODIUM-14.95)/6.58.
PROCESS IF (SELECT EQ 0).
QUICK CLUSTER ZCALORIE ZCOST ZALCOHOL ZSODIUM
   /CRITERIA=CLUSTERS(5) NOUPDATE
   /INITIAL=(.436   -.379    .342    .342
             .755   1.85     .704   -.639
             .689   -.793    .638   1.45
            -.767   -.254   -.447   -.722
           -2.06    -.532  -2.42    -.676).
```

Classification Cluster Centers.

Cluster	ZCALORIE	ZCOST	ZALCOHOL	ZSODIUM
1	.4360	-.3790	.3420	.3420
2	.7550	1.8500	.7040	-.6390
3	.6890	-.7930	.6380	1.4500
4	-.7670	-.2540	-.4470	-.7220
5	-2.0600	-.5320	-2.4200	-.6760

The cases in the new data set are standardized using the means and standard deviations of the original data set. These values are shown in Figure 9.2c. For each case the Euclidean distance (Chapter 8) to each of the cluster centers is calculated. For example, the first new beer to be classified is Miller High Life. Its standardized value for calories is 0.55, for cost is −0.53, for alcohol is 0.34, and for sodium is 0.31. Its Euclidean distance to Cluster 1 is

Equation 9.2a

$$\sqrt{(0.55-0.44)^2 + (-0.53-(-0.38))^2 + (0.34-0.34)^2 + (0.31-0.34)^2} = 0.19$$

Distances to the other cluster centers are computed in the same way. The distance to Cluster 2 is 2.6, to Cluster 3 is 1.21, to Cluster 4 is 1.87, and to Cluster 5 is 3.92. Since the distance is smallest to Cluster 1, Miller High Life is assigned to it.

Figure 9.2c   Original and standardized values for the 15 beers

```
COMPUTE ZCALORIE=(CALORIES-132.4)/30.26.
COMPUTE ZCOST=(COST-49.65)/14.38.
COMPUTE ZALCOHOL=(ALCOHOL-4.44)/.76.
COMPUTE ZSODIUM=(SODIUM-14.95)/6.58.
FORMATS ZCALORIE ZCOST ZALCOHOL ZSODIUM (F5.2).
PROCESS IF (SELECT EQ 0).
LIST VAR=BEER CALORIES SODIUM ALCOHOL COST
         ZCALORIE ZSODIUM ZALCOHOL ZCOST.
```

BEER	CALORIES	SODIUM	ALCOHOL	COST	ZCALORIE	ZSODIUM	ZALCOHOL	ZCOST
MILLER HIGH LIFE	149	17	4.7	.42	.55	.31	.34	-3.42
MICHELOB	162	10	5.0	.50	.98	-.75	.74	-3.42
LABATTS	147	17	5.0	.53	.48	.31	.74	-3.42
MOLSON	154	17	5.1	.56	.71	.31	.87	-3.41
HENRY WEINHARD	149	7	4.7	.61	.55	-1.21	.34	-3.41
ANCHOR STEAM	154	17	4.7	1.20	.71	.31	.34	-3.37
SCHMIDTS	147	7	4.7	.30	.48	-1.21	.34	-3.43
PABST BLUE RIBBON	152	8	4.9	.38	.65	-1.06	.61	-3.43
OLYMPIA	153	27	4.6	.44	.68	1.83	.21	-3.42
DOS EQUIS	145	14	4.5	.70	.42	-.14	.08	-3.40
SCOTCH BUY (SAFEWAY)	145	18	4.5	.27	.42	.46	.08	-3.43
BLATZ	144	13	4.6	.30	.38	-.30	.21	-3.43
ROLLING ROCK	144	8	4.7	.36	.38	-1.06	.34	-3.43
TUBORG	155	13	5.0	.43	.75	-.30	.74	-3.42
ST PAULI GIRL	144	21	4.7	.77	.38	.92	.34	-3.40

Number of cases read =   15   Number of cases listed =   15

Figure 9.2d contains the cluster numbers to which the new beers are assigned, as well as the Euclidean distance from the case to the center of the cluster to which it is assigned. As shown in Figure 9.2e, ten beers are assigned to Cluster 1, four to Cluster 2, and one to Cluster 3. No beers are assigned to the last two clusters.

Figure 9.2d   Case listing of cluster membership

```
QUICK CLUSTER ZCALORIE ZCOST ZALCOHOL ZSODIUM
  /CRITERIA=CLUSTERS(5) NOUPDATE
  /INITIAL=( .436  -.379   .342    .342
             .755  1.85    .704   -.639
             .689  -.793   .638   1.45
            -.767  -.254  -.447   -.722
            -2.06  -.532  -2.42   -.676)
  /PRINT=ID(BEER) CLUSTER.
```

```
Case listing of Cluster membership.

BEER                      Cluster      Distance

  MILLER HIGH LIFE           1           .192
  MICHELOB                   1          1.345
  LABATTS                    1           .730
  MOLSON                     1          1.014
  HENRY WEINHARD             2          1.274
  ANCHOR STEAM               2          3.208
  SCHMIDTS                   1          1.839
  PABST BLUE RIBBON          1          1.502
  OLYMPIA                    3           .699
  DOS EQUIS                  2           .969
  SCOTCH BUY (SAFEWAY)       1          1.231
  BLATZ                      1          1.184
  ROLLING ROCK               1          1.511
  TUBORG                     1           .817
  ST PAULI GIRL              2          1.643
```

Figure 9.2e   Number of cases in each cluster

```
Number of Cases in each Cluster.

Cluster     unweighted cases    weighted cases

   1              10.0              10.0
   2               4.0               4.0
   3               1.0               1.0
   4               0.0               0.0
   5               0.0               0.0

Missing            0
Total             15.0              15.0
```

Once the beers have been assigned to clusters, it is possible to calculate the actual centers of the resulting clusters, which are just the average values of the variables for cases in the cluster. These values, labeled **Final Cluster Centers,** are shown in Figure 9.2f. Since no cases were assigned to the last two clusters, system-missing values are printed. From this table, we can see that the clusters do not differ much in average calories, since all three have similar standardized values. Cluster 2 has the beers with the highest cost, while Cluster 3 contains the high-sodium beers.

Figure 9.2f   Final cluster centers

```
Final Cluster Centers.

Cluster     ZCALORIE      ZCOST      ZALCOHOL     ZSODIUM

   1          .5783       -.6363       .5000      -.3267
   2          .5155       2.2497       .2763      -.0304
   3          .6808       -.3929       .2105      1.8313
   4            .            .           .           .
   5            .            .           .           .
```

Once clusters have been formed, it is useful to assess how "well-separated" they are by calculating the distances between their centers. Hopefully, the clusters will have centers that are far apart, with cases within a cluster hovering fairly closely to the cluster's center.

Euclidean distances between pairs of final cluster centers are displayed in Figure 9.2g. For example, the distance between Clusters 1 and 2 is

Equation 9.2b

$$\sqrt{(0.58-0.52)^2 + (-0.64-2.25)^2 + (0.50-0.28)^2 + (0.33-(-0.03))^2} = 2.91$$

Similarly, the distance between Clusters 1 and 3 is 2.19, while the distance between Clusters 2 and 3 is 3.24.

Figure 9.2g   Euclidean distances between clusters

```
QUICK CLUSTER ZCALORIE ZCOST ZALCOHOL ZSODIUM
  /CRITERIA=CLUSTERS(5) NOUPDATE
  /INITIAL=(.436  -.379    .342    .342
            .755  1.85     .704   -.639
            .689  -.793    .638   1.45
           -.767  -.254   -.447   -.722
           -2.06  -.532  -2.42    -.676)
  /PRINT=DISTANCE.
```

Distances between Final Cluster centers.					
Cluster	1	2	3	4	5
1	0.0				
2	2.9104	0.0			
3	2.1933	3.2374	0.0		
4	.	.	.	0.0	
5	.	.	.	.	0.0

The table of final cluster centers (Figure 9.2f) contains the average values of the variables for each cluster but provides no idea of the variability. One way of assessing the between-cluster to within-cluster variability is to compute a one-way analysis of variance for each of the variables and examine the ratio of the between-cluster to within-cluster mean squares.

Figure 9.2h contains the mean squares for examining differences between the clusters. The between-clusters mean square is labeled **Cluster MS**, and the within-cluster mean square is labeled **Error MS**. Their ratio is in the column labeled **F**. Large ratios and small observed significance levels are associated with variables that differ between the clusters. However, the F tests should be used only for descriptive purposes since the clusters have been chosen to maximize the differences among cases in different clusters. The observed significance levels are not corrected for this and thus cannot be interpreted as tests of the hypothesis that the cluster means are equal.

Figure 9.2h   Cluster mean squares

```
QUICK CLUSTER ZCALORIE ZCOST ZALCOHOL ZSODIUM
  /CRITERIA=CLUSTERS(5) NOUPDATE
  /INITIAL=(.436  -.379    .342    .342
            .755  1.85     .704   -.639
            .689  -.793    .638   1.45
           -.767  -.254   -.447   -.722
           -2.06  -.532  -2.42    -.676)
  /PRINT=ANOVA.
```

Analysis of Variance.						
Variable	Cluster MS	DF	Error MS	DF	F	Prob
ZCALORIE	.0124	2	.0334	12.0	.3712	.698
ZCOST	12.0558	2	1.2003	12.0	10.0438	.003
ZALCOHOL	.0952	2	.0586	12.0	1.6256	.237
ZSODIUM	2.1316	2	.5242	12.0	4.0665	.045

As expected from Figure 9.2f, the CALORIES variable does not differ between the clusters. The F value is small, and the associated significance level is large.

Beers in the three clusters also have fairly similar alcohol content. However, they do seem to be different in sodium and cost.

9.3
Classification When Cluster Centers Are Unknown

In the previous example, the cluster centers for classifying cases were already known. The initial cluster solution and the center values were obtained from the CLUSTER solution. In many situations the center values for the clusters are not known in advance. Instead, they too must be estimated from the data. Several different methods for estimating cluster centers are available. Most of them involve examining the data several times.

Good cluster centers separate the cases well. One strategy is to choose cases that have large distances between them and use their values as initial estimates of the cluster centers. The number of cases selected is the number of clusters specified.

The algorithm for this strategy proceeds as follows. The first k cases in the data file, where k is the number of clusters requested, are selected as temporary centers. As subsequent cases are processed, a case replaces a center if its smallest distance to a center is greater than the distance between the two closest centers. The center that is closer to the case is replaced. A case also replaces a center if the smallest distance from the case to a center is larger than the smallest distance between that center and all other centers. Again, it replaces the center closest to it.

To illustrate the basics of the QUICK CLUSTER procedure when centers are estimated from the data, let's consider the beers again, this time using QUICK CLUSTER to cluster all 35 beers into 5 clusters.

9.4
Selecting Initial Cluster Centers

The first step of cluster formation, as previously described, is selection of the first guesses at cluster centers. Although we need not specify anything else about the clusters, we must indicate the number of clusters to be formed. Figure 9.4a contains the values of five centers selected by the program. They are labeled **Initial Cluster Centers.** Each center corresponds to a beer. The first center is Schlitz Light, the second, Kronenbourg, the third, Pabst Extra Light, the next, Anchor Steam, and the last, Heileman's Old Style. These are, in terms of the variables under consideration, well-separated beers. Schlitz Light is a low-calorie beer; Kronenbourg is a low-sodium beer; Pabst Extra Light is a very light beer; Anchor Steam is a very expensive beer; and Heileman's Old Style is a rather average beer, though somewhat higher in sodium than most.

Figure 9.4a   Initial cluster centers for all 35 beers

```
DESCRIPTIVES CALORIES (ZCAL) SODIUM (ZSOD) ALCOHOL (ZALC) COST(ZCST)
   /OPTIONS=3.
QUICK CLUSTER ZCAL ZSOD ZALC ZCST
   /CRITERIA=CLUST(5).
```

Initial Cluster Centers.				
Cluster	ZCAL	ZSOD	ZALC	ZCST
1	−1.7496	−1.2461	−.6255	−.1907
2	1.2365	−1.2461	1.0330	1.1973
3	−2.9358	.0558	−3.7765	−.6711
4	.5820	.3813	.2038	3.7064
5	.1730	1.5204	.5354	−.4042

After the initial cluster centers have been selected, all cases are grouped into the cluster with the closest center. Once all cases have been assigned to clusters, average values for the variables are computed from the cases that have been assigned to each cluster and the cases that were the initial cluster centers. These values, shown in Figure 9.4b, are labeled **Classification Cluster Centers,** since they will be used to classify the cases at the next step.

Figure 9.4b   Classification cluster centers

```
Classification Cluster Centers.

  Cluster       ZCAL        ZSOD        ZALC        ZCST

        1     -1.5138      -.9695      -.6928      -.2315
        2       .8498     -1.0563       .7817       .8577
        3     -2.9085      -.1534     -3.6521      -.6237
        4       .5820       .3813       .2038      3.7064
        5       .3333       .8370       .4196      -.3716
```

Examination of the classification cluster centers shows that the "average profile" of the clusters has not changed much from that suggested by the initial centers. The first cluster remains the light beers; the second, low-sodium beers; and so forth. The fourth cluster contains only Anchor Steam, a beer far removed from the others because of its very steep price, almost four standard deviations above the rest.

**9.5
A Second Round of
Classification**

Although at this step all cases have been allocated to clusters based on the initial center values, clustering results can be improved by classifying the cases again using the classification cluster centers. Again, the same rule is used for the formation of clusters. Each case is assigned to the cluster for which its distance to the classification center is smallest. Beer names, cluster numbers, and distances to the cluster centers are shown in Figure 9.5a for the first 10 beers. The count of the number of cases in each cluster is shown in Figure 9.5b.

Figure 9.5a   Case listing of cluster membership

```
QUICK CLUSTER ZCAL ZSOD ZALC ZCST
  /CRITERIA=CLUST(5)
  /PRINT=ID(BEER) CLUSTER.
```

```
Case listing of Cluster membership.

BEER                     Cluster      Distance

  MILLER HIGH LIFE          5          .513
  BUDWEISER                 5          .827
  SCHLITZ                   5          .217
  LOWENBRAU                 5          .904
  MICHELOB                  2          .942
  LABATTS                   5          .735
  MOLSON                    5          .953
  HENRY WEINHARD            2          .827
  KRONENBOURG               2          .603
  HEINEKEN                  2          .805
    .
    .
    .
```

Figure 9.5b   Number of cases in each cluster

```
Number of Cases in each Cluster.

  Cluster     unweighted cases     weighted cases

        1            5.0                5.0
        2            9.0                9.0
        3            2.0                2.0
        4            1.0                1.0
        5           18.0               18.0

  Missing            0
  Total             35.0               35.0
```

Once the cases have been classified a second time, average values of the variables are again computed. These are termed final cluster centers and are shown in Figure 9.5c. The resulting five clusters are quite similar to those obtained with the CLUSTER procedure (Chapter 8) using a subset of the beers. Cluster 1 is the light beers, Cluster 3 is the very light beers, and Cluster 5 is the average beers. Anchor Steam, which was not included in the previous analysis, constitutes a separate cluster.

Figure 9.5c   Final cluster centers

```
Final Cluster Centers.

   Cluster        ZCAL          ZSOD          ZALC          ZCST

        1       -1.2505        -.7253        -.7913        -.2440
        2         .5093        -.9748         .4617         .3491
        3       -2.8540        -.6765       -3.2790        -.4576
        4         .5820         .3813         .2038        3.7064
        5         .3775         .7429         .3420        -.2618
```

Euclidean distances between the final cluster centers are shown in Figure 9.5d. Based on this, one can assess how different the final clusters are. The largest distance is between the very light beers and Anchor Steam; the smallest distance is between the average beers and the light beers. From Figure 9.5e, it appears that for all of the variables, variability within a cluster is less than the variability between the clusters.

Figure 9.5d   Euclidean distances between clusters

```
QUICK CLUSTER ZCAL ZSOD ZALC ZCST
  /CRITERIA=CLUST(5)
  /PRINT=DISTANCE.
```

```
Distances between Final Cluster centers.

  Cluster          1             2             3             4             5

        1        0.0
        2        2.2541        0.0
        3        2.9678        5.1034        0.0
        4        4.6020        3.6307        6.5110        0.0
        5        2.4679        1.8318        5.0603        3.9923        0.0
```

Figure 9.5e   Cluster mean squares

```
QUICK CLUSTER ZCAL ZSOD ZALC ZCST
  /CRITERIA=CLUST(5)
  /PRINT=ANOVA.
```

```
Analysis of Variance.

  Variable    Cluster MS   DF      Error MS      DF          F       Prob
  ZCAL          7.3370     4         .1551     30.0      47.3136     .000
  ZSOD          5.5445     4         .3941     30.0      14.0701     .000
  ZALC          7.1748     4         .1767     30.0      40.6070     .000
  ZCST          4.1961     4         .5738     30.0       7.3123     .000
```

9.6
RUNNING PROCEDURE QUICK CLUSTER

The QUICK CLUSTER procedure allocates cases to clusters when the number of clusters to be formed is known. It is particularly useful when the number of cases is large, since it requires substantially less computer memory and computation time than does the CLUSTER procedure. The algorithm classifies cases into clusters based on distances to the cluster centers. Cluster centers can either be specified by the user or estimated from the data.

Available output includes estimates of initial, updated, and final cluster centers, distances between all pairs of final cluster centers, cluster membership and distance to the cluster center for all cases, and analysis of variance tables for variables used in the clustering. For each case, cluster membership and distance can be saved as new variables on the active file.

9.7
Specifying the Variables

The only required specification for QUICK CLUSTER is the list of variables to be used for forming the clusters. The command

```
QUICK CLUSTER ZCALORIE ZCOST ZALCOHOL ZSODIUM.
```

produces a default clustering of cases into two groups based on the values of the four variables. The variable list must precede any optional subcommands.

9.8
Specifying the Number of Clusters

The CRITERIA subcommand is used to specify various options for the clustering algorithm. The following keywords are available:

CLUSTERS(k) *Number of clusters to be formed.* The default is two clusters.

NOUPDATE *Initial cluster centers are used for classification.* The centers are not updated to the observed means of the initial clusters. This keyword is required if cluster centers specified with the INITIAL subcommand are to be used for classification.

For example, the command

```
QUICK CLUSTER ZCALORIE ZCOST ZALCOHOL ZSODIUM
  /CRITERIA=CLUST(5).
```

asks for 5 clusters.

9.9
Specifying the Cluster Centers

The INITIAL subcommand specifies either the selection method for initial cluster centers or the actual values for the centers. These centers are then updated to actual cluster means for classification purposes. If the NOUPDATE keyword is used on the CRITERIA subcommand (see Section 9.8), the initial cluster centers are used for classification.

Available keywords are:

SELECT *Select well-spaced cases from the data file as initial centers.* This requires an extra pass of the data. This is the default.

FIRST *The first k cases in the data file are used as initial cluster centers, where k is the number of clusters.* This does not require an extra pass of the data but may result in a poor solution.

(value list) *Values for the initial cluster centers.* The values must be enclosed in parentheses. List all the values for each cluster together. For example, if there are two clusters, the values of all variables for Cluster 1 are followed by the values of all variables for Cluster 2.

For example, the command

```
QUICK CLUSTER ZCALORIE ZCOST ZALCOHOL ZSODIUM
  /CRITERIA=CLUSTERS(5) NOUPDATE
  /INITIAL=( .436   -.379    .342     .342
             .755   1.85     .704    -.639
             .689   -.793    .638    1.45
            -.767   -.254   -.447    -.722
           -2.06    -.532  -2.42     -.676).
```

requests 5 clusters. The values for the initial cluster centers are given, and the NOUPDATE keyword on the CRITERIA subcommand specifies that these initial cluster centers be used for classification.

9.10
Displaying Optional Output

By default, QUICK CLUSTER prints the initial cluster centers, the centers used for classification, and, when clustering is complete, average values for the variables in each cluster as well as the number of cases in each cluster. The PRINT subcommand with the following keywords is used to obtain additional output:

CLUSTER *Displays for each case an identifying number or label, the number of the cluster to which it is assigned, and its Euclidean distance to the center of the cluster.* (See Figures 9.2d and 9.5a.)

ID(varname) *Identifies cases on output by the values of the variable specified.* By default, cases are identified by their sequential number in the active file. (See Figures 9.2d and 9.5a.)

DISTANCE *Displays Euclidean distances between all pairs of final cluster centers.* (See Figures 9.2g and 9.5d.)

ANOVA *Displays an analysis of variance table for each variable used for classification.* (See Figures 9.2h and 9.5e.)

For example, the command

```
QUICK CLUSTER ZCALORIE ZCOST ZALCOHOL ZSODIUM
  /CRITERIA=CLUSTERS(5) NOUPDATE
  /INITIAL=( .436   -.379    .342      .342
             .755   1.85     .704     -.639
             .689   -.793    .638     1.45
            -.767   -.254   -.447     -.722
           -2.06    -.532  -2.42      -.676)
  /PRINT=DISTANCE ANOVA.
```

requests that the Euclidean distances between pairs of final clusters and an analysis of variance table be included in the display.

9.11
Missing Values

By default, QUICK CLUSTER eliminates from the analysis cases with system- or user-missing values for any variable on the variable list. Use the MISSING subcommand with one of the following four keywords to change the missing-value treatment:

LISTWISE   *Delete cases with missing values on any variable.* This is the default.

PAIRWISE   *Assign cases to clusters based on distances computed from all variables with non-missing values.*

INCLUDE   *Treat user-defined missing values as non-missing.*

DEFAULT   *Same as LISTWISE.*

For example, the command

```
QUICK CLUSTER ZCALORIE ZCOST ZALCOHOL ZSODIUM
  /MISSING=INCLUDE.
```

requests that user-missing values be included as non-missing.

9.12
Saving Cluster Membership and Distance

The SAVE subcommand saves cluster membership and distance as new variables on the active file. To use these results for use in subsequent sessions, you must save the active file using the SAVE or EXPORT commands.

Available keywords for SAVE are

CLUSTER(varname)   *The cluster number of each case is stored in the variable name specified.* The numbers range from 1 to k, where k is the number of clusters.

DISTANCE(varname)   *For each case the distance to the cluster center is stored in the variable name specified.*

For example, the subcommand

```
/SAVE=CLUSTER(MEMBER)
```

requests that the cluster number of each case be stored in the variable MEMBER.

9.13
Writing the Final Cluster Centers

The WRITE subcommand writes the final cluster centers onto the results file specified on the SET command (the default is SPSS.PRC). By editing this file, you can use these cluster centers on an INITIAL subcommand in a subsequent session. The WRITE subcommand has no specifications.

9.14
Annotated Example

The following SPSS/PC+ commands created the output in Figures 9.2b, 9.2d, 9.2e, 9.2f, 9.2g, and 9.2h.

```
DATA LIST FREE /SELECT RATING BEER (A21) ORIGIN AVAIL
        PRICE COST CALORIES SODIUM ALCOHOL CLASS LIGHT.
COMPUTE ZCALORIE=(CALORIES-132.4)/30.26.
COMPUTE ZCOST=(COST-49.65)/14.38.
COMPUTE ZALCOHOL=(ALCOHOL-4.44)/.76.
COMPUTE ZSODIUM=(SODIUM-14.95)/6.58.
BEGIN DATA.
data lines
END DATA.
PROCESS IF (SELECT EQ 0).
QUICK CLUSTER ZCALORIE ZCOST ZALCOHOL ZSODIUM
  /CRITERIA=CLUSTERS(5) NOUPDATE
  /INITIAL=(.436   -.379    .342     .342
            .755   1.85     .704    -.639
            .689   -.793    .638    1.45
           -.767   -.254   -.447    -.722
          -2.06    -.532   -2.42    -.676)
  /PRINT=ID(BEER) CLUSTER DISTANCE ANOVA.
FINISH.
```

- The DATA LIST command defines the variables names and tells SPSS/PC+ that the data are in freefield format.

- The four COMPUTE commands create the standardized variables needed for input to the QUICK CLUSTER command. COMPUTE statements, rather than procedure DESCRIPTIVES, are used so that the standardized values are based on the means and standard deviations of the original 20 beers analyzed in Chapter 8.

- PROCESS IF command temporarily selects only those beers that were not analyzed in Chapter 8. The variable SELECT is coded 0 for the new beers and 1 for the beers previously analyzed.

- The QUICK CLUSTER command names the four standardized variables as the variables to be used for forming clusters. The CRITERIA subcommand tells SPSS/PC+ to form 5 clusters. Since the values of the initial cluster centers are given on the INITIAL subcommand, the keyword NOUPDATE is included on the CRITERIA sucommand. The PRINT subcommand asks for all available output, with the values of string variable BEER used to label cases.

Contents

10 Reliability Analysis: Procedure RELIABILITY

From the moment we're born, the world begins to "score" us. One minute after birth, we're rated on the 10-point Apgar scale, followed closely by the 5-minute Apgar scale, and then on to countless other scales that will track our intelligence, creditworthinesss, likelihood of hijacking a plane, and so forth. A dubious mark of maturity is when we find ourselves administering these scales.

10.1 CONSTRUCTING A SCALE

When we wish to measure characteristics such as driving ability, mastery of course materials, or the ability to function independently, we must construct some type of measurement device. Usually we develop a scale or test that is composed of a variety of related items. The responses to each of the items can be graded and summed, resulting in a score for each case. A question that frequently arises is, How good is our scale? In order to answer this question, let's consider some of the characteristics of a scale or test.

When we construct a test to measure how well college students have learned the material in an introductory psychology course, the questions actually included in the test are a small sample from all of the items that may have been selected. Though we have selected a limited number of items for inclusion in a test, we want to draw conclusions about the students' mastery of the entire course contents. In fact, we'd like to think that even if we changed the actual items on the test, there would be a strong relationship between students' scores on the test actually given and the scores they would have received on other tests we could have given. A good test is one which yields stable results. That is, it's *reliable.*

10.2 Reliability and Validity

Everyone knows the endearing qualities of a reliable car. It goes anytime, anywhere, for anybody. It behaves the same way under a wide variety of circumstances. Its performance is repeatable. A reliable measuring instrument behaves similarly: the test yields similar results when different people administer it and when alternative forms are used. When conditions for making the measurement change, the results of the test should not.

A test must be reliable to be useful. But it's not enough for a test to be reliable; it must also be *valid.* That is, the instrument must measure what it is intended to measure. A test that requires students to do mirror drawing and memorize nonsense syllables may be quite reliable, but it is a poor indicator of mastery of the concepts of psychology. The test has poor validity.

There are many different ways to assess both reliability and validity. In this chapter, we will be concerned only with measures of reliability.

10.3
Describing Test Results

Before embarking on a discussion of measures of reliability, let's take a look at some of the descriptive statistics that are useful for characterizing a scale. We will be analyzing a scale of the physical activities of daily living in the elderly. The goal of the scale is to assess an elderly person's competence in the physical activities of daily living. Three hundred and ninety-five people were rated on the eight items shown in Figure 10.3a. For each item, a score of 1 was assigned if the patient was unable to perform the activity, 2 if the patient was able to perform the activity with assistance, and 3 if the patient required no assistance to perform the activity.

Figure 10.3a   Physical activity items

```
RELIABILITY /VARIABLES = ITEM1 TO ITEM8
   ...
```

```
   1.    ITEM1        Can eat
   2.    ITEM2        Can dress and undress
   3.    ITEM3        Can take care of own appearance
   4.    ITEM4        Can walk
   5.    ITEM5        Can get in and out of bed
   6.    ITEM6        Can take a bath or shower
   7.    ITEM7        Can get to bathroom on time
   8.    ITEM8        Has been able to do tasks for 6 months
```

When we summarize a scale, we want to look at the characteristics of the individual items, the characteristics of the overall scale, and the relationship between the individual items and the entire scale. Figure 10.3b contains descriptive statistics for the individual items.

Figure 10.3b   Univariate descriptive statistics

```
RELIABILITY /VARIABLES = ITEM1 TO ITEM8
   /STATISTICS DESCRIPTIVES
   ...
```

		MEAN	STD DEV	CASES
1.	ITEM1	2.9266	.3593	395.0
2.	ITEM2	2.8962	.4116	395.0
3.	ITEM3	2.9165	.3845	395.0
4.	ITEM4	2.8684	.4367	395.0
5.	ITEM5	2.9114	.3964	395.0
6.	ITEM6	2.8506	.4731	395.0
7.	ITEM7	2.7873	.5190	395.0
8.	ITEM8	1.6582	.4749	395.0

You see that the average scores for the items range from 2.93 for item 1 to 1.66 for item 8. Item 7 has the largest standard deviation, 0.5190.

Figure 10.3c   Interitem correlation coefficients

```
RELIABILITY /VARIABLES = ITEM1 TO ITEM8
   /STATISTICS DESCRIPTIVES CORRELATIONS
   ...
```

CORRELATION MATRIX

	ITEM1	ITEM2	ITEM3	ITEM4	ITEM5
ITEM1	1.0000				
ITEM2	.7893	1.0000			
ITEM3	.8557	.8913	1.0000		
ITEM4	.7146	.7992	.7505	1.0000	
ITEM5	.8274	.8770	.8173	.8415	1.0000
ITEM6	.6968	.8326	.7684	.8504	.7684
ITEM7	.5557	.5736	.5340	.5144	.5497
ITEM8	.0459	.1427	.0795	.2108	.0949

	ITEM6	ITEM7	ITEM8
ITEM6	1.0000		
ITEM7	.5318	1.0000	
ITEM8	.2580	.1883	1.0000

The correlation coefficients between the items are shown in Figure 10.3c. The only item that appears to have a small correlation with the other items is item 8. Its highest correlation is 0.26, with item 6.

Additional statistics for the scale as a whole are shown in Figure 10.3d and 10.3e.

Figure 10.3d Scale statistics

```
RELIABILITY /VARIABLES = ITEM1 TO ITEM8
  /STATISTICS DESCRIPTIVES CORRELATIONS SCALE
  ...
```

STATISTICS FOR	MEAN	VARIANCE	STD DEV	# OF VARIABLES
SCALE	21.8152	7.3896	2.7184	8

Figure 10.3e Summary statistics for items

```
RELIABILITY /VARIABLES = ITEM1 TO ITEM8
  /STATISTICS DESCRIPTIVES CORRELATIONS SCALE
  /SUMMARY = MEANS VARIANCES CORRELATIONS
  ...
```

	MEAN	MINIMUM	MAXIMUM	RANGE	MAX/MIN	VARIANCE
ITEM MEANS	2.7269	1.6582	2.9266	1.2684	1.7649	.1885
ITEM VARIANCES	.1891	.1291	.2694	.1403	2.0864	.0022
INTER-ITEM CORRELATIONS	.5843	.0459	.8913	.8454	19.4033	.0790

The average score for the scale is 21.82, and the standard deviation is 2.7 (Figure 10.3d). The average score on an item (Figure 10.3e) is 2.73, with a range of 1.27. Similarly, the average of the item variances is 0.19, with a minimum of 0.13 and a maximum of 0.27. The correlations between items range from 0.046 to 0.891. The ratio between the largest and smallest correlation is 0.891/.046, or 19.4. The average correlation is 0.584.

10.4
Relationship between the Scale and the Items

Now let's take a look at the relationship between the individual items and the composite score.

Figure 10.4 Item-total summary statistics

```
RELIABILITY /VARIABLES = ITEM1 TO ITEM8
  /STATISTICS DESCRIPTIVES CORRELATIONS SCALE
  /SUMMARY = MEANS VARIANCES CORRELATIONS TOTAL
  ...
```

ITEM-TOTAL STATISTICS

	SCALE MEAN IF ITEM DELETED	SCALE VARIANCE IF ITEM DELETED	CORRECTED ITEM- TOTAL CORRELATION	SQUARED MULTIPLE CORRELATION	ALPHA IF ITEM DELETED
ITEM1	18.8886	5.8708	.7981	.7966	.8917
ITEM2	18.9190	5.5061	.8874	.8882	.8820
ITEM3	18.8987	5.7004	.8396	.8603	.8873
ITEM4	18.9468	5.4718	.8453	.8137	.8848
ITEM5	18.9038	5.6202	.8580	.8620	.8852
ITEM6	18.9646	5.3084	.8520	.8029	.8833
ITEM7	19.0278	5.6414	.5998	.3777	.9095
ITEM8	20.1570	6.7316	.1755	.1331	.9435

For each item, the first column of Figure 10.4 shows what the average score for the scale would be if the item were excluded from the scale. For example, we know from Figure 10.3d that the average score for the scale is 21.82. If item 1 were eliminated from the scale, the average score would be 18.89. This is computed by simply subtracting the average score for the item from the scale mean. In this case it's $21.82 - 2.93 = 18.89$. The next column is the scale variance if the item were eliminated. The column labeled **CORRECTED ITEM-TOTAL CORRELATION** is the correlation coefficient between the score on the individual item and the sum of the scores on the remaining items. For example, the correlation between the score on item 8 and the sum of the scores of items 1 through 7 is only 0.176. This indicates that there is not much of a relationship between the eighth item and the other items. On the other hand, item 2 has a very high correlation, 0.887, with the other items.

Another way to look at the relationship between an individual item and the rest of the scale is to try to predict a person's score on the item based on the scores obtained on the other items. We can do this by calculating a multiple regression equation with the item of interest as the dependent variable and all of the other items as independent variables. The multiple R^2 from this regression equation is displayed for each of the items in the column labeled **SQUARED MULTIPLE CORRELATION**. We can see that almost 80% of the observed variability in the responses to item 1 can be explained by the other items. As expected, item 8 is poorly predicted from the other items. Its multiple R^2 is only 0.13.

10.5
THE RELIABILITY COEFFICIENT

By looking at the statistics shown above, we've learned quite a bit about our scale and the individual items of which it is composed. However, we still haven't come up with an index of how reliable the scale is. There are several different ways to measure reliability:

- You can compute an estimate of reliability based on the observed correlations or covariances of the items with each other.
- You can correlate the results from two alternate forms of the same test or split the same test into two parts and look at the correlation between the two parts.

(See Lord and Novick, 1968, and Nunnally, 1978.)

One of the most commonly used reliability coefficients is *Cronbach's Alpha*. Alpha (or α) is based on the "internal consistency" of a test. That is, it is based on the average correlation of items within a test, if the items are standardized to a standard deviation of 1; or on the average covariance among items on a scale, if the items are not standardized. We assume that the items on a scale are positively correlated with each other because they are measuring, to a certain extent, a common entity. The average correlation of an item with all other items in the scale tells us about the extent of the common entity. If items are not positively correlated with each other, we have no reason to believe that they are correlated with other possible items we may have selected. In this case, we do not expect to see a positive relationship between this test and other similar tests.

10.6
Interpreting Cronbach's Alpha

Cronbach's α has several interpretations. It can be viewed as the correlation between this test or scale and all other possible tests or scales containing the same number of items, which could be constructed from a hypothetical universe of items that measure the characteristic of interest. In the physical activities scale, for example, the eight questions actually selected for inclusion can be viewed as a sample from a universe of many possible items. The patients could have been asked whether they can walk up a flight of stairs, or get up from a chair, or cook a meal, or whether they can perform a myriad of other activities related to daily living. Cronbach's α tells us how much correlation we expect between our scale and all other possible 8-item scales measuring the same thing.

Another interpretation of Cronbach's α is the squared correlation between the score a person obtains on a particular scale (the observed score) and the score he would have obtained if questioned on *all* of the possible items in the universe (the true score).

Since α can be interpreted as a correlation coefficient, it ranges in value from 0 to 1. (Negative α values can occur when items are not positively correlated among themselves and the reliability model is violated.)

Figure 10.6 Cronbach's Alpha

```
RELIABILITY /VARIABLES = ITEM1 TO ITEM8
  /STATISTICS DESCRIPTIVES CORRELATIONS SCALE
  /SUMMARY = MEANS VARIANCES CORRELATIONS TOTAL
  /SCALE (ALPHA) = ALL
  /MODEL = ALPHA.
```

```
RELIABILITY COEFFICIENTS       8 ITEMS

ALPHA =   .9089          STANDARDIZED ITEM ALPHA =   .9183
```

Cronbach's α for the physical activity scale is shown in Figure 10.6. Note that the value, 0.91, is large, indicating that our scale is quite reliable. The other entry in Figure 10.6, labeled **STANDARDIZED ITEM ALPHA,** is the α value that would be obtained if all of the items were standardized to have a variance of 1. Since the items in our scale have fairly comparable variances, there is little difference between the two αs. If items on the scale have widely differing variances, the two αs may differ substantially.

Cronbach's α can be computed using the following formula:

$$\alpha = \frac{(k)\text{cov}/\text{var}}{1 + (k-1)\text{cov}/\text{var}}$$

Equation 10.6a

where k is the number of items in the scale, *cov* is the average covariance between items, and *var* is the average variance of the items. If the items are standardized to have the same variance, the formula can be simplified to

$$\alpha = \frac{k\,r}{1+(k-1)r}$$

Equation 10.6b

where r is the average correlation between items.

Looking at Equation 10.6b, we can see that Cronbach's α depends on both the length of the test (k in the formula) and the correlation of the items on the test. For example, if the average correlation between items is 0.2 on a 10-item scale, α is 0.71. If the number of items is increased to 25, α is 0.86. You can have large reliability coefficients even when the average interitem correlation is small, if the number of items on the scale is large enough.

10.7
Alpha If Item Deleted

When we are examining individual items, as in Figure 10.4, we may wish to know how each of the items affects the reliability of the scale. This can be accomplished by calculating Cronbach's α when each of the items is removed from the scale. These αs are shown in the last column of Figure 10.4. You can see that eliminating item 8 from the physical activity scale causes α to increase from 0.9089 (as in Figure 10.6) to 0.9435 (Figure 10.4). From the correlation matrix in Figure 10.3c we saw that item 8 is not strongly related to the other items, so we would expect that eliminating it from the scale would increase the overall reliability of the scale. Elimination of any of the other items from the scale causes little change in α.

10.8
THE SPLIT-HALF RELIABILITY MODEL

Cronbach's α is based on correlations of items on a single scale. It's a measure based on the internal consistency of the items. Other measures of reliability are based on splitting the scale into two parts and looking at the correlation between the two parts. Such measures are called *split-half* coefficients. One of the disadvantages of this method is that the results depend on the allocation of items to halves. The coefficient you get depends on how you split your scale. Sometimes split-half methods are applied to situations in which two tests are administered, or the same test is administered twice.

Figure 10.8a Split-half statistics

```
RELIABILITY /VARIABLES = ITEM1 TO ITEM8
   /STATISTICS DESCRIPTIVES CORRELATIONS SCALE
   /SUMMARY – MEANS VARIANCES CORRELATIONS TOTAL
   /SCALE (SPLIT) = ALL /MODEL = SPLIT.
```

```
    # OF CASES =        395.0

                                                # OF
STATISTICS FOR      MEAN     VARIANCE   STD DEV  VARIABLES
        PART 1    11.6076     2.1527     1.4672     4
        PART 2    10.2076     1.8959     1.3769     4
        SCALE     21.8152     7.3896     2.7184     8

ITEM MEANS          MEAN     MINIMUM    MAXIMUM    RANGE     MAX/MIN    VARIANCE
        PART 1     2.9019     2.8684     2.9266     .0582     1.0203     .0007
        PART 2     2.5519     1.6582     2.9114    1.2532     1.7557     .3575
        SCALE      2.7269     1.6582     2.9266    1.2684     1.7649     .1885

ITEM VARIANCES      MEAN     MINIMUM    MAXIMUM    RANGE     MAX/MIN    VARIANCE
        PART 1      .1593      .1291      .1907     .0616     1.4774     .0007
        PART 2      .2190      .1571      .2694     .1123     1.7147     .0021
        SCALE       .1891      .1291      .2694     .1403     2.0864     .0022

INTER-ITEM
CORRELATIONS        MEAN     MINIMUM    MAXIMUM    RANGE     MAX/MIN    VARIANCE
        PART 1      .8001      .7146      .8913     .1768     1.2474     .0039
        PART 2      .3985      .0949      .7684     .6735     8.0973     .0606
        SCALE       .5843      .0459      .8913     .8454    19.4033     .0790


ITEM-TOTAL STATISTICS

              SCALE         SCALE       CORRECTED
              MEAN          VARIANCE    ITEM-                SQUARED      ALPHA
              IF ITEM       IF ITEM     TOTAL                MULTIPLE     IF ITEM
              DELETED       DELETED     CORRELATION          CORRELATION  DELETED

ITEM1        18.8886        5.8708       .7981                .7966        .8917
ITEM2        18.9190        5.5061       .8874                .8882        .8820
ITEM3        18.8987        5.7004       .8396                .8603        .8873
ITEM4        18.9468        5.4718       .8453                .8137        .8848
ITEM5        18.9038        5.6202       .8580                .8620        .8852
ITEM6        18.9646        5.3084       .8520                .8029        .8833
ITEM7        19.0278        5.6414       .5998                .3777        .9095
ITEM8        20.1570        6.7316       .1755                .1331        .9435
```

Figure 10.8a contains summary statistics that would be obtained if we split the physical ability scale into two equal parts. The first 4 items are part 1, while the second 4 items are part 2. Note that separate descriptive statistics are given for each of the parts, as well as for the entire scale. Reliability statistics for the split model are shown in Figure 10.8b.

Figure 10.8b Split-half reliability

```
RELIABILITY /VARIABLES = ITEM1 TO ITEM8
   /STATISTICS DESCRIPTIVES CORRELATIONS SCALE
   /SUMMARY = MEANS VARIANCES CORRELATIONS TOTAL
   /SCALE (SPLIT) = ALL /MODEL = SPLIT.
```

```
RELIABILITY COEFFICIENTS      8 ITEMS

CORRELATION BETWEEN FORMS =     .8269     EQUAL LENGTH SPEARMAN-BROWN =     .9052

GUTTMAN SPLIT-HALF =            .9042     UNEQUAL-LENGTH SPEARMAN-BROWN =   .9052

ALPHA FOR PART 1 =              .9387     ALPHA FOR PART 2 =                .7174

    4 ITEMS IN PART 1                         4 ITEMS IN PART 2
```

The correlation between the two halves, labeled on the output as **CORRELATION BETWEEN FORMS**, is 0.8269. This is an estimate of the reliability of the test if it has 4 items. The equal length Spearman-Brown coefficient, which has a value of 0.9052 in this case, tells us what the reliability of the 8-item test would be if it was made up of two equal parts that have a 4-item reliability of 0.8269.

(Remember, the reliability of a test increases as the number of items on the test increase, provided that the average correlation between items does not change.) If the number of items on each of the two parts is not equal, the unequal length Spearman-Brown coefficient can be used to estimate what the reliability of the overall test would be. In this case, since the two parts are of equal length, the two Spearman-Brown coefficients are equal. The Guttman split-half coefficient is another estimate of the reliability of the overall test. It does not assume that the two parts are equally reliable or have the same variance. Separate values of Cronbach's α are also shown for each of the two parts of the test.

10.9
OTHER RELIABILITY MODELS

In the previous models we've considered, we didn't make any assumptions about item means or variances. If we have information about item means and variances, we can incorporate this additional information in the estimation of reliability coefficients. Two commonly used models are the *strictly parallel* model and the *parallel* model. In the strictly parallel model, all items are assumed to have the same means, the same variances for the true (unobservable) scores, and the same error variances over replications. When the assumption of equal means is relaxed, we have what's known as a parallel model.

Additional statistics can be obtained from a strictly parallel or parallel model. Figure 10.9a contains a test of the goodness-of-fit for the parallel model applied to the physical activity data. (This model is not appropriate for these data. We'll use it, however, to illustrate the output for this type of model.)

Figure 10.9a   Goodness-of-fit for parallel model

```
RELIABILITY /VARIABLES = ITEM1 TO ITEM8
  /STATISTICS DESCRIPTIVES CORRELATIONS SCALE
  /SUMMARY = MEANS VARIANCES CORRELATIONS TOTAL
  /SCALE (ML) = ALL /MODEL = PARALLEL.
```

```
    TEST FOR GOODNESS OF FIT OF MODEL          PARALLEL

    CHI SQUARE  =      1660.1597      DEGREES OF FREEDOM =       34
    LOG OF DETERMINANT OF UNCONSTRAINED MATRIX =    -21.648663
    LOG OF DETERMINANT OF CONSTRAINED MATRIX   =    -17.403278
    PROBABILITY =   .0000
```

As you can see, the chi-square value is very large and we must reject the hypothesis that the parallel model fits. If the parallel model were appropriate we could consider the results, which are shown in Figure 10.9b.

Figure 10.9b   Maximum-likelihood reliability estimate

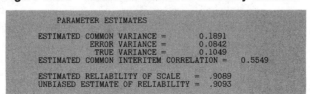

```
    PARAMETER ESTIMATES

    ESTIMATED COMMON VARIANCE =        0.1891
               ERROR VARIANCE =        0.0842
                TRUE VARIANCE =        0.1049
    ESTIMATED COMMON INTERITEM CORRELATION =    0.5549

    ESTIMATED RELIABILITY OF SCALE   =  .9089
    UNBIASED ESTIMATE OF RELIABILITY =  .9093
```

The first entry is an estimate of the common variance for an item. It is the sum of the true variance and the error variance, which are displayed below it. An estimate of the common interitem correlation, based on the model, is also shown. Figure 10.9b also shows two reliability coefficients. The first is a maximum likelihood estimate of the reliability coefficient, while the second is the maximum likelihood estimate corrected for bias. If either the parallel or the strictly parallel model fits the data, then the best linear combination of the items is simply their sum.

10.10
RUNNING PROCEDURE RELIABILITY

Use RELIABILITY to analyze *additive* scales: scales formed by simply adding a number of component variables, or items. RELIABILITY can efficiently analyze different groups of items to help you choose the best scale. RELIABILITY does not create the scale for you. After choosing the items that you want, on the basis of the reliability analysis, use the COMPUTE command to form the scale as the sum of the items.

10.11
Specifying Variables

The VARIABLES subcommand specifies a group of variables for subsequent analysis. It must be the first subcommand. You can enter more than one VARIABLES subcommand; each one specifies variables for the following SCALE subcommands, up to the next VARIABLES subcommand (if any). You can specify VARIABLES=ALL to use all variables in your active file as scale components.

10.12
Specifying a Scale

After a VARIABLES subcommand, enter one or more SCALE subcommands. Each SCALE subcommand defines a scale for analysis. Specifications on SCALE consist of a scale name of up to eight characters, in parentheses, and a list of the variables making up the scale. Specify ALL to use all the variables on the VARIABLES subcommand. For example:

```
RELIABILITY VARIABLES=ITEM1 TO ITEM8 /SCALE (SUM) = ALL.
```

• The scale name SUM will be used to label the reliability analysis.
• The scale includes all the variables from ITEM1 to ITEM8.

You can use more than one SCALE subcommand to analyze the items on the preceding VARIABLES subcommand:

```
RELIABILITY VARIABLES=ITEM1 TO ITEM8
  /SCALE (ALL) = ALL
  /SCALE (ALLBUT8) = ITEM1 TO ITEM7
  /SCALE (FIRST4) = ITEM1 TO ITEM4.
```

When you use the keyword TO on the SCALE subcommand, as in this example, it refers to the order that variables were listed on the preceding VARIABLES subcommand, and not to their order in the active file.

10.13
Choosing a Model

The default model for reliability analysis is ALPHA, which calculates Cronbach's α coefficient for each SCALE subcommand. To use a different model, specify the MODEL subcommand after the SCALE to which the model applies. Available models are:

ALPHA — *Cronbach's α.* This is the default.

SPLIT (n) — *Split-half coefficients.* A split-half reliability analysis is performed, based on the order in which you named the items on the preceding SCALE subcommand. The first half of the items (rounding up if the number of items is odd) form the first part, and the remaining items form the second part. After the keyword SPLIT, you can specify in parentheses the number of items to be placed in the *second* part. Thus, /MODEL=SPLIT(5) indicates that the last five items on the SCALE subcommand should form the second part, and the items that precede them should form the first part.

GUTTMAN — *Guttman's lower bounds for true reliability.*

PARALLEL — *Maximum likelihood reliability estimate under parallel assumptions.* This model assumes that the items all have equal variance.

STRICTPARALLEL — *Maximum likelihood reliability estimate under strictly parallel assumptions.* This model assumes that the items have the same variance and the same mean.

You can only specify MODEL once after a single SCALE subcommand. To use more than one model on the same scale, specify several SCALE subcommands, each followed by MODEL:

```
RELIABILITY VARIABLES=ITEM1 TO ITEM8
  /SCALE (ALPHA)=ALL /MODEL=ALPHA
  /SCALE (SPLIT)=ALL /MODEL=SPLIT
  /SCALE (ML)=ALL    /MODEL=PARALLEL.
```

10.14
Obtaining Statistics

Use the STATISTICS and SUMMARY subcommands for additional statistics from RELIABILITY. Use these subcommands only once; they apply to all the SCALE subcommands that you enter.

SUMMARY provides comparisons of various statistics over all items in a scale, as well as comparisons of each item to the others taken as a group. Available keywords are:

MEANS — *Summary statistics for item means.* The average item mean, the largest, smallest, range, and variance of item means, and the ratio of the largest to the smallest item mean.

VARIANCES — *Summary statistics for item variances.* Same statistics as those displayed for MEANS.

COVARIANCES — *Summary statistics for interitem covariances.* Same statistics as those displayed for MEANS.

CORRELATIONS — *Summary statistics for interitem correlations.* Same statistics as those displayed for MEANS.

TOTAL — *Summary statistics comparing each item to the scale composed of the other items.* Scale mean and variance if the item were deleted; correlation between the item and the scale if it were deleted; squared multiple correlation with the other items; Cronbach's α if the item were deleted.

ALL — *All available summary statistics.*

For example, Figures 10.3e and 10.4 were obtained by specifying

```
RELIABILITY /VARIABLES = ITEM1 TO ITEM8
  /SUMMARY = MEANS VARIANCES CORRELATIONS TOTAL
  ...
```

The STATISTICS command computes a variety of descriptive and diagnostic statistics. The keywords for it are:

DESCRIPTIVES — *Item means and standard deviations.*

COVARIANCES — *Interitem variance-covariance matrix.*

CORRELATIONS — *Interitem correlation matrix.*

SCALE — *Scale mean and variance.*

ANOVA — *Repeated-measures analysis of variance table.*

TUKEY — *Tukey's estimate of the power to which the scale must be raised to achieve additivity.* This tests the assumption that there is no multiplicative interaction among the items.

HOTELLING — *Hotelling's T^2.* This tests for violations of the assumption that item means are equal, for scales with more than two items.

FRIEDMAN — *Friedman's chi-square and Kendall's coefficient of concordance.* Request this in addition to ANOVA if your items have the form of ranks. The chi-square test replaces the usual F test in the ANOVA table.

COCHRAN — *Cochran's Q.* You can request this in addition to ANOVA if your items are all dichotomies. The Q statistic replaces the usual F test in the ANOVA table.

ALL — *All available statistics.*

For example, Figures 10.3b, 10.3c, and 10.3d were obtained by specifying

```
RELIABILITY /VARIABLES = ITEM1 TO ITEM8
  /STATISTICS DESCRIPTIVES CORRELATIONS SCALE
  ...
```

10.15
Annotated Example

The following commands produced the output in Figures 10.3a through 10.9b.

```
DATA LIST FREE/ ID ITEM1 TO ITEM8.
VARIABLE LABELS ITEM1 'Can eat'
    ITEM2 'Can dress and undress'
    ITEM3 'Can take care of own appearance'
    ITEM4 'Can walk'
    ITEM5 'Can get in and out of bed'
    ITEM6 'Can take a bath or shower'
    ITEM7 'Can get to bathroom on time'
    ITEM8 'Has been able to do tasks for 6 months'.
VALUE LABELS ITEM1 TO ITEM8 1 'Unable to perform'
    2 'Needs assistance' 3 'Needs no assistance'.
BEGIN DATA.
3433 3 3 3 3 3 2 2
1418 3 3 3 3 3 3 2
2180 3 2 3 2 3 2 1
 ...
END DATA.
RELIABILITY VARIABLES = ITEM1 TO ITEM8
  /STATISTICS = DESCRIPTIVES CORRELATIONS SCALE
  /SUMMARY = MEANS VARIANCES CORRELATIONS TOTAL
  /SCALE (DEFAULT) ALL /MODEL ALPHA
  /SCALE (SPLIT) ALL    /MODEL SPLIT
  /SCALE (ML) ALL       /MODEL PARALLEL.
```

- The DATA LIST command indicates that the variables ID and ITEM1 to ITEM8 are to be read in free format.

- The VARIABLE LABELS and VALUE LABELS commands provide descriptive labels.

- The RELIABILITY command names all eight items on the VARIABLES subcommand.

- The STATISTICS subcommand requests descriptive statistics (Figure 10.3b), the correlation matrix (Figure 10.3c), and scale statistics (Figure 10.3d).

- The SUMMARY subcommand requests summary tables of means, variances, and correlations (Figure 10.3e), as well as item-total summary statistics (Figure 10.4).

- A series of SCALE subcommands follow. Each provides a scale name (in parentheses) and specifies that all eight variables should be included in the scale. Scale names are arbitrary (although limited to 8 letters or numbers); these were chosen to indicate the model used for each scale.

- Each SCALE subcommand is followed by a MODEL subcommand that specifies the model for that scale.

Bibliography _____

Anderson, R., and S. Nida. 1978. Effect of physical attractiveness on opposite and same-sex evaluations. *Journal of Personality* 46(3): 401–413.

Anderberg, M. R. 1973. *Cluster analysis for applications.* New York: Academic Press.

Belsley, D. A., E. Kuh, and R. E. Welsch. 1980. *Regression diagnostics: Identifying influential data and sources of collinearity.* New York: John Wiley & Sons.

Cattell, R. B. 1966. The meaning and strategic use of factor analysis. In *Handbook of multivariate experimental psychology,* ed. R. B. Cattell. Chicago: Rand McNally.

Churchill, G. A., Jr. 1979. *Marketing research: Methodological foundations.* Hinsdale, Illinois: Dryden Press.

Consumer Reports, July 1983.

Cook, R. D. 1977. Detection of influential observations in linear regression. 1977. *Technometrics* 19: 15–18.

Daniel, C., and F. Wood. 1980. *Fitting equations to data,* rev. ed. New York: John Wiley & Sons.

Davis, H., and E. Ragsdale. 1983. Unpublished working paper. Chicago: University of Chicago Graduate School of Business.

Dillon, W. R., and M. Goldstein. 1984. *Multivariate analysis: Methods and applications.* New York: John Wiley & Sons.

Dineen, L. C., and B. C. Blakesley. 1973. Algorithm AS 62: A generator for the sampling distribution of the Mann-Whitney *U* statistic. *Applied Statistics* 22: 269–273.

Draper, N. R., and H. Smith. 1981. *Applied regression analysis.* New York: John Wiley & Sons.

Everitt, B. S. 1980. *Cluster analysis,* 2nd ed. London: Heineman Educational Books Ltd.

Frane, J. W. 1976. Some simple procedures for handling missing data in multivariate analysis. *Psychometrika* 41: 409–415.

Greeley, A. M., W. C. McCready, and G. Theisen. 1980. *Ethnic drinking subcultures.* New York: Praeger Publishers.

Harman, H. H. 1967. *Modern factor analysis,* 2nd ed. Chicago: University of Chicago Press.

Jonassen, C. T., and S. H. Peres. 1960. *Interrelationships of dimensions of community systems.* Columbus: Ohio State University Press.

Judge, G. G., W. E. Griffiths, R. C. Hill, H. Lutkepohl, and T. C. Lee. 1985. *The theory and practice of econometrics,* 2nd ed. New York: John Wiley & Sons.

Kaiser, H. F. 1974. An index of factorial simplicity. *Psychometrika* 39: 31–36.

Kim, J. O., and C. W. Mueller. 1978. *Introduction to factor analysis.* Beverly Hills, California: Sage Press.

King, M. M., et al. 1979. Incidence and growth of mammary tumors induced by 7,12-dimethylbenz(a) anthracene as related to the dietary content of fat and antioxident. *Journal of the National Cancer Institute* 63(3): 657–663.

Kleinbaum, D. G., and L. L. Kupper. 1978. *Applied regression analysis and other multivariable methods.* North Scituate, Massachusetts: Duxbury Press.

Lee, E. T. 1980. *Statistical methods for survival data analysis.* Belmont, California: Lifetime Learning Publications.

Lord, F. M., and M. R. Novick. 1968. *Statistical theories of mental test scores.* Reading, Massachusetts: Addison-Wesley.

Meyer, L. S., and M. S. Younger. 1976. Estimation of standardized coefficients. *Journal of the American Statistical Association* 71: 154–157.

Milligan, G. W. 1980. An examination of the effect of six types of error perturbation on fifteen clustering algorithms. *Psychometrika* 45: 325–342.

Neter, J., W. Wasserman, and R. Kutner. 1985. *Applied linear statistical models,* 2nd ed. Homewood, Illinois: Richard D. Irwin Inc.

Nunnally, J. 1978. *Psychometric theory,* 2nd ed. New York: McGraw-Hill.

Overall, J. E., and C. Klett. 1972. *Applied multivariate analysis.* New York: McGraw-Hill.

Roberts, H. V. 1980. Statistical bases in the measurement of employment discrimination. In *Comparable worth: Issues and alternatives,* ed. E. Robert Livernash, 173–195. Washington, D.C.: Equal Employment Advisory Council.

Romesburg, H. C. 1984. *Cluster analysis for researchers.* Belmont, California: Lifetime Learning Publications.

Siegel, S. 1956. *Nonparametric statistics for the behavioral sciences.* New York: McGraw-Hill.

Sigall, H., and N. Ostrove. 1975. Beautiful but dangerous: Effects of offender attractiveness and nature of the crime on juridic judgment. *Journal of Personality and Social Psychology* 31: 410–414.

Sneath, P. H. A., and R. R. Sokal. 1973. *Numerical taxonomy.* San Francisco: W. H. Freeman and Co.

Snedecor, G. W., and W. G. Cochran. 1967. *Statistical methods.* Ames, Iowa: Iowa State University Press.

Stoetzel, J. 1960. A factor analysis of liquor preference of French consumers. *Journal of Advertising Research* 1(1): 7–11.

Tucker, L. R. 1971. Relations of factor score estimates to their use. *Psychometrika* 36: 427–436.

Tucker, R. F., R. F. Koopman, and R. L. Linn. 1969. Evaluation of factor analytic research procedures by means of simulated correlation matrices. *Psychometrika* 34: 421–459.

Winer, B. J. 1971. *Statistical principles in experimental design.* New York: McGraw-Hill.

Wynder, E. L. 1976. Nutrition and cancer. *Federal Proceedings* 35: 1309–1315.

Command Reference

Symbol	Variable	Coordinates	
1	FEMEMPLD	.012	.909
2	RETAILNG	.815	-.236
3	INDUSTZN	.794	-.364
4	UNEMPLOY	-.558	.632
5	DWELGNEW	.891	-.106
6	MIGRNPOP	.873	.083

Contents

ANOVA

```
ANOVA [VARIABLES=] varlist BY varlist(min,max) [WITH varlist]
      [/[VARIABLES=] varlist ...]

      [/OPTIONS=option numbers]

      [/STATISTICS={statistic numbers}]
                   {ALL                }
```

Options:

1 Include user-missing values
2 Suppress labels
3 Suppress all interaction terms
4 Suppress three-way terms
5 Suppress four-way terms
6 Suppress five-way terms
7 Covariates with main effects
8 Covariates after main effects
9 Regression approach
10 Hierarchical approach
11 Narrow format

Statistics:

1 Multiple classification analysis (MCA) table
2 Unstandardized regression coefficients for covariates
3 Display cell means and counts

Example:

```
ANOVA VARIABLES=YVAR1,YVAR2 BY XVAR(1,3) ZVAR1,ZVAR2(1,2)
  /OPTIONS=4
  /STATISTICS=3.
```

Overview

Procedure ANOVA performs analysis of variance for factorial designs. The default is the full factorial model if there are five or fewer factors. ANOVA tests the hypothesis that the group means of the dependent variable are equal. The dependent variable is interval level, and one or more categorical variables define the groups. These categorical variables are termed *factors*. ANOVA also allows you to include continuous explanatory variables, termed *covariates*. Other SPSS/PC+ procedures that perform analysis of variance are MEANS (see *SPSS/PC+ Base Manual*) and ONEWAY.

Defaults

By default, the model includes all interaction terms up to five-way interactions. In the default model, the sums of squares are decomposed using the classical experimental approach, in which covariates, main effects, and ascending orders of interaction are assessed separately in that order. The default display includes an analysis of variance table with variable labels, sums of squares, degrees of freedom, mean square, *F*, probability of *F* for each effect, and a count of valid and missing cases. By default, a case that has a missing value for any variable in an analysis list is omitted from the analysis.

Tailoring

Statistical Display. You can choose among three methods for controlling the order in which covariates and main effects are assessed. You can also select among three methods for decomposing the sums of squares, and you can pool interaction effects in the error term. In addition, you can request a labeled *multiple classification analysis* (MCA) table, a table of means of the dependent variable within groups formed by the factors, and unstandardized regression coefficients for the covariates.

Display Format. You can suppress the display of variable labels on all tables and the display of value labels on the MCA table.

Missing Values. You can include cases with user-missing values in the analysis.

Syntax

• The minimum specification is a single VARIABLES subcommand with an analysis list. The actual keyword VARIABLES may be omitted.

• The minimum analysis list specifies a list of dependent variables, the keyword BY, a list of factor variables, and the minimum and maximum integer values of the factors in parentheses.

• Subcommands can be specified in any order and must be separated by slashes.

Operations
- ANOVA causes the data to be read.
- A separate analysis of variance is performed for each dependent variable in an analysis list, using the same factors and covariates.
- With the exception of cell means and counts (Statistic 3), the output is always displayed in narrow format, regardless of the width defined on SET.

Limitations
- Maximum 5 VARIABLES subcommands.
- Maximum 1 each STATISTICS and OPTIONS subcommands.
- Maximum 5 dependent variables per VARIABLES subcommand.
- Maximum 10 factors per VARIABLES subcommand.
- Maximum 10 covariates per VARIABLES subcommand.
- Maximum 5 interaction levels.
- Maximum 25 value labels per variable displayed in the MCA table.
- The combined number of categories for all factors in an analysis list plus the number of covariates must be less than the sample size.
- Memory requirements for ANOVA are roughly proportional to the square of the product of the number of values for each independent variable.
- Both the number of categories in each factor and the number of interaction terms included in the model will determine the amount of workspace required.

Example
```
ANOVA VARIABLES=YVAR1,YVAR2 BY XVAR(1,3) ZVAR1,ZVAR2(1,2)
  /OPTIONS=4
  /STATISTICS=3.
```
- The VARIABLES subcommand specifies two three-way analyses of variance: YVAR1 by XVAR, ZVAR1, and ZVAR2; and YVAR2 by XVAR, ZVAR1, and ZVAR2.
- Variables ZVAR1 and ZVAR2 both have the values 1 and 2 included in the analysis.
- The OPTIONS subcommand pools all three-way interaction terms into the error sum of squares.
- The STATISTICS subcommand requests the display of a table of cell means of YVAR1 and YVAR2 within the combined categories of XVAR, ZVAR1, and ZVAR2.

VARIABLES Subcommand

The VARIABLES subcommand specifies the analysis list. The actual keyword VARIABLES may be omitted.

- Variables named before the BY keyword are dependent variables.
- Variables named after the BY in the analysis list are factor (independent) variables. All factors are used simultaneously in the analysis of variance requested by that analysis list.
- Every factor variable must have a value range indicating its minimum and maximum values. The values must be separated by a space or comma and enclosed in parentheses.
- Variables named after the keyword WITH are covariates.
- Each analysis list can include only one BY and one WITH keyword.
- Factor variables must be integer. Noninteger values for factors are truncated.
- Cases with values outside the range specified for a factor are excluded from the analysis.
- If two or more factors have the same value range, you can specify the value range once following the last factor to which it applies.
- You can specify a single minimum and maximum value range that encompasses the ranges of all factors in the list. However, this may reduce performance and cause memory problems if the specified range is larger than the actual range.
- You can specify multiple VARIABLES subcommands on a single ANOVA command. The slash between subcommands is required; the VARIABLES keyword is not.

Suppressing Interaction Effects

By default, all interaction effects up to and including fifth-order interaction effects are tested. You can suppress any of these higher-order interactions and pool them into the error (residual) sums of squares by specifying Option 3, 4, 5, or 6. When you specify any of these options, cell means corresponding to suppressed interaction terms are not displayed.

Option 3 *Suppress all interaction terms.*

Option 4 *Suppress three-way and higher-order interaction terms.*

Option 5 *Suppress four-way and higher-order interaction terms.*

Option 6 *Suppress five-way and higher-order interaction terms.*

Specifying Order of Entry of Covariates

By default, covariates are assessed first and main effects are assessed after adjusting for the covariates. To change this order, use Option 7 or 8.

Option 7 *Process covariates concurrently with main effects for factors.*

Option 8 *Process covariates after main effects for factors.* Option 8 is ignored when Option 9 is in effect.

Decomposing Sums of Squares

By default, each type of effect is assessed separately in the following order (unless Option 7 or 8 has been specified):

• Effects of covariates.
• Main effects of factors.
• Two-way interaction effects.
• Three-way interaction effects.
• Four-way interaction effects.
• Five-way interaction effects.

To change this order, specify Option 9 or 10.

Option 9 *Regression approach.* All effects are assessed simultaneously, with each effect adjusted for all other effects in the model. Option 9 overrides Options 7 and 8. Statistics 1 and 3 are not available with Option 9.

Option 10 *Hierarchical approach.* Factor main effects and covariate effects are assessed hierarchically. Factor main effects are adjusted only for factor main effects already assessed, and covariate effects are adjusted only for covariates already assessed. Factors are assessed in the order they are listed in the analysis list on the ANOVA command.

Table A shows how effects would be assessed under Options 9, 10, and the default for the following command:

```
ANOVA VARIABLES=Y BY A B C (0 3).
```

Table A Terms adjusted for under each option

Effect	Default	Option 9	Option 10
A	B,C	ALL OTHERS	NONE
B	A,C	ALL OTHERS	A
C	A,B	ALL OTHERS	A,B
AB	A,B,C,AC,BC	ALL OTHERS	A,B,C,AC,BC
AC	A,B,C,AB,BC	ALL OTHERS	A,B,C,AB,BC
BC	A,B,C,AB,AC	ALL OTHERS	A,B,C,AB,AC
ABC	A,B,C,AB,AC,BC	ALL OTHERS	A,B,C,AB,AC,BC

Summary of Analysis Methods

Table B describes the results obtained with various combinations of methods for controlling entry of covariates and decomposing the sums of squares.

Table B Summary of analysis methods

	Assessments between types of effects	Assessments within the same type of effect
Default	**Covariates** *then* **Factors** *then* **Interactions**	**Covariates:** Adjust for all other covariates **Factors:** Adjust for covariates and all other factors **Interactions:** Adjust for covariates, factors, and all other interactions of the same and lower orders
Option 7	**Factors** **Covariates** concurrently *then* **Interactions**	**Covariates:** Adjust for factors and all other covariates **Factors:** Adjust for covariates and all other factors **Interactions:** Adjust for covariates, factors, and all other interactions of the same and lower orders
Option 8	**Factors** *then* **Covariates** *then* **Interactions**	**Factors:** Adjust for all other factors **Covariates:** Adjust for factors and all other covariates **Interactions:** Adjust for covariates, factors, and all other interactions of the same and lower orders
Option 9	**Covariates** **Factors** **Interactions** simultaneously	**Covariates:** Adjust for factors, interactions, and all other covariates **Factors:** Adjust for covariates, interactions, and all other factors **Interactions:** Adjust for covariates, factors, and all other interactions
Option 10	**Covariates** *then* **Factors** *then* **Interactions**	**Covariates:** Adjust for preceding covariates **Factors:** Adjust for covariates and preceding factors **Interactions:** Adjust for covariates, factors, and all other interactions of the same and lower orders
Options 7 and 10	**Factors** **Covariates** concurrently *then* **Interactions**	**Factors:** Adjust only for preceding factors **Covariates:** Adjust for factors and preceding covariates **Interactions:** Adjust for covariates, factors, and all other interactions of the same and lower orders
Options 8 and 10	**Factors** *then* **Covariates** *then* **Interactions**	**Factors:** Adjust only for preceding factors **Covariates:** Adjust for factors and preceding covariates **Interactions:** Adjust for covariates, factors, and all other interactions of the same and lower orders

Multiple Classification Analysis

Multiple classification analysis is useful for displaying the results of analysis of variance when there are no significant interaction effects (see Andrews et al., 1973).

• For each category of each factor, the MCA table presents the unadjusted mean of the dependent variable expressed as a deviation from the grand mean; the deviation from the grand mean of the category mean adjusted for other factors;

and the deviation from the grand mean of the category mean adjusted for both factors and covariates.

• For each factor, the complete MCA display includes: the correlation ratio (eta) with the unadjusted deviations (the square of eta indicates the proportion of variance explained by all categories of the factor); a partial beta equivalent to the standardized partial regression coefficient that would be obtained by assigning the unadjusted deviations to each factor category and regressing the dependent variable on the resulting variables; and the parallel partial betas from a regression that includes covariates in addition to the factors, and the multiple R and R^2 from this regression.

To obtain an MCA table, specify Statistic 1 on the STATISTICS subcommand.

Statistic 1   *Multiple classification analysis.* The MCA display is affected by the form of analysis specified by Options 7 through 10 or their defaults. When covariates are specified, a complete MCA table can be obtained only in conjunction with Option 8, Options 8 and 10 together, or Options 7 and 10 together. With a model in which factors are not processed first, effects adjusted only for factors do not appear. The MCA table cannot be produced when Option 9 is in effect.

Statistical Display

You can request the following optional statistics on the STATISTICS subcommand:

Statistic 2   *Display unstandardized regression coefficients for covariates.* The regression coefficients are computed when the covariates are entered into the equation. Thus, their values depend on the design you specify with Options 7 through 10 or the defaults.

Statistic 3   *Display cell means and counts for the dependent variable.* A table is created by crossing all factors. Marginal means and counts as well as cell means and counts are displayed. With Options 3 through 6, cells corresponding to the suppressed interaction terms are not displayed. Statistic 3 is not available when Option 9 is in effect.

ALL   *Display all statistics.* Includes display produced by Statistics 2 and 3.

Display Format

In the default display, the ANOVA table is labeled with the variable labels and the MCA table includes value labels. In addition, the table of cell means and counts (Statistic 3) uses the available width. To change these defaults, specify the following on the OPTIONS subcommand:

Option 2   *Suppress variable and value labels.*

Option 11   *Narrow format.* Restricts the display produced by Statistic 3 to narrow width regardless of the width defined on SET.

Missing Values

By default, a case that has a missing value for any variable named on a VARIABLES subcommand is omitted from all analyses requested by that subcommand. You can change the treatment of missing values by specifying Option 1 on the OPTIONS subcommand:

Option 1   *Include user-missing values.* User-missing value specifcations are ignored. A case with a system-missing value for any variable named on a VARIABLES subcommand is omitted from the analyses requested by that subcommand.

Reference

Andrews, F., J. Morgan, J. Sonquist, and L. Klein. 1973. *Multiple classification analysis.* 2nd ed. Ann Arbor: University of Michigan.

C

Command Reference

CLUSTER

```
CLUSTER {varlist} [/MISSING={LISTWISE**} {INCLUDE}]
        {ALL     }          {DEFAULT**  }

[/READ=[SIMILAR] [{TRIANGLE}]]  [/WRITE=[DISTANCE]]
                 {LOWER   }

[/MEASURE={SEUCLID**}]  [/METHOD={BAVERAGE**}[(rootname)][,...]]
          {DEFAULT** }           {DEFAULT**  }
          {EUCLID    }           {WAVERAGE   }
          {COSINE    }           {SINGLE     }
          {POWER(p,r)}           {COMPLETE   }
          {BLOCK     }           {CENTROID   }
          {CHEBYCHEV }           {MEDIAN     }
                                 {WARD       }

[/SAVE=CLUSTER({level  })]  [/ID=varname]
               {min,max}

[/PRINT=[CLUSTER({level  })]  [{SCHEDULE**}]]
                 {min,max}     {DEFAULT** }

     [DISTANCE]  [NONE]

[/PLOT=[VICICLE** [(({1,n-1,1       })]]  [DENDROGRAM]]
                    {min[,max[,inc]]}

     [HICICLE [(({1,n-1,1       })]]  [NONE]
                {min[,max[,inc]]}
```

**Default if subcommand is omitted.

Example:
```
CLUSTER VARA TO VARD
  /PLOT=DENDROGRAM
  /PRINT=CLUSTER (2 4).
```

Overview   The CLUSTER procedure produces hierarchical clusters of items based on their dissimilarity or similarity on one or more variables. Cluster analysis is discussed in Anderberg (1973).

Defaults   By default, CLUSTER assumes that the items being clustered are cases and uses the squared Euclidean distances between cases on the variables in the analysis as the measure of distance. Cases are clustered using the method of average linkage between groups. The default display includes the number of cases in the analysis, the agglomeration schedule for the clustering, and a vertical icicle plot. Cases are identified by case number. By default, CLUSTER reads cases for the analysis and omits cases with missing values for any variable in the analysis.

Tailoring   **Cluster Measures and Methods.** You can use one of six similarity or distance measures and can cluster items using any one of seven methods: single, complete, or between- or within-groups average linkage, or the median, centroid, or Ward method. You can request more than one clustering method on a single CLUSTER command.

Display and Plots. You can display cluster membership, the distance or similarity matrix used to cluster variables or cases, and the agglomeration schedule for the cluster solution. You can request either a horizontal or vertical icicle plot or a dendrogram of the cluster solution, and you can control the cluster levels displayed on the icicle plot. You can also specify a variable to be used as a case identifier in the display.

Adding Variables to the Active File. You can save cluster membership for specified solutions as new variables in the active file.

Writing and Reading Matrices. You can write out the distance matrix and use it in subsequent CLUSTER analyses. You can also read in matrices produced by other procedures (e.g., CORRELATION) to cluster other items, such as variables.

Missing Values. You can include cases with user-missing values for the clustering variables in the analysis.

Syntax
- The minimum specification is a list of variables.
- The variables list must come first. Other subcommands can be specified in any order.
- Subcommands must be separated by slashes.
- The variables list and subcommands can each be specified once.
- More than one clustering method can be used on a matrix.

Operations
- CLUSTER causes the data to be read.
- The CLUSTER procedure involves four steps:

First, CLUSTER obtains distance measures of similarities between or distances separating initial clusters (individual cases or variables being clustered).

Second, it combines the two nearest clusters to form a new cluster.

Third, it recomputes similarities or distances of existing clusters to the new cluster.

Fourth, CLUSTER returns to the second step until all items are combined in one cluster.

- Clustering requires that valid values be present for most items.
- CLUSTER identifies clusters in solutions by sequential integers (1, 2, 3, and so on).
- When a narrow width is defined on the SET command, plots exceeding the defined width are broken into two sections and are printed one after the other.
- The BLOCK specification on the SET command controls the character used in the dendrogram.

Limitations
- The number of variables allowed on the variables list is the same as the system limit.
- CLUSTER stores both items and a lower-triangular matrix of similarities or distances in memory. Storage requirements increase rapidly with the number of items (cases). You should be able to cluster about 100 items using a small number of variables in a 64K workspace.
- Maximum 1 variable list and 1 each of the optional subcommands.

Example
```
CLUSTER VARA TO VARD
  /PLOT=DENDROGRAM
  /PRINT=CLUSTER (2 4).
```

- This example clusters cases based on their values for all variables between and including VARA and VARD on the active file.
- The analysis uses the default measure of distance (squared Euclidean) and the default clustering method (average linkage between groups).
- The PLOT subcommand requests a dendrogram.
- The PRINT subcommand requests a table that gives the cluster membership of each case for the two-, three-, and four-cluster solutions.

C

Command Reference

Variable List   When cases are read, the variable list identifies the variables used to compute similarities or distances between cases. When a distance or similarity matrix is read, the variable list uses the names for the items in the matrix.

- The variable list is required and must be specified before the optional subcommands.
- You can use keyword ALL to refer to all user-defined variables in the active file.
- You can use keyword TO to refer to consecutive variables in the active file.

MEASURE Subcommand   The MEASURE subcommand specifies the distance or similarity measure to be used in clustering cases.

- If the MEASURE subcommand is omitted or included with no specifications, squared Euclidean distances are used.
- Only one measure can be specified.

The following measures are available:

SEUCLID   *Squared Euclidean distances.* The distance between two cases is the sum of the squared differences in values on each variable. SEUCLID is the measure commonly used with centroid, median, and Ward's methods of clustering. SEUCLID is the default and can also be requested with the keyword DEFAULT.

EUCLID   *Euclidean distances.* The distance between two cases is the square root of the sum of the squared differences in values on each variable.

COSINE   *Cosine of vectors of variables.* This is a pattern similarity measure.

BLOCK   *City-block or Manhattan distances.* The distance between two cases is the sum of the absolute differences in values on each variable.

CHEBYCHEV   *Chebychev distance metric.* The distance between two cases is the maximum absolute difference in values for any variable.

POWER(p,r)   *Distances in an absolute power metric.* The distance between two cases is the rth root of the sum of the absolute differences to the pth power of values on each variable. Appropriate selection of integer parameters p and r yields Euclidean, squared Euclidean, Minkowski, city-block, minimum, maximum, and many other distance metrics.

METHOD Subcommand   The METHOD subcommand specifies one or more clustering methods.

- If the METHOD subcommand is omitted or included with no specifications, the method of average linkage between groups is used.
- Only one METHOD subcommand can be used, but more than one method can be specified on it.
- When you have a large number of items (cases), CENTROID and MEDIAN require significantly more CPU time than other methods.

The following methods can be specified:

BAVERAGE   *Average linkage between groups (UPGMA).* BAVERAGE is the default and can also be requested with the keyword DEFAULT.

WAVERAGE   *Average linkage within groups.*

SINGLE   *Single linkage or nearest neighbor.*

COMPLETE   *Complete linkage or furthest neighbor.*

CENTROID   *Centroid clustering (UPGMC).* Square Euclidean distances are commonly used with this method.

MEDIAN   *Median clustering (WPGMC).* Squared Euclidean distances are commonly used with this method.

WARD   *Ward's method.* Squared Euclidean distances are commonly used with this method.

Example   CLUSTER AVAR BVAR CVAR
                     /METHOD=SINGLE COMPLETE WARDS.

• This example clusters cases based on their values for variables AVAR, BVAR, and CVAR, and uses three clustering methods: single linkage, complete linkage, and Ward's method.

PRINT Subcommand

The PRINT subcommand controls the display of cluster output (except plots, which are controlled by the PLOT subcommand).

• If the PRINT subcommand is omitted or included with no specifications, an agglomeration schedule is displayed. If other keywords are specified on PRINT, the agglomeration schedule is displayed only if explicitly requested.

• CLUSTER automatically displays summary information (the clustering method and measure used and the number of cases) for each method named on the METHOD subcommand. This summary is displayed regardless of specifications on PRINT.

You can specify any or all of the following on the PRINT subcommand:

SCHEDULE
: *Agglomeration schedule.* Displays the order in which and distances at which items and clusters combine to form new clusters. It also shows the last cluster level at which an item joined the cluster. SCHEDULE is the default and can also be requested with keyword DEFAULT.

CLUSTER(min,max)
: *Cluster membership.* For each item, the display includes the value of the case identifier (or the variable name if matrix input is used), the case sequence number, and a value (1, 2, 3, etc.) identifying the cluster to which that case belongs in a given cluster solution. Specify either a single integer value in parentheses indicating the number of cluster solutions or a minimum and maximum value in parentheses indicating a range of solutions for which display is desired. If the number of clusters specified exceeds the number produced, the largest number of clusters is used (number of items minus 1). If CLUSTER is specified more than once, the last specification is taken.

DISTANCE
: *Matrix of distances or similarities between items.* DISTANCE displays the matrix read or computed. The type of matrix produced (similarities or dissimilarities) depends upon the measure selected. DISTANCE produces a large volume of output and uses significant CPU time when the number of cases to cluster is large.

NONE
: *None of the above.* NONE overrides any other keywords specified on PRINT.

Example   CLUSTER AVAR BVAR CVAR/PRINT=CLUSTER(3,5).

• This example requests the display of cluster membership for each case for the three-, four-, and five-cluster solutions.

PLOT Subcommand

The PLOT subcommand controls the plots produced for each method specified on the METHOD subcommand. For icicle plots, PLOT allows you to control the cluster solution at which the plot begins and ends and the increment for displaying intermediate cluster solutions.

• If the PLOT subcommand is omitted or included with no specifications, a vertical icicle plot is produced.

• If keywords are specified on the PLOT subcommand, only those plots requested are produced.

• If there is not enough memory for a dendrogram or an icicle plot, the plot is skipped and a warning is issued.

• A large plot can be avoided by specifying range values or an increment for VICICLE or HICICLE. Smaller plots require significantly less workspace and time.

<table>
<tr><td>VICICLE(min,max,inc)</td><td>Vertical icicle plot. This is the default. The range specifications are optional. If used, they must be integer and must be enclosed in parentheses. min is the cluster solution at which to start the display (the default is 1) and max is the cluster solution at which to end the display (the default is the number of cases minus 1). If max is greater than the number of cases minus 1, the default is used. inc is the increment to use between cluster solutions (the default is 1). If max is specified, min must be specified, and if inc is specified, both min and max must be specified. If VICICLE is specified more than once, the last specification is used.</td></tr>
<tr><td>HICICLE(min,max,inc)</td><td>Horizontal icicle plot. All specifications for VICICLE apply to HICICLE. If both VICICLE and HICICLE are specified, the last one specified is used.</td></tr>
<tr><td>DENDROGRAM</td><td>Tree diagram. The dendrogram is scaled by the joining distances of the clusters.</td></tr>
<tr><td>NONE</td><td>No plots.</td></tr>
</table>

Example   `CLUSTER AVAR BVAR CVAR/PLOT=VICICLE(1,20).`

- This example produces a vertical icicle plot for the one-cluster through the twenty-cluster solution.

Example   `CLUSTER AVAR BVAR CVAR`
`  /PLOT=VICICLE(1,151,5).`

- This example produces a vertical icicle plot for every fifth cluster solution starting with 1 and ending with 151 (1 cluster, 6 clusters, 11 clusters, and so on).
- In this example, the vertical dimension of the icicle plot fits on a single printed page.

ID Subcommand

The ID subcommand names a string variable to be used as the case identifier in cluster membership tables, icicle plots, and dendrograms. If the ID subcommand is omitted, cases are identified by case number.

SAVE Subcommand

The SAVE subcommand allows you to save cluster membership at specified solution levels as new variables on the active file.

- The only specification on SAVE is the CLUSTER keyword, followed by an equals sign and either the number of a single cluster solution or a range of solutions separated by a comma or blank. The solution number or range must be enclosed in parentheses.
- Both the CLUSTER keyword and a solution number or range are required. There are no default specifications.
- For each method for which you want to save cluster membership you must specify a rootname on the METHOD subcommand. The METHOD subcommand is therefore required when you use the SAVE subcommand. The rootname is specified in parentheses after the keyword on the METHOD subcommand. You can specify a rootname for only one method.
- The solution number or range applies to all methods for which you supply a rootname on METHOD.
- The new variables derive their names from the rootname and the number of the cluster solution.
- If the variables created by SAVE cause you to exceed the 200-variable limit, the entire CLUSTER command is not executed.

Example   `CLUSTER A B C`
`  /METHOD=BAVERAGE (CLUSMEM)`
`  /SAVE=CLUSTERS(3,5).`

- This command creates three new variables, CLUSMEM5, CLUSMEM4, and CLUSMEM3, containing the cluster membership for each case at the five-, four-, and three-cluster solutions.

• The order of the new variables on the active file will be CLUSMEM5, CLUSMEM4, and CLUSMEM3, since this is the order in which the solutions are obtained.

WRITE Subcommand

The WRITE subcommand allows you to write a computed distance or similarity matrix based on a measure of similarity or dissimilarity to the results file named on the SET command.

• If the WRITE subcommand is omitted, no file is written.

• If the WRITE subcommand is included without specifications, a square distance matrix of similarities or dissimilarities (depending on the measure selected) is written.

• Matrix elements are written in fixed 16-column fields with 5 decimal places. Thus, there are 5 matrix elements on each 80-character record.

• The dimensions of the matrix depend on the number of items clustered. If cases are read, the distance matrix is dimensioned by the number of cases clustered.

• Each row of the matrix begins on a new line.

• The WRITE subcommand writes the matrix to the results file named on the SET command or to the default results file (SPSS.PRC). Any existing contents of the results file are overwritten.

DISTANCE   *Write a distance or similarity matrix.* This is the default.

Example
```
SET RESULTS='GSS80.MAT'.
DATA LIST FILE='GSS80.DAT'/SUICIDE1 TO SUICIDE4 2-9.
N 35.
CLUSTER  SUICIDE1 TO SUICIDE4
  /WRITE DISTANCE.
```

• This example produces a default clustering of 35 cases. It uses all variables between and including SUICIDE1 to SUICIDE4 on the active file.

• A matrix of squared Euclidean distances is written to the file GSS80.MAT.

READ Subcommand

By default, CLUSTER assumes that the data file it uses contains cases. Use the READ subcommand to indicate that the data file contains a matrix. The general conventions for matrix materials are described in DATA LIST: Matrix Materials (see *SPSS/PC+ Base Manual*).

• If the READ subcommand is included without specifications, the matrix is assumed to be a square distance matrix. This is the default matrix written by CLUSTER.

• If any keywords are specified on READ, only the defaults that are specifically changed are altered.

• If you use the READ subcommand on CLUSTER, you must first use a DATA LIST command specifying matrix input. The DATA LIST command also assigns a variable name to each item that dimensions the matrix.

• All items named on the CLUSTER variables list must be defined on the DATA LIST command.

• The order in which items are named on the variables list must be the same as their order in the matrix.

• The MEASURE subcommand is ignored with matrix input.

• All methods specified on METHOD will accept either similarity or dissimilarity distance matrices as input. Incorrect results will be obtained for all methods if a similarity matrix is read and not identified as such.

• CLUSTER can read more than one distance matrix from the same file. Each matrix must be of the same type (similarity or dissimilarity) and must have the same dimensions.

• CLUSTER can also read other matrices such as a correlation matrix created by CORRELATION or another SPSS/PC+ procedure. This allows you to cluster variables as well as cases or to use a distance or similarity measure not available in CLUSTER.

Use the following keywords to read a matrix other than the default. TRIANGLE and LOWER are alternatives.

SIMILAR   *Distance matrix based on a similarity measure.* By default, the distance matrix is assumed to be based on a measure of dissimilarity, or distance.

TRIANGLE   *Lower-triangular matrix.* Same as LOWER but includes the diagonal elements. By default, the matrix is assumed to be square.

LOWER   *Lower-subdiagonal matrix.* Same as TRIANGLE but without the diagonal elements. By default, the matrix is assumed to be square.

Example
```
DATA LIST MATRIX FILE='GSS80.MAT'/CASE1 TO CASE35.
CLUSTER CASE1 TO CASE35/READ.
```

- The DATA LIST command names the file and the items in the matrix. The matrix is assumed to be in the fixed format written by CLUSTER.

- The variable list indexes the matrix to be read by naming the variable that stands for each matrix item. In this case, the items are the cases on which the matrix was calculated.

- The READ subcommand specifies that a matrix is to be read. By default, CLUSTER will assume that the matrix was based on a measure of distance.

Example   This example will read a matrix that was produced by the following commands:
```
SET RESULTS='VARS.MAT'.
DATA LIST FILE='VARS.DAT'/VA VB VC 1-3.
CORRELATION VARIABLES=VA VB VC/OPTIONS=2 4.
```

- The CORRELATION procedure computes correlations among the three variables and writes the matrix to the file VARS.MAT.

The commands to read this matrix into CLUSTER are
```
DATA LIST MATRIX FREE FILE='VARS.MAT'/VA VB VC.
CLUSTER VA VB VC
   /PRINT=DISTANCE/READ=SIMILAR.
```

- The DATA LIST command specifies that a matrix will be read in freefield format (keyword FREE) from the VARS.MAT file and assigns variable names to the items in the matrix. FREE is specified because the matrix to be read is not in the default format produced by CLUSTER. In this example, the items being clustered are variables.

- The variables list on CLUSTER names the same variables as the DATA LIST command and in the same order. This identifies the entries of the input matrix.

- The PRINT subcommand allows you to verify that the matrix is being read properly.

- The READ subcommand specifies that a matrix will be read instead of cases. The matrix is a square matrix and contains a measure of similarity.

- CLUSTER will read both the correlation matrix and the matrix of *n*'s written by CORRELATION. You should ignore the warning message and analysis produced by the matrix of *n*'s.

- This analysis clusters variables across cases by the default between-groups average-linkage method.

MISSING Subcommand

The MISSING subcommand controls the treatment of cases with missing values. By default, a case that has a missing value for any variable in the variable list is omitted from the analysis.

LISTWISE   *Delete cases with missing values listwise.* Only cases with nonmissing values on all variables in the variable list are used. LISTWISE is the default and can also be requested with keyword DEFAULT.

INCLUDE   *Include cases with user-missing values.* Only cases with system-missing values are excluded.

References

Anderberg, M. J. 1973. *Cluster analysis for applications.* New York: Academic Press.

CORRELATION

```
CORRELATION [VARIABLES=] {varlist} [WITH varlist] [/varlist ...]
                         {ALL    }

            [/OPTIONS=option numbers]

            [/STATISTICS={statistic numbers}]
                         {ALL             }
```

Options:

1 Include user-missing values   4 Write count and correlation matrix
2 Exclude missing values pairwise 5 Display count and probability
3 Two-tailed probability

Statistics:

1 Univariate mean, standard deviation, and count
2 Cross-product deviations and covariance

Example:

```
CORRELATION VARIABLES=WVAR XVAR YVAR
  /VARIABLES=ZVAR1 TO ZVAR5 WITH ZVAR6 TO XVAR8
  /OPTIONS=2 3
  /STATISTICS=1.
```

Overview   Procedure CORRELATION produces Pearson product-moment correlations with one-tailed probabilities and, optionally, univariate statistics, covariances, and cross-product deviations. Other procedures that read and write correlation matrices are FACTOR and REGRESSION.

Defaults   By default, CORRELATION displays a rectangular matrix of correlation coefficients for each analysis list. The default display includes the coefficient and the number of valid cases used in the computation of the matrix. An asterisk (*) indicates that a coefficient has a one-tailed probability of less than 0.01, and two asterisks (**) indicate a probability of less than 0.001. Cases that have missing values for any variable in the matrix are excluded.

Tailoring   **Statistical Display.** You can display counts and probabilities in the matrix of coefficients, two-tailed probabilities, univariate statistics for each variable, and cross-product deviations and covariances for each pair of variables.

Writing Matrices. You can write out a square matrix containing correlation coefficients and the number of cases for use in other SPSS/PC+ procedures (see FACTOR and REGRESSION: Matrix Materials).

Missing Values. Missing-value options allow you to include cases with user-missing values in the computation of each coefficient. Alternatively, you can exclude cases with missing values on a pairwise basis.

Syntax   • The minimum specification is the VARIABLES subcommand with a single analysis list. The actual keyword VARIABLES can be omitted.

• Subcommands are separated by slashes.

Operations   • CORRELATION causes the data to be read.

• A correlation of a variable with itself is displayed as 1.0000.

• A correlation that cannot be computed is displayed as a period (.).

• Correlation coefficients are displayed with four decimal places. Optional statistics are displayed with four decimal places where possible.

• Long or short string variables on an analysis list prevents execution of CORRELATION.

• The display uses the width set on the SET command.

C

Command Reference

Limitations
- The maximum number of variables that can be named on a CORRELATION command is the same as the system limit.
- Maximum 40 VARIABLES subcommands per CORRELATION command.
- Maximum 1 each of the OPTIONS and STATISTICS subcommands.
- Maximum 250 individual elements per CORRELATION command. Variable names, keywords, and special delimiters count as 1. Variables implied by the TO keyword do not count.

Example
```
CORRELATION VARIABLES=WVAR XVAR YVAR
   /VARIABLES=ZVAR1 TO ZVAR5 WITH ZVAR6 TO ZVAR8
   /OPTIONS=2 3
   /STATISTICS=1.
```

- The first VARIABLES subcommand requests a square matrix of correlation coefficients among variables WVAR, XVAR, and YVAR.
- The second VARIABLES subcommand requests a rectangular correlation matrix in which variables ZVAR1 through ZVAR5 are the rows and ZVAR6 through ZVAR8 are the columns.
- Option 2 specifies pairwise deletion. All cases with valid values for the pair of variables used to compute a coefficient are included in the computation of that coefficient.
- Option 3 requests two-tailed probabilities.
- Statistic 1 asks for univariate statistics for all variables named on the VARIABLES subcommands.

VARIABLES Subcommand

The VARIABLES subcommand specifies the analysis list. The actual keyword VARIABLES can be omitted.

- An analysis list composed of a simple variable list produces a square matrix of correlations of each variable with every other variable.
- An analysis list that consists of a list of variables and keyword WITH produces a rectangular correlation matrix. Variables listed before WITH define the rows of the matrix and those listed after WITH define the columns.
- The keyword ALL can be used in an analysis list to refer to all user-defined variables.
- You can specify multiple VARIABLES subcommands on a single CORRELATION command. The slash between the subcommands is required; the keyword VARIABLES is not.

Statistical Display

By default, the correlation matrix and number of valid cases on which the matrix is based are displayed. One-tailed probabilities of less than 0.01 are indicated by an asterisk (*) and less than 0.001 by two asterisks (**). In addition, you can request the following on the OPTIONS and STATISTICS subcommands:

Option 3   *Two-tailed probability.* Two-tailed probabilities less than 0.01 are indicated by an asterisk (*) and less than 0.001 by two asterisks (**). With Options 3 and 5, the exact two-tailed probabilties are displayed.

Option 5   *Display count and probability.* The number of cases used to compute each coefficient and exact probability are displayed.

Statistic 1   *Univariate mean, standard deviation, and count.* Displays the mean, standard deviation, and number of nonmissing cases for each variable. Cases with missing values are excluded on a variable-by-variable basis regardless of the missing-value option in effect.

Statistic 2   *Cross-product deviations and covariance.*

ALL   *Display all statistics.* Includes statistics available with Statistics 1 and 2. Specify ALL on the STATISTICS subcommand.

Writing Matrices   By default, matrices are written only to the display file. Optionally, you can write matrices to the results file named on the SET command for use in other procedures by specifying Option 4 on the OPTIONS subcommand.

- Any VARIABLES subcommand that contains the keyword WITH is ignored when matrices are written.
- With listwise deletion of cases with missing values (the default), the correlation matrix precedes a record containing the *n* used to compute all coefficients in the matrix.
- With pairwise deletion of cases with missing values (Option 2), each correlation matrix precedes a matrix of the *n*'s used to compute the coefficients.
- Correlation matrices are written with F10.7 format.
- Matrices of *n*'s are written with an F10.0 format.
- Each row of a matrix begins on a new record.
- Each record has a maximum of eight values.
- A matrix of coefficients followed by the number of cases is written for each VARIABLES subcommand in the order in which the VARIABLES subcommands are specified.
- If the results file named on the SET command is not empty when CORRELA-TION is executed, the contents of the file will be overwritten. Use the SET command immediately before the CORRELATION command to control the destination of the matrix that is being written.

Option 4   *Write count and correlation matrix.* The correlation matrix and number of cases used to compute each coefficient are written for each analysis list to the results file named on the SET command. Option 4 is ignored for VARIABLES subcommands with the keyword WITH.

Example
```
SET RESULTS='SAVINGS.MAT'.
DATA LIST FILE='SAVINGS.DAT'/ VAR1 TO VAR10 1-20.
CORRELATION VARIABLES=VAR1 TO VAR10
  /OPTIONS=4.
```

- This example writes one matrix of correlations followed by a single *n* to file SAVINGS.MAT.

Missing Values   By default, a case with a user- or system-missing value on any variable in a matrix is excluded from the computation of that matrix. Alternatively, you can specify the following missing-value treatments on the OPTIONS subcommand:

Option 1   *Include user-missing values.* Cases with user-missing values are considered valid when listwise or pairwise deletion of cases with missing values is performed.

Option 2   *Exclude missing values pairwise.* Cases with valid values for the variables used to compute a coefficient are included in the computation of that coefficient, regardless of whether the cases have missing values for other variables named on the analysis list.

C

Command Reference

FACTOR

```
FACTOR VARIABLES={varlist} [/MISSING=[{LISTWISE**}] [INCLUDE]]
                 {ALL    }           {PAIRWISE }
                                     {MEANSUB  }
                                     {DEFAULT**}

      [/WIDTH=[{width on SET**}] ]
              {n            }

      [/ANALYSIS={varlist}...]
                 {ALL**  }

      [/FORMAT=[SORT] [BLANK(n)] [DEFAULT**]]

      [/PRINT=[DEFAULT**] [INITIAL] [EXTRACTION] [ROTATION]
              [UNIVARIATE] [CORRELATION] [DET] [INV] [REPR] [AIC]
              [KMO] [FSCORE] [SIG] [ALL] ]

      [/PLOT=[EIGEN] [ROTATION (n1,n2) (n3,n4)...]]

      [/DIAGONAL={DEFAULT** }]
                 {value list}

      [/CRITERIA=[FACTORS(n)] [MINEIGEN({1.0})] [ITERATE({25})]
                                        {eig}            {ni}

              [RCONVERGE({0.0001})] [DELTA({0})]
                         {rl    }          {d}

              [ECONVERGE({0.001})] [{KAISER }]
                         {el    }    {NOKAISER}
              [DEFAULT**]]

      [/EXTRACTION={PC**    }]
                   {DEFAULT**}
                   {PA1**   }
                   {PAF     }
                   {ALPHA   }
                   {IMAGE   }
                   {ULS     }
                   {GLS     }
                   {ML      }
                   {PA2     }

      [/ROTATION={VARIMAX**}]
                 {DEFAULT**}
                 {EQUAMAX  }
                 {QUARTIMAX}
                 {OBLIMIN  }
                 {NOROTATE }

      [/SAVE={REG    } ({ALL} rootname)]
             {BART   }  {n  }
             {AR     }
             {DEFAULT}

      [/ANALYSIS...]

      [/CRITERIA...]             [/EXTRACTION...]

      [/SAVE...]                 [/ROTATION...]
```
**Default if subcommand is omitted.

Example:

FACTOR VARIABLES=VAR1 TO VAR12.

Overview   Procedure FACTOR performs factor analysis using one of seven extraction methods. For information on writing and reading matrices, see FACTOR: Matrix Materials.

Defaults   By default, FACTOR performs principal components analysis with a varimax rotation on all variables in the analysis using default criteria. A case that has a missing value for any variable on the FACTOR command is omitted from all analyses.

The default display includes the initial communalities, eigenvalues of the correlation matrix, and percent of variance associated with each; communalities, eigenvalues, and unrotated factor loadings; the rotated factor pattern matrix; and the factor transformation matrix. If you specify an oblique rotation (oblimin), the display also includes the factor structure matrix and the factor correlation matrix.

Tailoring   **Analysis Block Display.** You can tailor the statistical display for an analysis block to include correlation matrices, reproduced correlation matrices, and other statistics. You can control the order of entries in the factor pattern and structure matrices. You can also request scree plots and plots of the variables in factor space for all analyses within an analysis block.

Extraction Phase Options. You can choose among six extraction methods in addition to the default principal components extraction: principal axis factoring, alpha factoring, image factoring, unweighted least squares, generalized least squares, and maximum likelihood. You can supply initial diagonal values for principal axis factoring. You can also select the statistical criteria used in the extraction.

Rotation Phase Options. You can control the criteria for factor rotation. You can also choose among three rotation methods (equamax, quartimax, and oblimin) in addition to the default varimax rotation, or specify no rotation.

Factor Scores. You can save factor scores as new variables on the active file, using any of three methods.

Display Format. You can control the width of the display within FACTOR.

Writing and Reading Matrices. The optional subcommands used to write and read matrices are discussed in FACTOR: Matrix Materials.

Missing Values. You can request pairwise deletion of cases with missing values or assign the variable mean to cases with missing values. You can also include cases with user-missing values.

Syntax   • The minimum specification is the VARIABLES subcommand with a variable list.

• Subcommands are separated by slashes.

• The global subcommands VARIABLES, MISSING, and WIDTH can be specified only once and are in effect for the entire FACTOR procedure. WIDTH can be specified anywhere, while VARIABLES and MISSING must precede any of the other subcommands.

• The subcommands ANALYSIS, PRINT, PLOT, DIAGONAL, and FORMAT are *analysis block* subcommands. ANALYSIS specifies a subset of variables; the other subcommands apply to all analyses performed on those variables until another ANALYSIS subcommand is entered.

• You can request more than one analysis block within a FACTOR procedure.

• The subcommands CRITERIA and EXTRACTION are *extraction block* subcommands. EXTRACTION triggers the extraction of factors according to a specified method. CRITERIA can be used one or more times in an extraction block to set parameters governing any *subsequent* EXTRACTION and ROTATION subcommands.

• You can request more than one extraction block within an analysis block.
• The subcommands SAVE and ROTATION are *rotation block* subcommands. ROTATION triggers a rotation of the factors in the current extraction block, and SAVE adds factor scores for the following rotation to the active file.
• You can request more than one rotation block within an extraction block.
• You can save factor scores more than once within a rotation block.

Some subcommands (VARIABLES, ANALYSIS, EXTRACTION, SAVE, ROTATION) perform or initiate an action. For any specific analysis, you should enter these subcommands, or as many of them as you need, in the following order:

• VARIABLES causes the calculation of a correlation matrix, which is the basis for all further analysis.
• ANALYSIS initiates an analysis block, in which specifications for the analysis of a subset of variables are collected.
• EXTRACTION triggers the actual extraction of factors.
• SAVE defines new variables containing factor scores and adds them to the active file.
• ROTATION rotates the most recently extracted factors.

Other subcommands set specifications which remain in effect thereafter:

• The FORMAT and CRITERIA subcommands remain in effect until you explicitly change them.
• The PRINT, PLOT, and DIAGONAL subcommands remain in effect for the current analysis block. However, defaults are restored when an ANALYSIS subcommand is subsequently specified.

Operations
• FACTOR causes the data to be read.
• FACTOR builds a correlation matrix of variables named on the VARIABLES subcommand before it produces any factor results.
• The width specified on the WIDTH subcommand, if any, overrides the width defined on SET.

Limitations
• The number of variables allowed on the VARIABLES subcommand is the same as the system limit. However, the size of the correlation matrix that can actually be computed is limited by the memory available for workspace.
• Maximum 1 VARIABLES subcommand.
• Maximum 1 MISSING subcommand.
• Maximum 1 WIDTH subcommand.
• Maximum 10 ANALYSIS subcommands.
• Maximum 1 DIAGONAL subcommand within an analysis block.
• There is no fixed limit on other subcommands.

Example   FACTOR VARIABLES=VAR1 TO VAR12.

• This example produces the default principal components analysis of twelve variables. Those with eigenvalues greater than 1 (the default criterion for extraction) are rotated using varimax (the default rotation method).

Subcommand Order   • The standard subcommand order is illustrated in Figure A.

Figure A   Subcommand order

```
FACTOR VARIABLES=...
  /MISSING=...
  /WIDTH=...
  /READ
```

```
┌────────────────────────────────────────────────────────────┐
│                      Analysis Blocks                         │
│  /ANALYSIS=...                                               │
│  /PRINT=...                                                  │
│  /PLOT=...                                                   │
│  /DIAGONAL=...                                               │
│  /FORMAT=...                                                 │
│  /WRITE=...                                                  │
│    ┌──────────────────────────────────────────────────────┐ │
│    │                  Extraction Blocks                    │ │
│    │  /CRITERIA=(extraction criteria)                      │ │
│    │  /EXTRACTION=...                                      │ │
│    │    ┌────────────────────────────────────────────────┐ │ │
│    │    │               Rotation Blocks                   │ │ │
│    │    │  /CRITERIA=(rotation criteria)                  │ │ │
│    │    │  /ROTATION=...                                  │ │ │
│    │    │  /SAVE=...                                      │ │ │
│    │    └────────────────────────────────────────────────┘ │ │
│    └──────────────────────────────────────────────────────┘ │
└────────────────────────────────────────────────────────────┘
```

• Boxes indicate the hierarchy of subcommands. Subcommands listed in the analysis block apply to all extraction and rotation blocks within that analysis block. Subcommands listed in the extraction block apply to all rotation blocks within that extraction block.

• Each analysis block can contain multiple extraction blocks, and each extraction block can contain multiple rotation blocks.

• The CRITERIA and FORMAT subcommands remain in effect until explicitly overridden. Other subcommands affect only the block in which they are contained.

• The order of subcommands can be different from the order shown in Figure A. However, any analysis that can be performed with procedure FACTOR can be performed using this order, repeating rotation, extraction, and analysis blocks as needed.

Because of this structured syntax, which allows rotation blocks nested within extraction blocks nested within analysis blocks, you can get unexpected results if you specify commands out of order.

• If you enter any subcommand other than the global subcommands (VARIA-BLES, MISSING, WIDTH, READ) before the first ANALYSIS subcommand, an implicit analysis block including all variables on the VARIABLES subcommand is activated. Factors are extracted and rotated for this implicit block before any explicitly requested analysis block is activated.

• If you enter a SAVE or ROTATION subcommand before the first EXTRAC-TION in any analysis block, an implicit extraction block using the default method (principal components) is activated. Factors are extracted and rotated for this implicit block before any explicitly requested extraction block is activated.

• If you enter CRITERIA *after* an EXTRACTION or ROTATION subcommand, the assigned criteria do not affect that extraction or rotation.

Example
```
FACTOR VAR=VAR1 TO VAR12
  /CRITERIA=FACTORS(3)
  /ANALYSIS=VAR1 TO VAR8
  /EXTRACTION=PAF
  /ROTATION=QUARTIMAX.
```

- The CRITERIA subcommand activates an analysis block of all twelve variables. FACTOR extracts three factors using the default extraction method (principal components) and rotation (varimax) before entering the analysis block with VAR1 to VAR8, where different extraction and rotation methods are requested.

Example
```
FACTOR VARIABLES=VAR1 TO VAR12
  /SAVE DEFAULT (ALL,FAC)
  /EXTRACTION=PAF
  /ROTATION=OBLIMIN.
```

- The SAVE subcommand activates an extraction block using the default extraction method (principal components) and rotation (varimax). These factors are saved on the active file as FAC1, FAC2, and so on.
- The next extraction block uses principal axis factoring and oblimin rotation but does not contain a SAVE subcommand, so no factor scores are saved in the active file.

Example
```
FACTOR VAR1 TO VAR12
  /EXTRACTION PAF
  /CRITERIA FACTORS(5).
```

- Since no CRITERIA subcommand precedes EXTRACTION, default criteria are used, and the CRITERIA subcommand is ignored.

VARIABLES Subcommand

The required VARIABLES subcommand names all the variables to be used in the FACTOR procedure. FACTOR computes a correlation matrix that includes all the variables named. This matrix is used by all analysis blocks that follow.

- The specification on VARIABLES is a list of variables.
- There can be only one VARIABLES subcommand and only the MISSING and WIDTH subcommands can precede it.
- Variables must be numeric.
- Keyword ALL on VARIABLES refers to all variables on the active file.
- All variables named on subsequent subcommands must first be named on the VARIABLES subcommand.

MISSING Subcommand

Use the MISSING subcommand to control the treatment of cases with missing values.

- The MISSING subcommand can be specified only once.
- If the MISSING subcommand is omitted or included without specifications, listwise deletion is in effect.
- The MISSING subcommand must precede any analysis block subcommands.
- The MISSING specification controls all analyses requested on the FACTOR command.
- The LISTWISE, PAIRWISE, and MEANS keywords on MISSING are alternatives describing how missing data should be treated in computing the correlation matrix. Any of these may be requested in combination with INCLUDE, which specifies whether user-missing data should be treated as missing or valid.

The following keywords can be specified on MISSING:

LISTWISE *Delete cases with missing values listwise.* Only cases with nonmissing values for all variables named on the VARIABLES subcommand are used. Listwise deletion may also be requested with keyword DEFAULT.

PAIRWISE *Delete cases with missing values pairwise.* All cases with nonmissing values for each pair of variables correlated are used to compute that correlation, regardless of whether the cases have missing values on any other variable.

MEANSUB *Replace missing values with the variable mean.* All cases are used after the substitution is made. If INCLUDE is also specified, user-missing values are included in the computation of the means, and means are substituted only for the system-missing value.

INCLUDE *Include user-missing values.* Cases with user-missing values are treated as valid, regardless of whether LISTWISE, PAIRWISE, or MEANSUB is in effect.

WIDTH Subcommand

Use the WIDTH subcommand to control the width of the display.

- WIDTH can be specified anywhere and affects all FACTOR displays. If more than one width is specified, the last is in effect.
- The only specification on WIDTH is an integer ranging from 72 to 132.
- If the WIDTH subcommand is omitted, the width specified on the SET command is used.
- If the WIDTH subcommand is entered without specifications, a width of 132 is used.

ANALYSIS Subcommand

The optional ANALYSIS subcommand specifies a subset of the variables named on VARIABLES for use in subsequent analyses. It can also be used to perform different analyses on the same set of variables.

- The specification for ANALYSIS is a list of variables, all of which must have been named on the VARIABLES subcommand.
- Each use of ANALYSIS explicitly initiates an analysis block. The analysis block ends when another ANALYSIS subcommand or the end of the FACTOR procedure is reached.
- Within an analysis block, only those variables named on the ANALYSIS subcommand are available.
- If the ANALYSIS subcommand is omitted, all variables named on the VARIABLES subcommand are used in all extractions.
- Keyword TO in a variable list on ANALYSIS refers to the order in which variables are named on the VARIABLES subcommand, not to their order on the active file.
- Keyword ALL refers to all variables named on the VARIABLES subcommand.

Example

```
FACTOR VARIABLES=VAR1 VAR2 VAR3 VAR4 VAR5 VAR6
  /ANALYSIS=VAR1 TO VAR4
  /ANALYSIS=VAR4 TO VAR6.
```

- This example specifies two analysis blocks. Variables VAR1, VAR2, VAR3, and VAR4 are included in the first analysis block. Variables VAR4, VAR5, and VAR6 are in the second analysis block.
- The keyword TO on the ANALYSIS subcommand refers to the order of variables on the variable list, not to their order on the active file.
- A default principal components analysis with a varimax rotation will be performed for each analysis block.

FORMAT Subcommand

Use the FORMAT subcommand to reformat the display of factor pattern and structure matrices to increase interpretability.

- FORMAT can be specified once in each analysis block. If more than one FORMAT is encountered in an analysis block, the last is in effect.
- If the FORMAT subcommand is omitted or included without specifications, variables appear in the order in which they are named and all matrix entries are printed.
- Once specified, FORMAT stays in effect until it is overridden.

C

Command Reference

The following keywords may be specified on FORMAT:

SORT   *Order the factor loadings in descending order by the magnitude of the first factor.*

BLANK(n) *Suppress coefficients lower in absolute value than threshold* n.

DEFAULT   *Turn off keywords SORT and BLANK.*

Example
```
FACTOR VARIABLES=VAR1 TO VAR12
   /MISSING=MEANSUB
   /FORMAT-SORT BLANK(.3)
   /EXTRACTION=ULS
   /ROTATION=NOROTATE.
```

• This example specifies a single analysis block. All variables between and including VAR1 and VAR12 on the active file are included.

• The MISSING subcommand requests that variable means be substituted for missing values.

• The FORMAT subcommand requests that variables be ordered in factor pattern matrices by descending value of loadings. Factor loadings with an absolute value less than 0.3 will be omitted.

• Factors are extracted using unweighted least squares.

• The factors are not rotated.

PRINT Subcommand

Use the PRINT subcommand to control the statistical display for an analysis block, and all extraction and rotation blocks within it.

• If the PRINT subcommand is omitted or included without keywords, the displays indicated by the keywords INITIAL, EXTRACTION, and ROTATION are produced for the current analysis block.

• If any keywords are specified, only those displays specifically requested are produced for the current analysis block.

• The defaults are reinstated when an ANALYSIS subcommand is encountered.

• The statistics requested include only the variables named in the analysis block.

• PRINT can be placed anywhere within the analysis block. If more than one PRINT subcommand is specified, the last one encountered is in effect.

The following keywords can be specified on PRINT:

UNIVARIATE   *Valid n's, means, and standard deviations.*

INITIAL   *Initial communalities for each variable, eigenvalues of the unreduced correlation matrix for each factor, and percent of variance for each.*

CORRELATION   *Correlation matrix.*

SIG   *Matrix of significance levels of correlations.*

DET   *The determinant of the correlation matrix.*

INV   *The inverse of the correlation matrix.*

AIC   *The anti-image covariance and correlation matrices* (Kaiser, 1970). *The measure of sampling adequacy for the individual variable is printed on the diagonal of the anti-image correlation matrix.*

KMO   *The Kaiser-Meyer-Olkin measure of sampling adequacy and Bartlett's test of sphericity.* Tests of significance are not computed with matrix input if an N command is not used.

EXTRACTION   *Factor pattern matrix, revised communalities, the eigenvalue of each factor retained, and the percent of variance each eigenvalue represents.*

REPR   *Reproduced correlations and residual correlations.*

ROTATION	*Rotated factor pattern and factor transformation matrices.* Displayed for all rotations except oblimin. For oblimin rotations, the factor pattern, factor structure, and factor correlation matrices are displayed.
FSCORE	*The factor score coefficient matrix.* Factor score coefficients are calculated using the regression method.
ALL	*All available statistics.*
DEFAULT	*INITIAL, EXTRACTION, and ROTATION.*

Example
```
FACTOR VARS=VAR1 TO VAR12
  /MISS=MEANS
  /PRINT=DEF AIC KMO REPR
  /EXTRACT=ULS
  /ROTATE=VARIMAX.
```

• This example specifies a single analysis block that includes all variables between and including VAR1 and VAR12 on the active file.

• Variable means are substituted for missing values.

• In addition to the default display, the display includes the anti-image correlation and covariance matrices, the Kaiser-Meyer-Olkin measure of sampling adequacy, and the reproduced residual and correlation matrix.

• Factors are extracted using unweighted least squares.

• The factor pattern matrix is rotated using the varimax rotation.

PLOT Subcommand

Use the PLOT subcommand to request scree plots or plots of variables in rotated factor space.

• If the PLOT subcommand is omitted, no plots are produced.

• If the PLOT subcommand is used without specifications, it is ignored.

• PLOT is in effect only for analyses in the analysis block where it is specified. The default (no plots) is reinstated when the next ANALYSIS subcommand is encountered.

• PLOT can be placed anywhere within an analysis block. If more than one PLOT subcommand is specified, the last one encountered is in effect.

The following keywords may be specified on PLOT:

EIGEN	*Display the scree plot* (Cattell, 1966). The eigenvalues from each extraction are plotted in descending order.
ROTATION(n1 n2) (n3 n4)...	*Plot the variables in factor space for each rotation.* Specify a pair of factor numbers in parentheses for each plot desired. Always enter the ROTATION subcommand explicitly when you enter this keyword on the PLOT subcommand.

DIAGONAL Subcommand

The DIAGONAL subcommand specifies values for the diagonal in conjunction with principal axis factoring.

• Only one DIAGONAL subcommand can be specified in each analysis block.

• DIAGONAL is in effect for all principal axis factoring extractions within the analysis block.

• DIAGONAL is ignored with extraction methods other than principal axis factoring.

• If the DIAGONAL subcommand is omitted or included without specifications, FACTOR uses the default method for specifying the diagonal.

• Default communality estimates for principal axis factoring (and for other methods, except principal components) are squared multiple correlations. If these cannot be computed, the maximum absolute correlation between the variable and any other variable in the analysis is used.

The following may be specified on DIAGONAL:

valuelist   *Diagonal values.* The number of values supplied must equal the number of variables in the analysis block. Use the notation n* before a value to indicate the value is repeated *n* times.

DEFAULT   *Initial communality estimates.*

Example
```
FACTOR VARIABLES=VAR1 TO VAR12
  /DIAGONAL=.56 .55 .74 2*.56 .70 3*.65 .76 .64 .63
  /EXTRACTION=PAF
  /ROTATION-VARIMAX.
```

- A single analysis block includes all variables between and including VAR1 and VAR12 on the active file.
- DIAGONAL specifies 12 values to use as initial estimates of communalities in principal axis factoring.
- The factor pattern matrix is rotated using varimax rotation.

CRITERIA Subcommand

Use the CRITERIA subcommand to control extraction and rotation criteria.

- CRITERIA can be specified before any implicit or explicit request for an extraction or rotation.
- Only defaults specifically altered are changed.
- Any criterion that is altered remains in effect for *all* subsequent analysis blocks until it is explicitly overridden. CRITERIA subcommands thus have cumulative effects.

The keywords listed below may be specified on CRITERIA.

- The FACTORS, MINEIGEN, and ECONVERGE keywords apply to extractions.
- The RCONVERGE, KAISER, NOKAISER, and DELTA keywords apply to rotations.
- ITERATE applies to both extrations and rotations.

FACTORS(nf)   *Number of factors extracted.* The default is the number of eigenvalues greater than MINEIGEN.

MINEIGEN(eg)   *Minimum eigenvalue used to control the number of factors extracted.* The default is 1.

ECONVERGE(e1)   *Convergence criterion for extraction.* The default is 0.001.

ITERATE(ni)   *Number of iterations for the solutions in the extraction or rotation phases.* The default is 25.

RCONVERGE(e2)   *Convergence criterion for rotation.* The default is 0.0001.

KAISER   *Kaiser normalization in the rotation phase.* This is the default. The alternative is NOKAISER.

NOKAISER   *No Kaiser normalization.*

DELTA(d)   *Delta for direct oblimin rotation.* DELTA affects the ROTATION subcommand only when oblimin rotation is requested. The default is 0.

DEFAULT   *Reestablish default values for all criteria.*

Example
```
FACTOR VARIABLES=VAR1 TO VAR12
  /CRITERIA=FACTORS(6)
  /EXTRACTION=PC
  /ROTATION=NOROTATE
  /CRITERIA=DEFAULT
  /EXTRACTION=ML
  /ROTATION=VARIMAX
  /PLOT=ROTATION(1 2) (1 3).
```

- This example initiates a single analysis block that analyzes all variables between and including VAR1 and VAR12 on the active file.
- Six factors are extracted in the first extraction. The extraction uses the default principal components method and the factor pattern matrix is not rotated.

- The default criteria are reinstated for the second extraction, which uses the maximum likelihood method. The second factor pattern matrix is rotated using the varimax rotation.
- The PLOT subcommand requests plots of the variables in the factor space defined by the first and second factors and of variables in the factor space defined by the first and third factors. The PLOT subcommand applies to both extractions, since there is only a single analysis block.

EXTRACTION Subcommand

Use the EXTRACTION subcommand to specify the factor extraction technique to be used.

- Multiple EXTRACTION subcommands can be specified within an analysis block.
- If EXTRACTION is not specified or if it is included without specifications, the default principal components extraction is used.
- If you specify criteria for an extraction, the CRITERIA subcommand must precede the EXTRACTION subcommand.
- When you specify EXTRACTION, you should always explicitly specify a rotation method (or ROTATION=NOROTATE).

The following extraction techniques may be specified on EXTRACTION:

PC   *Principal components analysis* (Harman, 1967). This is the default. PC can also be requested with keyword PA1 or DEFAULT.

PAF   *Principal axis factoring.* PAF can also be requested with keyword PA2.

ALPHA *Alpha factoring* (Kaiser, 1963).

IMAGE *Image factoring* (Kaiser & Caffry, 1963).

ULS   *Unweighted least squares* (Harman & Jones, 1966).

GLS   *Generalized least squares.*

ML   *Maximum likelihood* (Jöreskog & Lawley, 1968).

Example
```
FACTOR VARIABLES=VAR1 TO VAR12
  /EXTRACTION=ULS
  /ROTATION=NOROTATE
  /ANALYSIS=VAR1 TO VAR6
  /EXTRACTION=ULS
  /ROTATION=NOROTATE
  /EXTRACTION=ML
  /ROTATION=NOROTATE.
```

- This example specifies two analysis blocks.
- In the first analysis block, variables VAR1 through VAR12 are analyzed using unweighted least-squares extraction. The factor pattern matrix is not rotated.
- In the second analysis block, variables VAR1 through VAR6 are analyzed first with an unweighted least-squares extraction and then with a maximum likelihood extraction. No rotation is performed for either extraction.

ROTATION Subcommand

The ROTATION subcommand specifies the factor rotation method. It can also be used to suppress the rotation phase entirely.

- You can specify multiple ROTATION subcommands after each extraction.
- Rotations are performed on the matrix resulting from the previous extraction.
- If you omit both the EXTRACTION and ROTATION subcommands, you implicitly initiate a rotation phase with a varimax rotation.
- If you include the ROTATION subcommand without specifications, the default varimax rotation is used.
- If you include an EXTRACTION subcommand but omit the ROTATION subcommand, the rotation phase may be suppressed.
- Keyword NOROTATE on the ROTATION subcommand produces a plot of variables in unrotated factor space if the PLOT subcommand is also included in the analysis block.

The following can be specified on ROTATION:

VARIMAX   *Varimax rotation.* This is the default if EXTRACTION and ROTATION are both omitted or if EXTRACTION is omitted and ROTATION is entered without specifications. Varimax can also be specified with keyword DEFAULT.

EQUAMAX   *Equamax rotation.*

QUARTIMAX   *Quartimax rotation.*

OBLIMIN   *Direct oblimin rotation.*

NOROTATE   *No rotation.*

Example
```
FACTOR VARIABLES=VAR1 TO VAR12
   /EXTRACTION=ULS
   /ROTATION
   /ROTATION=OBLIMIN.
```

• The first ROTATION subcommand specifies the default varimax rotation.

• The second ROTATION subcommand specifies an oblimin rotation based on the same extraction of factors.

SAVE Subcommand

The SAVE subcommand allows you to save factor scores from any rotated or unrotated extraction as new variables on the active file. You can use any of three methods for computing the factor scores.

• SAVE must follow the ROTATION subcommand specifying the rotation for which factor scores are to be saved. If no ROTATION subcommand precedes SAVE, factor scores are saved for the unrotated factors, regardless of whether they have previously been rotated.

• Specifications for SAVE consist of a keyword specifying a method for computing the scores and, in parentheses, the number of scores to save and a rootname with which to form variable names.

• You can specify SAVE more than once in a rotation block. Thus, you can calculate factor scores using different methods for a single rotation.

• Each specification applies to the next rotation or to the unrotated factors if no rotation follows.

• The new variables are added to the end of the active file.

• If adding the new variables results in an active file with more than 200 variables, SPSS/PC+ prints an error message and stops processing the FACTOR command.

Keywords to specify the method of computing factor scores are:

REG   *The regression method.* REG can also be specified with keyword DEFAULT.

BART   *The Bartlett method.*

AR   *The Anderson-Rubin method.*

After one of the above keywords, specify in parentheses the number of scores to save and a rootname to use in naming the variables.

• You can specify either an integer or the keyword ALL.

• The maximum number of scores you can specify is the number of factors retained in the solution.

• SPSS/PC+ forms variable names by appending sequential numbers to the rootname you specify.

• The rootname must begin with a letter and otherwise conform to the rules for SPSS/PC+ variable names.

• The rootname must be no longer than seven characters. If ten or more scores are being saved, the rootname must be short enough that the variable names formed will not exceed eight characters.

• The new names formed must be unique within the active file.

• FACTOR automatically generates variable labels for the new variables.

Example
```
FACTOR VARIABLES=VAR1 TO VAR12
   /CRITERIA FACTORS(4)
   /ROTATION
   /SAVE REG (4,PCOMP)
   /CRITERIA DEFAULT
   /EXTRACTION PAF
   /ROTATION
   /SAVE DEF (ALL,FACT).
```

• Since there is no EXTRACTION subcommand before the first ROTATION, the first extraction will be the default principal components.

• The first CRITERIA subcommand specifies that four principal components should be extracted.

• The first SAVE subcommand requests that scores be calculated by the regression method. Four scores will be added to the file, and they will be named PCOMP1, PCOMP2, PCOMP3, and PCOMP4.

• The first ROTATION subcommand requests the default varimax rotation for the principal components. The varimax-rotated scores will be saved as PCOMP1, PCOMP2, PCOMP3, and PCOMP4.

• The next CRITERIA subcommand restores default criteria. Here it implies that subsequent extractions should extract all factors with eigenvalues greater than 1.

• The second EXTRACTION subcommand specifies principal axis factoring.

• The second SAVE subcommand requests that scores be calculated by the default method (which is the regression method, as before). The number of scores added to the file is the number extracted, and their names are FACT1, FACT2, and so on.

• The final ROTATION subcommand requests varimax rotation for PAF factors, so the varimax-rotated factor scores are saved. If this subcommand had been omitted, the rotation phase would have been skipped, and scores for unrotated factors would then be added to the file.

References

Cattell, R. B. 1966. The meaning and strategic use of factor analysis. In *Handbook of multivariate experimental psychology,* ed. R. B. Cattell. Chicago: Rand McNally.

Harman, H. H. 1967. *Modern factor analysis.* Chicago: University of Chicago Press.

Harman, H. H., and W. H. Jones. 1966. Factor analysis by minimizing residuals (minres). *Psychometrika* 31: 351–368.

Jöreskog, K. G., and D. N. Lawley. 1968. New methods in maximum likelihood factor analysis. *British Journal of Mathematical and Statistical Psychology* 21: 85–96.

Kaiser, H. F. 1970. A second-generation Little Jiffy. *Psychometrika* 35: 401–415.

Kaiser, H. F. 1963. Image analysis. In *Problems in Measuring Change,* ed. C. W. Harris. Madison: University of Wisconsin Press.

Kaiser, H. F., and J. Caffry. 1965. Alpha factor analysis. *Psychometrika* 30: 1–14.

FACTOR: Matrix Materials

```
FACTOR VARIABLES=varlist

[/READ=[{CORRELATION [TRIANGLE]}]]
        {DEFAULT                }
        {FACTOR(n)              }

[/WRITE=[{CORRELATION}]]
         {DEFAULT    }
         {FACTOR     }
```

Examples:

```
SET RESULTS 'FACT.MAT'.
FACTOR VARIABLES=SUICIDE1 TO SUICIDE4
  /WRITE.

DATA LIST MATRIX FILE='FACT.MAT' / SUICIDE1 TO SUICIDE4.
FACTOR VARIABLES=SUICIDE1 TO SUICIDE4
  /READ
  /ROTATION=OBLIMIN.
```

Overview

The FACTOR procedure can write a correlation matrix or a factor-loading matrix to the results file named on SET for use in subsequent SPSS/PC+ sessions. It can also read either type of matrix, instead of a case file, for further analysis. Matrix materials to be read can be in either fixed or freefield format but must conform to certain record and format specifications (see DATA LIST: Matrix Materials in *SPSS/PC+ Base Manual*). Matrices written by the FACTOR procedure are suitable for input under either format.

When reading matrix input, FACTOR only performs analyses that are possible with that type of matrix input. Subcommands that cannot be executed are ignored.

Syntax

• WRITE is an analysis block subcommand. With WRITE=CORRELATION (or simply WRITE), a correlation matrix is written once for the analysis block in which the WRITE subcommand appears. With WRITE=FACTOR, a factor matrix is written once for each extraction performed in the analysis block.

• The READ subcommand must be specified before the first analysis block. Only VARIABLES, MISSING, and WIDTH can precede the READ subcommand.

• READ and WRITE cannot be used in the same FACTOR procedure.

• Any of the other FACTOR subcommands can be used when READ= CORRELATION (or simply READ) is specified.

• When READ=FACTOR(n) is specified, the VARIABLES subcommand must precede the READ subcommand.

• When READ=FACTOR(n) is specified, factor rotation is the only analysis that can be performed.

Operations

• FACTOR writes fixed-column matrices, with each matrix entry in a 10-column field. There are thus up to 8 entries on each record. Each row of the matrix begins on a new record.

• If the results file named on SET is not empty when you specify WRITE, FACTOR will overwrite the contents of the file. Use the SET command to specify the name of the results file before you execute FACTOR. The default is SPSS.PRC.

• When FACTOR reads correlation matrices written by other procedures such as CORRELATION, it skips the record or matrix of n's and prints a message for each line of the matrix of n's.

• When a correlation matrix is read, the MISSING subcommand and the UNIV specification on the PRINT subcommand are ignored (see FACTOR).

• When a factor matrix is read, the MISSING, ANALYSIS, DIAGONAL, and EXTRACTION subcommands are ignored. Only rotation plots are available on the PLOT subcommand. The only printed output available is the communalities and rotation information; requests for other output are ignored (see FACTOR).

Limitations

• Only one matrix can be read.

WRITE Subcommand

Use the WRITE subcommand to write a correlation or factor matrix to the results file.

• WRITE is an analysis block subcommand and can be specified within any analysis block.

• The variables in the analysis block are the only variables included in the matrix.

• When WRITE is included without keywords, FACTOR writes a correlation matrix.

• The matrix is written to the results file specified on the SET command (by default, SPSS.PRC).

• If FACTOR writes a correlation matrix, the matrix is indexed by the number and order of variables on the ANALYSIS subcommand immediately preceding WRITE. If no ANALYSIS subcommand precedes WRITE, the list on the VARIABLES subcommand is used.

• If FACTOR writes a factor matrix, each variable in the analysis defines a row and each factor extracted defines a column.

• One factor matrix is written for each extraction in the analysis block.

• The factor matrix that is written is unrotated.

• Unless you edit the results file, only the first factor matrix written to the file can be read into a subsequent FACTOR procedure.

The following can be specified on WRITE:

CORRELATION   *Write a correlation matrix.* The correlation matrix can also be requested with keyword DEFAULT.

FACTOR   *Write an unrotated factor matrix for each EXTRACTION subcommand in the analysis block.*

Example
```
DATA LIST FREE FILE='GSS80.DAT'
  /ABANY,ABDEFECT,ABHLTH,ABNOMORE,ABPOOR,ABRAPE,ABSINGLE.
SET RESULTS='GSS80.MAT'.
FACTOR VAR=ABANY TO ABSINGLE
  /WRITE FACTOR.
```

• The DATA LIST command requests that data be read from the file GSS80.DAT. DATA LIST also specifies that the data will be read in freefield format and provides names for the variables.

• The SET command identifies GSS80.MAT as the results file.

• In the first analysis block, all variables in the active file are analyzed. The default principal components extraction and varimax rotation are performed.

• The WRITE subcommand writes out a factor matrix of the unrotated factors.

READ Subcommand

Use the READ subcommand to indicate that a correlation or factor matrix is to be read.

• READ is a global subcommand and can be specified only once on the FACTOR subcommand.

• The VARIABLES subcommand must be the first subcommand specified when you use READ.

• READ must be specified before the first analysis block.

• When READ is included without specifications, FACTOR assumes that it is reading a correlation matrix that is in the same format as the matrices FACTOR writes.

C

Command Reference

- When you specify READ on FACTOR, you must first specify a DATA LIST MATRIX command that points to the file containing the matrix materials and names the variables that will be read (see the example below).
- Only a single factor matrix can be read from a file, regardless of how many matrices were written (by multiple EXTRACTION subcommands) in the analysis block containing the WRITE command.
- The number and order of variables named on DATA LIST MATRIX must match the number and order of variables in the correlation or factor matrix.
- You can analyze a subset of variables when you read a correlation matrix but not when you read a factor matrix.
- Because FACTOR does not read the number of cases with matrix materials, specify an N command before FACTOR to obtain significance levels for extraction techniques using a chi-square test or when PRINT KMO is specified.

The following can be specified on the READ subcommand:

CORRELATION   *Read a correlation matrix.* A correlation matrix can also be specified with keyword DEFAULT or by entering the READ subcommand with no specifications.

TRIANGLE   *Read a correlation matrix in lower-triangular form.* TRIANGLE can be specified only after the CORRELATION keyword.

FACTOR(nf)   *Read a factor matrix. nf* is the number of factors (columns) in the matrix.

Example
```
DATA LIST MATRIX FREE
  /ABANY,ABDEFECT,ABHLTH,ABNOMORE,ABPOOR,ABRAPE,ABSINGLE.
BEGIN DATA
  .6747329    .2183443
  .6522527    .1644450
  .3511271    .8334249
 -.0181689    .8180816
  .6998996   -.0986098
  .6363841   -.1623558
  .7479211   -.4813617
END DATA.
FACTOR VAR=ABANY TO ABSINGLE
  /READ FAC (2)
  /ROTATION=EQUAMAX
  /ROTATION=QUARTIMAX.
```

- This example reads a factor matrix computed on seven variables. Two factors were extracted when the matrix was computed.
- The DATA LIST MATRIX command is required in order to read matrix input. Here the matrix is inline.
- The matrix is analyzed using equamax and quartimax rotations.

NPAR TESTS

```
NPAR TESTS  [CHISQUARE=varlist [(lo,hi)]]

    [/EXPECTED={EQUAL**    }]
                {fl,f2, ...fn}

    [/K-S ({UNIFORM [,lo,hi]})=varlist]
           {NORMAL [,m,sd]  }
           {POISSON [,m]     }

    [/RUNS ({MEAN  })=varlist]
            {MEDIAN}
            {MODE  }
            {value }

    [/BINOMIAL [({.5})]=varlist ({valuel,value2})]
                {p }            {value         }

    [/MCNEMAR=varlist [WITH varlist]]

    [/SIGN=varlist [WITH varlist]]

    [/WILCOXON=varlist [WITH varlist]]

    [/COCHRAN=varlist]

    [/FRIEDMAN=varlist]

    [/KENDALL=varlist]

    [/MEDIAN [(value)]=varlist BY var (valuel,value2)]

    [/M-W=varlist BY var (valuel,value2)]

    [/K-S=varlist BY var (valuel,value2)]

    [/W-W=varlist BY var (valuel,value2)]

    [/MOSES[(n)]=varlist BY var (valuel,value2)]

    [/K-W=varlist BY var (valuel,value2)]

    [/OPTIONS=option numbers]

    [/STATISTICS=statistic numbers]
```

**Default if subcommand is omitted.

Options:

1 Include user-missing values   3 Sequential pairing of variables
2 Exclude missing values   for two related samples
   listwise   4 Random sampling

Statistics:

1 Mean, maximum, minimum, standard deviation, and count
2 Quartiles and count

Example:

```
NPAR TESTS K-S(UNIFORM)=AVAR/ K-S(NORMAL,0,1)=BVAR.
```

Overview   Procedure NPAR TESTS is a collection of nonparametric tests that make minimal assumptions about the underlying distribution of data. All of these tests are described in Siegel (1956).

The tests available in NPAR TESTS can be grouped into three broad categories, based on how the data are organized: one-sample tests, related-samples tests, and independent-samples tests. A one-sample test analyzes one variable. A test for related samples compares two or more variables for the same set of cases. An independent-samples test analyzes one variable grouped by categories of another variable. Following the list of available tests below, each test is described in detail.

One-sample tests are:

• BINOMIAL.
• CHISQUARE.
• K-S (Kolmogorov-Smirnov).
• RUNS.

Tests for two related samples are

• MCNEMAR.
• SIGN.
• WILCOXON.

Tests for *k* related samples are

• COCHRAN.
• FRIEDMAN.
• KENDALL.

Tests for two independent samples are

• M-W (Mann-Whitney).
• K-S (Kolmogorov-Smirnov).
• W-W (Wald-Wolfowitz).
• MOSES.

Tests for *k* independent samples are

• K-W (Kruskal-Wallis).
• MEDIAN.

Defaults   There are no default tests; each test must be requested by its subcommand keyword. By default, cases with missing values are deleted on a test-by-test basis within subcommands.

Tailoring   **Statistical Display.** In addition to the tests, you can request univariate statistics, quartiles, and counts for all variables named on the command. You can also control the pairing of variables in two-related-samples tests.

Random Sampling. NPAR TESTS must store cases in memory for tests that use ranks. You can use random sampling when there is not enough space to store all cases.

Missing Values. You can include cases with user-missing values in all tests. Optionally, you can exclude cases with missing values for any variable named on any subcommand from all tests.

Syntax   • The minimum specification is a single test subcommand and its arguments.

• Each test subcommand specifies a test and a list of variables to be tested. Some tests require additional specifications. CHISQUARE has an optional subcommand.

• The OPTIONS and STATISTICS subcommands are optional. Each can be specified only once per NPAR TESTS command.

• You can request any or all tests, and you can specify a test subcommand more than once on a single NPAR TESTS command.

• Subcommands must be separated by slashes.

• You can use keyword ALL in any variable list to refer to all user-defined variables in the active file.

• Keyword WITH controls pairing of variables in two-related-samples tests.
• Keyword BY introduces the grouping variable in two- and *k*-independent-samples tests.

Operations
• NPAR TESTS causes the data to be read.
• The display always uses narrow format.
• Specifying a string variable on any subcommand will stop execution of NPAR TESTS.
• When ALL is used, requests for tests of variables with themselves are ignored and a warning is printed.

Limitations
• The amount of memory required is directly proportional to the number of cases being analyzed.
• Maximum 1 each of the OPTIONS and STATISTICS subcommands.
• Maximum 100 subcommands per NPAR TESTS command.
• The maximum number of variables is the same as the system limit.
• The maximum range of values on the CHISQUARE subcommand is 200.

BINOMIAL Subcommand
```
NPAR TESTS BINOMIAL [({.5})]=varlist[({value,value})]
                       {p }              {value       }
```
BINOMIAL tests whether the observed distribution of a dichotomous variable is the same as that expected from a specified binomial distribution. By default, each variable named is assumed to have only two values, and the distribution of each variable named is compared to a binomial distribution with *p* (the proportion of cases expected in the first category) equal to 0.5. The default display includes the number of valid cases in each group, the test proportion, and the two-tailed probability of the observed proportion.

Syntax
• The minimum specification is a list of variables to be tested.
• To change the default 0.5 test proportion, specify a value in parentheses immediately after the BINOMIAL subcommand keyword.
• A single value in parentheses following the variable list is used as a cutting point. Cases with values equal to or less than the cutting point form the first category; the remaining cases form the second.
• If two values appear in parentheses after the variable list, cases with values equal to the first value form the first category, and cases with values equal to the second value form the second category.
• If no values are specified, the variables must be dichotomous.

Operations
• The proportion observed in the first category is compared to the test proportion. Then the probability of the observed proportion occurring given the test proportion and a binomial distribution is computed.
• If the test proportion is the default (0.5), a two-tailed probability is displayed. For any other test proportion, a one-tailed probability is displayed. The output label will always say two-tailed, however.
• A test statistic is calculated for each variable.

Example
```
NPAR TESTS BINOMIAL(.667)=YVAR(0,1).
```
• This example requests the one-tailed probability that, for cases having value 0 or 1 for YVAR, the proportion with value 0 is greater or less than 0.667.

CHISQUARE Subcommand
```
NPAR TESTS CHISQUARE=varlist [(lo,hi)]
                              [/EXPECTED={EQUAL**     }]
                                        {f1,f2,... fn}
```
The CHISQUARE (alias CHI-SQUARE) one-sample test tabulates a variable into categories and computes a chi-square statistic based on the differences between observed and expected frequencies. By default, equal frequencies are expected in each category. The display includes the frequency distribution, expected frequencies, residuals, chi-square, degrees of freedom, and probability.

Syntax
- The minimum specification is a list of variables to be tested.
- Optionally, you can specify a value range in parentheses following the variable list.
- You can also specify expected proportions with the EXPECTED subcommand.
- If you use the EXPECTED subcommand to specify unequal expected frequencies, you must specify a value greater than 0 for each observed category of the variable or the keyword EQUAL.
- The expected frequencies are specified in ascending order of category value.
- You can use the notation $n*f$ to indicate that frequency f is expected for n consecutive categories.
- Specifying keyword EQUAL on the EXPECTED subcommand has the same effect as omitting the EXPECTED subcommand.
- EXPECTED applies to all variables named on the CHISQUARE subcommand.
- Use multiple CHISQUARE and EXPECTED subcommands to specify different expected proportions for variables.
- You can request CHISQUARE with its alias CHI-SQUARE.

Operations
- If no range is specified for the variables to be tested, each distinct value encountered defines a category.
- If a range is specified, integer-valued categories are established for each value within the range. Noninteger values are truncated before classification. Cases with values outside the specified range are excluded.
- EXPECTED values are interpreted as proportions, not absolute values. Values are summed, and then each value is divided by the total to calculate the proportion of cases expected in the corresponding category.
- A test statistic is calculated for each variable named.

Example
`NPAR TESTS CHISQUARE=AVAR (1,5)/EXPECTED= 12, 3*16, 18.`
- This example requests the chi-square test for values 1 through 5 of variable AVAR.
- The observed frequencies for variable AVAR are compared with the hypothetical distribution of 12/78 occurrences of value 1; 16/78 occurrences each of values 2, 3, and 4; and 18/78 occurrences of value 5.

COCHRAN Subcommand
`NPAR TESTS COCHRAN=varlist`

COCHRAN calculates Cochran's Q, which tests whether the distribution of values of k dichotomous variables is the same for all the variables. The display shows the frequency distribution for each variable, degrees of freedom, and probability.

Syntax
- The minimum specification is a list of two variables.
- Variables must be dichotomous and must be coded with the same two values.

Operations
- A $2 \times k$ contingency table (category vs. variable) is constructed for dichotomous variables and the proportions for each variable are computed.
- Cochran's Q statistic has approximately a chi-square distribution.
- A single test comparing all variables is performed.

Example
`NPAR TESTS COCHRAN=RVAR1 TO RVAR3.`
- This example tests whether the distribution of values 0 and 1 for RVAR1, RVAR2, and RVAR3 is the same.

FRIEDMAN Subcommand
`NPAR TESTS FRIEDMAN=varlist`

FRIEDMAN tests whether k related samples have been drawn from the same population. The display shows the mean rank for each variable, number of valid cases, chi-square, degrees of freedom, and probability.

Syntax
- The minimum specification is a list of two variables.
- Variables should be at least at the ordinal level of measurement.

Operations
- The values of *k* variables are ranked from 1 to *k* for each case and the mean rank is calculated for each variable over all cases.
- The test statistic has approximately a chi-square distribution.
- A single test statistic comparing all variables is calculated.

Example
```
NPAR TESTS FRIEDMAN=SVAR TVAR UVAR
  /STATISTICS = 1.
```
- This example tests variables SVAR, TVAR, and UVAR, and requests univariate statistics for all three.

K-S Subcommand (One Sample)

```
NPAR TESTS K-S({NORMAL [mean,stddev]})=varlist
              {POISSON [mean]        }
              {UNIFORM [min,max]     }
```

The K-S (alias KOLMOGOROV-SMIRNOV) one-sample test compares the cumulative distribution function for a variable with a uniform, normal, or Poisson distribution and tests whether the distributions are homogeneous. The parameters of the test distribution can be specified; the defaults are the observed parameters. The display shows the number of valid cases, parameters of the test distribution, most-extreme absolute, positive, and negative differences, K-S *Z*, and two-tailed probability for each variable.

Syntax
- The minimum specification is a distribution keyword and a list of variables. The distribution keywords are

NORMAL *Normal distribution.* Default parameters are the observed mean and standard deviation.

POISSON *Poisson distribution.* The default parameter is the observed mean.

UNIFORM *Uniform distribution.* Default parameters are the observed minimum and maximum values.

- The distribution keyword and its optional parameters must be enclosed within parentheses.
- The distribution keyword must be separated from its parameters by blanks or commas.
- You can request K-S with its alias KOLMOGOROV-SMIRNOV.

Operations
- The Kolmogorov-Smirnov *Z* is computed from the largest difference in absolute value between the observed and test distribution functions.
- The K-S probability levels assume that the test distribution is specified entirely in advance. The distribution of the test statistic and resulting probabilities change when the parameters of the test distribution are estimated from the sample. No correction is made.
- For a mean of 100,000 or larger, a normal approximation to the Poisson distribution is used.
- A test statistic is calculated for each variable.

Example
```
NPAR TESTS K-S(UNIFORM)=AVAR/ K-S(NORMAL,0,1)=BVAR.
```
- The first K-S subcommand compares the distribution of AVAR with a uniform distribution that has the same range as AVAR.
- The second K-S subcommand compares the distribution of BVAR with a normal distribution with a mean of 0 and a standard deviation of 1.

K-S Subcommand (Two Sample)

```
NPAR TESTS K-S=varlist BY variable(valuel,value2)
```

K-S (alias KOLMOGOROV-SMIRNOV) tests whether the distribution of a variable is the same in two independent samples defined by a grouping variable. The test is sensitive to any difference in median, dispersion, skewness, and so forth, between the two distributions. The display shows the count in each group, the largest absolute, positive, and negative differences between the two groups, K-S *Z*, and the two-tailed probability for each variable.

Syntax	• The minimum specification is a test variable, the keyword BY, a grouping variable, and a pair of values in parentheses.
	• The test variable should be at least at the ordinal level of measurement.
	• Cases with the first value form one group and cases with the second value form the other. The order in which values are specified determines which difference is the largest positive and which is the largest negative.
	• You can request K-S with its alias KOLMOGOROV-SMIRNOV.
Operations	• The observed cumulative distributions for both groups and the maximum positive, negative, and absolute differences are computed.
	• Cases with values other than those specified for the grouping variable are excluded.
	• A test statistic is calculated for each variable named before BY.
Example	NPAR TESTS K-S=YVAR1 YVAR2 BY NVAR(0,1).
	• This example specifies two tests. The first compares the distribution of YVAR1 for cases with value 0 for NVAR with the distribution of YVAR1 for cases with value 1 for NVAR.
	• A parallel test is calculated for YVAR2.

K-W Subcommand

NPAR TESTS K-W=varlist BY variable(valuel,value2)

K-W (alias KRUSKAL-WALLIS) tests whether k independent samples defined by a grouping variable are from the same population. The display shows the number of valid cases, mean rank of the variable in each group, chi-square, probability, and chi-square and probability after correcting for ties.

Syntax	• The minimum specification is a test variable, the keyword BY, a grouping variable, and a pair of values in parentheses.
	• Every value in the range defined by the pair of values forms a group.
	• You can request K-W with its alias KRUSKAL-WALLIS.
Operations	• Cases from the k groups are ranked in a single series and the rank sum for each group is computed.
	• Kruskal-Wallis H has approximately a chi-square distribution.
	• Cases with values other than those specified for the grouping variable are excluded.
	• A test statistic is calculated for each variable named before BY.
Example	NPAR TESTS K-W=YVAR BY IVAR(0,4).
	• This example tests YVAR for groups defined by values 0 through 4 of IVAR.

KENDALL Subcommand

NPAR TESTS KENDALL=varlist

KENDALL tests whether k related samples are from the same population. W is a measure of agreement among judges where each case is one judge's rating of several entities (variables). The display includes the mean rank for each variable, valid count, W, chi-square, degrees of freedom, and probability.

Syntax	• The minimum specification is a list of two variables.
Operations	• The values of the k variables are ranked from 1 to k for each case and the mean rank is calculated for each variable over all cases.
	• Kendall's W and a corresponding chi-square statistic are calculated, correcting for ties.
	• W ranges between 0 (no agreement) and 1 (complete agreement).
	• A single test statistic is calculated for all variables.

Example
```
DATA LIST /XVAR1 TO XVAR5 1-10.
BEGIN DATA.
2 5 4 5 1
3 3 4 5 3
3 4 4 6 2
2 4 3 6 2
END DATA.
NPAR TESTS KENDALL=ALL.
```

• This example tests four judges (cases) on five entities (variables XVAR1 through XVAR5).

M-W Subcommand
```
NPAR TESTS M-W=varlist BY variable(value1,value2)
```

M-W (alias MANN-WHITNEY) compares two independent samples defined by a grouping variable on a single test variable. The test statistic uses the rank of each case to test whether the groups are drawn from the same population. The display shows the mean rank of the variable within each group, the valid count for each group, the Mann-Whitney U, Wilcoxon W (the rank sum of the smaller group), the two-tailed probability of U (or W), the Z statistic, and the two-tailed probability of Z corrected for ties.

Syntax
• The minimum specification is a test variable, the keyword BY, a grouping variable, and a pair of values in parentheses.

• Cases with the first value form one group and cases with the second value form the other. Order is unimportant.

• You can request M-W with its alias MANN-WHITNEY.

Operations
• Cases are ranked in order of increasing size, and test statistic U—the number of times a score from Group 1 precedes a score from Group 2—is computed.

• For fewer than than 30 cases, an exact significance level is computed.

• For more than 30 cases, U is transformed into a normally distributed Z statistic.

• Cases with values other than those specified for the grouping variable are excluded.

• A test statistic is calculated for each variable named before BY.

Example
```
NPAR TESTS M-W=YVAR BY XVAR(1,2).
```

• This example tests YVAR based on the two groups defined by values 1 and 2 of XVAR.

MCNEMAR Subcommand
```
NPAR TESTS MCNEMAR=varlist [WITH varlist]
[/OPTIONS=3]
```

MCNEMAR tests whether the changes in proportions are the same for pairs of dichotomous variables. The display shows the 2×2 contingency table, number of valid cases, and two-tailed probability for each pair of variables.

Syntax
• The minimum specification is a list of two variables.

• Variables must be dichotomous and must have the same two values.

• Without keyword WITH, each variable pair in the list is tested.

• With keyword WITH, each variable before WITH is tested with each variable following WITH.

• With Option 3 and no WITH, the first variable is paired with the second, the second with the third, the third with the fourth, and so on.

• With Option 3 and WITH, the first variable before WITH is paired with the first variable after WITH, the second variable before WITH with the second variable after WITH, and so on.

• With Option 3 and WITH, the number of variables specified before and after WITH must be the same.

C

Command Reference

Operations	• A 2×2 table is constructed for each pair of dichotomous variables and a chi-square statistic is computed for cases having different values for the two variables.
	• If fewer than 10 cases change values from the first variable to the second variable, the binomial distribution is used to compute the probability.
Example	`NPAR TESTS MCNEMAR=YVAR1 YVAR2 YVAR3.`
	• This example performs the MCNEMAR test on variable pairs YVAR1 and YVAR2, YVAR1 and YVAR3, and YVAR2 and YVAR3.

MEDIAN Subcommand

`NPAR TESTS MEDIAN [(value)]=varlist BY variable(value1,value2)`

MEDIAN tests whether the median of a variable is the same in k independent samples defined by a grouping variable. For each variable, the display shows a table of the number of cases greater than and less than or equal to the median in each category of the grouping variable, the median, chi-square, degrees of freedom, and probability. By default, the median tested is calculated from all cases included in the test.

Syntax

• The minimum specification is a single test variable, the keyword BY, a grouping variable, and two values in parentheses.

• If the first grouping value is less than the second, every value in the range defined by the pair of values forms a group and a k-sample test is performed.

• If the first value is greater than the second, two groups are formed using the two values and a two-sample test is performed.

• To override the default median, specify a median value in parentheses following the MEDIAN subcommand keyword.

Operations

• A $2 \times k$ contingency table is constructed with counts of the number of cases greater than the median and less than or equal to the median for the k groups.

• For more than 30 cases, a chi-square statistic is computed.

• For 30 or fewer cases, Fisher's exact procedure (one-tailed) is used instead of chi-square.

• For a two-sample test, cases with values other than the two specified are excluded.

• A test statistic is calculated for each variable named before BY.

Example

```
NPAR TESTS MEDIAN(8.4)=YVAR BY XVAR(1,2)/
    MEDIAN=YVAR BY XVAR(1,2)/ MEDIAN=YVAR BY ZVAR(1,4)/
    MEDIAN=YVAR BY ZVAR(4,1).
```

• The first two MEDIAN subcommands test variable YVAR grouped by values 1 and 2 of variable XVAR. The first test specifies a median of 8.4 and the second uses the observed median.

• The third MEDIAN subcommand requests a four-samples test, dividing the sample into four groups based on values 1, 2, 3, and 4 of variable ZVAR.

• The last MEDIAN subcommand requests a two-samples test, grouping cases based on values 1 and 4 of ZVAR and ignoring all other cases.

MOSES Subcommand

`NPAR TESTS MOSES[(n)]=varlist BY variable(value1,value2)`

The MOSES test of extreme reactions tests whether the range of an ordinal variable is the same in a control group and a comparison group defined by a grouping variable. For each variable tested, the display includes the count in the two groups, the number of outliers removed, the span of the control group before and after outliers are removed, and the one-tailed probability of the span with and without outliers. By default, 5% of the cases are trimmed from each end of the range of the control group to remove outliers.

Syntax

• The minimum specification is a test variable, the keyword BY, a grouping variable, and two values in parentheses.

• The test variable must be at least at the ordinal level of measurement.

- The first value of the grouping variable defines the control group, and the second value defines the comparison group.
- You can override the default 5% of cases to be trimmed from each end of the control group by specifying a value in parentheses following the subcommand keyword MOSES. This value represents an actual number of cases, not a percentage.

Operations
- Scores from the groups are arranged in a single ascending sequence.
- The span of the control group is computed as the number of cases in the sequence containing the lowest and highest control score.
- No adjustments are made for tied cases.
- Cases with values other than those specified for the grouping variable are excluded.
- A test statistic is calculated for each variable named before BY.

Example   NPAR TESTS MOSES=YVAR BY NVAR(0,1)/MOSES=YVAR BY NVAR(1,0).

- The first MOSES subcommand tests YVAR using value 0 of NVAR to define the control group and value 1 for the experimental group. The second MOSES subcommand reverses the experimental and control groups.

RUNS Subcommand

```
NPAR TESTS RUNS({MEAN  })=varlist
               {MEDIAN}
               {MODE  }
               {value }
```

RUNS tests whether the sequence of values of a dichotomized variable is random. The display includes the test value (cutting point used to dichotomize the variable tested), number of runs, number of cases below the cutting point, number of cases equal to or greater than the cutting point, and test statistic Z with its one-tailed probability.

Syntax
- The minimum specification is a cutting point in parentheses followed by a test variable.
- The cutting point can be specified by an exact value or one of the keywords MEAN, MEDIAN, or MODE.

Operations
- All variables tested are treated as dichotomous: values less than the cutting point form one category, and values equal to or greater than the cutting point form the other category.
- A test statistic is calculated for each variable named.

Example   NPAR TESTS RUNS(MEDIAN)=XVAR/RUNS(24.5)=XVAR/RUNS(1)=ZVAR.

- This example performs three runs tests. The first two test variable XVAR, first using the median and then using 24.5 as the cutting point.
- The third test is for variable ZVAR, with value 1 specified as the cutting point.

SIGN Subcommand

```
NPAR TESTS SIGN=varlist [WITH varlist]
[/OPTION=3]
```

SIGN tests whether the number of positive and negative differences between two paired ordinal variables in a two-related-samples test is equal. The display includes the number of positive differences, number of negative differences, number of ties, and the two-tailed binomial probability.

Syntax
- The minimum specification is a list of two variables.
- Variables should be at least at the ordinal level of measurement.
- Without keyword WITH, each variable in the list is paired with every other variable in the list.
- With keyword WITH, each variable before WITH is paired with each variable after WITH.
- With Option 3 and no WITH, the first variable is paired with the second, the second with the third, the third with the fourth, and so on.

- With Option 3 and WITH, the first variable before WITH is paired with the first variable after WITH, the second variable before WITH with the second variable after WITH, and so on.
- With Option 3 and WITH, the number of variables specified before and after WITH must be the same.

Operations
- The positive and negative differences between the pair of variables are counted. Ties are ignored.
- The probability is taken from the binomial distribution if 25 or fewer differences are observed. Otherwise, the probability comes from the Z distribution.
- Under the null hypothesis for large sample sizes, Z is approximately normally distributed with a mean of 0 and a variance of 1.

Example
```
NPAR TESTS SIGN=NVAR1,MVAR1 WITH NVAR2,MVAR2
/OPTION=3.
```
- In this example, NVAR1 is tested with NVAR2, and MVAR1 is tested with MVAR2.

W-W Subcommand

```
NPAR TESTS W-W=varlist BY variable(value1,value2)
```

W-W (alias WALD-WOLFOWITZ) tests whether the distribution of a variable is the same in two independent samples. A runs test is performed with group membership as the criterion. The display includes the number of valid cases in each group, the number of runs, Z, and the one-tailed probability of Z. If ties are present, the minimum and maximum number of ties possible, their Z statistics, and one-tailed probabilities are displayed.

Syntax
- The minimum specification is a single test variable, the keyword BY, a grouping variable, and two values in parentheses.
- Cases with the first value form one group and cases with the second value form the other. Order is unimportant.
- You can request W-W with its alias WALD-WOLFOWITZ.

Operations
- Cases are combined from both groups and ranked from lowest to highest.
- A runs test is performed using group membership as the criterion.
- For ties involving cases from both groups, both the minimum and maximum number of runs possible are calculated.
- For a sample size of 30 or less, the exact one-tailed probability is calculated.
- For a sample size greater than 30, the normal approximation is used.
- Cases with values other than those specified for the grouping variable are excluded.
- Test statistics are calculated for each variable named before BY.

Example
```
NPAR TESTS W-W=YVAR BY NVAR(0,1).
```
- This example ranks cases from lowest to highest based on their values for YVAR. A runs test on the group variable is done.

WILCOXON Subcommand

```
NPAR TESTS WILCOXON=varlist [WITH varlist]
[/OPTION=3]
```

WILCOXON tests the hypothesis that there are no differences between two paired populations of ordered-metric scores. The test takes into account the magnitude of the differences between two paired variables. The display includes the number of positve and negative differences and their respective means, the number of ties, the valid count, Z, and the probability of Z.

Syntax
- The minimum specification is a list of two variables.
- Without keyword WITH, each variable is paired with every other variable in the list.
- With keyword WITH, each variable before WITH is paired with each variable after WITH.
- With Option 3 and no WITH, the first variable is paired with the second, the second with the third, the third with the fourth, and so on.

- With Option 3 and WITH, the first variable before WITH is paired with the first variable after WITH, the second variable before WITH with the second variable after WITH, and so on.
- With Option 3 and WITH, the number of variables specified before and after WITH must be the same.

Operations
- The differences between the pair of variables are counted, the absolute differences ranked, the positive and negative ranks summed, and the test statistic Z computed from the positive and negative rank sums.
- Under the null hypothesis for large sample sizes, Z is approximately normally distributed with a mean of 0 and a variance of 1.

Example
```
NPAR TESTS WILCOXON=VARA VARB VARC
  /OPTIONS=3.
```
- This example pairs VARA and VARB and then VARB and VARC.

Statistical Display

The following options and statistics are available in NPAR TESTS. Option 3 can be specified only for two-related-samples tests (MCNEMAR, SIGN, and WIL-COXON).

Option 3 *Sequential pairing of variables for two related samples.* With a simple variable list, sequential pairs are tested. With keyword WITH, the first variable before WITH is tested with the first variable after WITH, and so on. The variable lists on both sides of WITH must have the same number of variables.

Statistic 1 *Mean, maximum, minimum, standard deviation, and count.*

Statistic 2 *Quartiles and count.* Values corresponding to the 25th, 50th, and 75th percentiles and the number of valid cases are displayed.

Example
```
NPAR TESTS MCNEMAR=XVAR YVAR ZVAR
  /OPTION=3.
```
- This example tests XVAR with YVAR and YVAR with ZVAR, but not XVAR with ZVAR, as is the case without Option 3.

Random Sampling

Option 4 *Random sampling.* Use if there is insufficient memory. Ignored for the RUNS subcommand.

Missing Values

By default, cases with missing values are deleted on a test-by-test basis. For subcommands specifying several tests, each test is evaluated separately.

Option 1 *Include user-missing values.* Cases with user-defined missing values are included in all tests requested on the NPAR TESTS command.

Option 2 *Exclude missing values listwise.* Cases missing on any variable named on any subcommand are excluded from all tests.

Reference

Siegel, S. 1956. *Nonparametric statistics for the behavioral sciences.* New York: McGraw-Hill.

ONEWAY

```
ONEWAY [VARIABLES=]varlist BY varname(min,max)

[/POLYNOMIAL=n]

[/CONTRAST=coefficient list] [/CONTRAST=...]

[/RANGES={SNK          }] [RANGES=...]
         {BTUKEY       }
         {TUKEY        }
         {ranges values}
         {LSD          }  [({.05  })]
         {DUNCAN       }    {alpha}
         {MODLSD       }
         {SCHEFFE      }

[/OPTIONS=option numbers]

[/STATISTICS={statistic numbers}]
             {ALL              }
```

Options:

1 Include user-missing values
2 Exclude missing values listwise
3 Suppress variable labels
4 Write matrix of counts, means, and standard deviations
6 Use value labels as group labels
7 Read matrix of counts, means, and standard deviations
8 Read matrix of counts, means, pooled variance, and degrees of freedom
10 Harmonic mean of all group sizes as sample sizes in range tests

Statistics:

1 Group descriptive statistics
2 Fixed- and random-effects statistics
3 Homogeneity-of-variance tests

Example:

```
ONEWAY VARIABLES=YVAR BY XVAR(1,4).
```

Overview

Procedure ONEWAY produces a one-way analysis of variance for an interval-level dependent variable by one numeric independent variable that defines the groups for the analysis. Other SPSS/PC+ procedures that perform analysis of variance are MEANS, ANOVA, and MANOVA (in Advanced Statistics). Some tests not included in the other procedures are available as options in ONEWAY.

Defaults

By default, ONEWAY produces a labeled table for each dependent variable by the independent variable. The table contains the between- and within- groups sums of squares, mean squares, and degrees of freedom. The F ratio and the probability of F for the test are displayed. Cases that are missing on both variables used in each test are excluded from the calculation of the test statistics.

Tailoring

Trends, Contrasts, and Ranges. You can partition the between-groups sums of squares into linear, quadratic, cubic, and higher-order trend components. You can specify up to 10 contrasts to be tested with the t statistic. You can also specify seven different range tests for comparisons of all possible pairs of group means, or "multiple comparisons."

Display Format. You can suppress the display of variable labels. You can also label groups with the value labels of the independent variable.

Statistical Display. In addition to the default display, you can obtain means, standard deviations, and other descriptive statistics for each group. Fixed- and random-effects statistics as well as several tests for homogeneity of variance are also available. The harmonic mean of all group sizes can be used as the sample size for each group in range tests.

Writing and Reading Matrices. ONEWAY can write out or read a matrix of group frequencies, means, and standard deviations for use in subsequent analyses. ONEWAY also reads matrix materials consisting of group frequencies, means, pooled variance, and degrees of freedom for the pooled variance.

Missing Values. You can include cases with user-missing values in the analysis or omit cases with missing values for any variable in the analysis list from all calculations.

Syntax
- The minimum specification is the VARIABLES subcommand with a single analysis list. The actual keyword VARIABLES may be omitted.
- The minimum analysis list specifies a dependent variable, the keyword BY, an independent variable, and the minimum and maximum values of the independent variable in parentheses.
- The VARIABLES subcommand must be specified first. Other subcommands can be specified in any order.
- Subcommands must be separated by a slash.

Operations
- ONEWAY causes the data to be read.
- Noninteger values for the independent variable are truncated.
- Cases with values outside the range specified for the independent variable are omitted from the analysis.
- Specifying a string variable as an independent or dependent variable stops execution of ONEWAY.
- The display uses the width defined on SET.
- If SPSS/PC+ encounters more than one each of the POLYNOMIAL, OPTIONS, or STATISTICS subcommands, it uses the last one of each type.

Limitations
- Maximum 100 dependent variables.
- Maximum 1 independent variable.
- The number of categories for the independent variable is limited only by available memory.
- Maximum 1 VARIABLES subcommand.
- Maximum 1 POLYNOMIAL subcommand.
- Maximum 10 CONTRAST subcommands.
- Maximum 10 RANGES subcommands.
- Maximum 1 OPTIONS subcommand.
- Maximum 1 STATISTICS subcommand.
- Contrasts tests are not performed if the range of values for the independent variable exceeds 50.
- Range tests are not performed if there are more than 50 nonempty categories.
- Range tests are not performed on less than 3 groups.

Example

```
ONEWAY VARIABLES=YVAR BY XVAR(1,4).
```

- This example names YVAR as the dependent variable and XVAR as the independent variable with a minimum value of 1 and a maximum value of 4.

VARIABLES Subcommand

The VARIABLES subcommand specifies the analysis list. The actual keyword VARIABLES may be omitted.

- An analysis list specifies a dependent variable list, the keyword BY, an independent variable, and the minimum and maximum values of the independent variable in parentheses.
- There can be only one VARIABLES subcommand and it must be specified before any of the optional subcommands.
- All variables named must be numeric.
- The minimum and maximum values of the independent variable must be separated by a comma or a space and enclosed in parentheses. These values must be integers.

C

Command Reference

POLYNOMIAL Subcommand

The POLYNOMIAL subcommand partitions the between-groups sums of squares into linear, cubic, quadratic, or higher-order trend components. The display is an expanded analysis of variance table that provides the degrees of freedom, sums of squares, mean square, F, and probability of F for each partition.

- The value specified on POLYNOMIAL denotes the highest-degree polynomial to be used.
- The polynomial value must be a positive integer less than or equal to 5. If the polynomial specified is greater than the number of groups, the highest-degree polynomial possible is assumed.
- With balanced designs, ONEWAY computes the sums of squares for each order polynomial from weighted polynomial contrasts, using the group code as the metric. These contrasts are orthogonal.
- With unbalanced designs and equal spacing between groups, ONEWAY also computes sums of squares using the unweighted polynomial contrasts. These contrasts are not orthogonal.
- The deviation sums of squares are always calculated from the weighted sums of squares (Speed, 1976).
- Only one POLYNOMIAL subcommand can be specified per ONEWAY command.

Example

```
ONEWAY VARIABLES=WELL BY EDUC6 (1,6)
   /POLYNOMIAL=2.
```

- This example requests an analysis of variance of WELL by EDUC6 with second-order (quadratic) polynomial contrasts.

CONTRAST Subcommand

Use the CONTRAST subcommand to specify a priori contrasts to be tested by the t statistic. Contrasts are specified as a vector of coefficients, where each coefficient corresponds to a category of the independent variable. The display for each contrast list is the value of the contrast, the standard error of the contrast, the t statistic, the degrees of freedom for t, and the two-tailed probability of t. Both pooled- and separate-variance estimates are displayed.

- A contrast must be specified or implied for every group in the range specified for the independent variable, even if the group is empty. If the number of contrast values is less than the number of groups, contrast values of 0 are assumed for the remaining groups.
- Only one set of contrast coefficients can be specified per CONTRAST subcommand. Additional contrasts on a single CONTRAST subcommand are ignored.
- You can use the notation $n*c$ to indicate that coefficient c is repeated n times.
- Coefficients are assigned to empty and nonempty groups defined by ascending integer values of the independent variable.
- Trailing coefficients of 0 do not need to be expressed.
- A warning is issued when sets of contrasts do not sum to 0.

Example

```
ONEWAY VARIABLES=YVAR BY XVAR(1,4)
   /CONTRAST = -1 -1 1 1
   /CONTRAST = -1 0 0 1
   /CONTRAST = -1 0 .5 .5.
```

- The first CONTRAST subcommand contrasts the combination of the first two groups with the combination of the last two groups.
- The second CONTRAST subcommand contrasts the first group with the last group.
- The third CONTRAST subcommand contrasts the first group with the combination of the third and fourth groups.

Example

```
ONEWAY VARIABLES=YVAR BY XVAR(1,4)
   /CONTRAST = -1 1 2*0
   /CONTRAST = -1 1 0 0
   /CONTRAST = -1 1.
```

• All three CONTRAST subcommands specify the the same contrast coefficients for a four-group analysis. The first group is contrasted with the second group in all three cases.

• The first CONTRAST uses the $n*c$ notation and the last CONTRAST omits the trailing zero coefficients.

RANGES Subcommand

Each RANGES subcommand specifies one of seven different tests for multiple comparisons between means. The RANGES display always includes multiple comparisons between all groups. Nonempty group means are sorted in ascending order, with asterisks indicating significantly different groups. In addition, homogeneous subsets are calculated for balanced designs. The means of the groups included within a subset are not significantly different.

• By default, the range tests use sample sizes of the two groups being compared. This is equivalent to using the harmonic mean of the sample size of the two groups begin compared. You can use Option 10 to change this default.

• The default alpha for all tests is 0.05. For some tests, you can specify a different alpha.

The tests available on the RANGES subcommand are

LSD(p)   *Least-significant difference.* Alpha can be specified between 0 and 1. The default is 0.05.

DUNCAN(p)   *Multiple range test.* Alpha can be specified as 0.01, 0.05, and 0.10 only. The default is 0.05. DUNCAN uses 0.01 if the alpha specified is less than 0.05; 0.05 if the alpha specified is greater than or equal to 0.05 but less than 0.10; 0.10 if the alpha specified is greater than or equal to 0.10; and 0.05 if no alpha is specified.

SNK   *Student-Newman-Keuls.* Alpha is 0.05.

BTUKEY   *Tukey's alternate procedure.* Alpha is 0.05.

TUKEY   *Honestly significant difference.* Alpha is 0.05.

MODLSD(p)   *Modified LSD.* Alpha can be specified between 0 and 1. The default is 0.05.

SCHEFFE(p) *Scheffé's test.* Alpha can be specified between 0 and 1. The default is 0.05.

Alternatively, you can use any other type of range by specifying range values:

• Specify the range values separated by commas or blanks.

• Up to $k-1$ range values can be specified in ascending order, where k is the number of groups and where the range value times the standard error of the combined subset is the critical value.

• If less than $k-1$ values are specified, the last value specified is used for the remaining range values.

• You can use the notation $n*r$ to indicate that the range r is repeated n times.

• To use a single critical value for all subsets, specify one range value.

Example
```
ONEWAY VARIABLES=WELL BY EDUC6 (1,6)
  /RANGES=SNK
  /RANGES=SCHEFFE (.01).
```

• This example requests two different range tests. The first uses the Student-Newman-Keuls test and the second uses Scheffé's test with an alpha of 0.01.

Example
```
ONEWAY VARIABLES=WELL BY EDUC (1,6)
  /RANGES=2.81, 3.34, 3.65, 3.88, 4.05.
```

• The RANGES subcommand specifies five range values.

Harmonic Means

By default, range tests use the harmonic mean of the sizes of the two groups being compared. Use Option 10 on the OPTIONS subcommand to change this default.

Option 10 *Use the harmonic mean of* all *group sizes as the sample size for each group in range tests.* If Option 10 is used for unbalanced designs, ONEWAY determines homogeneous subsets for all range tests.

C

Command Reference

Display Format   The default display labels groups as GRP1, GRP2, and so forth, and includes variable labels. You can change these defaults by specifying the following on the OPTIONS subcommand:

Option 3   *Suppress variable labels.*

Option 6   *Use value labels for group labels.* Use the first eight characters from the value labels of the independent variable as group labels.

Statistical Display   By default, ONEWAY displays the between- and within-groups sums of squares, mean squares, degrees of freedom, the *F* ratio, and the probability of *F* for the test. You can obtain additional statistics by specifying the following on the STATISTICS subcommand:

Statistic 1   *Group descriptive statistics.* Displays the count, mean, standard deviation, standard error, minimum, maximum, and 95% confidence interval for each group for each dependent variable.

Statistic 2   *Fixed- and random-effects statistics.* Displays the standard deviation, standard error, and 95% confidence interval for the fixed-effects model and the standard error, 95% confidence interval, and estimate of between-component variance for the random-effects model.

Statistic 3   *Homogeneity-of-variance tests.* Displays Cochran's *C*, Bartlett-Box *F*, and Hartley's *F* max.

ALL   *All statistics.*

Writing Matrices   ONEWAY writes matrix materials that it can read in subsequent analyses.

• To write matrix materials, specify Option 4 on the OPTIONS subcommand.

• Matrix materials are written to the results file named on the SET command (the default is SPSS.PRC).

• If the results file is not empty when ONEWAY is executed with Option 4, the contents of the file are overwritten. Use the SET command to specify a different results file.

Option 4   *Write a matrix containing vectors of counts, means, and standard deviations.* For each dependent variable, Option 4 writes a vector of group frequencies, followed by a vector of group means and a vector of group standard deviations. Vectors are written 80 characters per line with each vector beginning on a new line. The format for the frequencies vector is F10.2. The format for the means and standard deviation vectors is F10.4. There is thus a maximum of eight values per line.

Example
```
SET RESULTS='WELL.MAT'.
DATA LIST FILE='GSS80.DAT'
 /WELL 2-3 EDUC 4-5.
RECODE EDUC (0 THRU 8=1) (9 10 11=2) (12=3) (13 14 15=4)
 (16=5) (17 THRU 20=6).
ONEWAY VARIABLES=WELL BY EDUC (1,6)
 /OPTIONS=4.
```

• The SET command defines file WELL.MAT in the current directory as the results file.

• Option 4 writes group counts, means, and standard deviations for WELL by EDUC to the results file using the format supplied by ONEWAY.

Reading Matrices   You can read matrix materials in fixed or free format by specifying Option 7 or 8 on the OPTIONS subcommand. The general conventions for matrix materials are described in DATA LIST: Matrix Materials.

• If you specify Option 7 or 8 in ONEWAY, you must first use a DATA LIST command specifying matrix materials.

• All variables named on the ONEWAY analysis list must be named on the DATA LIST command.

- The analysis list on the ONEWAY command must be the same as the analysis list that was used when the matrix was written.
- There must be an entry for each group in the vectors of counts, means, and (with Option 7) standard deviations. Entries should be in ascending order of the values of the independent variable.
- Each user-generated vector must begin on a new line or record and can be entered in either fixed or freefield format.

Option 7 *Read matrix materials containing vectors of counts, means, and standard deviations.* ONEWAY expects a vector of counts for each group, followed by a vector of group means and a vector of group standard deviations like those written by Option 4.

Option 8 *Read matrix materials containing vectors of counts and means, followed by the pooled variance and the degrees of freedom.* ONEWAY expects a vector of counts for each group, followed by a vector of means, followed by the a record containing the pooled variance (within-groups mean square) and another record containing the (within-groups) degrees of freedom for the pooled variance. If the degrees of freedom are omitted, then $n-k$ degrees of freedom are assumed, where n is the number of cases and k is the number of groups. Statistics 1, 2, and 3, and the separate variance estimate for contrasts named on the CONTRAST command are not available.

Example
```
DATA LIST FREE MATRIX
  /WELL EDUC.
BEGIN DATA.
65 95 181 82 40 37
2.6462 2.7737 4.1796 4.5610 4.6625 5.2297
6.2699
494
END DATA.
ONEWAY VARIABLES=WELL BY EDUC(1,6)
  /OPTIONS=8.
```

- The DATA LIST command specifies matrix input in freefield format.
- The counts for the six analysis groups (the six categories of EDUC, in this example) are on the first line of matrix input, the means for the six groups are on the second line, the within-groups mean square is on the third line, and the within-groups degrees of freedom are on the fourth line.
- Each vector to be read begins on a new line.
- Option 8 requests that matrix materials be read consisting of vectors of counts and means, plus the pooled variance and degress of freedom.

Missing Values   By default, cases with missing values on either the independent or dependent variable are excluded from the test. You can change the handling of cases with missing values by specifying one of the following on the OPTIONS subcommand:

Option 1 *Include cases with user-missing values.* Cases with user-missing values are included in the analyses.

Option 2 *Exclude cases with missing values listwise.* Cases that have missing values for any of the variables named in the analysis list are excluded from all analyses.

References   Speed, M. F. 1976. Response curves in the one way classification with unequal numbers of observations per cell. *Proceedings of the statistical computing section, American Statistical Association.*

C

Command Reference

QUICK CLUSTER

```
QUICK CLUSTER {varlist} [/INITIAL = [{SELECT**   }]]
              {ALL     }              {FIRST      }
                                      {(value list)}

    [/CRITERIA = [CLUSTERS({2     })] [NOUPDATE]]
                           {number}

    [/PRINT = [CLUSTER] [ID(varname)] [INITIAL**]]
              [DISTANCE] [ANOVA]

    [/WRITE]

    [/SAVE = [CLUSTER(varname)] [DISTANCE(varname)]]

    [/MISSING = {LISTWISE**}
                {PAIRWISE  }
                {INCLUDE   }]
                {DEFAULT** }
```

**Default if subcommand is omitted.

Example:

```
QUICK CLUSTER VARA TO VARD
  /CRITERIA=CLUSTERS(4)
  /SAVE=CLUSTER(GROUP).
```

Overview

The QUICK CLUSTER procedure groups cases efficiently into clusters, when the desired number of clusters is known. It is not as flexible as CLUSTER, but it uses considerably less processing time and memory, especially when the number of cases is large.

Defaults

By default, QUICK CLUSTER forms two clusters and chooses well-spaced cases as initial cluster centers. It then assigns each case to the nearest cluster, updating the cluster center every time a case is added, so that the center will be at the mean value of all the cases included in the cluster. After all cases have been used to update the cluster centers, each case is assigned to the nearest of the updated centers. (This will often, but not always, be the one to which it was joined during the updating phase.)

Default output consists of the initial cluster centers, the centers used for the final assignment of cases, the actual centers of the final clusters, and the number of cases in each cluster. By default, cases are deleted from the analysis if they have any missing values on the variables used in clustering.

Tailoring

Clustering Criteria. You can specify the number of clusters to be formed. You can suppress the updating phase and simply assign cases to the initial cluster centers to classify cases very rapidly into clusters whose centers have already been determined.

Initial Cluster Centers. You can specify the points to be used as initial cluster centers. Alternatively, you can use the first k cases in the file that have nonmissing data as initial centers (where k is the number of clusters requested) to avoid the search for widely spaced cases.

Saving Cluster Centers. You can write the final cluster centers to the results file, possibly for use as initial cluster centers in a later run.

Adding Results to the Active File. You can add a new variable to your active file to indicate the cluster membership of each case. You can also add a variable indicating the distance of each case from its cluster center.

Display Output. You can display cluster membership and distance from the final cluster center for each case. Cases are identified either by sequential numbers or by the values of any variable in your file. You can ask to see the distances between each final cluster center and the other final centers. You can also request descriptive F tests for each variable used in the clustering and a covariance matrix.

Missing Values. You can request pairwise deletion of missing data, in which a case is assigned to the nearest cluster on the basis of variables for which the case has valid data. You can also include user-missing values in the calculation of distances.

Syntax

- The minimum specification is a list of variables.
- The variable list must be specified first. Other subcommands can be specified in any order.
- Subcommands must be separated from each other and from the variable list by slashes.

Operations

- QUICK CLUSTER causes the data to be read.
- The procedure involves three steps:

  First, QUICK CLUSTER selects initial cluster centers according to the method specified on the INITIAL subcommand.

  Second, the cluster centers are updated by joining each case to the nearest center. After each case is joined, the cluster center is updated to the (new) mean value of all cases in the cluster plus the initial cluster center.

  Third, the cases are examined again, and each is assigned to the cluster whose final updated center location is closest to it.

- By default, initial cluster centers are formed by choosing one case (with valid data for the clustering variables) for each cluster requested. These cases are chosen to be well separated from one another, so this initial selection requires a pass through the data.
- Two other methods are available for choosing initial cluster centers (see INITIAL Subcommand).
- If CRITERIA=NOUPDATE is specified, the updating of cluster centers is suppressed and cases are simply assigned to the nearest initial cluster center.
- Variables measured on different scales should be standardized prior to their use in QUICK CLUSTER. Otherwise, the scale on which different variables are measured will affect the distances used in forming clusters.

Limitations

- The number of variables allowed on the variable list is the same as the system limit.
- Since QUICK CLUSTER processes cases sequentially rather than storing them in memory, memory requirements depend on the number of variables and the number of clusters, but not on the number of cases.
- Only 1 variable list and 1 each of the optional subcommands can be specified.

Example

```
QUICK CLUSTER VARA TO VARD
  /CRITERIA=CLUSTERS(4)
  /WRITE.
```

- This example clusters cases based on their values for all variables between and including VARA and VARD on the active file.
- Four clusters, rather than the default two, will be formed.
- Initial cluster centers will be chosen by the default method, by finding four widely spaced cases.
- The four final cluster centers will be written to the resulting file specified on the SET command (SPSS.PRC by default).

C

Command Reference

Variable List
The variable list identifies the variables on which cases are to be clustered.

• The variable list is required and must be the first specification on QUICK CLUSTER.

• You can use the keyword ALL to refer to all user-defined variables in the active file.

• You can use the keyword TO to refer to consecutive variables in the active file.

CRITERIA Subcommand
Use the CRITERIA subcommand to specify the number of clusters desired or to suppress the updating of initial cluster centers. If updating is suppressed, QUICK CLUSTER simply assigns cases to the initial centers.

• If you do not specify the number of clusters on a CRITERIA subcommand, cases will be grouped into two clusters.

• QUICK CLUSTER uses the squared Euclidean distance measure in assigning cases to the nearest cluster center. In this algorithm, the unsquared Euclidean measure would assign cases in the same way.

The following criteria may be specified:

CLUSTERS(number) *Number of clusters to create.* If you do not specify a number, two clusters are formed.

NOUPDATE *Do not update the initial cluster centers.* Cases are simply assigned to the nearest of the initial cluster centers. This specification is normally used only if the initial centers are specified on the INITIAL subcommand.

INITIAL Subcommand
Use the INITIAL subcommand to specify the method by which initial cluster centers are chosen.

SELECT *Select widely spaced cases from the data file as initial centers.* QUICK CLUSTER searches through the data for cases that are widely separated on the clustering variables. This normally produces a good clustering solution. However, it requires that the data file be read an extra time in order to select the initial centers. SELECT is the default.

FIRST *Use the first* k *cases in the data file as initial centers,* where *k* is the number of clusters requested. This method saves the initial pass through the data and may be appropriate when a large number of clusters are to be formed and the order of cases in the data file is essentially random. It should not be used if the file is sorted on any of the clustering variables.

(value list) *Take cluster centers directly from the INITIAL subcommand.* Specify one value for each clustering variable for each of the requested clusters. For example, if there are five clustering variables and four clusters are requested, you should enter twenty values: five for the first initial center, five for the second, and so on. Values must be separated by spaces or commas, and the entire list should be enclosed in parentheses.

Example
```
QUICK CLUSTER A B
  /CRITERIA=CLUSTERS(3)
  /INITIAL=(1 6 7 7 22 9).
```

• This example forms three clusters of cases based on their values for variables A and B.

• The initial cluster centers will be at the points (A=1,B=6), (A=7,B=7), and (A=22,B=9).

PRINT Subcommand

QUICK CLUSTER always displays the initial cluster centers, the updated centers used to classify cases (classification cluster centers), the mean values of the cases in each cluster (final cluster centers), and the number of cases in each cluster. Use the PRINT subcommand to request additional output.

- Some PRINT options will markedly increase the volume of output or the processing time required for large cluster problems.

CLUSTER
: *Cluster membership for each case.* Each case displays an identifying number or value, the number of the cluster to which it was assigned, and its distance from the center of that cluster. This output is extensive when you process a large number of cases.

ID(varname)
: *Case identification in output.* SPSS/PC+ will use the value of the variable named to identify cases in output. By default, cases are identified by their sequential number in the active file.

DISTANCE
: *Pairwise distances between all final cluster centers.* When a very large number of clusters are requested, this output can consume a great deal of processing time.

ANOVA
: *Descriptive univariate* F *tests for the clustering variables.* Since cases are assigned to clusters so as to maximize differences between the clusters, it is not legitimate to interpret the F tests as tests of the null hypothesis that there are no differences between clusters. The tests are descriptive only.

Example
```
QUICK CLUSTER A B C D E
  /CRITERIA=CLUSTERS(6)
  /PRINT=CLUSTER ID(CASEID) DISTANCE.
```

- Six clusters are formed on the basis of the five variables A, B, C, D, and E.
- Cluster membership and distance from cluster center are displayed for each case in the file.
- Cases are identified by the values of the variable CASEID.
- Distances between all cluster centers are printed.

WRITE Subcommand

Use the WRITE subcommand to write the final cluster centers to the results file (SPSS.PRC by default). The file will include the values of all cluster variables for each final cluster center. By editing this file with REVIEW, you can use these cluster centers on an INITIAL subcommand in a subsequent execution of QUICK CLUSTER.

- The WRITE subcommand does not have any specifications.
- Cluster centers are written to the current results file and replace any existing data in that file.

SAVE Subcommand

Use the SAVE subcommand to save results of the cluster analysis as new variables in your active file.

- The SAVE subcommand affects only the active file. To preserve the clustering results for analysis in later sessions, you must use the SAVE command to save a system file on disk.

The following variables can be saved on the active file:

CLUSTER(varname)
: *The cluster number of each case.* Specify a variable name in parentheses. The value of this variable will be set to an integer from 1 to the number of clusters.

DISTANCE(varname)
: *The distance of each case from its cluster center.* Specify a variable name in parentheses. For each case, the value of this variable will be the distance of that case from its cluster center.

Example
```
QUICK CLUSTER A B C D
  /CRITERIA=CLUSTERS(6)
  /SAVE=CLUSTER(CLUSNUM) DISTANCE(DISTCNTR).
```

- Six clusters of cases are formed on the basis of variables A, B, C, and D.
- The variable CLUSNUM will be set to an integer between 1 and 6 to indicate cluster membership for each case.
- The variable DISTCNTR will be set to the Euclidean distance between a case and the center of the cluster to which it is assigned.

MISSING Subcommand

Use the MISSING subcommand with the following keywords to specify the treatment of cases with missing values.

LISTWISE *Delete cases with missing values listwise.* A case with a missing value on any of the clustering variables is deleted from the analysis and will not be assigned to a cluster. This is the default.

PAIRWISE *Assign each case to the nearest cluster on the basis of the clustering variables for which the case has nonmissing values.* Cases are deleted if they have missing values on all clustering variables.

INCLUDE *Treat user-missing values as valid.*

DEFAULT *Same as LISTWISE.*

Example

This example uses QUICK CLUSTER twice to classify cases in a very large data file.
```
GET FILE='BIGFILE.SYS'.
COMPUTE TEST = UNIFORM(100).
PROCESS IF (TEST < 1).
QUICK CLUSTER V1 TO V5
  /CRITERIA CLUSTERS(4)
  /WRITE.
```

This first QUICK CLUSTER procedure processes a sample of cases to reduce processing time.

- For each case, TEST is calculated as a random number between 0 and 100. The PROCESS IF command then selects approximately 1% of the cases for the first QUICK CLUSTER procedure.
- Using the default method of selecting initial centers, QUICK CLUSTER processes this small group of cases and writes the final centers to the procedure output file (SPSS.PRC by default).

```
QUICK CLUSTER V1 TO V5
  /INITIAL= (23.6  11.3  -2.71  55.0  19.2
             6.75   4.1   0.24  91.2  29.1
            10.2   -1.2   9.25   3.1  10.9
             2.0   10.0  -8.1   12.0  22.0 )
  /CRITERIA CLUSTERS(4) NOUPDATE
  /SAVE CLUSTER(CLUSNUM).
SAVE OUTFILE='CLUSTERD.SYS'.
```

- This QUICK CLUSTER procedure begins with the centers from the first procedure. A text editor was used to edit the contents of SPSS.PRC into a file for this run.
- Since NOUPDATE is specified on the CRITERIA subcommand, SPSS/PC+ simply classifies all cases to the nearest center.
- The cluster number (in this case, an integer from 1 to 4) is added to the active file as variable CLUSNUM.
- The SAVE command saves a system file containing CLUSNUM on disk.

REGRESSION

```
REGRESSION [VARIABLES={varlist     }]
                      {(COLLECT)**}
                      {ALL          }


           [/STATISTICS=[DEFAULTS**] [R] [COEFF] [ANOVA] [OUTS]
                        [ZPP] [CHA] [CI] [F] [BCOV] [SES] [TOL]
                        [COLLIN] [XTX] [HISTORY] [END]
                        [LINE] [ALL]] [SELECTION]


           [/CRITERIA=[DEFAULTS**] [TOLERANCE({.0001})] [MAXSTEPS({2v})]
                                              {value}                {n }

            [{PIN({0.05 })}]        [{POUT({0.10 })}]
             {    {value} }          {     {value} }
             {FIN({3.84 })}          {FOUT({2.71 })}      [CIN({95** })]
             {    {value} }          {     {value} }           {value}


           [/{NOORIGIN**}]
             {ORIGIN    }


           /DEPENDENT=varlist

           /[METHOD=]{STEPWISE [= varlist]      }  [/METHOD=...]
                     {FORWARD [=varlist]         }
                     {BACKWARD [=varlist]        }
                     {ENTER [=varlist]           }
                     {REMOVE=varlist             }
                     {TEST=(varlist) (varlist)}


           [/DESCRIPTIVES=[DEFAULTS] [MEAN] [STDDEV] [CORR]
                          [VARIANCE] [XPROD] [SIG] [N] [BADCORR]
                          [COV]      [ALL]   [NONE**]]


           [/SELECT={varname relation value}]


           [/MISSING=[{LISTWISE**      }] [INCLUDE]]
                      {PAIRWISE        }
                      {MEANSUBSTITUTION}


           [/WIDTH={value on SET**}]
                   {n              }

           [/REGWGT=variable]
```

**Default if subcommand is omitted.

Example:

```
REGRESSION VARIABLES=X1 TO X7,Y
  /DEPENDENT=Y
  /METHOD=ENTER X1 X2 X3
  /METHOD=ENTER X4 TO X7
  /METHOD=STEPWISE.
```

Overview   Procedure REGRESSION calculates multiple regression equations and associated statistics and plots. REGRESSION also calculates collinearity diagnostics, predicted values, r ls, measures of fit and influence, and several statistics based on these (see REGRESSION: Residuals).

Several methods for selecting variables into the equation are available. Display options include several types of plots, including partial residual plots.

Defaults   The minimum specification for REGRESSION is a dependent variable which begins the building of an equation (DEPENDENT) and a method for selecting blocks of independent variables for the equation (METHOD). For each block of variables selected, the default display includes statistics on the equation (including R^2 and analysis of variance), on the variables in the equation (including regression coefficients), and on variables being considered that are not in the equation. The default display uses the width specified on SET. By default, all cases in the active file with valid values for all the variables named on the VARIABLES subcommand are used to compute the correlation matrix on which the regression equations are based. The default equations include a constant (intercept).

Tailoring

The options for procedure REGRESSION can be grouped into logically related operations or specifications.

Global-Control Subcommands. These optional subcommands should be named only once and apply to the entire REGRESSION command. DESCRIPTIVES requests descriptive statistics on the variables in the analysis. SELECT estimates the model based on a subset of cases. MISSING specifies the treatment of cases with missing values.

Equation-Control Subcommands. These optional subcommands control the calculation and display of each equation. STATISTICS controls the statistics displayed as the equations are built, CRITERIA specifies the criteria used by the variable selection method, and ORIGIN specifies whether regression is through the origin.

Display Format. The WIDTH subcommand controls the width of the display for REGRESSION only. It applies to all output from the REGRESSION command.

Analysis of Residuals, Fit, and Influence. The optional subcommands that analyze and plot residuals, and optionally add new variables to the active file containing predicted values, residuals, or related information, are described in REGRESSION: Residuals. These subcommands apply to a specific final equation, as defined by a DEPENDENT subcommand after processing all METHOD subcommands.

Writing and Reading Matrices. The optional subcommands that read and write matrix materials are described in REGRESSION: Matrix Materials. These subcommands are global in scope.

Syntax

- The minimum specification is two subcommands and their specifications: DEPENDENT, which initiates equation(s) and specifies at least one dependent variable; and METHOD, which specifies a method to be used in selecting independent variables.

- The VARIABLES subcommand can be used only once. If used, VARIABLES must be specified before the DEPENDENT and METHOD subcommands. If omitted, VARIABLES defaults to (COLLECT).

- The MISSING, DESCRIPTIVES, and SELECT subcommands can be entered anywhere except between a DEPENDENT subcommand and the immediately following METHOD subcommands. If any of these subcommands appears more than once on the REGRESSION command, the last one of each type is in effect for the entire REGRESSION command.

- CRITERIA, STATISTICS, and ORIGIN subcommands remain in effect for all subsequent equations until replaced. These subcommands must not be placed between a DEPENDENT subcommand and its METHOD subcommand(s).

- More than one DEPENDENT subcommand can be used. An equation is estimated for each variable listed on a DEPENDENT subcommand.

- A DEPENDENT subcommand must be followed immediately by one or more METHOD subcommands.

- If no variable list is specified on METHOD, all variables named on VARIABLES but not on DEPENDENT will be considered for selection.

- The WIDTH subcommand can appear anywhere. The last WIDTH subcommand encountered is in effect for all REGRESSION displays.

- All subcommands must be separated by slashes.

Operations

- REGRESSION calculates a correlation matrix that includes all variables named on the VARIABLES subcommand. All equations requested on the REGRESSION command are calculated from the same correlation matrix.

- The MISSING, DESCRIPTIVES, and SELECT subcommands control the calculation of the correlation matrix and associated displays.

- The DEPENDENT subcommand and the METHOD subcommands that follow it control the building of an equation for each variable named on the DEPENDENT subcommand.
- The equation generated for each variable named on a DEPENDENT subcommand uses the same independent variables and methods contained in other equations generated by named variables.
- Multiple METHOD subcommands operate, in sequence, on the equations defined by the preceding DEPENDENT subcommand.
- All independent variables that pass the tolerance criterion are candidates for entry (see CRITERIA Subcommand).
- If the width set is less than 132, some statistics requested may not be displayed. The WIDTH subcommand within REGRESSION allows you to increase the display width and obtain all of the statistics available to you.

Limitations

- The number of variables that can be named on the VARIABLES subcommand depends on the memory available.

Example

```
REGRESSION VARIABLES=X1 TO X7,Y
   /DEPENDENT=Y
   /METHOD=ENTER X1 X2 X3
   /METHOD=ENTER X4 TO X7
   /METHOD=STEPWISE.
```

- VARIABLES requests that a correlation matrix of variables X1 to X7 and Y be calculated for use by REGRESSION.
- DEPENDENT defines a single equation, with Y as the dependent variable.
- The first METHOD subcommand requests that X1 to X3 be entered into the equation.
- The second METHOD subcommand requests that X4 to X7 be added to the equation containing X1 to X3.
- The last METHOD subcommand requests that the entire equation be evaluated using the stepwise method.

Subcommand Order

The standard subcommand order for REGRESSION is shown in Figure A.

Figure A Subcommand order

```
REGRESSION VARIABLES=...
   /DESCRIPTIVES=...
   /SELECT=...
   /MISSING=...
   /WIDTH=...
   /READ=...
   /WRITE=...
```

```
┌──────────────────────────────────────────────────────────┐
│                     Equation Blocks                        │
│                                                            │
│     /STATISTICS=...                                        │
│     /CRITERIA=...                                          │
│     /ORIGIN                                                │
│     /NOORIGIN                                              │
│     /DEPENDENT=...                                         │
│     ┌──────────────────────────────────────────────────┐  │
│     │                 Method Blocks                     │  │
│     │     /METHOD=...                                   │  │
│     └──────────────────────────────────────────────────┘  │
│                                                            │
│     /RESIDUALS=...                                         │
│     /CASEWISE=...                                          │
│     /SCATTERPLOT=...                                       │
│     /PARTIALPLOT=...                                       │
└──────────────────────────────────────────────────────────┘
```

C

Command Reference

• Subcommands listed outside the boxes apply to all analyses performed by the REGRESSION command. Subcommands listed in the equation block apply to all methods used in estimating that equation.

• A REGRESSION command can include multiple equation blocks, and each equation block can contain multiple METHOD subcommands. These methods are applied, one after the other, to the estimation of the equation.

• The STATISTICS, CRITERIA, and ORIGIN/NOORIGIN subcommands must precede the DEPENDENT subcommand for the equation to which they apply.

• The RESIDUALS, CASEWISE, SCATTERPLOT, and PARTIALPLOT subcommands must follow the last METHOD subcommand in an equation block and apply only to the final equation after all METHOD subcommands have been processed.

• This order of subcommands can be different from the order shown in Figure A. However, any analysis that can be performed with procedure REGRESSION can be performed using this order, repeating equation blocks and METHOD subcommands as needed.

VARIABLES Subcommand

VARIABLES names all the variables to be used in the analysis with either a variable list or a keyword.

• The minimum specification is a list of two variables or one of the keywords ALL or (COLLECT). The default is (COLLECT).

• There cannot be more than one VARIABLES subcommand, and it must precede any DEPENDENT or METHOD subcommands.

• You can name any user-defined variable in the active system file.

• You can use the TO keyword in the variable list to refer to consecutive variables on the active file.

• The order of variables in the correlation matrix constructed by REGRESSION is the same as their order on the VARIABLES subcommand.

• If you omit the VARIABLES subcommand or explicitly specify the keyword (COLLECT), the order of variables in the correlation matrix is the order in which they are first referred to on the DEPENDENT and METHOD subcommands.

You can specify either of the following keywords instead of a variable list:

ALL   *Include all user-defined variables in the active file.*

(COLLECT)   *Include all variables named on the DEPENDENT and METHOD subcommands. If (COLLECT) is used, the METHOD subcommands must have variable lists.*

Example

```
REGRESSION VARIABLES=(COLLECT)
  /DEPENDENT=Y
  /METHOD=STEP B C D E F G
  /METHOD=ENTER H
  /DEPENDENT=H
  /METHOD=ENTER G.
```

• (COLLECT) requests that the correlation matrix include Y, B, C, D, E, F, G, and H. Since (COLLECT) is the default, the VARIABLES subcommand could have been omitted in this example.

• The first DEPENDENT subcommand defines a single equation in which Y is the dependent variable.

• The first METHOD subcommand requests that the block of variables B to G be considered for inclusion using a stepwise procedure.

• The second METHOD subcommand specifies that variable H be added to the equation, provided that it satisfies the default tolerance criterion.

• A second DEPENDENT subcommand requests an equation in which H is the dependent variable.

• Variable G will be entered into this equation, provided that it satisfies the default tolerance criterion.

DEPENDENT Subcommand

The required DEPENDENT subcommand specifies a list of variables and requests that an equation be built for each.

- The minimum specification is a single variable. There is no default variable list.
- You can specify more than one DEPENDENT subcommand. Each must be followed by at least one METHOD subcommand.
- The keyword TO on a DEPENDENT subcommand refers to the order variables are named on the VARIABLES subcommand. If VARIABLES=(COLLECT) was specified, TO refers to the order of variables in the active file.
- If the DEPENDENT subcommand names more than one variable, an equation is built for each using the same independent variable(s) and methods.
- No variable named on the DEPENDENT subcommand can be specified as an independent variable on associated METHOD subcommands.

METHOD Subcommand

The required METHOD subcommand specifies a variable selection method and names a block of variables to be evaluated using that method.

- The minimum specification is a method keyword and, for some methods, a list of variables. The actual keyword METHOD may be omitted.
- The default variable list for methods FORWARD, BACKWARD, STEPWISE, and ENTER consists of all variables named on the VARIABLES subcommand that are not named on the preceding DEPENDENT subcommand.
- There is no default variable list for the REMOVE and TEST methods.
- If you omit the VARIABLES subcommand or explicitly specify the default VARIABLES=(COLLECT), you must name the variables.
- The keyword TO in a variable block named on METHOD refers to the order variables are named on the VARIABLES subcommand. If VARIABLES= (COLLECT) was specified, TO refers to the order of variables in the active file.
- At least one METHOD subcommand must follow each DEPENDENT subcommand.
- When you specify more than one method for a single DEPENDENT subcommand, the methods are cumulative.

The available stepwise methods are:

BACKWARD *Backward elimination.* Variables in the block are considered for removal. At each step, the variable with the largest probability-of-F value is removed, provided that the value is larger than POUT (see CRITERIA Subcommand). If no variables are in the equation when BACKWARD is specified, all independent variables are first entered.

FORWARD *Forward entry.* Variables in the block are added to the equation one at a time. At each step, the variable not in the equation with the smallest probability of F is entered if the value is smaller than PIN (see CRITERIA Subcommand).

STEPWISE *Stepwise selection.* If there are independent variables already in the equation, the variable with the largest probability of F is removed if this value is larger than POUT. The equation is recomputed omitting the removed variable and the evaluation process is repeated until no more independent variables can be removed. Then the independent variable not in the equation with the smallest probability of F is entered if this value is smaller than PIN. Finally, all variables in the equation are again examined for removal. This process continues until no variables in the equation need to be removed and no variables not in the equation are eligible for entry, or until the maximum number of steps has been reached (see CRITERIA Subcommand).

C

Command Reference

The methods that enter or remove the entire variable block in a single step are:

ENTER   *Forced entry.* All variables in the block are entered in a single step in order of decreasing tolerance. If the order in which variables are entered is important, use multiple METHOD=ENTER subcommands.

REMOVE   *Forced removal.* All variables are removed in a single step. REMOVE requires a variable list.

TEST   *Test indicated subsets of independent variables using* R^2 *change and its test of significance.* This method first builds a model that includes all variables named on that METHOD=TEST subcommand by adding any variables that are not already in the equation. Variables already in the equation are not removed. Test statistics are printed for the subsets, usually in addition to any other statistics that may have been requested. Specify test subsets in parentheses. A variable can be used in more than one subset, and each subset can include any number of variables. Variables named on TEST remain in the equation when the METHOD subcommand is completed.

Example
```
REGRESSION VARIABLES=X1 TO X7,Y
 /DEPENDENT=Y
 /METHOD=STEPWISE
 /METHOD=ENTER.
```

- STEPWISE applies the stepwise procedure to variables X1 to X7.

- Any variables not in the equation when the STEPWISE method is complete will be forced into the equation with ENTER.

Example
```
REGRESSION VARIABLES=(COLLECT)
 /DEPENDENT=ZVAR
 /METHOD=TEST(QVAR15 TO QVAR20)(QVAR15,PVAR)
 /METHOD=ENTER XVAR.
```

- The VARIABLES=(COLLECT) specification assembles a correlation matrix that includes all variables named on the DEPENDENT and METHOD subcommands. QVAR15 TO QVAR20 refers to all variables between and including QVAR15 and QVAR20 on the active file.

- REGRESSION first builds the full equation of all the variables named on the first METHOD subcommand: ZVAR regressed on QVAR15 to QVAR20 and PVAR. For each set of test variables, the R^2 change, F, probability, sums of squares, and degrees of freedom are displayed.

- XVAR is added to the equation by the second METHOD subcommand. Variables QVAR15 to QVAR20 and PVAR are still in the equation when this subcommand is executed.

STATISTICS Subcommand

The optional STATISTICS subcommand controls the display of statistics for the equation and for the independent variables.

- The minimum specification is simply the subcommand keyword.

- If the STATISTICS subcommand is omitted or if it is included with no keywords, R, ANOVA, COEFF, and OUTS are displayed (see below).

- If any statistics are specified on STATISTICS, only statistics specifically requested are displayed.

- The statistical displays for stepwise methods (BACKWARD, FORWARD, and STEPWISE) are sometimes different from those for methods that enter and remove blocks of variables. In particular, some statistical displays are not produced for method TEST if the equation has not changed since the last variable block.

- Method TEST always produces its own display in addition to other statistics.

- A STATISTICS subcommand affects any equations that are subsequently defined and remains in effect until overridden by another STATISTICS subcommand.

• A STATISTICS subcommand may not be placed between the DEPENDENT and METHOD subcommands.

• If the width is set to less than 132, some requested statistics may not be displayed.

Global Statistics

DEFAULTS *R, ANOVA, COEFF, and OUTS.* These are displayed if the STATISTICS subcommand is omitted or if it is specified without keywords.

ALL *Display all statistics except F, LINE, and END.*

Equation Statistics

R *Multiple* R. Includes R^2, adjusted R^2, and standard error of the estimate.

ANOVA *Analysis of variance table.* Includes regression and residual sum of squares, mean square, *F*, and probability of *F*.

CHA *Change in* R^2. Includes the change in R^2 between steps, *F* at the end of each step and its probability, and *F* for the equation and its probability. For stepwise methods (BACKWARD, FORWARD, and STEPWISE), these statistics are displayed at the end of each step. For other methods, the statistics are displayed for the variable block.

BCOV *Variance-covariance matrix for unstandardized regression coefficients.* Matrix has covariances below the diagonal, correlations above the diagonal, and variances on the diagonal.

XTX *Sweep matrix.*

COLLIN *Collinearity diagnostics.* COLLIN includes the variance inflation factors (VIF), the eigenvalues of the scaled and uncentered cross-products matrix, condition indices, and variance-decomposition proportions (Belsley et al., 1980).

SELECTION *Aids to selecting set of regressors.* SELECTION includes Akaike information criterion (AIK), Ameniya's prediction criterion (PC), Mallow's conditional mean squared error of prediction criterion (Cp), and Schwarz Bayesian criterion (SBC) (Judge et al., 1980).

Statistics for the Independent Variables

COEFF *Regression coefficients.* Includes regression coefficients (B), standard errors of the coefficients, standardized regression coefficients (beta), *t*, and two-tailed probability of *t*.

OUTS *Statistics for variables not yet in the equation that have been named on METHOD subcommands for the equation.* Displays beta, *t*, two-tailed probability of *t*, and minimum tolerance of the variable if it were the only variable entered next.

ZPP *Zero-order, part, and partial correlation.*

CI *95% confidence interval for the unstandardized regression coefficient.*

SES *Approximate standard error of the standardized regression coefficients.* (See Meyer & Younger, 1976.)

TOL *Tolerance.* Displays tolerance for variables in the equation and, for variables not in the equation, the tolerance each variable would have if it were the only variable entered next.

F F *value for* B *and its probability.* Displayed instead of the *t* value.

Step Summary Statistics

The full summary line displayed by keywords LINE, END, and HISTORY includes R, R^2, adjusted R^2, F, probability of F, R^2 change, F of the change, probability of R^2 change, and statistics on variables added or removed. For stepwise methods (BACKWARD, FORWARD, and STEPWISE), the statistics refer to each step. For other methods (ENTER, REMOVE, and TEST), the statistics refer to the entire variable block. If other statistics are requested, the summary line may not be produced for a block that does not entail steps.

LINE *Display a single summary line for each step, for stepwise methods only.* Does not affect direct methods. The default or requested statistics are displayed at the end of each method block for all methods.

END *Display the same summary line produced by LINE after each step for stepwise methods, and after each variable block for other methods.* For TEST, the summary line is displayed only if the equation changes. Other default or requested statistics are displayed at the completion of the last METHOD subcommand for the equation.

HISTORY *Display a final summary report.* HISTORY can be requested in addition to LINE or END. For stepwise methods, the report includes a summary line for each step. For ENTER and REMOVE, the report includes a summary line for each method; for TEST, the summary line is displayed only if the equation changes. If HISTORY is the only statistic requested, COEFF is displayed for the final equation.

CRITERIA Subcommand

The optional CRITERIA subcommand controls the statistical criteria used in building the regression equations. The way in which these criteria are used depends on the method specified on the METHOD subcommand. The default criteria are noted in the description of each CRITERIA keyword below.

• The minimum specification is a criterion keyword and its arguments, if any.

• If the CRITERIA subcommand is omitted or included with no specifications, the default criteria are in effect.

• Only default criteria that are changed explicitly on the CRITERIA subcommand are altered.

• A CRITERIA subcommand affects any subsequent DEPENDENT and METHOD subcommands and remains in effect until overridden by another CRITERIA subcommand.

• The CRITERIA subcommand may not be placed between the DEPENDENT subcommand and its METHOD subcommands.

Tolerance and Minimum Tolerance Criteria

Variables must pass both tolerance and minimum tolerance tests in order to enter and remain in a regression equation. Tolerance is the proportion of the variance of a variable in the equation that is not accounted for by other independent variables in the equation. The minimum tolerance of a variable not in the equation is the smallest tolerance any variable already in the equation would have if the variable being considered were included in the analysis.

If a variable passes the tolerance criteria, it is further tested according to the method in effect. These criteria are controlled by the CRITERIA subcommand or defaults in effect for the equations that the DEPENDENT subcommand builds.

Testing Independent Variables

The ENTER, REMOVE, and TEST methods use only the TOLERANCE criterion. The stepwise methods (BACKWARD, FORWARD, and STEPWISE) differ in the way they use criteria.

• BACKWARD selects variables according to the probability of *F*-to-remove (keyword POUT). Specify FOUT to use *F*-to-remove instead.

• FORWARD selects variables according to the probability of *F*-to-enter (keyword PIN). Specify FIN to use *F*-to-enter instead.

• STEPWISE uses both PIN and POUT (or FIN and FOUT) as criteria. If the criterion for entry (PIN or FIN) is less stringent than the criterion for removal (POUT or FOUT), the same variable may cycle in and out until the maximum number of steps is reached. Therefore, if PIN is larger than POUT or FIN is smaller than FOUT, REGRESSION adjusts POUT or FOUT and issues a warning.

DEFAULTS *PIN(0.05), POUT(0.10), and TOLERANCE(0.0001).* These are the defaults if the CRITERIA subcommand has not been specified. If criteria have been changed, keyword DEFAULTS restores these defaults.

PIN(value) *Probability of* F-*to-enter.* The default value is 0.05. Keywords PIN and FIN are alternatives. If more than one is used, the last mentioned is in effect.

FIN(value)	*F-to-enter*. If no value is specified, the value defaults to 3.84. Keywords PIN and FIN are alternatives. If more than one is used, the last mentioned is in effect.
POUT(value)	*Probability of F-to-remove*. The default value is 0.10. Keywords POUT and FOUT are alternatives. If more than one is used, the last mentioned is in effect.
FOUT(value)	*F-to-remove*. If no value is specified, the value defaults to 2.71. Keywords POUT and FOUT are alternatives. If more than one is used, the last mentioned is in effect.
TOLERANCE(value)	*Tolerance*. The default value is 0.0001. If the tolerance chosen is very low, REGRESSION issues a warning.
MAXSTEPS(n)	*Maximum number of steps*. The value of MAXSTEPS is the sum of the maximum number of steps over each method for the equation. The default values for the BACKWARD and FORWARD methods is the number of variables meeting PIN/POUT or FIN/FOUT criteria. The default value for the STEPWISE method is twice the number of independent variables.

Example
```
REGRESSION VARIABLES=X1 TO X7,Y
  /CRITERIA=PIN(.1) POUT(.15) TOL(.001)
  /DEPENDENT=Y
  /METHOD=FORWARD
  /CRITERIA=DEFAULTS
  /DEPENDENT=Y
  /METHOD=STEPWISE.
```

• The first CRITERIA subcommand relaxes the default criteria for the entry and removal of variables while the FORWARD method is used. Note that the specified PIN is less than POUT.

• The second CRITERIA subcommand reestablishes the defaults for the second equation.

Confidence Intervals

CIN(value)	*Reset the value of the percent for confidence intervals*. The default is 95, indicating 95%. This sets the percentage interval used in the computation of the temporary variable types MCIN and ICIN (see the Operations section in REGRESSION: Residuals).

Example
```
REGRESSION VARIABLES=POP15 TO GROWTH, SAVINGS
  /CRITERIA=PIN(.1) POUT(.15)
  /DEPENDENT=SAVINGS
  /METHOD=FORWARD
  /CRITERIA=DEFAULTS
  /DEPENDENT=SAVINGS
  /METHOD=STEPWISE.
```

• The first CRITERIA subcommand relaxes the default criteria for the entry and removal of variables while the FORWARD method is used. Note that the specified PIN is less than POUT.

• The second CRITERIA subcommand reestablishes the defaults for the second equation.

ORIGIN and NOORIGIN Subcommands

The optional ORIGIN and NOORIGIN subcommands control whether or not the constant is suppressed.

• The minimum specification is simply the ORIGIN or NOORIGIN subcommand. There are no additional specifications.

• ORIGIN and NOORIGIN must be specified before the DEPENDENT and METHOD subcommands they modify.

• ORIGIN and NOORIGIN are mutually exclusive.

• If neither ORIGIN nor NOORIGIN is specified, NOORIGIN is the default and all equations include a constant term (intercept).

• ORIGIN requests regression through the origin. The constant term is suppressed.

• Once specified, ORIGIN remains in effect until NOORIGIN is requested.

• If you specify ORIGIN, statistics requested on the DESCRIPTIVES subcommand are computed as if the mean were zero.

Example
```
REGRESSION VAR=(COL)
   /DEP=A
   /METHOD=ENTER B
   /ORIGIN
   /DEP=A
   /METHOD=ENTER B
   /NOORIGIN
   /DEP=B
   /METHOD=ENTER C.
```

• The subcommand VAR=(COL) builds a correlation matrix that includes A, B, and C.
• The REGRESSION command requests three equations. The first regresses A on B and includes a constant term because the default (NOORIGIN) is in effect. The second regresses A on B and suppresses the constant (ORIGIN). The third regresses B on C and includes a constant term because NOORIGIN has been specified.
• This example takes advantage of spelling permitted by three-character truncation of keywords.

DESCRIPTIVES Subcommand

By default, descriptive statistics are not displayed. Use the optional DESCRIPTIVES subcommand to request the display of correlation and descriptive statistics for variables in the correlation matrix.

• The minimum specification is simply the command keyword.
• If DESCRIPTIVES is specified without keywords, MEAN, STDDEV, and CORR are displayed.
• If DESCRIPTIVES is included and any keywords are specified, only those statistics specifically requested are displayed.
• Descriptive statistics are displayed only once for all variables named or implied on VARIABLES.
• Descriptive statistics are based on all valid cases for each variable if PAIRWISE or MEANSUBSTITUTION has been specified on MISSING. Otherwise, only cases included in the computation of the correlation matrix are included in the calculation of the descriptive statistics.
• If regression through the origin has been requested (subcommand ORIGIN), statistics are computed as if the mean were zero.

NONE   *Turn off all descriptive statistics. This is the default if the subcommand is omitted.*

DEFAULTS   *MEAN, STDDEV, and CORR. Same as specifying DESCRIPTIVES without specifications.*

MEAN   *Variable means.*

STDDEV   *Variable standard deviations.*

VARIANCE *Variable variances.*

CORR   *Correlation matrix.*

SIG   *One-tailed probabilities of the correlation coefficients.*

BADCORR   *Display the correlation matrix only if some coefficients cannot be computed.*

COV   *Covariance matrix.*

XPROD   *Cross-product deviations from the mean.*

N   *Numbers of cases used to compute correlation coefficients.*

ALL   *Display all descriptive statistics.*

Example
```
REGRESSION DESCRIPTIVES=DEFAULTS SIG COV
   /VARIABLES=X1 TO X7,Y
   /DEPENDENT=Y
   /METHOD=ENTER X1
   /METHOD=ENTER X2.
```

• The variable means, variable standard deviations, correlation matrix, one-tailed probabilities of the correlation coefficients, and covariance matrix are displayed.

- Statistics are displayed for all variables named on VARIABLES, even though only variables Y, X1, and X2 are used to build the equations.
- X1 is entered into the equation by the first METHOD subcommand; X2 is entered by the second METHOD subcommand.

SELECT Subcommand

By default, all cases on the active file are considered for inclusion in REGRESSION. Use the optional SELECT subcommand to include a subset of cases in the correlation matrix and resulting regression statistics.

- The minimum specification is a logical expression. The default is to include all cases if the subcommand is omitted.
- Do not include the variable named on SELECT on the VARIABLES subcommand.
- The logical expression on SELECT is of the form

```
/SELECT=varname relation value
```

where the relation can be EQ, NE, LT, LE, GT, or GE.
- Only cases for which the logical expression on SELECT is true are included in the calculation of the correlation matrix and regression statistics. All other cases, including those with missing values for the variable named on SELECT, are not selected.
- SELECT displays additional statistics describing the fit of the model estimated among the unselected cases.
- By default, residuals and predicted values are calculated and reported separately for both selected and unselected cases (see REGRESSION: Residuals).
- Cases deleted from the active file with the SELECT IF, PROCESS IF, or SAMPLE commands are not passed to REGRESSION. Such cases are not reviewed by the SELECT subcommand and are not included among either the selected or unselected cases.
- The display of the values of the variable named on SELECT is controlled by that variable's format (see DATA LIST in *SPSS/PC+ V4.0 Base Manual*).

Example
```
REGRESSION SELECT SEX EQ 'M'
  /VARIABLES=X1 TO X7,Y
  /DEPENDENT=Y
  /METHOD=STEP
  /RESIDUALS=NORMPROB.
```

- Only cases with the value M for SEX are included in the correlation matrix calculated by REGRESSION.
- Separate normal probability plots are displayed for cases with SEX equal to M and for other cases (see REGRESSION: Residuals).

MISSING Subcommand

By default, a case that has a user- or system-missing value for any variable named or implied on the VARIABLES subcommand is omitted from the computation of the correlation matrix on which all analyses are based. Use the optional MISSING subcommand to change the treatment of cases with missing values.

- The minimum specification is a keyword specifying a missing-value treatment.

The available keywords are

LISTWISE
: *Delete cases with missing values listwise.* This is the default. Only cases with valid values on all variables named on the current VARIABLES subcommand are used. If INCLUDE is also specified, only cases with system-missing values are deleted listwise. LISTWISE is the default if the MISSING subcommand is omitted.

PAIRWISE
: *Delete cases with missing values pairwise.* Each correlation coefficient is computed using cases with complete data for the pair of variables correlated. If INCLUDE is also specified, only cases with system-missing values are deleted pairwise.

MEANSUBSTITUTION   *Replace missing values with the variable mean.* All cases are included and the substitutions are treated as valid observations. If INCLUDE is also specified, user-missing values are included in the computation of the means. Mean substitution affects the computation of the correlation matrix and the calculation of predicted values and residuals.

INCLUDE   *Include cases with user-missing values.* All user-missing values are treated as valid values. This keyword can be specified along with the methods LISTWISE, PAIRWISE, or MEANSUBSTITUTION. Including user-missing values affects the computation of the correlation matrix and the calculation of predicted values and residuals.

Example
```
REGRESSION  VARIABLES=X1 TO X7,Y
  /DEPENDENT=Y
  /METHOD=STEP
  /MISSING=MEANS.
```

- Missing values are replaced with the means of the variables when the correlation matrix is calculated.
- The MEANS keyword takes advantage of spelling permitted by three-character truncation.

WIDTH Subcommand

The optional WIDTH subcommand controls the width of the display within the REGRESSION procedure.

- The minimum specification is an integer between 72 and 132.
- The default display uses the width specified on SET. The width specified on the WIDTH subcommand within REGRESSION overrides the width on SET for the REGRESSION display only.
- The WIDTH subcommand can appear anywhere.
- If more than one WIDTH subcommand is included, the last WIDTH specified will be in effect for the display.
- If the width is less than 132, some statistics may not be displayed.

REGWGT Subcommand

The only specification on REGWGT is the name of the variable containing the weights to be used in estimating a weighted least-squares model. With REGWGT the default display is the usual REGRESSION display.

- REGWGT is a global command.
- If more than one REGWGT subcommand is specified on a REGRESSION procedure, only the last one is executed.
- Residuals saved from equations using the REGWGT command are not weighted. To obtain weighted residuals, residuals created with SAVE should be multiplied by the square root of the weighting variable in a COMPUTE statement.
- REGWGT is in effect for all equations and determines how the correlation matrix is built. Thus, if REGWGT is specified on a REGRESSION procedure that writes matrix materials to a system file, subsequent REGRESSION procedures using that file also will be automatically weighted.

Example
```
REGRESSION VARIABLES=GRADE GPA STARTLEV TREATMNT
  /DEPENDENT=GRADE
  /METHOD=ENTER
  /SAVE PRED(P).
COMPUTE WEIGHT=1/(P*(1-P)).
REGRESSION VAR=GRADE GPA STARTLEV TREATMNT
  /REGWGT=WEIGHT
  /DEP=GRADE
  /METHOD=ENTER.
```

- VARIABLES builds a correlation matrix that includes GRADE, GPA, STARTLEV, and TREATMNT.

- DEPENDENT identifies GRADE as the dependent variable.
- METHOD regresses GRADE on GPA, STARTLEV, and TREATMNT.
- SAVE adds the predicted values from the regression equation to the active system file as the variable P (see REGRESSION: Residuals).
- COMPUTE creates the variable WEIGHT as a transformation of P.
- The second REGRESSION procedure performs a weighted regression analysis on the same set of variables using WEIGHT as the weighting variable.

Example

```
REGRESSION VAR=GRADE GPA STARTLEV TREATMNT
   /REGWGT=WEIGHT
   /DEP=GRADE
   /METHOD=ENTER
   /SAVE RESID(RGRADE).
COMPUTE WRGRADE=RGRADE * SQRT(WEIGHT).
```

- This example illustrates the use of COMPUTE with SAVE to weight the residuals.
- REGRESSION performs a weighted regression analysis of GRADE on GPA, STARTLEV, and TREATMNT, using WEIGHT as the weighting variable.
- SAVE saves the residuals as RGRADE (see REGRESSION: Residuals). These residuals are not weighted.
- COMPUTE computes weighted residuals as WRGRADE in the active system file.

References

Berk, K. N. 1977. Tolerance and condition in regression computation. *Journal of the American Statistical Association* 72: 863–866.

Meyer, L. S., and M. S. Younger. 1976. Estimation of standardized coefficients. *Journal of the American Statistical Association* 71: 154–157.

Command Reference

REGRESSION: Matrix Materials

```
REGRESSION [READ=[DEFAULTS] [MEAN] [STDDEV]

           [VARIANCE] {CORR} [N]]
                      {COV }

 [/WRITE=[DEFAULTS] [MEAN] [STDDEV]

         [VARIANCE] [CORR] [COV]

         [N] [NONE**]]]

 /VARIABLES=varlist/DEPENDENT=varlist/METHOD=method
```

**Default if subcommand is omitted.

Example:
```
REGRESSION  VARIABLES=AGE TO SUICIDE
  /DESCRIPTIVES
  /WRITE
  /DEP=SUICIDE
  /METHOD=ENTER
  /RESIDUALS.
```

Overview

Procedure REGRESSION can both read and write matrix materials. It accepts matrix materials written by REGRESSION or other SPSS/PC+ procedures such as CORRELATION, or entered directly from other sources provided that the appropriate keyword specifications are used. Such matrix materials can be processed more quickly than cases. Matrix materials to be read can be in either fixed or freefield format but must conform to certain format and record specifications (see DATA LIST: Matrix Materials in *SPSS/PC+ Base Manual*).

The subcommands for writing and reading matrix materials can be used in addition to the REGRESSION subcommands described in REGRESSION.

WRITE Subcommand

Use the WRITE subcommand to write the matrix materials used in the REGRESSION computations to an external file.

• The WRITE subcommand can be specified anywhere except between the DEPENDENT subcommand and the METHOD subcommands that define an equation.

• If the WRITE subcommand is included without specifications, REGRESSION writes a vector of means, a vector of standard deviations, a correlation matrix, and the number of cases.

• If any keyword specifications are given, only those materials specified are written.

• Matrix materials are written for all variables named on the VARIABLES subcommand.

• The order of variables in vectors and matrices is the same as the order in which variables are named on the VARIABLES subcommand.

• If (COLLECT) is used on the VARIABLES subcommand, the order of the variables in the matrix materials is the order in which they are first named on REGRESSION. Use keyword CORRELATION on the DESCRIPTIVES subcommand to display a listing of the matrix you write.

• Only one WRITE subcommand should be used. If more than one WRITE appears, the last one encountered will be in effect.

• Each type of matrix material written begins on a new record. Eight 10-column fields are used on each record.

• REGRESSION displays a format table describing the contents and format of the file it has written.

• The VARIABLES, SELECT, ORIGIN or NOORIGIN, and MISSING subcommands in effect for the REGRESSION procedure also affect the materials that are written.

• Matrix materials are written to the results file named on the SET command (by default, SPSS.PRC).

• If the results file named on SET is not empty when the WRITE subcommand is executed, its contents will be overwritten.

The following keywords can be specified on WRITE. These keywords should be specified in the order they are listed below.

DEFAULTS *Includes MEAN, STDDEV, CORR, and N. This is the default if the WRITE subcommand is used without specifications.*

MEAN *Write a vector of means.*

STDDEV *Write a vector of standard deviations.*

VARIANCE *Write a vector of variances.*

CORR *Write a correlation matrix.*

COV *Write a covariance matrix.*

N *Write out the n's of cases used to compute correlation coefficients. When the MISSING=LISTWISE specification is in effect, the number of cases is written as one item on the last record. When PAIRWISE or MEANSUBSTITUTION is specified on MISSING, a matrix of n's is written.*

NONE *No matrix output* (default).

Example
```
SET RESULTS='GSS82.MAT'.
DATA LIST FILE='GSS82.DAT'/AGE 5-6 INCOME 7-13
  ANOMIE1 TO ANOMIE7 14-20 SUICIDE 21.
REGRESSION  VARIABLES=AGE TO SUICIDE
  /DESCRIPTIVES
  /WRITE
  /DEP=SUICIDE
  /METHOD=ENTER
  /RESIDUALS.
```

• The SET command sets the results file to the file GSS82.MAT in the current directory.

• The DATA LIST command specifies variable names and column locations for raw data in file GSS82.DAT.

• The VARIABLES subcommand on REGRESSION requests that all variables in the active file between and including AGE and SUICIDE be included in the computation of the correlation matrix for the regression.

• The DESCRIPTIVES subcommand requests descriptive statistics for all variables in the analysis.

• The WRITE subcommand requests that default matrix materials be written to the file specified on the SET RESULTS command. GSS82.MAT will contain a vector of means, a vector of standard deviations, a correlation matrix, and the number of cases, in that order. All variables from AGE to SUICIDE will be included in the matrix materials.

• A regression of SUICIDE on all other variables implied by the VARIABLES subcommand will be computed and the default display produced (see REGRESSION).

• The RESIDUALS subcommand displays a histogram of the standardized residuals, a normal probability plot of the standardized residuals, the Durbin-Watson test statistic, and a listing of the 10 worst outliers based on the absolute value of the standardzied residuals (see REGRESSION: Residuals).

READ Subcommand

Use the READ subcommand to read matrix materials.

• There can be only one READ subcommand.

• The READ subcommand cannot be specified between the DEPENDENT and METHOD subcommands.

- If the READ subcommand is used without specifications, REGRESSION assumes that the matrix materials have the default structure: a vector of means, a vector of standard deviations, a correlation matrix, and the number of cases.

- If any keywords are specified on READ, only those matrix materials specified will be expected.

- The matrix materials you read must permit regression statistics to be calculated. You must read either a correlation or covariance matrix.

- When you specify READ on REGRESSION, you must first specify a DATA LIST MATRIX command that points to the file containing the matrix materials and names the variables that will be read (see DATA LIST: Matrix Materials in *SPSS/PC+ Base Manual*).

- All matrix materials read must be in a single input file.

- The order in which variables are named on the VARIABLES subcommand of REGRESSION must be the order of the variables in each vector or matrix that is read.

- If a correlation matrix is the only matrix material to be read, an N command must be entered prior to REGRESSION to specify the number of cases. Only standardized coefficients will be available.

- If more than one kind of matrix material is present, the matrix materials must be arranged in the input file in the following order: the vector of means, the vector of standard deviations, the vector of variances, the correlation or covariance matrix, and the *n*'s of cases.

- The specification on the MISSING and ORIGIN or NOORIGIN subcommands should agree with the options in effect when the matrix was written.

- The descriptive statistics available with the DESCRIPTIVES subcommand depend on which matrix materials are read.

- The RESIDUALS, CASEWISE, SCATTERPLOT, and PARTIALPLOT subcommands are not available when matrix materials are read.

- The (COLLECT) keyword on the VARIABLES subcommand is not allowed if the READ subcommand is used.

DEFAULTS *MEAN, STDDEV, CORR, and N.* If you specify READ without specifications, the input file must contain these materials in this order. Matrix materials written by REGRESSION are in this default format.

MEAN *The matrix is preceded by a vector of means.*

STDDEV *The matrix is preceded by a vector of standard deviations.*

VARIANCE *The matrix is preceded by a vector of variances.*

CORR *Correlation matrix.* Alternative to keyword COV.

COV *Covariance matrix.* Alternative to keyword CORR. A covariance matrix is not allowed if pairwise deletion of missing values is specified.

N *The number of cases used to compute correlation coefficients follows the matrix.* If the MISSING subcommand specifies MEANSUBSTITUTION or PAIRWISE, a symmetric matrix of *n*'s is expected. If the MISSING subcommand specifies LISTWISE or INCLUDE, all coefficients are based on the same number of cases and a single number is expected. If a single number of cases is expected, it will be read from the first 10 columns of the last record of the matrix file. If the keyword N is not specified, the *n* specified on the N command is used. If an *n* is read from the matrix file and an *n* is specified on the N command, the *n* read from the matrix file is used.

Example
```
DATA LIST FIXED MATRIX FILE='GSS82.MAT'
 /AGE INCOME ANOMIE1 TO ANOMIE7 SUICIDE.
REGRESSION READ
 /VARIABLES=AGE INCOME ANOMIE1 TO ANOMIE7 SUICIDE
 /DEPENDENT=SUICIDE
 /METHOD=ENTER ANOMIE1 TO ANOMIE7.
```

- The DATA LIST command specifies that the matrix input should be read from the file GSS82.MAT and names the variables in the file. The names of the variables on the DATA LIST command will be entered in the dictionary of the active file.
- The READ subcommand on REGRESSION requests that matrix materials be read and used for the procedure. Because no keyword specifications are given and the default listwise treatment of missing values is in effect, REGRESSION expects a vector of means, a vector of standard deviations, a correlation matrix, and a single n of cases.
- The VARIABLES subcommand names the variables in the order in which they appear in the vectors and matrix to be read.
- The DEPENDENT subcommand defines an equation in which SUICIDE is the dependent variable.
- The METHOD subcommand requests that the variables ANOMIE1 to ANOMIE7 be entered into the equation using the ENTER method.
- The variables AGE and INCOME are not used in the equation but must be named on the VARIABLES subcommand so that the locations of all variables in the matrix file are identified accurately.

REGRESSION: Residuals

```
REGRESSION VARIABLES=varlist/ DEPENDENT=varname/ METHOD=method

  [/RESIDUALS=[DEFAULTS] [ID(varname)] [DURBIN] [{SEPARATE}]
                                                {POOLED }
            [HISTOGRAM({ZRESID     })] [OUTLIERS({ZRESID     })]
                       {tempvarlist}             {tempvarlist}


            [NORMPROB({ZRESID     })] [SIZE({LARGE})]]
                      {tempvarlist}          {SMALL}


  [/CASEWISE=[DEFAULTS] [{OUTLIERS({3    })}]
                        {        {value} }
                        {ALL            }

            [PLOT({ZRESID })] [{DEPENDENT PRED RESID}]]
                  {tempvar}    {tempvarlist         }

  [/SCATTERPLOT=(varname,varname)... [SIZE({SMALL})]]
                                           {LARGE}

  [/PARTIALPLOT=[{ALL    }] [SIZE({SMALL})]]
                {varlist}        {LARGE}

  [/SAVE=tempvar(newname) [tempvar(newname)... ]]
```

Temporary variables available for residuals analysis include:

```
PRED    ZPRED  ADJPRED  SEPRED  RESID   ZRESID  SRESID  DRESID
SDRESID MAHAL  COOK     LEVER   DFBETA  SDBETA  DFFIT   SDFIT
COVRATIO MCIN  ICIN
```

SAVE FITS saves:

```
DFBETA  SDBETA  DFFIT  SDFIT  COVRATIO
```

Example:

```
REGRESSION VARIABLES=SAVINGS INCOME POP15 POP75
  /WIDTH=132
  /DEPENDENT=SAVINGS
  /METHOD=ENTER
  /RESIDUALS
  /CASEWISE
  /SCATTERPLOT (*ZRESID,*ZPRED)
  /PARTIALPLOT
  /SAVE ZRESID(STDRES) ZPRED(STDPRED).
```

Overview

REGRESSION automatically calculates predicted values, residuals, measures of fit and influence, and several statistics based on these. The distribution of these statistics can be examined and outliers can be identified. The temporary variables are available for analysis within REGRESSION by means of casewise plots, scatterplots, histograms, normal probability plots, and partial plots of the variables. In addition, any of of the residuals subcommands can be specified to obtain statistics on the predicted values, residuals, and their standardized versions. Any of the temporary variables can be added to the active system file with the SAVE command.

Defaults

All residuals analysis subcommands are optional but most have active defaults that can be requested by including the subcommand without any further specifications. These active defaults are described by subcommand below.

Tailoring

You can specify which residuals statistics are presented, which variables are added to the active file, which are plotted, and the size of plots.

Syntax

• The optional residuals subcommands RESIDUALS, CASEWISE, SCATTER-PLOT, and PARTIALPLOT follow the last METHOD subcommand for any equation for which residuals analysis is requested. If you specify more than one equation (more than one DEPENDENT subcommand), you can request residual analysis after each one.

- Residuals subcommands can be specified in any order.
- Residuals subcommands affect only the equation they follow.
- The residuals subcommands cannot be specified if matrix input is used.

Operations
- All calculations and plots requested on the RESIDUALS subcommand are based on the regression equation produced as a result of the last method specified.
- The temporary variables PRED, RESID, ZPRED, and ZRESID are calculated and descriptive statistics are printed for these variables whenever any RESIDUALS subcommand is specified. Referring to any of the other temporary variables (or specifying DEPENDENT on CASEWISE) causes additional temporary variables to be calculated.
- Predicted values and statistics based on predicted values are calculated for every observation that has valid values for all variables in the equation.
- Residuals and statistics based on residuals are calculated for all observations that have a valid predicted value and a valid value for the dependent variable.
- The missing-values option therefore affects the calculation of residuals and predicted values.
- The amount of information displayed in a casewise plot is limited by the display width (see REGRESSION).
- The widest page allows a maximum of eight variables in a casewise plot.
- No residuals or predictors are generated for cases deleted from the active file with the PROCESS IF, SELECT IF, or SAMPLE commands.
- All variables are standardized before plotting. If the unstandardized version of a variable is requested, the standardized version is plotted.
- For each analysis, REGRESSION can calculate several types of temporary variables:

PRED	*Unstandardized predicted values.*
ZPRED	*Adjusted predicted values.*
ADJPRED	*Standardized predicted values.*
SEPRED	*Standard errors of the predicted values.*
RESID	*Unstandardized residuals.*
ZRESID	*Standardized residuals.*
SRESID	*Studentized residuals.*
DRESID	*Deleted residuals.*
SDRESID	*Studentized deleted residuals.* (See Hoaglin & Welsch, 1978.)
MAHAL	*Mahalanobis' distances.*
COOK	*Cook's distances.* (See Cook, 1977.)
LEVER	*Leverage values.* (See Velleman & Welsch, 1981.)
DFBETA	*DFBETA.* This is the change in the regression coefficient that results from the deletion of the ith case. (See Belsley et al., 1980.) A DFBETA value is computed for each case for each regression coeffiecient generated in a model.
SDBETA	*Standardized DFBETA.* An SDBETA value is computed for each case for each regression coefficient generated in a model. (See Belsley et al., 1980.)
DFFIT	*DFFIT.* The change in the predicted value when the ith case is deleted. (See Belsley et al., 1980.)
SDFIT	*Standardized DFFIT.* (See Belsley et al., 1980.)

COVRATIO *COVRATIO.* Ratio of the determinant of the covariance matrix with the ith case deleted to the determinant of the covariance matrix with all cases included. (See Belsley et al., 1980.)

MCIN *Lower and upper bounds for the prediction interval of the mean predicted response.* A lower bound LMCIN and an upperbound UMCIN are generated. The default confidence interval is 95%. The interval may be reset with the CIN keyword of the CRITERIA subcommand. (See Dillon & Goldstein, 1984.)

ICIN *Lower and upper bounds for the prediction interval for a single observation.* A lower bound LICIN and an upperbound UICIN are generated. The default confidence interval is 95%. The interval may be reset with the CIN keyword of the CRITERIA subcommand. (See Dillon & Goldstein, 1984.)

Limitations

- If there is not enough storage available to assemble the requested plots, a warning is printed. Small plots are displayed and some plots may be deleted.

Example

```
REGRESSION VARIABLES=SAVINGS INCOME POP15 POP75
   /WIDTH=132
   /DEPENDENT=SAVINGS
   /METHOD=ENTER
   /RESIDUALS
   /CASEWISE
   /SCATTERPLOT (*ZRESID,*ZPRED)
   /PARTIALPLOT
   /SAVE ZRESID(STDRES) ZPRED(STDPRED).
```

- This REGRESSION command requests a single equation in which SAVINGS is the dependent variable and INCOME, POP15, and POP75 are independent variables.

- The RESIDUALS subcommand requests the default residuals output.

- Because residuals processing has been requested, statistics for predicted values, residuals, and standardized versions of predicted values and residuals are displayed.

- The CASEWISE subcommand requests a casewise plot of ZRESID of cases for which the absolute value of ZRESID is greater than 3. Values of the dependent variable, predicted value, and residual are listed for each case.

- The SCATTERPLOT subcommand requests a small plot of the standardized predicted value by the standardized residual.

- The PARTIALPLOT subcommand requests small partial residual plots of SAVINGS by POP75, SAVINGS by POP15, and SAVINGS by INCOME.

- The SAVE subcommand requests that the standardized residual and the standardized predicted value be added to the active file as new variables named STDRES and STDPRED.

RESIDUALS Subcommand

The RESIDUALS subcommand controls the display and labeling of summary information on outliers as well as the display of the Durbin-Watson test statistic plus histograms and normal probability plots for the temporary variables.

- The RESIDUALS subcommand without specifications displays a histogram of the standardized residuals, a normal probability plot of the standardized residuals, the values of $CASENUM and ZRESID for the 10 cases with the largest absolute value of ZRESID, and the Durbin-Watson test statistic. The default SIZE of both plots is LARGE when no specifications are given.

- If any keyword specifications are given for RESIDUALS, only the displays requested are produced.

DEFAULTS	*DURBIN, HISTOGRAM(ZRESID), OUTLIERS-(ZRESID), NORMPROB(ZRESID), SIZE(LARGE).* These are the defaults if the RESIDUALS subcommand is included without specifications.
SIZE(plotsize)	*Plot sizes.* The plot size can be SMALL or LARGE. The default is large plots if the display width is at least 120 (see REGRESSION) and the page length is at least 57 (see SET in *SPSS/PC+ Base Manual*). Four small histograms or normal probability plots can be displayed on a single page if the width is 132 (see REGRESSION) and the page length is 59.
HISTOGRAM(tempvarlist)	*Histogram of the standardized temporary variable or variables.* The default is ZRESID. The other temporary variables for which histograms are available are PRED, ZPRED, ADJPRED, RESID, SRESID, DRESID, and SDRESID. The specification of any temporary variable other than these will result in an error.
NORMPROB(tempvarlist)	*Normal probability (P-P) plot of standardized values.* The default is ZRESID. The other temporary variables available for normal probability plots are PRED, ZPRED, ADJPRED, RESID, SRESID, DRESID, and SDRESID. The specification of any temporary variable other than these will result in an error.
OUTLIERS(tempvarlist)	*The 10 cases with the largest absolute values of the specified temporary variables.* The default is ZRESID. The listing includes the value of $CASENUM and of the temporary variables for the 10 cases. The other temporary variables available for OUTLIERS are RESID, SRESID, DRESID, SDRESID, MAHAL, and COOK. The specification of any temporary variable other than these will result in an error.
DURBIN	*Durbin-Watson test statistic.*
ID(varname)	*The case identifier on outlier plots.* Any variable on the active file can be named. ID also labels the list of cases produced by CASEWISE.
POOLED	*Display pooled plots and statistics using all cases in the active file when the SELECT subcommand is in effect* (see REGRESSION). The alternative to POOLED is the default keyword SEPARATE, which requests separate reporting of residuals statistics and plots for selected and unselected cases.

Example   `/RESID=DEFAULT ID(SVAR)`

- DEFAULT produces the default residuals statistics: the Durbin-Watson test statistic, a normal probability plot and histogram of ZRESID, and an outlier plot of ZRESID.

- Descriptive statistics for ZRESID, RESID, PRED, and ZPRED are automatically displayed.

- ID(SVAR) names SVAR the case identifier on outlier plots. If the CASEWISE subcommand is also included, SVAR is used to label cases in the casewise plot.

CASEWISE Subcommand

The CASEWISE subcommand requests a casewise plot of residuals. On it you specify a temporary residual variable for casewise plotting (PLOT) and control the selection of cases for plotting (OUTLIERS or ALL). CASEWISE can also be used to specify variables to be listed for each case next to the plot.

- The CASEWISE subcommand without specifications displays a casewise plot of ZRESID for cases for which the absolute value of ZRESID is at least 3. By default the values of the case sequence number, DEPENDENT, PRED, and RESID are listed next to the plot entry for each case.

- Only those defaults specifically altered are changed.

DEFAULTS
OUTLIERS(3), PLOT(ZRESID), DEPENDENT, PRED, and RESID. These are the defaults if the CASEWISE subcommand is included without specifications.

OUTLIERS(value)
Plot only cases for which the absolute standardized value of the plotted variable is at least as large as the value given. The default value is 3. The alternative to a casewise plot of outliers is a plot of all cases (keyword ALL). The keyword OUTLIERS is ignored if the keyword ALL is also present.

ALL
Include all cases in the casewise plot. ALL is the alternative to the OUTLIERS keyword.

PLOT(tempvar)
Plot the standardized values of the temporary variable in the casewise plot. The default temporary variable is ZRESID. Other variables that can be plotted are RESID, DRESID, SRESID, and SDRESID.

tempvarlist
Display the values of these variables for each case next to its casewise plot entry. The default variables are DEPENDENT (the dependent variable), PRED, and RESID. Other variables that can be named are ZPRED, ADJPRED, SEPRED, ZRESID, SRESID, DRESID, SDRESID, MAHAL, COOK, and LEVER. If an ID variable is specified on the RESIDUALS subcommand, the ID variable is also listed if the width is sufficient.

Example
`/CASEWISE=DEFAULT ALL SRE MAH COOK SDR`

- This example requests a casewise plot of the standardized residuals for all cases.
- The dependent variable and the temporary variables PRED, RESID, SRESID, MAHAL, COOK, and SDRESID are also listed for all cases.

SCATTERPLOT Subcommand

The SCATTERPLOT subcommand names pairs of variables for scatterplots and controls the size of the plots.

- The minimum specification for SCATTERPLOT is a pair of variables in parentheses.
- There are no default specifications for SCATTERPLOT.
- The first variable named in each set of parentheses is plotted along the vertical axis, and the second variable is plotted along the horizontal axis.
- Specify as many pairs of variables in parentheses as you want.
- Plotting symbols are used to represent multiple points occurring at the same print position.
- Specify the temporary variable names with an asterisk prefix to distinguish temporary from user-defined variables.
- All scatterplots are standardized. That is, specifying *RESID is the same as specifying *ZRESID, and *PRED is the same as *ZPRED.

(varname,varname)
Plot the variables specified. Available temporary variables are PRED, RESID, ZPRED, ZRESID, DRESID, ADJPRED, SRESID, and SDRESID, along with any variable on the VARIABLES subcommand. The specification of any temporary variable other than these will result in an error.

SIZE(plotsize)
Plot sizes. The plot size can be either SMALL or LARGE. The default is always small. Four small scatterplots can be displayed on a single page if the width is at least 120 (see REGRESSION) and the page length is at least 57 (see SET in *SPSS/PC+ Base Manual*).

Example
`/SCATTERPLOT (*RES,*PRE)(*RES,SAVINGS)`

- This example specifies two scatterplots: residuals against predicted values and residuals against the values of the variable YVAR.

PARTIALPLOT Subcommand

Use the PARTIALPLOT subcommand to request partial residual plots and to control the size of the plots. Partial residual plots are scatterplots of the residuals of the dependent variable and an independent variable when both of these variables are regressed on the rest of the independent variables.

- If the PARTIALPLOT subcommand is included without specifications, a partial residual plot is produced for every independent variable in the equation.
- All plots are standardized.
- Plots are displayed in descending order of the standard error of *B*.

varlist   *List of variables to be plotted.* Any variable entered into the equation can be named. At least two independent variables must be in the equation for partial residual plots to be produced. The default is every independent variable in the equation. You can request the defaults with keyword ALL.

SIZE(plotsize)   *Plot sizes.* The plotsize can be either SMALL or LARGE. The default is always SMALL. Four small partialplots çan be displayed on a single page if the width is at least 120 (see REGRESSION) and the page length is at least 57 (see SET in *SPSS/PC+ Base Manual*).

Example
```
REGRESSION VARS=PLOT15 TO SAVINGS
   /DEP=SAVINGS
   /METH=ENTER
   /RESID=DEFAULTS
   /PARTIAL.
```

- A partial residual plot is produced for every independent variable in the equation.

SAVE Subcommand

Use SAVE to add new variables to the active system file containing one or more temporary residual or fit variables.

- Specifications for SAVE consist of one or more of the temporary variable types (see Operations) each optionally followed by a new variable name in parentheses.
- New variable names must be unique.
- If temporary variable types are specified without new variable names, the procedure generates a stem corresponding to a shortened form of the temporary variable name with a suffix to identify its creation sequence.
- If you specify DFBETA or SDBETA on the SAVE subcommand, the number of new variables saved is equal to the total number of variables in the equation.

FITS   *Save all influence statistics.* Save DFBETA, SDBETA, DFFIT, SDFIT, and COVRATIO. You cannot specify new variable names when using this keyword. Default names will be generated.

Example
```
/SAVE=PRED(PREDVAL) RESID(RESIDUAL) COOK(CDISTANC)
```

- This subcommand adds three variables to the end of the file: PREDVAL, containing the unstandardized predicted value for the case, RESIDUAL, containing the unstandardized residual for the case, and CDISTANC, containing Cook's distance for the case.

Example
```
/SAVE=PRED RESID
```

- This subcommand adds two variables, named PRE_1 and RES_1, to the end of the file.

Example
```
REGRESSION DEPENDENT=Y
   /METHOD=ENTER X1 X2
   /SAVE DFBETA(DFBVAR).
```

- The SAVE subcommand will create and save three new variables with the names DFBVAR0, DFBVAR1, and DFBVAR2.

Example
```
REGRESSION VARIABLES=SAVINGS INCOME POP15 POP75 GROWTH
   /DEPENDENT=SAVINGS
   /METHOD=ENTER INCOME POP15 POP75
   /SAVE=PRED(PREDV) SDBETA(BETA) ICIN.
```

Command Reference **C**

• The SAVE subcommand adds seven variables to the end of the file: PREDV, containing the unstandardized predicted value for the case; BETA0, the standardized DFBETA for the intercept; BETA1, BETA2, and BETA3, the standardized DFBETA's for the three independent variables in the model; LICL1, the lower bound for the prediction interval for an individual case; and UICL1, the upper bound for the prediction interval for an individual case.

References

Belsley, D. A., E. Kuh, and R. E. Welsch. 1980. *Regression diagnostics: Identifying influential data and sources of collinearity.* New York: John Wiley & Sons.

Cook, R. D. 1977. Detection of influential observations in linear regression. *Technometrics* 19: 15–18.

Dillon, W. R., and M. Goldstein. 1984. *Multivariate analysis: Methods and applications.* New York: John Wiley & Sons.

Hoaglin, D. C., and R. E. Welsch. 1978. The hat matrix in regression and ANOVA. *American Statistician* 32: 17–22.

Velleman, P. F., and R. E. Welsch. 1981. Efficient computing of regression diagnostics. *American Statistician* 35: 234–242.

RELIABILITY

```
RELIABILITY VARIABLES=varlist

[/SCALE(scalename)=varlist [/SCALE... ]]

[/MODEL={ALPHA          }] [/VARIABLES...]
        {SPLIT[(n)]     }
        {GUTTMAN        }
        {PARALLEL       }
        {STRICTPARALLEL }

[/MISSING={EXCLUDE}]
          {INCLUDE}

[/FORMAT={LABELS  }]
         {NOLABELS}

[/METHOD=COV]

[/STATISTICS=[DESCRIPTIVE] [SCALE    ] [{ANOVA    }] [ALL]]
             [COV        ] [TUKEY    ]  {FRIEDMAN }
             [CORR       ] [HOTELLING]  {COCHRAN  }

[/SUMMARY=[MEANS    ] [COV ] [TOTAL]]
          [VARIANCE ] [CORR] [ALL  ]
```

Example:

```
RELIABILITY /VARIABLES=SCORE1 TO SCORE10
    /SCALE (OVERALL) = ALL
    /MODEL = ALPHA
    /SUMMARY = MEANS TOTAL.
```

Overview   RELIABILITY estimates reliability statistics for the components of multiple-item additive scales. It uses any of five models for reliability analysis and offers a great variety of statistical displays.

Defaults   By default, RELIABILITY displays the number of cases, number of items, and Cronbach's α. Whenever possible, it uses an algorithm that does not require the calculation of the covariance matrix. Cases with a missing value for any variable in the analysis are excluded.

Tailoring   **Model type.** You can specify any of five models.

Statistical display. Available statistics include descriptive statistics, correlation and covariance matrices, a repeated-measures analysis of variance table, Hotelling's T^2, Tukey's test for additivity, Friedman's chi-square for the analysis of ranked data, and Cochran's Q.

Computational method. You can force RELIABILITY to use the covariance method, even when you are not requesting any output that requires it.

Missing data. You can include user-missing values in the computations.

Syntax   • The minimum specifications are the VARIABLES subcommand, a SCALE subcommand that provides a name for the scale, and either the names of the variables in that scale or keyword ALL.

• You must enter the VARIABLES subcommand first. You can enter it more than once.

• Other subcommands can be specified in any order and must be separated by slashes.

• The STATISTICS and SUMMARY subcommands are cumulative. You can enter them at any point after the VARIABLES subcommand. If you enter them more than once, all statistics that you request are produced for each scale.

Operations
- RELIABILITY causes the data to be read.
- If you request output that is not available for your model or for your data, RELIABILITY ignores the request.
- RELIABILITY uses an economical algorithm whenever possible but calculates a covariance matrix when necessary; see the METHOD subcommand for details.

Limitations
- Maximum 10 VARIABLES subcommands.
- Maximum 50 SCALE subcommands.
- Maximum 200 variables (the system limit) on any scale.

Example
```
RELIABILITY /VARIABLES=SCORE1 TO SCORE10
  /SCALE (OVERALL) = ALL
  /SCALE (ODD) = SCORE1 SCORE3 SCORE5 SCORE7 SCORE9
  /SUMMARY = MEANS TOTAL.
```
- This example analyzes two additive scales composed of the variables (or "items") from SCORE1 to SCORE10.
- One scale (labeled OVERALL in the display output) is composed of all 10 items. Another (labeled ODD) is composed of every other item.
- Summary statistics are displayed for each scale, showing item means and the relation of each item to the total scale.

VARIABLES Subcommand

The VARIABLES subcommand specifies the variables to be used in the analysis.
- The VARIABLES subcommand is required and must be specified first.
- You can use keyword ALL to refer to all user-defined variables in the active file.
- You can use keyword TO to refer to consecutive variables in the active file.
- You can specify VARIABLES more than once in a single RELIABILITY command.

SCALE Subcommand

The SCALE subcommand defines a scale for analysis, providing a name for the scale and specifying its component variables. After SCALE, specify:

- A name for the scale, in parentheses. This name is used only to label the output from RELIABILITY. The RELIABILITY command does *not* add any new variables to your active file. If the analysis is satisfactory, use COMPUTE to create a new variable containing the sum of the component items.
- A list of variables to be used as components for the additive scale. The keyword ALL refers to all variables named on the preceding VARIABLES subcommand.

RELIABILITY analyzes the scale formed by adding the component variables.

- Variables named on SCALE must have been named on the previous VARIABLES subcommand.
- To reference consecutive variables from the VARIABLES subcommand, you can specify the keyword TO.
- To analyze different groups of the component variables, you can specify SCALE more than once following a VARIABLES subcommand.

Example
```
RELIABILITY VARIABLES = ITEM1 TO ITEM20
  /SCALE (A) = ITEM1 TO ITEM10
  /SCALE (B) = ITEM1 ITEM3 ITEM5 ITEM16 TO ITEM20
  /SCALE (C) = ALL.
```
- This command analyzes three different scales: scale A has 10 items, scale B has 8 items, and scale C has 20 items.

MODEL Subcommand

The MODEL subcommand specifies the type of reliability analysis for the scale on the preceding SCALE subcommand. If you do not specify MODEL, ALPHA is the default.

Available models are:

ALPHA   *Cronbach's* α. Standardized item α is also displayed if you specify METHOD COV. This is the default.

SPLIT   *Split-half coefficients.* By default, the first half of the items is compared with the last half of the items (with the odd item, if any, going to the first half). You can specify a number in parentheses to override this default division, indicating how many items should be in the *second* half. For example, MODEL SPLIT (6) takes the last 6 variables for the second half, with all others in the first half.

GUTTMAN   *Guttman's lower bounds for true reliability.*

PARALLEL   *Maximum likelihood reliability estimate under parallel assumptions.* This model assumes that items have the same variance, but not necessarily the same mean.

STRICTPARALLEL   *Maximum likelihood reliability estimate under strictly parallel assumptions.* This model assumes that items have the same means, the same true score variances over a set of objects being measured, and the same error variance over replications.

STATISTICS Subcommand

The STATISTICS subcommand displays optional statistics. After STATISTICS, you can specify one or more of the following:

DESC   *Item means and standard deviations.*

COVARIANCES   *Inter-item variance-covariance matrix.*

CORRELATIONS   *Inter-item correlation matrix.*

SCALE   *Scale mean(s) and scale variance(s).*

TUKEY   *Tukey's test for additivity.* This helps determine whether a transformation of the items in your scale is needed to reduce non-additivity. The test prints an estimate of the power to which the items should be raised in order to be additive.

HOTEL   *Hotelling's* T^2. This is a test for equality of means among the items.

ANOVA   *Repeated-measures analysis of variance table.*

FRIEDMAN   *Friedman's chi-square and Kendall's coefficient of concordance.* These apply to ranked data. You must request ANOVA in addition to FRIEDMAN; the Friedman chi-square appears in place of the usual F test.

COCHRAN   *Cochran's* Q. This applies when all of the items are dichotomies. You must request ANOVA in addition to COCHRAN; the Q statistic appears in place of the usual F test.

ALL   *All applicable statistics.*

The STATISTICS subcommand is cumulative. If you enter it more than once, all statistics that you request are produced for each scale.

SUMMARY Subcommand

The SUMMARY subcommand displays summary statistics for each individual item in the scale. After SUMMARY, you can specify one or more of the following:

MEANS   *Statistics on item means,* including the average, minimum, maximum, range, ratio of maximum to minimum, and variance of the item means.

VARIANCE   *Statistics on item variances.* VARIANCE includes the same statistics as for MEANS.

C

Command Reference

COVARIANCES *Statistics on item covariances.* COVARIANCE includes the same statistics as for MEANS.

CORRELATIONS *Statistics on item correlations.* CORRELATIONS includes the same statistics as for MEANS.

TOTAL *Statistics comparing each individual item to the scale composed of the other items.* TOTAL includes the scale mean, variance, and Cronbach's α without the item, and the correlation between the item and the scale without it.

ALL *All applicable summary statistics.*

The SUMMARY subcommand is cumulative. If you enter it more than once, all statistics that you request are produced for each scale.

METHOD Subcommand

Two computational methods are available with the RELIABILITY procedure. The "space-saver" method does not require the calculation of a covariance matrix and is used whenever possible. RELIABILITY does compute the covariance matrix for all variables on each VARIABLES subcommand if *any* of the following is true:

• You specify a model other than ALPHA or SPLIT.

• You request COV, CORR, FRIEDMAN, or HOTELLING on the STATISTICS subcommand.

• You request anything other than TOTAL on the SUMMARY subcommand.

Even if none of these conditions applies, you can force RELIABILITY to use the covariance matrix with the METHOD subcommand. Only a single specification applies:

COVARIANCE *Calculate and use the covariance matrix,* even if it is not needed.

FORMAT Subcommand

By default, RELIABILITY prints the variable label of each variable in the scale before reporting on the analysis. The FORMAT subcommand lets you suppress this initial display of variable names and labels. The available keywords on FORMAT are:

LABELS *Display names and labels for all items* before the analysis. This is the default.

NOLABELS *Do not display names and labels.*

MISSING Subcommand

RELIABILITY deletes cases from analysis if they have a missing value for any variable named on the current VARIABLES subcommand. By default, both system-missing and user-missing values are excluded. You can use the MISSING subcommand to control deletion of missing data. Specify one of the following after MISSING:

EXCLUDE *Exclude user-missing as well as system-missing values.* This is the default.

INCLUDE *Treat user-missing values as valid,* excluding only system-missing values.

T-TEST

Independent Samples:

```
T-TEST GROUPS=varname [({1,2       })] /VARIABLES=varlist
                        {value     }
                        {value,value}


        [/OPTIONS=option numbers]
```

Paired Samples:

```
T-TEST PAIRS=varlist [WITH varlist] [/[PAIRS=] varlist ...]


        [/OPTIONS=option numbers]
```

Options:

1 Include user-missing values   3 Suppress variable labels
2 Exclude missing values listwise   5 Special pairing for WITH

Examples:

```
T-TEST GROUPS=XVAR(1,3)/VARIABLES=YVAR1 YVAR2 YVAR3.

T-TEST PAIRS=ZVAR1 ZVAR2 ZVAR3/ZVAR4 ZVAR5.
```

Overview

T-TEST compares sample means by calculating Student's t and displays the two-tailed probability of the difference between the means. Statistics are available for either independent samples (different groups of cases) or paired samples (different variables). Other procedures that compare group means are ANOVA and ONEWAY.

Defaults

In addition to Student's t, degrees of freedom, and two-tailed probabilities, T-TEST produces the mean, standard deviation, standard error, and count for each group or variable. The default display includes the variable label and always uses narrow format. Cases with missing values for the variables that specify a test are excluded from that test.

Independent-Samples Test. For independent-samples tests, both pooled- and separate-variance estimates are calculated, along with the F value used to test homogeneity of variance and its probability. The two-tailed probability is displayed for the t value.

Paired-Samples Test. For paired-samples tests, the default output includes the difference between the means, the two-tailed probability level for a test of the difference, the correlation coefficient for the two variables, and the two-tailed probability level for a test of the coefficient.

Tailoring

Display Format. You can suppress the printing of variable labels.

Statistical Display. You can control which variables are paired in paired-samples tests. There are no optional statistics. All statistics available are displayed by default.

Missing Values. You can include cases with user-missing values in the calculation of the statistics for each test. Alternatively, you can exclude cases with missing values for any of the variables named on the command from all analyses.

Syntax

- To request both independent- and paired-samples tests, specify GROUPS and VARIABLES first, then PAIRS.
- Subcommands can each be specified only once and must be separated by a slash.

Operations

- T-TEST is a procedure and causes the data to be read.
- If a GROUPS variable is a long string, only the short-string portion is used to identify groups in the analysis.
- Probability levels are two-tailed.
- The T-TEST display always uses narrow format regardless of the width defined on SET.
- The BOXSTRING subcommand controls the characters used in the table display (see SET).

C

Command Reference

Limitations	• Maximum 1 grouping variable per independent-samples test (the GROUPS subcommand).
	• Maximum 50 analysis variables per independent-samples test (the VARIABLES subcommand).
	• Maximum 1 each of the GROUPS, VARIABLES, and OPTIONS subcommands.
	• The maximum number of variables for paired-sample tests is the same as the system limit.

Example T-TEST GROUPS=XVAR(1,3)/VARIABLES=YVAR1 YVAR2 YVAR3.

• This independent-samples example compares the means of the two groups defined by XVAR for variables YVAR1, YVAR2, and YVAR3.

Example T-T PAIRS=ZVAR1 ZVAR2 ZVAR3/ZVAR4 ZVAR5.

• The first analysis list in this paired-samples example compares the means of ZVAR1 and ZVAR2, ZVAR1 and ZVAR3, and ZVAR2 and ZVAR3. The second analysis list compares the means of ZVAR4 and ZVAR5.

• This example takes advantage of spelling permitted by three-character truncation of keywords.

GROUPS and VARIABLES Subcommands

Independent samples t-tests are requested with the GROUPS and VARIABLES subcommands. The GROUPS subcommand names a variable used to group cases. The VARIABLES subcommand names the dependent variables.

• The minimum specification for an independent-samples test is the GROUPS subcommand with a variable name followed by the VARIABLES subcommand with a variable name.

• GROUPS can name only one variable, which can be numeric or string.

• The GROUPS variable can be followed by a range specification in parentheses.

• A single GROUPS value in parentheses groups all cases with a code equal to or greater than the value into one group and the remaining cases into the other group.

• Two GROUPS values in parentheses include cases with the first value in one group and cases with the second value in the other group. Cases with other values are excluded.

• If no GROUPS values are specified, (1,2) is assumed for numeric variables and (DEFAULT1, DEFAULT2) is assumed for string variables.

• VARIABLES names the variables being analyzed.

• VARIABLES can name only numeric variables.

PAIRS Subcommand

Use the PAIRS subcommand to request paired-samples tests.

• The minimum specification for a paired-samples test is the PAIRS subcommand with a single analysis list.

• The minimum analysis list is two variables.

• Analysis lists can name only numeric variables.

• An analysis list without keyword WITH compares each variable with every other variable.

• An analysis list with keyword WITH compares every variable to the left of the keyword with every variable to the right of the keyword.

• Multiple PAIRS subcommands can be used. The keyword PAIRS is required only on the first PAIRS subcommand.

• Use a slash to separate multiple PAIRS subcommands.

Display Format   The default display includes the variable label. You can change this default with the following option on the OPTIONS subcommand:

Option 3   *Suppress variable labels.*

Statistical Display   All statistics available with T-TEST are displayed automatically. However, you can control the pairing of variables in the analysis list with the following option on the OPTIONS subcommand:

Option 5   *Special pairing for paired-samples test.* Option 5 must be used with keyword WITH. The first variable before WITH is compared to the first variable after WITH, the second variable before WITH is compared to the second variable after WITH, and so forth. The same number of variables should be specified before and after WITH; unmatched variables are ignored. Option 5 is ignored with independent samples or when keyword WITH is not specified in the PAIRS subcommand.

Example   ```
T-TEST PAIRS=SCALE1 TO SCALE3 WITH SCALE4 TO SCALE6
  /OPTIONS=5.
```

• This analysis compares SCALE1 and SCALE4, SCALE2 and SCALE5, and SCALE3 and SCALE6.

**Missing Values**   For independent-samples tests, cases missing on either the grouping variable or the analysis variable are excluded from the analysis of that variable. For paired-samples tests, a case missing on either of the variables in a given pair is excluded from the analysis of that pair. You alter the handling of cases with missing values by specifying the following on the OPTIONS subcommand:

**Option 1**   *Include user-missing values.* Cases with user-missing values are included in the calculation of test statistics.

**Option 2**   *Exclude missing values listwise.* A case with a missing value for any variable named on the command is excluded from all analyses the command requests.
```

Examples

Contents

Examples

ANOVA   This example, illustrating the use of ANOVA, is a three-way analysis of variance with one covariate. The data are 500 cases from the 1980 General Social Survey. The variables are:

• PRESTIGE—the respondent's occupational prestige scale score. PRESTIGE is the dependent variable.

• EDUC—the respondent's education in years.

• RACE—the respondent's race, coded 1=WHITE, 2=BLACK, and 3=OTHER.

• SEX—the respondent's sex, coded 1=MALE and 2=FEMALE.

• REGION—the respondent's residence, coded as one of nine regions.

The task is twofold: determine the degree to which the American occupational structure differs across race, sex, and region; and measure the effect of the respondent's educational level, since education might prove to be a concomitant influence. The data are in an external file named AANOVA.DAT. The SPSS/PC+ commands in the command file named on the INCLUDE command are:

```
DATA LIST FILE='AANOVA.DAT'/
   PRESTIGE 1-2 EDUC 3-4 RACE 5 SEX 6 REGION 7.
VARIABLE LABELS PRESTIGE "Resp's Occupational Prestige Score"
                EDUC 'Highest Year School Completed'
                REGION 'Region of Interview'.
ANOVA PRESTIGE BY REGION(1,9) SEX,RACE(1,2) WITH EDUC
   /STATISTICS 2
   /OPTIONS 10,11.
FINISH.
```

• The DATA LIST command assigns variable names and gives column locations for the variables in the analysis (see DATA LIST).

• The VARIABLE LABELS command completes the file definition (see VARIABLE LABELS).

• The ANOVA command names PRESTIGE as the dependent variable; REGION, SEX, and RACE as the factors; and EDUC as the covariate. The minimum and maximum values for REGION are 1 and 9, and the minimum and maximum values for both SEX and RACE are 1 and 2. Since variable RACE actually has values 1, 2, and 3, cases with value 3 are eliminated from the model.

• Statistic 2 requests the regression coefficient for the covariate EDUC.

• Option 10 requests the hierarchical approach for decomposing sums of squares. First, the covariate EDUC is assessed to establish statistical control. Then the effect of REGION is assessed. Next, the effect of SEX is adjusted for REGION; then the effect of RACE is adjusted for REGION and SEX. Finally, each of the interaction effects is assessed.

• Option 11 tells SPSS/PC+ to display the results within a narrow width.

The display produced by ANOVA is on the following page. The exact appearance of the printed output depends on the characters available on the printer used.

D

Examples

ANOVA display

```
            PRESTIGE  Resp's Occupational Prestige Score
      BY    REGION    Region of Interview
            SEX
            RACE
      WITH  EDUC      Highest Year School Completed
```

SOURCE OF VARIATION	SUM OF SQUARES	DF	MEAN SQUARE	F	SIGNIF OF F
COVARIATES	23715.522	1	23715.522	191.701	0.000
EDUC	23715.522	1	23715.522	191.701	0.000
MAIN EFFECTS	2708.380	10	270.838	2.189	0.018
REGION	1260.552	8	157.569	1.274	0.255
SEX	22.413	1	22.413	0.181	0.671
RACE	1425.415	1	1425.415	11.522	0.001
2-WAY INTERACTIONS	3144.833	17	184.990	1.495	0.092
REGION SEX	1349.220	8	168.653	1.363	0.211
REGION RACE	1138.839	8	142.355	1.151	0.328
SEX RACE	534.154	1	534.154	4.318	0.038
3-WAY INTERACTIONS	1663.399	6	277.233	2.241	0.039
REGION SEX RACE	1663.399	6	277.233	2.241	0.039
EXPLAINED	31232.135	34	918.592	7.425	0.0
RESIDUAL	52205.957	422	123.711		
TOTAL	83438.092	456	182.978		

```
COVARIATE   RAW REGRESSION COEFFICIENT

EDUC            2.331


   500 CASES WERE PROCESSED.
    43 CASES (  8.6 PCT) WERE MISSING.
```

CLUSTER   This example clusters cities using data from the 1982 *Information Please Almanac.* These were the 25 most populous cities in the U.S. in 1980. The variables are:

- CITY—the city in question.
- CHURCHES—number of churches.
- PARKS—number of parks. Some cities only report total acreage and have a missing-value code of 9999 for number of parks.
- PHONES—number of telephones.
- TVS—number of television sets.
- RADIOST—number of radio stations.
- TVST—number of television stations.
- POP80—city population in 1980.
- TAXRATE—property tax rate in city.

We use these variables to cluster cities into groups that are relatively homogeneous with respect to these variables. Cities differ on these variables simply as a function of their population. We therefore rescale the variables to number of parks, etc., per person. The data are in an external file named ACLUS.DAT.

The SPSS/PC+ commands in the command file named on the INCLUDE command are:

```
DATA LIST FILE='ACLUS.DAT'/
    CITY 6-18(A) POP80 53-60
    CHURCHES 10-13 PARKS 14-17 PHONES 18-25 TVS 26-32
    RADIOST 33-35 TVST 36-38 TAXRATE 52-57(2)/.
MISSING VALUE PARKS (9999).
COMPUTE CHURCHES=CHURCHES/POP80.
COMPUTE PARKS=PARKS/POP80.
COMPUTE PHONES=PHONES/POP80.
COMPUTE TVS=TVS/POP80.
COMPUTE RADIOST=RADIOST/POP80.
COMPUTE TVST=TVST/POP80.
CLUSTER CHURCHES TO TAXRATE
    /METHOD=BAVERAGE
    /ID=CITY
    /PRINT=CLUSTER(3,5) DISTANCE SCHEDULE
    /PLOT=VICICLE HICICLE DENDROGRAM.
FINISH.
```

- DATA LIST names the file that contains the data and gives variable names and column locations. There are three records per case. No variables are read from the third record, so an extra slash is included to skip the unread record for each case.
- The MISSING VALUE command tells SPSS/PC+ to treat the value 9999 as a user-missing value for variable PARKS.
- The COMPUTE commands divide each measure by the population of the city in 1980. This yields the number of churches, phones, etc., per person.
- The CLUSTER variable specification names six variables using the TO convention.
- METHOD clusters cases by the method of average linkage between groups. It uses the default squared Euclidean distances over the six specified variables.
- The ID subcommand requests that the string variable CITY be used to label CLUSTER output.
- The cluster membership table is part of the default display (Figure A).
- PRINT requests the computed distances between cases; the cluster to which each case belongs for the 3-, 4-, and 5-cluster solutions; and the cluster agglomeration schedule (Figure B).
- PLOT presents the cluster solution as both a horizontal (Figure C) and a vertical (Figure D) icicle plot, as well as a dendrogram (Figure E).

The display is shown in Figures A through E. The exact appearance of the printed display will depend on the characters available on the printer used.

A Cluster membership of cases

```
Data Information

      22 unweighted cases accepted.
       3 cases rejected because of missing value.

Squared Euclidean measure used.

1 Agglomeration method specified.


Cluster Membership of Cases using Average Linkage (Between Groups)

                                   Number of Clusters

   Label            Case      5     4     3

   Baltimore          1       1     1     1
   Chicago            2       2     2     2
   Cleveland          3       1     1     1
   Columbus           4       3     1     1
   Dallas             5       4     3     3
   Denver             6       4     3     3
   Detroit            7       3     1     1
   Houston            8       4     3     3
   Indianapolis       9       5     4     2
   Jacksonville      10       4     3     3
   Los Angeles       11       4     3     3
   Memphis           12       3     1     1
   Nashville         13       1     1     1
   New Orleans       14       2     2     2
   New York          15       2     2     2
   Philadelphia      16       1     1     1
   Phoenix           17       4     3     3
   San Diego         18       3     1     1
   San Francisco     19       3     1     1
   San Jose          20       4     3     3
   Seattle           21       4     3     3
   Washington        22       4     3     3
```

B Agglomeration schedule for clustering

```
Agglomeration Schedule using Average Linkage (Between Groups)
             Clusters Combined                    Stage Cluster 1st Appears   Next
   Stage    Cluster 1  Cluster 2   Coefficient    Cluster 1    Cluster 2    Stage
      1         5         20          .213571          0            0          8
      2        17         22          .261159          0            0          6
      3         4         18          .292620          0            0         11
      4         8         21          .656814          0            0          8
      5         3         13         3.067433          0            0         14
      6        10         17         3.173483          0            2         16
      7         1         16         5.655860          0            0         14
      8         5          8         8.083633          1            4         12
      9         7         12        13.270877          0            0         11
     10        14         15        16.843185          0            0         13
     11         4          7        33.221954          3            9         15
     12         5         11        38.605591          8            0         17
     13         2         14        48.604095          0           10         19
     14         1          3        73.268372          7            5         18
     15         4         19        88.134521         11            0         18
     16         6         10        97.164627          0            6         17
     17         5          6       250.892181         12           16         20
     18         1          4       651.010742         14           15         20
     19         2          9      1026.891846         13            0         21
     20         1          5      1710.032959         18           17         21
     21         1          2      5559.281250         20           19          0
```

C Horizontal icicle plot

```
Horizontal Icicle Plot Using Average Linkage (Between Groups)

                          Number of Clusters

                          111111111122
         C A S E          12345678901234678901
    Label        Seq      ++++++++++++++++++++

    Indianapolis    9     XXXXXXXXXXXXXXXXXXXX
                          XXX
                          XXX
    New York       15     XXXXXXXXXXXXXXXXXXXX
                          XXXXXXXXXXXX
                          XXXXXXXXXXXX
    New Orleans    14     XXXXXXXXXXXXXXXXXXXX
                          XXXXXXXXX
                          XXXXXXXXX
    Chicago         2     XXXXXXXXXXXXXXXXXXXX
                          X
                          X
    Washington     22     XXXXXXXXXXXXXXXXXXXX
                          XXXXXXXXXXXXXXXXXX
                          XXXXXXXXXXXXXXXXXX
    Phoenix        17     XXXXXXXXXXXXXXXXXXXX
                          XXXXXXXXXXXXXXXX
                          XXXXXXXXXXXXXXXX
    Jacksonville   10     XXXXXXXXXXXXXXXXXXXX
                          XXXXX
                          XXXXX
    Denver          6     XXXXXXXXXXXXXXXXXXXX
                          XXXXX
                          XXXXX
    Los Angeles    11     XXXXXXXXXXXXXXXXXXXX
                          XXXXXXXXX
                          XXXXXXXXX
    Seattle        21     XXXXXXXXXXXXXXXXXXXX
                          XXXXXXXXXXXXXXXX
                          XXXXXXXXXXXXXXXX
    Houston         8     XXXXXXXXXXXXXXXXXXXX
                          XXXXXXXXXXXXX
                          XXXXXXXXXXXXX
    San Jose       20     XXXXXXXXXXXXXXXXXXXX
                          XXXXXXXXXXXXXXXXXX
                          XXXXXXXXXXXXXXXXXX
    Dallas          5     XXXXXXXXXXXXXXXXXXXX
                          XX
                          XX
    San Francisco  19     XXXXXXXXXXXXXXXXXXXX
                          XXXXXX
                          XXXXXX
    Memphis        12     XXXXXXXXXXXXXXXXXXXX
                          XXXXXXXXXXXXX
                          XXXXXXXXXXXXX
    Detroit         7     XXXXXXXXXXXXXXXXXXXX
                          XXXXXXXXXX
                          XXXXXXXXXX
    San Diego      18     XXXXXXXXXXXXXXXXXXXX
                          XXXXXXXXXXXXXXXX
                          XXXXXXXXXXXXXXXX
    Columbus        4     XXXXXXXXXXXXXXXXXXXX
                          XXXX
                          XXXX
    Nashville      13     XXXXXXXXXXXXXXXXXXXX
                          XXXXXXXXXXXXXXXX
                          XXXXXXXXXXXXXXXX
    Cleveland       3     XXXXXXXXXXXXXXXXXXXX
                          XXXXXXXX
                          XXXXXXXX
    Philadelphia   16     XXXXXXXXXXXXXXXXXXXX
                          XXXXXXXXXXXXX
                          XXXXXXXXXXXXX
    Baltimore       1     XXXXXXXXXXXXXXXXXXXX
```

D Vertical icicle plot

```
Vertical Icicle Plot using Average Linkage (Between Groups)

 (Down) Number of Clusters  (Across) Case Label and number

    I  N  N  C  W  P  J  D  L  S  H  S  D  S  M  D  S  C  N  C  P  B
    n  e  e  h  a  h  a  e  o  e  o  a  a  a  e  e  e  a  o  a  l  a
    d  w  w  i  s  o  c  n  s  a  u  n  l  n  m  t  n  l  s  e  h  l
    i     Y  c  h  e  k  v     t  s  l     n  p  r     u  h  v  l  t
    a  Y  O  a  i  n  s  e  A  t  t  J  a  F  h  o  D  m  v  e  a  i
    n  o  r  g  n  i  o  r  n  l  o  o  s  r  i  i  b  i  i  d  d  m
    a  r  l  o  g  x     n  g  e  n  s  e  a  n     g  l  l  e  e  o
    p  k  e  t     v     i  e  s  c  i        n     s  e  l     l  r
    o     a  o     i     l  l     i                    e  d     p  e
    l     n  n     l     l  e     s                          h
    i     s        l     e  s     c                          i
    s                          o                             a

    1  1        2  1  1     1  2     2     1  1     1     1  1     1
    9  5  4  2  2  7  0  6  1  1  8  0  5  9  2  7  8  4  3  3  6  1
 1 +XXXXXXXXXXXXXXXXXXXXXXXXXXXXXXXXXXXXXXXXXXXXXXXXXXXXXXXXXXXXXXXX
 2 +XXXXXXXXXX  XXXXXXXXXXXXXXXXXXXXXXXXXXX  XXXXXXXXXXXXXXXXXXXXXXXX
 3 +XXXXXXXXXX  XXXXXXXXXXXXXXXXXXXXXXXXXXX  XXXXXXXXXXXXXXXXXXXXXXXX
 4 +X XXXXXXXX  XXXXXXXXXXXXXXXXXXXXXXXXXXX  XXXXXXXXXXXXXXXXXXXXXXXX
 5 +X XXXXXXXX  XXXXXXXXXXXXXXXXXXXXXXXXXXX  XXXXXXXXXXXX  XXXXXXXXXX
 6 +X XXXXXXXX  XXXXXXXXXX  XXXXXXXXXXXXXXX  XXXXXXXXXXXX  XXXXXXXXXX
 7 +X XXXXXXXX  XXXXXXXX  X  XXXXXXXXXXXXXX  XXXXXXXXXXXX  XXXXXXXXXX
 8 +X XXXXXXXX  XXXXXXX  X  XXXXXXXXXXXXXX X XXXXXXXXXXX  XXXXXXXXXX
 9 +X XXXXXXXX  XXXXXXX  X  XXXXXXXXXXXXXX X XXXXXXXXXXX  XXXX  XXXX
10 +X XXXX  X  XXXXXXX  X  XXXXXXXXXXXXXX X XXXXXXXXXXX  XXXX  XXXX
11 +X XXXX  X  XXXXXXX  X X  XXXXXXXXXX  X  XXXXXXXXXXX  XXXX  XXXX
12 +X XXXX  X  XXXXXXX  X X  XXXXXXXXXX  X  XXXX  XXXX  XXXX  XXXX
13 +X X  X  X  XXXXXXX  X X  XXXXXXXXXX  X  XXXX  XXXX  XXXX  XXXX
14 +X X  X  X  XXXXXXX  X X  XXXXXXXXXX  X  X  X  XXXX  XXXX  XXXX
15 +X X  X  X  XXXXXXX  X X  XXXX  XXXX  X  X  X  XXXX  XXXX  XXXX
16 +X X  X  X  XXXXXXX  X X  XXXX  XXXX  X  X  X  XXXX  XXXX  X  X
17 +X X  X  X  XXXX  X  X X  XXXX  XXXX  X  X  X  XXXX  XXXX  X  X
18 +X X  X  X  XXXX  X  X X  XXXX  XXXX  X  X  X  XXXX  X  X  X  X
19 +X X  X  X  XXXX  X  X X  X  X  XXXX  X  X  X  XXXX  X  X  X  X
20 +X X  X  X  XXXX  X  X  X  X  X  XXXX  X  X  X  X  X  X  X  X  X
21 +X X  X  X  X  X  X  X  X  X  XXXX  X  X  X  X  X  X  X  X  X  X
```

E Dendrogram

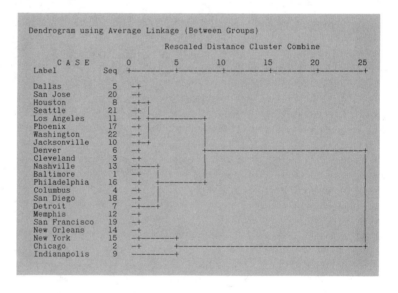

```
Dendrogram using Average Linkage (Between Groups)

                              Rescaled Distance Cluster Combine

         C A S E          0         5        10        15        20        25
    Label          Seq    +---------+---------+---------+---------+---------+

    Dallas           5     -+
    San Jose        20     -+
    Houston          8     -+-+
    Seattle         21     -+ |
    Los Angeles     11     -+ +-----------+
    Phoenix         17     -+ |           |
    Washington      22     -+-+           |
    Jacksonville    10     -+-+           |
    Denver           6     -+             +-----------------------+
    Cleveland        3     -+             |                       |
    Nashville       13     -+---+         |                       |
    Baltimore        1     -+   |         |                       |
    Philadelphia    16     -+   +---------+                       |
    Columbus         4     -+   |                                 |
    San Diego       18     -+   |                                 |
    Detroit          7     -+-+-+                                 |
    Memphis         12     -+                                     |
    San Francisco   19     -+                                     |
    New Orleans     14     -+                                     |
    New York        15     -+--------+                            |
    Chicago          2     -+        +---------------------------+
    Indianapolis     9     ----------+
```

CORRELATION   This example analyzes 1979 prices and earnings in 45 cities around the world, compiled by the Union Bank of Switzerland. The variables are:

- FOOD—the average net cost of 39 different food and beverage items in the city, expressed as a percentage above or below that of Zurich, where Zurich equals 100%.
- RENT—the average gross monthly rent in the city, expressed as a percentage above or below that of Zurich, where Zurich equals 100%.
- SERVICE—the average cost of 28 different goods and services in the city, expressed as a percentage above or below that of Zurich, where Zurich equals 100%.
- PUBTRANS—the average cost of a three-mile taxi ride within city limits, expressed as a percentage above or below that of Zurich, where Zurich equals 100%.
- TEACHER, COOK, ENGINEER, MECHANIC, BUS—the average gross annual earnings of primary-grade teachers in public schools, cooks, electrical engineers, automobile mechanics, and municipal bus drivers; working from 5 to 10 years in their respective occupations. Each of these variables is expressed as a percentage above or below those of Zurich, where Zurich equals 100%.

This example analyzes the degree to which variation in the costs of goods and services in a city is related to variation in earnings in several occupations. CORRELATION is used to compute correlations between the average costs of various goods and services and the average gross earnings in five different occupations. The data are in an external file ACORR.DAT. The SPSS/PC+ commands in the file named on the INCLUDE command are:

```
DATA LIST FILE='ACORR.DAT'/
   FOOD 2-4 RENT 6-8 PUBTRANS 10-12 TEACHER 14-16 COOK 18-20
   ENGINEER 22-24 SERVICE 26-28 MECHANIC 30-32 BUS 34-36.
CORRELATION VARIABLES=FOOD RENT PUBTRANS TEACHER COOK ENGINEER/
          SERVICE PUBTRANS WITH MECHANIC BUS
   /STATISTICS=1,2.
FINISH.
```

- The DATA LIST command assigns variable names and gives column locations for the variables in the analysis (see DATA LIST).
- The CORRELATION command requests two correlation matrices. The first variable list produces correlation coefficients for each variable with every other variable. The second variable list produces four coefficients, pairing SERVICE with MECHANIC and BUS, and PUBTRANS with MECHANIC and BUS.
- The STATISTICS subcommand requests the mean, standard deviation, and number of nonmissing cases for each variable, and the cross-product deviations and covariance for each pair of variables. The statistics for all the variable lists precede all the correlation matrices in the CORRELATION display.

The display produced by CORRELATION is on the following page. The exact appearance of the printed display will depend on the characters available on the printer used.

A CORRELATION statistics

Variable	Cases	Mean	Std Dev
FOOD	43	70.9767	18.8319
RENT	43	122.2558	95.7054
PUBTRANS	43	48.8837	24.9258
TEACHER	43	38.3023	25.4797
COOK	43	64.9767	30.5626
ENGINEER	43	60.1163	26.4802
SERVICE	43	73.5116	18.9892
PUBTRANS	43	47.8372	24.0445
MECHANIC	43	50.4884	31.0762
BUS	43	42.9535	27.3652

Variables		Cases	Cross-Prod Dev	Variance-Covar
FOOD	RENT	43	18459.2558	439.5061
FOOD	PUBTRANS	43	11121.8837	264.8068
FOOD	TEACHER	43	11244.3023	267.7215
FOOD	COOK	43	9574.9767	227.9756
FOOD	ENGINEER	43	10106.1163	240.6218
RENT	PUBTRANS	43	-3527.7209	-83.9934
RENT	TEACHER	43	-2515.3256	-59.8887
RENT	COOK	43	17443.2558	415.3156
RENT	ENGINEER	43	26859.7209	639.5172
PUBTRANS	TEACHER	43	18659.5116	444.2741
PUBTRANS	COOK	43	19394.8837	461.7829
PUBTRANS	ENGINEER	43	17621.5814	419.5615
TEACHER	COOK	43	20326.3023	483.9596
TEACHER	ENGINEER	43	18627.4884	443.5116
COOK	ENGINEER	43	25524.1163	607.7171

Variables		Cases	Cross-Prod Dev	Variance-Covar
SERVICE	MECHANIC	43	11965.2558	284.8870
SERVICE	BUS	43	12806.0233	304.9053
PUBTRANS	MECHANIC	43	23496.4186	559.4385
PUBTRANS	BUS	43	21561.6744	513.3732

B CORRELATION matrices

Correlations:	FOOD	RENT	PUBTRANS	TEACHER	COOK	ENGINEER
FOOD	1.0000	.2439	.5641**	.5579**	.3961*	.4825**
RENT	.2439	1.0000	-.0352	-.0246	.1420	.2523
PUBTRANS	.5641**	-.0352	1.0000	.6995**	.6062**	.6357**
TEACHER	.5579**	-.0246	.6995**	1.0000	.6215**	.6573**
COOK	.3961*	.1420	.6062**	.6215**	1.0000	.7509**
ENGINEER	.4825**	.2523	.6357**	.6573**	.7509**	1.0000

N of cases: 43   1-tailed Signif: * - .01 ** - .001

" . " is printed if a coefficient cannot be computed

Correlations:	MECHANIC	BUS
SERVICE	.4828**	.5868**
PUBTRANS	.7487**	.7802**

N of cases: 43   1-tailed Signif: * - .01 ** - .001

" . " is printed if a coefficient cannot be computed

FACTOR This example uses six items from a 500-case sample from the 1980 General Social Survey. Respondents indicate whether they favor or oppose abortion in the following contexts:

- ABHLTH—if the woman's health is seriously endangered.
- ABRAPE—if the woman is pregnant as a result of rape.
- ABDEFECT—if there is a strong chance of a serious defect in the child.
- ABPOOR—if the woman has a low income and cannot afford more children.
- ABSINGLE—if the woman is not married and doesn't want the child.
- ABNOMORE—if the woman is married and wants no more children.

The data are in an external file named AFACTOR.DAT. The SPSS/PC+ commands in the command file named on the INCLUDE command are:

```
DATA LIST FREE FILE='AFACTOR.DAT'/
   ABDEFECT ABNOMORE ABHLTH ABPOOR ABRAPE ABSINGLE.
RECODE  ABDEFECT TO ABSINGLE(1=1)(2=0)(ELSE=9).
MISSING VALUE ABDEFECT TO ABSINGLE (9).
VALUE LABELS  ABDEFECT TO ABSINGLE
   0 'NO' 1 'YES' 9 'MISSING'.
FACTOR  VARIABLES=ABDEFECT TO ABSINGLE
  /MISSING=MEANSUB
  /FORMAT=SORT BLANK(.3)
  /PLOT=ROTATION(1 2)
  /EXTRACTION=ULS
  /ROTATION=OBLIMIN.
FINISH.
```

- The DATA LIST command names the file that contains the data and assigns variable names. Keyword FREE indicates that the data are in freefield format.
- The RECODE and MISSING VALUE commands redefine the variables, and VALUE LABELS provides labels for the redefined responses.
- The VARIABLES subcommand on FACTOR names all the variables that are used in this FACTOR procedure.
- The MISSING subcommand forces mean substitution for missing data.
- The FORMAT subcommand displays the factor loadings in descending order of magnitude and suppresses the printing of factor loadings less than 0.3.
- The PLOT subcommand requests a plot of the variables in factor space, where 1 and 2 are the factor numbers to be plotted.
- The EXTRACTION subcommand specifies unweighted least squares as the method of extraction.
- The ROTATION subcommand specifies an oblimin rotation.

Portions of the output produced by this set of commands appear in Figures A through D. The exact appearance of printed output depends on the characters available on your printer.

- Figure A contains initial statistics, which are produced by default. Initial statistics are the initial communalities, eigenvalues of the correlation matrix, and percentage of variance explained.
- Figure B contains extraction statistics, which are produced by default. Extraction statistics are the communalities, eigenvalues, and unrotated factor loadings. Note the effect of specifying SORT and BLANK on the FORMAT subcommand.
- Figure C contains rotation statistics, which are produced by default if the model is rotated. These statistics are the rotated factor pattern and structure matrices (since this is an oblimin rotation) and the factor correlation matrix.
- Figure D contains a plot of the variables in rotated factor space. Although the rotation is oblimin, the axes are orthogonal.

A Initial statistics

```
Initial Statistics:

Variable      Communality  *  Factor   Eigenvalue   Pct of Var   Cum Pct
                           *
ABDEFECT         .44988    *    1        3.38153        56.4        56.4
ABNOMORE         .66747    *    2        1.19287        19.9        76.2
ABHLTH           .35555    *    3         .50823         8.5        84.7
ABPOOR           .66600    *    4         .40867         6.8        91.5
ABRAPE           .39760    *    5         .28847         4.8        96.3
ABSINGLE         .60394    *    6         .22024         3.7       100.0
```

B Extraction statistics

```
Factor Matrix:

              FACTOR  1      FACTOR  2

ABPOOR          .81970       -.32158
ABNOMORE        .81704       -.34273
ABSINGLE        .78051
ABDEFECT        .65764        .46888
ABRAPE          .62257        .33014
ABHLTH          .53469        .44445

Final Statistics:

Variable      Communality  *  Factor   Eigenvalue   Pct of Var   Cum Pct
                           *
ABDEFECT         .65233    *    1        3.05462        50.9        50.9
ABNOMORE         .78502    *    2         .81821        13.6        64.5
ABHLTH           .48344    *
ABPOOR           .77532    *
ABRAPE           .49658    *
ABSINGLE         .68014    *
```

C Rotation statistics

```
Pattern Matrix:

              FACTOR  1      FACTOR  2

ABNOMORE        .90007
ABPOOR          .88136
ABSINGLE        .80050

ABDEFECT                      .80734
ABHLTH                        .72675
ABRAPE                        .63777


Structure Matrix:

              FACTOR  1      FACTOR  2

ABNOMORE        .88574        .46583
ABPOOR          .88052        .48028
ABSINGLE        .82393        .48046

ABDEFECT        .44195        .80767
ABRAPE          .45976        .69852
ABHLTH          .33632        .69342


Factor Correlation Matrix:

              FACTOR  1      FACTOR  2

FACTOR  1      1.00000
FACTOR  2       .54667       1.00000
```

D Factor plot

```
Horizontal Factor  1   Vertical Factor  2        Symbol Variable   Coordinates

                                                     1    ABDEFECT   .001   .807
                                                     2    ABNOMORE   .900  -.026
              3 1                                     3    ABHLTH    -.061   .727
                  5                                   4    ABPOOR     .881  -.002
                                                     5    ABRAPE     .111   .638
                                                     6    ABSINGLE   .801   .043



                                     6
      ---------------------------------------------
                                    4 2
```

NPAR TESTS The following example requests two chi-square tests on inline data. First, the frequencies for all categories of POSTPOS are compared against equal expected frequencies. The second CHISQUARE subcommand specifies eight expected proportions. The SPSS commands are:

```
TITLE  'CHISQUARE TEST, SIEGEL, P. 45'.
DATA LIST  /POSTPOS 1-2 NWINS 4-5.
VAR LABELS  POSTPOS 'POST POSITION'.
WEIGHT  BY NWINS.
BEGIN DATA
 2 19
 7 15
 4 25
 5 17
 8 11
 3 18
 6 10
 1 29
END DATA.
NPAR TESTS  CHISQUARE=POSTPOS
  /CHISQUARE=POSTPOS
  /EXPECTED=22,20,4*18,16,14.
```

- The TITLE command prints a title on each page of the display output.
- The DATA LIST command defines two variables, POSTPOS and NWINS. Because the FILE subcommand is omitted, data must be inline.
- The VARIABLE LABELS command assigns a label to variable POSTPOS.
- The WEIGHT command weights cases according to the values of variable NWINS.
- NPAR TESTS requests two chi-square tests. The first test assumes equal expected frequencies because the EXPECTED subcommand is omitted. The second test uses the proportions specified on EXPECTED.

The output is shown below. For each test, the display shows the number of observed cases and expected cases in each category of variable POSTPOS; the residual (observed minus expected) for each category; and the chi-square statistic, degrees of freedom, and significance of the chi-square.

One-sample chi-square test

```
- - - - - Chi-Square Test

   POSTPOS   POST POSITION

              Cases
   Category  Observed  Expected  Residual

        1        29     18.00     11.00
        2        19     18.00      1.00
        3        18     18.00       .00
        4        25     18.00      7.00
        5        17     18.00     -1.00
        6        10     18.00     -8.00
        7        15     18.00     -3.00
        8        11     18.00     -7.00
                 ---
   Total        144

       Chi-Square         D.F.      Significance
        16.333              7            .022

- - - - - Chi-Square Test

   POSTPOS   POST POSITION

              Cases
   Category  Observed  Expected  Residual

        1        29     22.00      7.00
        2        19     20.00     -1.00
        3        18     18.00       .00
        4        25     18.00      7.00
        5        17     18.00     -1.00
        6        10     18.00     -8.00
        7        15     16.00     -1.00
        8        11     14.00     -3.00
                 ---
   Total        144

       Chi-Square         D.F.      Significance
         9.316              7            .231
```

ONEWAY   This example analyzes a 500-case sample from the 1980 General Social Survey. The variables are:

- WELL—the respondent's score on a scale measuring sense of well-being. WELL is the dependent variable, computed from measures of happiness, health, life, helpfulness of others, trust of others, and satisfaction with city, hobbies, family life and friendships.
- EDUC—the respondent's education in six categories, where the original codes are years of education completed.

In this example we determine the degree to which sense of well-being differs across educational levels. The data are in an external file named AONE.DAT. The SPSS/PC+ commands in the command file named on the INCLUDE command are:

```
DATA LIST FILE='AONE.DAT'/
    EDUC 1-2 HAPPY 3 HEALTH 4 LIFE 5 HELPFUL 6 TRUST 7 SATCITY 8
    SATHOBBY 9 SATFAM 10 SATFRND 11.
COUNT  X1=HAPPY HEALTH LIFE HELPFUL TRUST SATCITY SATHOBBY
            SATFAM SATFRND(1).
COUNT  X2=HAPPY HEALTH SATCITY SATHOBBY SATFAM SATFRND(2).
COUNT  X3=HEALTH HELPFUL TRUST (3).
COUNT  X4=SATCITY SATHOBBY SATFAM SATFRND(6).
COUNT  X5=HAPPY LIFE (3).
COUNT  X6=SATCITY SATHOBBY SATFAM SATFRND(7).
COMPUTE WELL=X1 + X2* .5 - X3* .5 - X4* .5 - X5 - X6.
VAR LABELS  WELL 'Sense of Well-Being Scale'.
COMPUTE EDUC6=EDUC.
RECODE  EDUC6 (0 THRU 8=1)(9,10,11=2)(12=3)(13,14,15=4)
            (16=5)(17,18,19,20=6).
VAR LABELS  EDUC6 'Education in 6 Categories'.
VALUE LABELS  EDUC6 1 'Grade School or Less' 2 'Some High School'
                3 'High Sch Grad' 4 'Some College'
                5 'College Grad' 6 'Grad Sch'.
ONEWAY  VARIABLES=WELL BY EDUC6 (1,6)
  /POLYNOMIAL=2
  /CONTRAST= 2* -1, 2* 1
  /CONTRAST=2* 0,2* -1,2* 1
  /CONTRAST=2* -1,2* 0,2* 1
  /RANGES=SNK
  /RANGES=SCHEFFE(.01)
  /STATISTICS=ALL.
FINISH.
```

- The DATA LIST names the file that contains the data and gives the column locations of the variables in the analysis (see DATA LIST).
- The COUNT and COMPUTE commands create variable WELL by counting the number of "satisfied" responses for each variable on the scale and computing a weighted sum of these responses (see COUNT and COMPUTE).
- A copy of EDUC is created with COMPUTE and then recoded into six categories with RECODE (see COMPUTE and RECODE).
- The VARIABLE LABELS and VALUE LABELS commands assign labels to the new variables, WELL and EDUC6 (see VARIABLE LABELS and VALUE LABELS).
- The ONEWAY command names WELL as the dependent variable and EDUC6 as the independent variable. The minimum and maximum values for EDUC6 are 1 and 6.
- The POLYNOMIAL subcommand specifies second-order polynomial contrasts. The sum of squares using the unweighted polynomial contrasts is calculated because the analysis design is unbalanced. (See Figure A.)
- The CONTRAST subcommands request three different contrasts. (See Figure B.)
- The RANGES subcommands calculate multiple comparisons between means using the Student-Newman-Keuls and Scheffe tests. (See Figure C.)
- The STATISTICS subcommand requests all optional statistics. (See Figure D.)

The display produced by ONEWAY begins on the following page. The exact appearance of the printed display will depend on the printer used and the LENGTH and WIDTH that govern the display (see SET). This example uses the default settings.

A ONEWAY polynomial contrasts

```
- - - - -   - - - - - - - - - O N E W A Y - - - - - - - - - - - - - - - -

         Variable   WELL      Sense of Well-Being Scale
         By Variable  EDUC6    Education in 6 Categories

                              Analysis of Variance

                                   Sum of       Mean            F      F
          Source          D.F.    Squares      Squares        Ratio  Prob.

Between Groups             5      361.3217     72.2643       11.5255  .0000

  Unweighted  Linear Term  1      257.3422    257.3422       41.0439  .0000
  Weighted    Linear Term  1      307.2051    307.2051       48.9966  .0000
  Deviation from Linear    4       54.1166     13.5291        2.1578  .0727

  Unweighted  Quad. Term   1        6.6073      6.6073        1.0538  .3051
  Weighted    Quad. Term   1       16.6406     16.6406        2.6540  .1039
  Deviation from Quad.     3       37.4759     12.4920        1.9924  .1142

Within Groups            494     3097.3463      6.2699

Total                    499     3458.6680
```

B ONEWAY contrasts

```
- - - - -   - - - - - - - - - O N E W A Y - - - - - - - - - - - - - - -

         Variable   WELL      Sense of Well-Being Scale
         By Variable  EDUC6    Education in 6 Categories

Contrast Coefficient Matrix

           Grp 1      Grp 3      Grp 5
               Grp 2      Grp 4      Grp 6

Contrast 1  -1.0  -1.0   1.0   1.0   0.0   0.0

Contrast 2   0.0   0.0  -1.0  -1.0   1.0   1.0

Contrast 3  -1.0  -1.0   0.0   0.0   1.0   1.0


                                    Pooled Variance Estimate
                    Value    S. Error   T Value   D.F.       T Prob.

Contrast 1          3.3207    0.5230     6.349    494.0       0.000

Contrast 2          1.1517    0.6613     1.742    494.0       0.082

Contrast 3          4.4724    0.6990     6.398    494.0       0.000


                                    Separate Variance Estimate
                    Value    S. Error   T Value   D.F.       T Prob.

Contrast 1          3.3207    0.5401     6.148    252.5       0.000

Contrast 2          1.1517    0.6108     1.886    123.2       0.062

Contrast 3          4.4724    0.6984     6.404    172.7       0.000
```

C ONEWAY multiple comparisons

```
- - - - - - - - - - - - - - - O N E W A Y - - - - - - - - - - - - - - -

        Variable  WELL       Sense of Well-Being Scale
      By Variable  EDUC6      Education in 6 Categories


Multiple Range Test


Student-Newman-Keuls Procedure
Ranges for the 0.050 level -

        2.81   3.34   3.65   3.88   4.05

The ranges above are table ranges.
The value actually compared with Mean(J)-Mean(I) is..
        1.7706 * Range * Sqrt(1/N(I) + 1/N(J))


  (*) Denotes pairs of groups significantly different at the 0.050 level

        Variable  WELL       Sense of Well-Being Scale
        (Continued)


                          G G G G G
                          r r r r r
                          p p p p p

      Mean      Group     1 2 3 4 5 6

      2.6462    Grp 1
      2.7737    Grp 2
      4.1796    Grp 3     * *
      4.5610    Grp 4     * *
      4.6625    Grp 5     * *
      5.2297    Grp 6     * *
- - - - - - - - - - - - - - - O N E W A Y - - - - - - - - - - - - - - -

        Variable  WELL       Sense of Well-Being Scale
      By Variable  EDUC6      Education in 6 Categories


Multiple Range Test


Scheffe Procedure
Ranges for the 0.010 level -

        5.53   5.53   5.53   5.53   5.53

The ranges above are table ranges.
The value actually compared with Mean(J)-Mean(I) is..
        1.7706 * Range * Sqrt(1/N(I) + 1/N(J))


  (*) Denotes pairs of groups significantly different at the 0.010 level

        Variable  WELL       Sense of Well-Being Scale
        (Continued)


                          G G G G G
                          r r r r r
                          p p p p p

      Mean      Group     1 2 3 4 5 6

      2.6462    Grp 1
      2.7737    Grp 2
      4.1796    Grp 3     * *
      4.5610    Grp 4     * *
      4.6625    Grp 5     * *
      5.2297    Grp 6     * *
```

D ONEWAY statistics

Group	Count	Mean	Standard Deviation	Standard Error	95 Pct Conf Int for Mean		
Grp 1	65	2.6462	2.7539	.3416	1.9638	To	3.3285
Grp 2	95	2.7737	2.8674	.2942	2.1896	To	3.3578
Grp 3	181	4.1796	2.4220	.1800	3.8243	To	4.5348
Grp 4	82	4.5610	2.1450	.2369	4.0897	To	5.0323
Grp 5	40	4.6625	2.3490	.3714	3.9113	To	5.4137
Grp 6	37	5.2297	2.3291	.3829	4.4532	To	6.0063
Total	500	3.8920	2.6327	.1177	3.6607	To	4.1233
Fixed Effects Model			2.5040	.1120	3.6720	To	4.1120
Random Effects Model				.4492	2.7374	To	5.0466

Random Effects Model — Estimate of Between Component Variance   0.8491

Group	Minimum	Maximum
Grp 1	-4.0000	8.5000
Grp 2	-5.0000	8.5000
Grp 3	-4.0000	9.0000
Grp 4	-.5000	9.0000
Grp 5	-1.0000	8.0000
Grp 6	-1.5000	9.0000
Total	-5.0000	9.0000

Tests for Homogeneity of Variances

```
Cochrans C = Max. Variance/Sum(Variances) =  .2209, P =  .093 (Approx.)
Bartlett-Box F =                            1.905 , P =  .090
Maximum Variance / Minimum Variance         1.787
```

QUICK CLUSTER

This example uses Fisher's classic data on irises to group the irises into clusters. The clusters are then compared with the actual botanical classification. The variables used are:

- SEPLEN—sepal length.
- SEPWID—sepal width.
- PETLEN—petal length.
- PETWID—petal width.
- IRISTYPE—type of iris.

The data are in an external file named AQCLUST.DAT. The SPSS/PC+ commands in the command file named on the INCLUDE command are:

```
DATA LIST FILE='AQCLUST.DAT'/
   SEPLEN 1-2 SEPWID PETLEN PETWID 3-11 IRISTYPE 13.
VARIABLE LABELS   SEPLEN  'SEPAL LENGTH'
                  SEPWID  'SEPAL WIDTH'
                  PETLEN  'PETAL LENGTH'
                  PETWID  'PETAL WIDTH'
                  IRISTYPE 'TYPE OF IRIS'.
VALUE LABELS   IRISTYPE  1 'SETOSA' 2 'VERSICOLOR'  3 'VIRGINICA'.
QUICK CLUSTER   SEPLEN TO PETWID
   /CRITERIA=CLUSTERS(3)
   /PRINT=INITIAL ANOVA
   /SAVE=CLUSTER(CLUSTMEM).
VARIABLE LABELS CLUSTMEM 'CLUSTERS FROM DEFAULT METHOD'.
CROSSTABS TABLES=IRISTYPE BY CLUSTMEM
   /STATISTICS=1,4,5.
FINISH.
```

- The DATA LIST command names the file that contains the data and defines the five variables.
- The VARIABLE LABELS command assigns descriptive labels to the variables. The VALUE LABELS command assigns labels to the three values of variable IRISTYPE—three types of irises.
- The QUICK CLUSTER command bases clustering on the values of four variables: SEPLEN, SEPWID, PETLEN, and PETWID.
- The CRITERIA subcommand specifies three clusters.
- The PRINT subcommand requests the display of initial cluster centers and an analysis of variance table describing differences between clusters for each of the four clustering variables (Figure A).
- The SAVE subcommand saves the cluster membership of each case in a new variable, CLUSTMEM, on the SPSS/PC+ active file.
- The VARIABLE LABELS commands assigns a descriptive label to the new variable CLUSTEM.
- The CROSSTABS command crosstabulates the cluster membership variable with variable IRISTYPE, which identifies the actual type of iris. The STATISTICS subcommand requests a chi-square test of significance plus two measures of the predictability of iris types from the cluster types (Figure B). The CROSSTABS output shows that the clusters are strongly associated with the actual classifications.

The display is shown in Figures A and B. The exact appearance of printed display depends on the characters available on your printer.

A QUICK CLUSTER output for the iris data

```
Initial Cluster Centers.

    Cluster      SEPLEN         SEPWID         PETLEN         PETWID

       1        58.0000        40.0000        12.0000         2.0000
       2        77.0000        38.0000        67.0000        22.0000
       3        49.0000        25.0000        45.0000        17.0000
- - - - - - - - - - - - - - - - - - - - - - - - - - - - - - - - - - - -
Classification Cluster Centers.

    Cluster      SEPLEN         SEPWID         PETLEN         PETWID

       1        51.0091        35.5029        13.5981         2.3147
       2        72.7018        34.1981        63.3840        21.8201
       3        59.9192        27.5660        47.4896        16.9838
- - - - - - - - - - - - - - - - - - - - - - - - - - - - - - - - - - - -
Final Cluster Centers.

    Cluster      SEPLEN         SEPWID         PETLEN         PETWID

       1        50.0600        34.2800        14.6200         2.4600
       2        70.8696        31.2609        60.1304        21.4348
       3        60.1558        27.9610        45.7532        15.3636
- - - - - - - - - - - - - - - - - - - - - - - - - - - - - - - - - - - -
Analysis of Variance.

    Variable    Cluster MS   DF       Error MS      DF             F    Prob

    SEPLEN      3645.6374     2        19.9018    147.0     183.1817   0.0
    SEPWID       611.6477     2        10.9347    147.0      55.9365   .000
    PETLEN     21598.9198     2        22.0048    147.0     981.5565   0.0
    PETWID      3734.5515     2         8.0809    147.0     462.1462   0.0
- - - - - - - - - - - - - - - - - - - - - - - - - - - - - - - - - - - -
Number of Cases in each Cluster.

    Cluster     unweighted cases    weighted cases

       1             50.0                50.0
       2             23.0                23.0
       3             77.0                77.0

    Missing            0
    Total          150.0               150.0
```

B Comparing clusters to the actual botanical classifications

```
Crosstabulation:     IRISTYPE   TYPE OF IRIS
                By CLUSTMEM   CLUSTERS FROM DEFAULT METHOD

CLUSTMEM-> Count                                    Row
                        1|      2|      3|  Total
IRISTYPE    --------+-------+-------+-------+
               1  |   50  |       |       |    50
    SETOSA        |       |       |       |  33.3
                  +-------+-------+-------+
               2  |       |       |   50  |    50
    VERSICOLOR    |       |       |       |  33.3
                  +-------+-------+-------+
               3  |       |   23  |   27  |    50
    VIRGINICA     |       |       |       |  33.3
                  +-------+-------+-------+
           Column     50      23      77     150
           Total    33.3    15.3    51.3   100.0

Chi-Square     D.F.    Significance      Min E.F.      Cells with E.F.< 5
- - - - - -    - -                                   
 194.80521       4        .0000           7.667           None

                                                  With IRISTYPE    With CLUSTMEM
        Statistic               Symmetric         Dependent        Dependent

Lambda                            .71098            .73000           .68493
Uncertainty Coefficient           .73144            .69729           .76910
Number of Missing Observations =       0
```

REGRESSION   The example attempts to predict the average aggregate personal savings rate of a
country as a function of the age distribution of the population, the average level of
real per capita disposable income, and the average percentage growth rate of real
per capita disposable income. The data are 50 cases taken from an example in
Belsley, Kuh, and Welsch (1980).

The variables are:

- COUNTRY—the country in question.
- SAVINGS—the average aggregate personal savings rate in a country over the period
1960–1970.
- POP15—the average percentage of the population under 15 years of age over the
period 1960–1970.
- POP75—the average percentage of the population over 75 years of age over the period
1960–1970.
- INCOME—the average level of real per capita disposable income in a country over
the period 1960–1970, measured in United States dollars.
- GROWTH—the average percentage growth rate of INCOME over the period
1960–1970.

The data are in an external file named AREG.DAT. The SPSS/PC+ commands
are:

```
DATA LIST FILE='AREG.DAT'/
   COUNTRY 1-8(A) SAVINGS POP15 POP75
   INCOME GROWTH 11-60.
VAR LABELS     SAVINGS 'Avg Agg Personal Savings Rate'
               POP15 'Avg % Pop Under 15 Years Old'
               POP75 'Avg % Pop Over 75 Years Old'
               INCOME 'Avg Level Real Per-Cap Disposable Inc'
               GROWTH 'Avg % Growth Rate of DPI'.
REGRESSION  VARIABLES=SAVINGS TO GROWTH
  /DEP=SAVINGS
  /ENTER
  /RESID=DEFAULT SIZE(SMALL) ID(COUNTRY)
  /SCATTERPLOT (*RES,*PRE).
```

- The DATA LIST command names the file that contains the data, names the variables,
and gives their column locations.
- The VAR LABELS command assigns labels to the variables (see VARIABLE
LABELS).
- The REGRESSION command requests a direct-entry regression analysis with
variable SAVINGS as the dependent variable.
- The RESIDUALS subcommand requests the default residuals results. In addition, the
SIZE(SMALL) keyword overrides the default plot sizes so that small plots are
displayed. The ID(COUNTRY) keyword specifies that the values for variable
COUNTRY are to be used to label outlier plots. Figure A shows the residuals statistics
and outlier plots. Figure B displays the histogram of the standardized residual and the
normal probability plot.
- The SCATTERPLOT subcommand requests a plot of the residuals against the
predicted values. Since *RES is specified first, it is plotted along the vertical axis (see
Figure C).

The display produced by REGRESSION begins on the following page. The exact
appearance of the printed display depends on the printer used and the LENGTH
and WIDTH that govern the display (see SET). This example uses the default
settings.

A REGRESSION residuals statistics and outliers

```
Residuals Statistics:

                   MIN         MAX      MEAN   STD DEV   N

*PRED           5.5874     15.8185    9.6710    2.6066  50
*RESID         -8.2422      9.7509     .0000    3.6441  50
*ZPRED         -1.5666      2.3584    -.0000    1.0000  50
*ZRESID        -2.1675      2.5642     .0000     .9583  50

Total Cases =        50


Durbin-Watson Test =    1.68579


Outliers - Standardized Residual

   Case #  COUNTRY       *ZRESID

       50  Zambia        2.56423
        7  Chile        -2.16749
       36  Philippi      1.75534
       35  Peru          1.71969
       18  Iceland      -1.63321
       34  Paraguay     -1.61093
       24  Korea        -1.60598
       10  Denmark       1.42014
       23  Japan         1.38890
        9  Costa Ri      1.34776
```

B REGRESSION histograms and normal probability plots

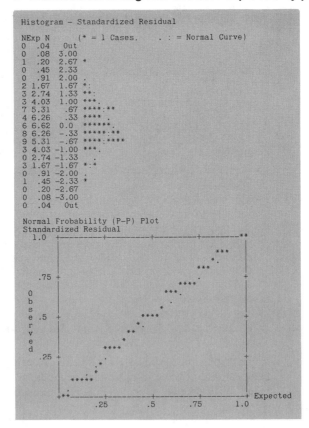

C Residuals against predicted values

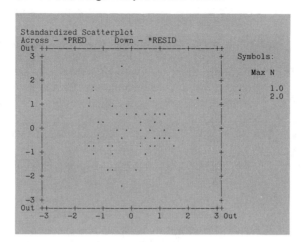

RELIABILITY The following example demonstrates the use of RELIABILITY to analyze an attitude scale of confidence in institutions in the United States. The data come from a 500-case sample of the 1980 General Social Survey. Respondents were asked how much confidence they have in the people running the following institutions: banks and financial institutions, major companies, organized religion, education, the executive branch of the federal government, organized labor, the press, medicine, television, the United States Supreme Court, the scientific community, Congress, and the military. The SPSS/PC+ commands are:

```
GET FILE='GSS80.SYS'.
RELIABILITY VARIABLES=CONFINAN TO CONARMY
  /SCALE (CONSCALE)=ALL
  /MODEL=SPLIT
  /SUMMARY=TOTAL
  /STATISTICS=ANOVA TUKEY HOTELLING.
```

- The GET command makes the data from the system file named GSS80.SYS available for analysis.
- The RELIABILITY command analyzes the scale formed from the 13 confidence variables CONFINAN to CONARMY.
- The SCALE subcommand supplies a name (CONSCALE) for the scale.
- The MODEL subcommand specifies a split-half analysis.
- The SUMMARY subcommand produces item-total statistics.
- The STATISTICS subcommand produces the analysis of variance table, the Tukey test for additivity, and Hotelling's T^2.

Portions of the output produced by these commands appear in Figures A through D.

- Figure A contains the item-total statistics produced by the SUMMARY subcommand.
- Figure B contains the analysis of variance table. The F statistic for variation between measures is significant, indicating that the items have significantly different means. F for nonadditivity is not significant, so we can accept the hypothesis that the items are additive.
- Figure C contains Tukey's test for non-additivity and Hotelling's T^2. Tukey's test is close to 1, which again indicates that the items are additive. Hotelling's T^2 is significant, which indicates that we can reject the hypothesis that the items have equal means in the population.
- Figure D contains the split-half reliability coefficients.

A Item-total statistics

```
        # OF CASES =      415.0


ITEM-TOTAL STATISTICS

                SCALE          SCALE      CORRECTED
                 MEAN        VARIANCE       ITEM-         SQUARED        ALPHA
               IF ITEM       IF ITEM        TOTAL        MULTIPLE      IF ITEM
               DELETED       DELETED     CORRELATION    CORRELATION    DELETED

CONFINAN      22.8361       17.8958         .4550         .2989         .7831
CONBUS        22.8410       18.6317         .3556         .2424         .7918
CONCLERG      22.8554       18.3172         .3693         .1671         .7912
CONEDUC       22.8458       18.0679         .4652         .2321         .7823
CONFED        22.4578       18.0459         .4692         .2961         .7820
CONLABOR      22.5181       18.4242         .3763         .2102         .7902
CONPRESS      22.7108       18.8147         .3215         .2220         .7947
CONMEDIC      23.1036       18.0158         .4962         .2740         .7798
CONTV         22.5518       18.5909         .3670         .1938         .7908
CONJUDGE      22.7446       17.5771         .5061         .3125         .7783
CONSCI        23.1036       18.6632         .3910         .2185         .7887
CONLEGIS      22.4145       18.0790         .5277         .3481         .7779
CONARMY       22.7952       17.7381         .4930         .2903         .7796
```

B ANOVA table

```
                      ANALYSIS OF VARIANCE

SOURCE OF VARIATION      SUM OF SQ.     DF     MEAN SQUARE      F        PROB.

BETWEEN PEOPLE            669.7412      414       1.6177
WITHIN PEOPLE           1858.9231     4980        .3733
   BETWEEN MEASURES       240.9631       12      20.0803     61.6571    .0000
   RESIDUAL             1617.9600     4968        .3257
      NONADDITIVITY         .0041        1        .0041        .0125    .9109
      BALANCE           1617.9559     4967        .3257
TOTAL                   2528.6643     5394        .4688

GRAND MEAN =               1.8960
```

C Tukey and Hotelling tests

```
TUKEY ESTIMATE OF POWER TO WHICH OBSERVATIONS
MUST BE RAISED TO ACHIEVE ADDITIVITY            =       0.9778


HOTELLINGS T-SQUARED =     694.5944       F =      56.3449      PROB. =   .0000
   DEGREES OF FREEDOM:            NUMERATOR =      12     DENOMINATOR =    403
```

D Split-half reliability estimates

```
RELIABILITY COEFFICIENTS    13 ITEMS

CORRELATION BETWEEN FORMS =     .6583    EQUAL LENGTH SPEARMAN-BROWN =     .7940

GUTTMAN SPLIT-HALF =            .7923    UNEQUAL-LENGTH SPEARMAN-BROWN =   .7948

ALPHA FOR PART 1 =             .6446    ALPHA FOR PART 2 =                .6955

   7 ITEMS IN PART 1                       6 ITEMS IN PART 2
```

T-TEST This example uses T-TEST to analyze 1979 prices and earnings in 45 cities around the world, compiled by the Union Bank of Switzerland. The variables are:

- WORLD—the economic class of the country in which the city is located. The 45 cities are divided into three groups: cities in economically developed nations such as the United States and most European nations; cities in nations that are members of the Organization for Petroleum Exporting Countries (OPEC); and cities in underdeveloped countries. These groups are coded from 1 to 3 and are labeled 1ST WORLD, PETRO WORLD, and 3RD WORLD, respectively.
- NTCPRI—the city's net price level, based on more than 100 goods and services weighted by consumer habits. NTCPRI is expressed as the percentage above or below that of Zurich, where Zurich equals 100%.
- NTCSAL—the city's net salary level, calculated from average net hourly earnings in 12 occupations. NTCSAL is expressed as a percentage above or below that of Zurich, where Zurich equals 100%.
- NTCPUR—the city's net purchasing power level, calculated as the ratio of labor expended (measured in number of working hours) to the cost of more than 100 goods and services, weighted by consumer habits. NTCPUR is expressed as a percentage above or below that of Zurich, where Zurich equals 100%.
- WCLOTHES—the cost of medium-priced women's clothes, expressed as the percentage above or below that of Zurich, where Zurich equals 100%.
- MCLOTHES—the cost of medium-priced men's clothes, expressed as the percentage above or below that of Zurich, where Zurich equals 100%.

This example compares mean price, salary and purchasing power for cities grouped by economic class. It also compares the mean costs of women's and men's clothes. The data are in an external file named ATTEST.DAT. The SPSS/PC+ commands in the command file specified on the INCLUDE command are:

```
DATA LIST FILE='ATTEST.DAT'/
   NTCPRI 9-11 NTCSAL 20-22 NTCPUR 31-33 WCLOTHES 42-44
   MCLOTHES 53-55 WORLD 66.
VARIABLE LABELS NTCPRI 'Net Price Level'/
                NTCSAL 'Net Salary Level'/
                NTCPUR 'Net Purchasing Level'/
                WCLOTHES "Medium-Priced Women's Clothes"/
                MCLOTHES "Medium-Priced Men's Clothes"/.
T-TEST GROUPS=WORLD(1,3)
  /VARIABLES=NTCPRI NTCSAL NTCPUR
  /PAIRS=WCLOTHES MCLOTHES/
   NTCPRI WITH NTCPUR NTCSAL.
FINISH.
```

- The DATA LIST command assigns variable names and gives the column locations of the variables to be analyzed (see DATA LIST).
- The VARIABLE LABELS command completes the data definition of these variables (see VARIABLE LABELS).
- The T-TEST command requests an independent-samples test and a paired-samples test. For the independent-samples test, the variable WORLD specifies a grouping criterion that compares cities in first-world countries to cities in third-world countries. Cities in petro-world countries are not included.
- By default, the display is formatted within 79 columns.

The results produced by T-TEST are on the next page. The exact appearance of the printed display depends on the characters available on the printer used.

T-TEST display

```
Independent samples of WORLD

Group 1: WORLD  EQ 1            Group 2: WORLD  EQ 3


t-test for: NTCPRI   Net Price Level

                Number              Standard    Standard
                of Cases    Mean    Deviation    Error

      Group 1      25      83.8400   13.309      2.662
      Group 2      13      67.3077   14.773      4.097

                  | Pooled Variance Estimate | Separate Variance Estimate
                  |                          |
    F    2-Tail   |  t    Degrees of 2-Tail  |  t    Degrees of 2-Tail
  Value  Prob.    | Value  Freedom   Prob.   | Value  Freedom   Prob.

  1.23  0.637     | 3.50     36      0.001   | 3.38    22.28     0.003

Independent samples of WORLD

Group 1: WORLD  EQ 1            Group 2: WORLD  EQ 3


t-test for: NTCSAL   Net Salary Level

                Number              Standard    Standard
                of Cases    Mean    Deviation    Error

      Group 1      25      64.4000   19.026      3.805
      Group 2      12      25.6667   13.241      3.822

                  | Pooled Variance Estimate | Separate Variance Estimate
                  |                          |
    F    2-Tail   |  t    Degrees of 2-Tail  |  t    Degrees of 2-Tail
  Value  Prob.    | Value  Freedom   Prob.   | Value  Freedom   Prob.

  2.06  0.210     | 6.33     35      0.000   | 7.18    30.07     0.000

Independent samples of WORLD

Group 1: WORLD  EQ 1            Group 2: WORLD  EQ 3


t-test for: NTCPUR   Net Purchasing Level

                Number              Standard    Standard
                of Cases    Mean    Deviation    Error

      Group 1      25      76.7600   21.491      4.298
      Group 2      12      31.9167   17.573      5.073

                  | Pooled Variance Estimate | Separate Variance Estimate
                  |                          |
    F    2-Tail   |  t    Degrees of 2-Tail  |  t    Degrees of 2-Tail
  Value  Prob.    | Value  Freedom   Prob.   | Value  Freedom   Prob.

  1.50  0.493     | 6.28     35      0.000   | 6.74    26.26     0.000


Paired samples t-test:  WCLOTHES  Medium-Priced Woman's Clothes
                        MCLOTHES  Medium-Priced Men's Clothes

Variable    Number              Standard    Standard
            of Cases    Mean    Deviation    Error

WCLOTHES      45      80.7111   30.195      4.501
MCLOTHES      45      87.0444   26.192      3.905

(Difference) Standard  Standard  |         2-Tail  |  t    Degrees of 2-Tail
  Mean     Deviation    Error    | Corr.   Prob.   | Value  Freedom   Prob.

 -6.3333    17.916      2.671    | 0.807  0.000    | -2.37    44      0.022


Paired samples t-test:  NTCPRI   Net Price Level
                        NTCPUR   Net Purchasing Level

Variable    Number              Standard    Standard
            of Cases    Mean    Deviation    Error

NTCPRI        44      82.1591   19.773      2.981
NTCPUR        44      58.7045   28.806      4.343

(Difference) Standard  Standard  |         2-Tail  |  t    Degrees of 2-Tail
  Mean     Deviation    Error    | Corr.   Prob.   | Value  Freedom   Prob.

 23.4545    33.310      5.022    | 0.098  0.528    | 4.67     43      0.000


Paired samples t-test:  NTCPRI   Net Price Level
                        NTCSAL   Net Salary Level

Variable    Number              Standard    Standard
            of Cases    Mean    Deviation    Error

NTCPRI        44      82.1591   19.773      2.981
NTCSAL        44      50.3409   24.295      3.663

(Difference) Standard  Standard  |         2-Tail  |  t    Degrees of 2-Tail
  Mean     Deviation    Error    | Corr.   Prob.   | Value  Freedom   Prob.

 31.8182    22.753      3.430    | 0.482  0.001    | 9.28     43      0.000
```

Index

Index

SPSS/PC+ Statistics™ 4.0 Reference Card

This card provides a convenient reference to SPSS/PC+ Statistics™ 4.0. It is arranged by command in alphabetic order. The format diagrams for procedure and nonprocedure commands are constructed according to the following conventions:

Square brackets enclose optional specifications not necessary to the correct completion of the command.

Braces enclose alternative specifications. One of these specifications must be entered in order to complete the specifications correctly. The brackets and braces themselves should not be coded.

Elipses indicate the possibility of repeating an element in the specifications of the entire cycle of specifications.

Uppercase elements must be entered as they appear in the diagrams.

Lowercase elements describe information to be filled in by the user.

Boldface entries denote defaults. Two asterisks (**) indicate that a specification is a default when its associated subcommand is not specified.

ANOVA

```
ANOVA [VARIABLES=] varlist BY varlist(min,max) [WITH varlist]
      [/[VARIABLES=] varlist ...]
      [/OPTIONS=option numbers]
      [/STATISTICS={statistic numbers}]
                   {ALL              }
```

Options:
1	Include user-missing values	7	Covariates with main effects
2	Suppress labels	8	Covariates after main effects
3	Suppress all interaction terms	9	Regression approach
4	Suppress three-way terms	10	Hierarchical approach
5	Suppress four-way terms	11	Narrow format
6	Suppress five-way terms		

Statistics:
1 Multiple classification analysis (MCA) table
2 Unstandardized regression coefficients for covariates
3 Display cell means and counts

CLUSTER

```
CLUSTER {varlist} [/MISSING={LISTWISE**} {INCLUDE}]
        {ALL    }          {DEFAULT** }
        [/READ=[SIMILAR] [{TRIANGLE}]] [/WRITE=[DISTANCE]]
                          {LOWER   }
        [/MEASURE={SEUCLID**  }] [/METHOD={BAVERAGE**}[(rootname)]]
                  {DEFAULT**  }           {DEFAULT** }
                  {EUCLID     }           {WAVERAGE  }
                  {COSINE     }           {SINGLE    }
                  {POWER(p,r) }           {COMPLETE  }
                  {BLOCK      }           {CENTROID  }
                  {CHEBYCHEV  }           {MEDIAN    }
                                          {WARD      }
        [/SAVE=CLUSTER({level  })]  [/ID=varname]
                      {min,max}
        [/PRINT=[CLUSTER({level  })]  [{SCHEDULE**}]]
                        {min,max}      {DEFAULT** }
                [DISTANCE]  [NONE]
        [/PLOT=[VICICLE** [({1,n-1,1      })]] [DENDROGRAM]]
                            {min[,max[,inc]]}
               [HICICLE [({1,n-1,1      })]]  [NONE]
                         {min[,max[,inc]]}
```
**Default if subcommand is omitted.

CORRELATION

```
CORRELATION [VARIABLES=] {varlist} [WITH varlist] [/varlist ...]
                         {ALL    }
            [/OPTIONS=option numbers]
            [/STATISTICS={statistic numbers}]
                         {ALL              }
```

Options:
1	Include user-missing values	4	Write count and correlation matrix
2	Exclude missing values pairwise	5	Display count and probability
3	Two-tailed probability		

Statistics:
1 Univariate mean, standard deviation, and count
2 Cross-product deviations and covariance

FACTOR

```
FACTOR VARIABLES={varlist} [/MISSING=[{LISTWISE**}] [INCLUDE]]
                 {ALL    }            {PAIRWISE  }
                                      {MEANSUB   }
                                      {DEFAULT** }
       [/WIDTH=[{width on SET**}] ]
               {n             }
       [/ANALYSIS={varlist}...]
                  {ALL**  }
       [/FORMAT=[SORT] [BLANK(n)] [DEFAULT**]]
       [/PRINT=[DEFAULT**] [INITIAL] [EXTRACTION] [ROTATION]
               [UNIVARIATE] [CORRELATION] [DET] [INV] [REPR] [AIC]
               [KMO] [FSCORE] [SIG] [ALL]
       [/PLOT=[EIGEN] [ROTATION (nl,n2) (n3,n4)...]]
       [/DIAGONAL={DEFAULT** }]
                  {value list}
       [/CRITERIA=[FACTORS(n)] [MINEIGEN({1.0})] [ITERATE({25})]
                                         {eig}            {ni}
                  [RCONVERGE({0.0001})] [DELTA({0})]
                            {rl     }          {d}
                  [ECONVERGE({0.001})] [{KAISER  }]
                            {el    }    {NOKAISER}
                  [DEFAULT**]]
       [/EXTRACTION={PC**    }]
                    {DEFAULT**}
                    {PA1**   }
                    {PAF     }
                    {ALPHA   }
                    {IMAGE   }
                    {ULS     }
                    {GLS     }
                    {ML      }
                    {PA2     }
       [/ROTATION={VARIMAX**}]
                  {DEFAULT**}
                  {EQUAMAX  }
                  {QUARTIMAX}
                  {OBLIMIN  }
                  {NOROTATE }
       [/SAVE={REG    } ({ALL} rootname)]
              {BART   }  {n  }
              {AR     }
              {DEFAULT}
       [/ANALYSIS...]
       [/CRITERIA...]                      [/EXTRACTION...]
       [/SAVE...]                          [/ROTATION...]
```
**Default if subcommand is omitted.

FACTOR: Matrix Materials

```
FACTOR VARIABLES=varlist
       [/READ=[{CORRELATION [TRIANGLE]}]]
               {DEFAULT               }
               {FACTOR(n)             }
       [/WRITE=[{CORRELATION}]]
                {DEFAULT    }
                {FACTOR     }
```

NPAR TESTS

```
NPAR TESTS [CHISQUARE=varlist [(lo,hi)]]
           [/EXPECTED={EQUAL**     }]
                      {f1,f2, ...fn}
           [/K-S ({UNIFORM [,lo,hi]})=varlist]
                 {NORMAL [,m,sd]    }
                 {POISSON [,m]      }
           [/RUNS ({MEAN  })=varlist]
                  {MEDIAN}
                  {MODE  }
                  {value }
           [/BINOMIAL [({.5})]=varlist ({valuel,value2})]
                       {p }            {value        }
           [/MCNEMAR=varlist [WITH varlist]]
           [/SIGN=varlist [WITH varlist]]
           [/WILCOXON=varlist [WITH varlist]]
           [/COCHRAN=varlist]
           [/FRIEDMAN=varlist]
           [/KENDALL=varlist]
           [/MEDIAN [(value)]=varlist BY var (valuel,value2)]
           [/M-W=varlist BY var (valuel,value2)]
           [/K-S=varlist BY var (valuel,value2)]
           [/W-W=varlist BY var (valuel,value2)]
           [/MOSES[(n)]=varlist BY var (valuel,value2)]
           [/K-W=varlist BY var (valuel,value2)]
           [/OPTIONS=option numbers]
           [/STATISTICS=statistic numbers]
```
**Default if subcommand is omitted.

Options:
1	Include user-missing values	3	Sequential pairing of variables for two related samples
2	Exclude missing values listwise	4	Random sampling

Statistics:
1 Mean, maximum, minimum, standard deviation, and count
2 Quartiles and count

ONEWAY

```
ONEWAY [VARIABLES=]varlist BY varname(min,max)
  [/POLYNOMIAL=n]
  [/CONTRAST=coefficient list] [/CONTRAST=...]
  [/RANGES={SNK          }] [RANGES=...]
           {BTUKEY       }
           {TUKEY        }
           {ranges values}
           {LSD          }  [({.05  })]
           {DUNCAN       }   {alpha}
           {MODLSD       }
           {SCHEFFE      }

  [/OPTIONS=option numbers]
  [/STATISTICS={statistic numbers}]
              {ALL              }
```

Options:

1 Include user-missing values
2 Exclude missing values listwise
3 Suppress variable labels
4 Write matrix of counts, means, and standard deviations
6 Use value labels as group labels
7 Read matrix of counts, means, and standard deviations
8 Read matrix of counts, means, pooled variance, and degrees of freedom
10 Harmonic mean of all group sizes as sample sizes in range tests

Statistics:

1 Group descriptive statistics
2 Fixed- and random-effects statistics
3 Homogeneity-of-variance tests

QUICK CLUSTER

```
QUICK CLUSTER {varlist} [/INITIAL = [{SELECT**     }]]
             {ALL    }                {FIRST        }
                                      {(value list)}
  [/CRITERIA = [CLUSTERS({2     })] [NOUPDATE]]
                        {number}
  [/PRINT = [CLUSTER] [ID(varname)] [INITIAL**]]
           [DISTANCE] [ANOVA]
  [/WRITE]
  [/SAVE = [CLUSTER(varname)] [DISTANCE(varname)]]
  [/MISSING = {LISTWISE**}]
             {PAIRWISE  }
             {INCLUDE   }
             {DEFAULT** }
```

**Default if subcommand is omitted.

REGRESSION

```
REGRESSION [VARIABLES={varlist     }]
                     {(COLLECT)**}
                     {ALL         }
  [/STATISTICS=[DEFAULTS**] [R] [COEFF] [ANOVA] [OUTS]
              ZPP] [CHA] [CI] [F] [BCOV] [SES] [TOL]
              COLLIN] [XTX] [HISTORY] [END]
              LINE] [ALL]] [SELECTION]
  [/CRITERIA=[DEFAULTS**] [TOLERANCE({.0001})] [MAXSTEPS({2v})]]
                                   {value }            {n }

  [{{PIN({0.05 })}]     [{POUT({0.10 })}]
     {value}             {value}
   {FIN({3.84 })}]      {FOUT({2.71 })}      [CIN({95** })]
     {value}             {value}                 {value}
  [/{NOORIGIN**}]
    {ORIGIN    }
  /DEPENDENT=varlist
  /[METHOD=]{STEPWISE [ = varlist]}     [/METHOD=...]
           {FORWARD [=varlist]   }
           {BACKWARD [=varlist]  }
           {ENTER [ =varlist]    }
           {REMOVE=varlist       }
           {TEST=(varlist) (varlist)}
  [/DESCRIPTIVES=[DEFAULTS] [MEAN] [STDDEV] [CORR]
                [VARIANCE] [XPROD] [SIG] [N] [BADCORR]
                [COV]      [ALL]    [NONE**]]
  [/SELECT={varname relation value}]
  [/MISSING=[{LISTWISE**       }] [INCLUDE]]
            {PAIRWISE         }
            {MEANSUBSTITUTION }
  [/WIDTH={value on SET**}]
         {n             }
  [/REGWGT=variable]
```

**Default if subcommand is omitted.

REGRESSION: Matrix Materials

```
REGRESSION [READ=[DEFAULTS] [MEAN] [STDDEV]
                 [VARIANCE] {CORR} [N]]
                            {COV }
  [/WRITE=[DEFAULTS] [MEAN] [STDDEV]
          [VARIANCE] [CORR] [COV]
          [N] [NONE**]]
  /VARIABLES=varlist/DEPENDENT=varlist/METHOD=method
```

**Default if subcommand is omitted.

REGRESSION: Residuals

```
REGRESSION  VARIABLES=varlist/ DEPENDENT=varname/ METHOD=method
  [/RESIDUALS=[DEFAULTS] [ID(varname)] [DURBIN] [{SEPARATE}]
                                                {POOLED  }
            [HISTOGRAM({ZRESID     })] [OUTLIERS(({ZRESID     })]
                      {tempvarlist}              {tempvarlist}
            [NORMPROB({ZRESID     })]  [SIZE({LARGE})]]
                     {tempvarlist}           {SMALL}
  [/CASEWISE=[DEFAULTS] [{OUTLIERS({3    })}]
                        {         {value}}
                        {ALL              }
            [PLOT({ZRESID })]  [{DEPENDENT PRED RESID}]]
                 {tempvar}      {tempvarlist         }
  [/SCATTERPLOT=(varname,varname)... [SIZE({SMALL})]]
                                          {LARGE}
  [/PARTIALPLOT=[{ALL    }] [SIZE({SMALL})]]
                {varlist}        {LARGE}
  [/SAVE=tempvar(newname) [tempvar(newname)... ]]
```

Temporary variables available for residuals analysis include:

```
PRED     ZPRED    ADJPRED  SEPRED   RESID    ZRESID   SRESID   DRESID
SDRESID  MAHAL    COOK     LEVER    DFBETA   SDBETA   DFFIT    SDFIT
COVRATIO MCIN     ICIN
```

SAVE FITS saves:

```
DFBETA  SDBETA  DFFIT  SDFIT  COVRATIO
```

RELIABILITY

```
RELIABILITY VARIABLES=varlist
  [/SCALE(scalename)=varlist [/SCALE... ]]
  [/MODEL={ALPHA         }] [/VARIABLES...]
         {SPLIT[(n)]    }
         {GUTTMAN       }
         {PARALLEL      }
         {STRICTPARALLEL}
  [/MISSING={EXCLUDE}]
           {INCLUDE}
  [/FORMAT={LABELS  }]
          {NOLABELS}
  [/METHOD=COV]
  [/STATISTICS=[DESCRIPTIVE] [SCALE    ] [{ANOVA   }] [ALL]]
               [COV        ] [TUKEY    ]  {FRIEDMAN}
               [CORR       ] [HOTELLING]  {COCHRAN }
  [/SUMMARY=[MEANS    ] [COV ] [TOTAL]]
            [VARIANCE ] [CORR] [ALL  ]
```

T-TEST

Independent Samples:

```
T-TEST GROUPS=varname [(({1,2        })] /VARIABLES=varlist
                          {value      }
                          {value,value}
       [/OPTIONS=option numbers]
```

Paired Samples:

```
T-TEST PAIRS=varlist [WITH varlist] [/[PAIRS=] varlist ...]
       [/OPTIONS=option numbers]
```

Options:

1 Include user-missing values
2 Exclude missing values listwise
3 Suppress variable labels
5 Special pairing for WITH

SPSS Inc.
444 North Michigan Avenue
Chicago, Illinois 60611
(312) 329-3500